The Psychoanalysis of the Absurd

The Psychoanalysis of the Absurd offers an interdisciplinary study of Existentialism and Phenomenology and their importance to the clinical work of Contemporary Psychotherapy and Psychoanalysis. The concept of Absurdity, developed by Camus, has never been applied to the therapeutic situation or directly contrasted with its antithesis; the search for personal meaning.

The book begins with narrative accounts of the historical development of Psychoanalysis, Existentialism and Phenomenology in 20th century Europe. The focus here is on fin de siècle Vienna and Paris between the Wars as the principal incubators of the two disciplines. Accompanied by composite case illustrations, Leffert then explores his own development of the Psychoanalysis of the Absurd, drawing on the work of Camus, Heidegger and Sartre. Absurdity is first discussed in relation to the Bio-Psycho-Social Self and Dasein is posited as a bridge concept, with personal meaning as the antithesis to Absurdity, before being discussed in relation to the world and how it impinges on self. A final chapter attempts to tie together particular issues raised by the book: Subjective Well-Being, Meaning, thrownness, Absurdity, Death and Death Anxiety and how we have become technologically enhanced human beings.

Existential psychotherapy and psychoanalysis have, until now, largely gone their own way: the goal of this book is to fold them back into Contemporary Psychoanalysis. Establishing that the concept of Absurdity is of singular clinical importance to both diagnosis and therapeutic action, this book will be of great interest to clinicians, philosophers, and interdisciplinary scientists.

Mark Leffert has been on the faculty of five psychoanalytic institutes and has been a Training and Supervising Analyst at four of them. He has taught, and supervised psychoanalysts, psychologists, and psychiatrists for 50 years. He is the author of many papers and six books. He has been engaged in an interdisciplinary reformulation of clinical psychoanalysis drawing on phenomenology, neuroscience, network studies, and (among others), heuristics and biases. He is in private practice in Santa Barbara, California.

"Over the past decade Mark Leffert has been on a creative journey resulting in this, his sixth volume, extending the contact, confrontation and integration of psychoanalysis with developments in a multitude of interdisciplinary domains. He is confronting us with findings in fields ranging from neuroscience, to chaos and complexity theories, to post-modern studies and in this book to Existentialism and Phenomenology to enrich psychoanalysis in both theoretical and clinical understanding of the human mind and condition. In his hands, psychoanalysis is getting solidly ensconced in the intellectual, scientific and cultural climate of the 21st Century. He is willing to seek outside the usual boxes of psychoanalytic discourse. We should go there with him."

Erik Gann, M.D., *Past President of the San Fransisco Center for Psychoanalysis and Chair of the Psychoanalytic Scholarship Forum of the American Psychoanalytic Association.*

"Leffert has an open, questioning mind, a keen sense of history, an orignal fresh stance to the clinical enterprise of psychoanalysis, and a clear and charming way of making his existential point. This book is a must read for all mental health clinicians."

Peter Loewenberg *is a Professor Emeritus of Modern European History and Political Psychology at UCLA, a Training and Supervising Analyst and former Dean of the New Center of Psychoanalysis, Los Angeles. Currently he teaches Psychoanalysis and Culture in China.*

The Psychoanalysis of the Absurd

Existentialism and Phenomenology in Contemporary Psychoanalysis

Mark Leffert

LONDON AND NEW YORK

First published 2021
by Routledge
2 Park Square, Milton Park, Abingdon, Oxon OX14 4RN

and by Routledge
52 Vanderbilt Avenue, New York, NY 10017

Routledge is an imprint of the Taylor & Francis Group, an informa business

© 2021 Mark Leffert

The right of Mark Leffert to be identified as author of this work has been asserted by him in accordance with sections 77 and 78 of the Copyright, Designs and Patents Act 1988.

All rights reserved. No part of this book may be reprinted or reproduced or utilised in any form or by any electronic, mechanical, or other means, now known or hereafter invented, including photocopying and recording, or in any information storage or retrieval system, without permission in writing from the publishers.

Trademark notice: Product or corporate names may be trademarks or registered trademarks, and are used only for identification and explanation without intent to infringe.

British Library Cataloguing-in-Publication Data
A catalogue record for this book is available from the British Library

Library of Congress Cataloging-in-Publication Data
A catalog record has been requested for this book

ISBN: 978-0-367-36736-7 (hbk)
ISBN: 978-0-367-36737-4 (pbk)
ISBN: 978-0-429-35106-8 (ebk)

Typeset in Bembo
by Integra Software Services Pvt. Ltd.

For Nancy

It is a Slippery Slope from Epiphany to Identity Category
—*Mark Leffert*

Contents

Acknowledgements x
Introduction xi

1 **Psychoanalytic knowing: A *brief* history of Psychoanalysis and Psychotherapy** 1

  Introduction 1
  The broad sweep of Psychoanalytic history 3
  The educational and practice traditions of Psychotherapists 11
  The Psychotherapists 12
  The Psychoanalysts 14
  Theoretical plurality 16
  What do psychoanalysts and psychotherapists actually do with their patients? 22
  Metapsychology and différance 25
  References 28

2 **Existentialism: The cafés of Vienna and Paris and beyond** 32

  Introduction 32
  Kierkegaard 36
  Nietzsche 38
  Schopenhauer 40
  Fin de siècle Vienna 41
  Husserl 47
  Heidegger 48
  Paris between the wars and beyond 51
  Sartre 54
  Being and no-thing-ness 54
  Existentialism is a Humanism 55
  No Exit 56
  Nausea 57

Camus and the "Three Absurds" 58
The Stranger 59
The Myth of Sisyphus 60
Caligula 63
Whatever happened to Existentialism? 64
References 65

3 Existentialist: Psychoanalysis and Psychotherapy   69

Introduction 69
Origins 71
The sixties 75
The Existentialist approach to the therapeutic situation 77
Existentialist Psychology today 84
Two cases 86
Daseinanalysis 87
The North Americans and the British 89
Yalom on Death 91
Anxiety 96
Despair 99
The beginning of a long case 100
References 104

4 The Psychotherapy and Psychoanalysis of the Absurd   108

Introduction 108
Absurdity and Meaning in the work of Camus and beyond 111
Everydayness (Alltäglichkeit) explained 113
The Self, Dasein, the Eigenwelt, and Absurdity 115
The neural hardware of the Self and its relationship to the Absurd and the Everyday 117
Affective neuroscience and the neuroevolutionary basis of human emotion 119
Heuristics and Biases 120
Subjective Well-Being 124
The Absurdity of development across the life cycle (from uterus to grave) 127
The biology and the psychology of Development 128
The Existential 131
The art of Existential interpretation 133
Some final thoughts about Absurdity 134
References 135

Contents ix

5 Culture and History: How Self engages World   **140**

Introduction 140
Unknowability and its post-structural effects on the ontology of the Self 142
Dasein: the bridge between Self and World 144
Culture and society 144
The American Dream 146
Anxieties—ecological and political 151
The Ecoanxieties 153
Political Anxiety 158
The inner world—the Microbiome 161
The mechanics—the Social Network and the Mirror Neuron System 164
The Mirror Neuron System (MNS) 165
The Social Networks that make us who we are 167
References 168

6 Meaning, Subjective Well-Being, Thrownness, and Death: A summing up   **173**

Introduction 173
Subjective Well-Being 175
Meaning, Absurdity, Thrownness, Happiness, and Subjective Well-Being 177
Meaning 179
Death and Death Anxiety 183
Charles 187
Dennis 188
Empirical studies of Death Anxiety 190
Technologically enhanced Human Beings 192
Background 192
Cyborgs 193
A final note on Postphenomenology 197
References 197

Index   202

Acknowledgements

There are a number of people without whom this book would not have been possible. Kate Hawes, my editor, has helped me to make a literary home at Taylor & Francis and has supported my work through, now, six volumes, beginning a decade ago. Three colleagues, Erik Gann, Peter Loewenberg, and Jeff Seitelman, have reviewed portions of this book and, kindly, offered endorsements. My friend Marshall Sashkin has offered his interest and support over a half-century. Kristopher Spring has served as my personal editor for over a decade. He has copy-edited my books from the beginning and has always been available to discuss fine points of meaning. Finally, my wife, Nancy Leffert, has supported me and my work throughout the complexities that life has thrown our way over 44 years of marriage.

Introduction

This is the sixth in a series of books (Leffert, 2010, 2013, 2016, 2017, 2018) in which I have taken the widest possible interdisciplinary lens to the Human condition in general and the Psychotherapeutic enterprise in particular. It offers a tightly reasoned account of Phenomenology and Existentialism and, at its conclusion, brings us to the edge of what is now being called Postphenomenology or Experimental Phenomenology (Idhe, 2012). It takes up the Psychoanalysis of Absurdity—Camus' concept of Existential failure—and how to characterize it, contrast it with personal Meaning, and clinically address it. This is a problem of Being-in-the-World. In Heidegger's terms, Absurdity is an illness of Dasein. I have consistently argued that while we Psychoanalysts have been able to formulate somewhat successful *clinical* theories of Therapeutic Action, we have only been able to formulate largely unsuccessful theory theories of personality and therapeutic technique. Psychoanalytic writers and clinicians have either chosen to spend their careers oriented to a chosen Metapsychology—another name for such theory theories—or have (e.g., LaFarge, 2017) eclectically chosen to borrow from each on an ad hoc basis (I made this latter choice for myself early in my career and held to it prior to the millennium). Such positions lack either consensus or empirical validation. This should trouble us in our everyday lives much more than it seems to. (Attachment theory, while an exception to this, is, after all, a psychology rather than a metapsychology, and it has a sound research base built on the observation of infants, young children, and their mothers.) Although many, perhaps most, clinicians recognize the failure of such epistemological positions, they hold to them nonetheless.

The problem with Metapsychologies, that goes largely unrecognized, is not whether or not they are true or false, but rather that they are only constructs. Constructs are just that: They have only limited epistemological standing and easily slip into being identity categories; they are best dealt with as subjects of *deconstruction*. The implicit response of most clinicians to this observation is that it is mitigated by their clinical experience, that what they see with their patients confirms their suppositions. They fail to recognize that these intuitions are based on statistically insignificant small samples lacking in validation. I am now far from alone in these observations: There are many authors

(Birksted-Breen, 2008; Blass, 2017; Rudden & Bronstein, 2017; Tuckett, 2008a, 2008b; Tuckett, et al., 2008, to name but a few) now trying to gather data and make sense of our predicament. Their experiences are already taking them away from Metapsychology.

I ultimately decided to follow the advice of Detective Sergeant Joe Friday—the long-forgotten hero of the police drama *Dragnet*—and stick to "just the facts [Ma'am]," or to put it more elegantly (not more simply) following Husserl, to "return to the things themselves." I have come to insist on a phenomenal, albeit interdisciplinary inquiry that in turn insists on holding to the knowable, even the Subjectively known, rather than the believed, and to treat as a given the premise that even the Subjective is capable of Objective study.

This amounts to an inquiry into our nature as Human Beings and the problems we face—internally and externally—in existing, in *Being* in the World. (That is to say, it is a Phenomenological and Existential inquiry.) While familiar psychoanalytic ideas of whatever theoretical ilk are of help in understanding and treating *some* of these problems, they are not helpful for many, possibly most(?), others, and can, in some cases, cause harm. These other problems involve the search for or absence of Personal Meaning and addressing the inevitability of biological Death and Death Anxiety—a universal condition in its own right, largely unrecognized by standard theory and practice. The way I will organize these issues is as either a struggle against, or a submission to, Absurdity. I would stress that, in doing so, I do not mean to discard psychoanalytic ideas as such but to treat them instead as a sometimes-useful subset of tools stored in an Existential toolbox. Psychoanalytic ideas concerning mental illness apply to a subset of ill Human Beings who lives have lost Meaning and who are terrified by Death. Conditions such as neuroses and pathological narcissism are, in effect, species of Absurdity. I differ as well from classical Phenomenological and Existential thought in that I insist on an Interdisciplinary foundation for all of these ideas. This in turn validates the presence of other tools: Neuroscience and Psychopharmacology.

Let me say something about the two terms, Existentialism and Phenomenology, and their relation to each other. First, there is no agreement on this question, but many authors, while steadfastly not commenting on the distinction, refer to themselves as one or the other. My choice is not to make a distinction between the terms or to assign contradictory ideas to them. Instead, I treat them as *complimentary narratives* that cover the same ground from different points of view. Phenomenological narratives are grounded in its concepts surrounding World, Being-in-the-World, and Existence, with pride of place given to Heidegger's shorthand condensation of all three: Dasein. Issues like Meaning, Death, and Absurdity are dealt with implicitly as they pertain to Everydayness, Thrownness, and Fallenness. The Existentialists tend to express themselves in Human narratives: novels, plays, poetry, art. A careful deconstruction reveals that they are ultimately talking about the same things. In keeping all of these threads in play, I have argued that it is *Absurdity in Being* that is the failing that summarizes the Existential/

Phenomenological problems that we have to help our patients deal with and around which I have organized this book.

Chapter 1 offers a sort of flyover history of mental health care, clinical and metapsychological psychoanalytic theory, and the professionals involved in them from the prehistoric beginnings of healing, to the inception (Breuer & Freud, (1893-1895)/1955) of Psychoanalysis, to the present. This is only one of many possible narratives of these millennia and the 125-year history of Psychoanalysis and claims no sort of primacy. For purposes of simplicity and readability, I am offering this as a linear narrative—it is not. It is rather a Post-Structural account (Derrida, 1972/1991), which is to say that it is non-serial and non-linear. It is a sheaf of simultaneous narrative threads, maintained in a state of sometime-tension, at times in conflict with one another. It is the sheaf whose whole offers up its meaning. (This, in effect, summarizes the Postmodern critique of Phenomenology but treats it instead as a supplement to Phenomenal inquiry, offering a capacity to simultaneously deal with multiple Phenomenal threads.)

An important thread in this account involves examining the academic disciplines from which mental health professionals come and how those disciplines effect the way they go about their work with patients. These threads inevitably involve issues of power relations (Lukes, 2005) that distort knowledge claims, also a thread in our account of Psychoanalysis and its history.

The chapter addresses in some depth the way different analysts (e.g., Blass, 2017; Cooper, 2017; LaFarge, 2017; Zimmer, 2017) address the multiple versus single Metapsychology problem that faces us all, including seeing the forest through the trees of countertransference. It hinges on the premise that therapists and analysts each have uniquely personal theory theories and clinical theories: I also stress that there remains a distinction between what everyone says they do, what they think they do, and what they actually do. One way for clinicians to deal with these distinctions is by making themselves conscious of them and, to the extent possible, make some headway in defining them. The important thing about such inquiries is to recognize the limits of their objective *evidential* value. Again, this need not be a problem so long as we realize we are dealing with constructions residing in Post-Structural epistemologies. To integrate a Phenomenological frame of reference into the conversation, we are dealing only with Everyday (*Alltäglich*) (Heidegger, 1927/2010) tools kept ready for the work-at-hand, for immediate use, be it with a patient or at a conference. It does not involve the *thrownness* that we often wish to attribute to it.

Where thrownness *is* to be found is in the new ways (Rudden & Bronstein, 2017; Tuckett, 2008a) of studying clinical process in depth utilizing moderator-led small groups. The work is to be studied, not crypto-supervised, and conscious efforts are made to render the discourse experience-near and free of theoretical terminology. The method yields a rich clinical discourse that can be brought back by the participants to their individual communities.

If Chapter 1 is about the development, history, and deployment of Mental Health care and of Psychoanalytic knowledges, Chapter 2 is about the development, history, and deployment of Existential and Phenomenological knowledges and their applications to Psychotherapy. As psychoanalysis began in Bergasse 19 (Engelman, 1976), I locate the origins of Phenomenology and Existentialism in, after a brief stint in Copenhagen, the cafés of Vienna and Paris. This chapter is written at a level that makes it readily available to a reader with a beginning (or higher) level of knowledge of Existentialism and Phenomenology. It will be clear to the more advanced reader that I, like other analyst-philosophers, am offering my own interpretations of Phenomenology, Existentialism, and, later Postphenomenology. As such, I would expect some inevitable disagreement and ask only for a reading.

It cannot be overstated that definitions of the terms Existentialism and Phenomenology are both fluid and unstable; neither are they subject to widespread agreement. I treat them as overlapping, with Phenomenology referring to an ontological geography and Existentialism to its Human and often literary expression. There may not be a lot of agreement with this position among philosophers but it seems most serviceable to me in dealing with the Philosophy-at-hand.

If, in the service of offering a usable account, we were to take a somewhat reductionist approach to the origins of Existentialism and Phenomenology, it would involve seven names (all men): Kierkegaard, Nietzsche, Schopenhauer, Husserl, Heidegger, Sartre, and Camus. Even then, only a limited view of their extensive *oeuvre* is possible.

Kierkegaard and Nietzsche both called themselves and can be considered early psychologists. They were taken up with the problem of Man and his constant need to search for meaning, a subject that will echo throughout this volume. If Kierkegaard turned to Christianity in his search for meaning, Nietzsche turned to Paganism, particularly the Dionysus myth, the god of ecstasy and tragedy, torn to pieces for what he brought to Man. They struggled with what might be called the animal nature of Man, just as Freud (1930/1961) did in *Civilization and Its Discontents*. Nietzsche offered up many of the ideas we would find in *fin de siècle* psychoanalysis, only in a less tightly organized form.

Kierkegaard brought forth Existentialism around *the special kind of existence unique to Human Beings*. He defined the latter with the term *existenz* and Heidegger would later polish it into Dasein, *Da-sein*, Being-there (with varying emphasis on either word). *Truth* became *relational truth*. He offered a lifelong discussion of Subjectivity, by which he meant *to exist humanly*, and described problems in Being that we would engage Existentially a hundred years later. Kierkegaard also had a clinical and personal interest: despair. He thought the *capacity* for despair to be uniquely human (perhaps) and hence of great excellence, while the *experience* of despair is the greatest source of misfortune and misery.

Nietzsche posits that, ultimately, we only experience ourselves, foreshadowing the concept of Irreducible Subjectivity. For him, it was a statement of his nihilism, ignoring the influence of World on Self. Many of his ideas were taken up by Heidegger, who studied and taught them, finding a fuller expression in his Phenomenology. Nietzsche was much more interested in *inhibition*

(*Hemmung* in the German) as opposed to Unconsciousness with its implied change in state.

The cafés of *fin de siècle* Vienna and the wider European milieu they epitomized provided the rich soil in which Phenomenology took root with approximately 70 individuals (Janik & Toulmin, 1973/1996; Johnston, 1972) forming a vibrant Social Network (Christakis & Fowler, 2009) at the center of European thought going into the 20th century. The *Zeitgeist* was of a rich seductiveness, an alluring corruption leading to an enamored Death. It was an era that worshipped the Self in isolation. The psychiatrists, novelists, and playwrights were all describing the same characters. All were preoccupied with the study of the individual, the Self, in the disintegrating society of the last days of the *Belle Époque*. The result was a crisis in Being that would, in the decades that followed, give rise to Phenomenology and Existentialism.

Phenomenology is defined by three paradigms (Luft & Overgaard, 2012). The first is that it is about the "I" and what the I experiences: *It is a first-person ontology*. The second is that it describes the first-person experience: It attempts—often unsuccessfully—to hold history in abeyance. The third is that there is a directedness of Consciousness (and Unconsciousness); Intentionality is central to Phenomenology.

Husserl (1913/2001), from whom 20th century Phenomenologists and Existentialists are descended, broke with the search for underlying meaning that had preoccupied philosophers for 2,500 years in favor of, his famous battle cry, a "return to the things themselves." Psychology is, for Husserl, an empirical science. It is a science whose purview is the Being of Human Beings. That means we are to treat psychological processes Phenomenally as they present themselves to us, *as they are*, not as representatives of some putative deep structures.

Heidegger moves forward with the proposition that *"being is the proper and sole theme of philosophy"* (1975/1982, p. 11). Philosophy is the study of *Ontology*, the Being of Human Beings. That Being, being *there* (in the World), is Dasein (a complex term we will spend some time with). Heidegger defines two axes of Being organized around three kinds and places of Being: the World of things and animals (*Die Umwelt*), the world of other Human Beings (*Die Mitwelt*) and the world of the inner Self (*Die Eigenwelt*). Dasein can be in any of these places in an Everyday, a Thrown, or a Fallen state. This ontology will be discussed in some depth. It is seen developmentally in the work of Erikson (1950/1963) in which each of the eight stages of Man poses a developmental challenge that can be met or failed; the result is a thrown response or a fallen one.

Two further concepts that are not particularly well-covered by Heidegger are Temporality and Consciousness. Phenomenologists argue, successfully I believe, that there is no such thing as psychological *depth*, that everything, conscious and otherwise, is always fully deployed. What there *is* is temporality, or historicity, or Archeology (Foucault, 1969 & 1971/1972); the history of knowledge. The original Phenomenologists and Existentialists of course did not have access to works from our time on the neuroscience of Consciousness. Tulving (1985/2003, 2005), as we will see, defines three kinds of

Consciousness—Autonoetic, Noetic, and Anoetic—with the first possible in Thrown and Fallen states and the last two present in the Everyday.

It appears that Existentialism owes its origins to the meeting of three young philosophers—Simone de Beauvoir, Jean-Paul Sartre, and Raymond Aron—at the Bec-de-Gaz Bar in Montparnasse over the Christmas holidays of 1932. Aron had brought for them, from Berlin, material from a new philosophy that went by the name of Phenomenology. It reconnected philosophy with normal Human experience. Sartre brought his interests in Kierkegaard as well. He added an idea of his own—that literature could be a vehicle for doing philosophy—and, in so doing, gave rise to French Existentialism. It percolated through the cafés of 1930s Paris with its first major works (e.g., Camus, 1942/1989, 1942/1991; Sartre, 1943/2003) appearing during the Nazi occupation of World War II, somehow slipping past the Vichy censors. This background, the *there* of Dasein, involving rage, terror, depression, and a search for Meaning, appeared in a kind of code to bypass the censors.

For Sartre, and Existentialism, the fundamental issue facing Human Beings was not a search for thrownness, but Human freedom. It was freedom that set us apart from the world of things and animals; we define ourselves by our experience. Freedom, in the time of the Nazi occupation, was particularly precious. To practice Existentialism was considered an act of rebellion and Sartre & Co. started out as Marxist communists (although the German-Soviet non-aggression pact of 1938 spelled the latter's demise in France). Philosophy was *lived*, not just written about. Camus came a bit later to the group with the works (1944/1958, 1942/1989, 1942/1991) he called his "three Absurds."

Existentialism exploded on the global scene on October 29, 1945 when Sartre gave a lecture to a packed crowd at the Salle de Centraux on Paris' Left Bank entitled "Is Existentialism a Humanism" (Sartre, 1947/2007). It was the first media event of its kind and he and de Beauvoir became a golden couple. If Husserl's battle cry was a "Return to the things themselves," Sartre's was the equally famous ontological criticism of Kierkegaard, "Existence precedes essence." Sartre's Existentialism is contained in an explanation of the linked concepts Being and Nothingness described, albeit somewhat arcanely, in his magnum opus (1943/2003) by the same name. "Existence precedes essence" is both an expression of this and a critique of Kierkegaard's position that, in effect, essence precedes existence. For Kierkegaard, God provides the essence, the Soul if you will, of a Human Being who is then brought into physical existence as an [embodied] creature. For Sartre, Man is, through a role of the ontological dice (biology, temporality, the world of humans and things), thrown into existence and is then left to make of it what he will, to create his own essence.

Camus developed the philosophy of the Absurd. It is worth noting that while he maintained cordial relationships with the other Existentialists (no mean feat I can assure you!), they were never in agreement with these ideas. Absurdism at its most basic is about a fundamental discrepancy between Self and World (Heidegger's *Mitwelt* and *Umwelt*). It involves a failure to find

Meaning and Desire (Leffert, 2017). Camus sets out his ideas in his "Three Absurds": a novel, *The Stranger* (1942/1989) an essay, *The Myth of Sisyphus* (1942/1991), and a play, *Caligula* (1944/1958).

Chapter 3 takes up Existentialism and Phenomenology as clinical theories of Psychoanalysis and Psychotherapy. By the mid-20th century, therapists in Europe and the United States (May, Angel, & Ellenberger, 1958) were recognizing a failure of standard theories and techniques to fully address problems of anxiety and depression in states of subjective meaninglessness and anhedonia. They turned to Existentialism to study the psychopathology of Human Being. Prior to this, analysts, when faced with systematic failures in clinical practice would seek answers in the form of new theories arising within our discipline (e.g., Self Psychology). In this case, clinicians turned *outside* of psychoanalysis to philosophy in search of systematic answers. They found new tools for observation and clinical theories based on the Being of Human Beings. Existential Psychology arose simultaneously at multiple points across Europe in the postwar years and subsequently made its way to North America. They treated standard psychoanalytic theories as theories of psychopathology, technique, and cure, but refused to consider any of them a *Theory of Man* as analysts generally did and, to a degree, still do.

If Existentialism was born in the cafés of Paris between the wars and Existentialist Psychology appeared in the 1950s, then the social environment in which *it* flowered was the populist movement of the 1960s and its attendant pressure for social and personal change.

Rollo May (1958) was at the center of establishing Existential Psychotherapy in the United States. His aim was not to replace the established psychoanalytic therapies but rather to posit a place for them under the Existential umbrella. He did not credit the stark differences in therapeutic technique at mid-century—to no longer simply attempt to listen to the patient's "Unconscious" with free-floating attention and restrict one's comments to issues of transference and resistance—with being the revolution it was.

To talk about Existentialism and Phenomenology requires spending time on the language and this is hard work. On the one hand, the English language terms—Meaning, Being, Existential, thrown—have been used and reused in so many different ways that they have lost any meaning and require work to recover. On the other, there are the arcane foreign terms—Dasein, *Mitwelt*, *en-soi*—that require so much work to grasp that many simply don't bother. I have tried throughout this book to make these terms as easy as possible for the less informed reader.

In Existentialist terms it is emotion—anxiety, depression, despair, loneliness, and generalized emotional pain—that bring Human Beings to see us, seeking relief from pain and suffering. Overshadowing all is the sense that their lives lack meaning. It may take some time for this lack of Meaning to emerge in the Therapeutic Situation.

Existentialist and Phenomenological Psychology are vibrant movements within Contemporary Psychology, but they have become much less well-known outside of their immediate circles. The movement comprises a sheaf of three threads: the North American, the British, and the European. What they seek as a therapeutic outcome is openness to the world and the freedom to enjoy it. This is phenomenally not so dissimilar from what other therapeutic modalities seek, but the language and its implications are *very* different.

Irwin Yalom (1980) has most prominently continued the development of Existentialist thought in the United States. He writes for a wide range of Psychotherapists—is less well-known among Psychoanalysts—and, in the Existential Philosophical tradition, writes narrative histories that are also of great interest to a wide range of clinicians as well as the general, reading public. He describes four challenges facing the Human Condition—isolation, meaninglessness, mortality, and freedom—that can have functional or dysfunctional solutions. He emphasizes the treatment of Death as a major, perhaps *the* major, psychological issue facing us as Human Beings, where therapists adhering to other, or even eclectic, theoretical schools, reserve such considerations for cases of terminal illness.

The chapter stresses, through the use of clinical illustrations, the differences between Metapsychologically-based and Existentially-based approaches to patients and the suffering they bring to us.

Chapters 4 and 5 offer a reformulation of the arguments for an Existential approach to patients: the Psychotherapy and Psychoanalysis of the Absurd. Among these arguments is the premise that we have always been dealing clinically with these things, albeit under different names. Absurdity is the antithesis of meaning, but, even within the limits of nihilism, it is possible to find a path beyond it. We begin with Camus' ideas about absurdity, relating them to Heidegger's multifaceted concepts of Being—thrown, everyday, and fallen —and their locations—*Eigenwelt, Mitwelt,* and *Umwelt.* I would posit that the 21st century Bio-Psycho-Social Self is the contemporary formulation of Dasein and that the *Eigenwelt* is the location—its *Da*—of Self-experience and Self-reflection. To follow these arguments, we will have to touch on Systems Theory and Complexity. Chapter 4, in particular, takes up an interdisciplinary Phenomenology that includes the biology and psychology of development, subjective well-being, heuristics and biases, the neural hardware of the Self, and affective neuroscience. It takes up as well the place of interpretation in Existential psychotherapy as a tool that expands Meaning.

Chapter 5 explores the ways in which World impinges on and influences Self. Emphasizing this vector of the Self-World interaction highlights a fundamental difference between Phenomenologically based therapies and those based on the spectrum of standard Psychoanalytic theories. The latter focus on how impairments of the Self—however they are formulated—limit its ability to get the most out of the world, while the former focuses on how World impinges on Self for good or ill and, most recently, for ill. To talk about the latter is to take up two global crises: that of climate and that of politics. As Latour (1999) points out, the two are necessarily interreferential. Both frequently produce traumatic levels of anxiety.

The discussion of World is inseparable from that of Culture and History, how they shape Human Beings' subjective experience of the World they inhabit, and their judgments concerning Meaning and Absurdity. Writing, as we are, from an early 21st century perspective, we also have to consider the Postmodern critique of a Modernist Existentialism and how it has changed our reading of it and of Phenomenology. Unknowability is a central feature of Postmodern discourse that is highly relevant to these concerns.

Culture and Society have a profound effect on the Being of Human Beings. Meaning is to be found in relationships, work, play, and the pursuit of higher goods, all of which vary with the society one is a member of. A brief social history of the past 75 years or so offers a useful grounding of these issues. The concept of the rise and fall of the *American Dream* is a helpful way of organizing these events. The loss of possibility arising in the 21st century has led to an increase in Absurdity and a consequent decrease in Meaning.

In taking up the linked issues of Ecological and Political anxiety, the chapter argues that these issues belong solidly within the scope of Therapeutic Discourse. This is at odds with the position taken by many clinicians and shared with the American Psychiatric Association and its "Goldwater Rule." My position is that it is unethical *not* to talk with patients about these things. Having said that, I found that my position in the chapter and with patients was (to me) surprisingly *un*polemical. The effects of climate change and climate catastrophes on individual communities and societies as a whole are taken up. These are Phenomenological effects on Being.

Up until recently, Existential relationships with the *Umwelt* could remain unspecified; only the outside world need be considered. This has changed. It is known that we carry about three pounds of living bacteria in our gastrointestinal tracts that effect the Self—physically and psychologically—in profound and complex ways. This *inner* world is called the microbiome and the study of it is only beginning.

In considering the *mechanics* of our relations in the Mitwelt, the chapter discusses the Mirror Neuron System and Social Network Theory.

Chapter 6, the final chapter, consists of a kind of stock-taking. It highlights what seem to me to be the major issues taken up in the book: a last attempt at answering some questions and raising others that will have to be considered in the future. It begins with a brief critique of Existentialism and Phenomenology focusing not on their errors but rather on what they have failed to consider. These shortcomings have in part to do with absent knowledges that have come into being towards the end of the millennium. We are looking at the concepts of Meaning, SWB, Happiness, and Thrownness and how they all play out against Death Anxiety and Death. The goal here is to offer a wider account of SWB than I have done before, fleshing it out with empirical studies.

The chapter reviews the development of empirical tools created to measure and validate meaning of life as experienced by individuals. They validate the premise that personal Meaning, a subjective assessment of Being, is, objectively, both measurable and quantifiable outside of the subjective assessments made of them by Human Beings, among them patients and their psychotherapists. They also validate subjective assessments of personal Meaning as useful assessments of therapeutic outcome.

I am also offering another assessment of Death and Death Anxiety, a difficult subject that is still incomplete. I posit that Death Anxiety is an implement of homeostasis regulation and that climate change and the current national and global political situation are experienced as threats to that homeostasis. These bring with them an Existential instability. Death Anxiety has phylogenetic roots that can be understood through the work of Jaak Panksepp (1998) on basic emotional states validated through cross-Mammalian studies. Phenomenologically, Death and Death Anxiety can appear in any of the three modes of Being—Thrownness, Everydayness, or Fallenness. The chapter offers two case illustrations of working with patients struggling with Death Anxiety.

As with the consideration of Meaning, it is also possible to empirically study Death Anxiety and how to classify and quantify it. It turns out to be a fairly stable personality trait involving negative cognitive and emotional reactions to Death and dying. In studying Death Anxiety, we find alternative responses to Death, among them different forms of Death *Acceptance*.

Finally, the chapter offers an introduction to an aspect of Postphenomenology: how Dasein has been expanded by the elaboration of digital connections between Self and World. It is my premise that the advent of cellphone usage, particularly in the last decade, has fundamentally changed ourselves, making Human Beings into new kinds of *Cyborgs*. The cellphone has massively increased the connectedness that Christakis and Fowler have talked about. There are advantages and disadvantages to this that most of us are already aware of. The premise is that cellphones fundamentally change the Self by adding another pathway for *mentalizing homeostasis*.

What has become clear is that the chapter fails to adequately tie up the loose ends of the preceding five chapters, but rather makes a case for the impossibility of such a simple procedure. Instead, it systematically organizes topics that will be considered in a subsequent volume.

References

Birksted-Breen, D. (2008). Introductory forward. In D. Tuckett, R. Basile, D. Birksted-Breen, T. Böhm, P. Denis, A. Ferro, H. Hinz, A. Jemstedt, P. Mariotti & J. Schubert (Eds), *Psychoanalysis comparable and incomparable: The evolution of a method to describe and compare psychoanalytic approaches* (pp. 1–4). London: Routledge.

Blass, R. B. (2017). Committed to a single model and open to reality. *Journal of the American Psychoanalytic Association, 65*, 845–858.

Breuer, J., & Freud, S. (1955). Studies in hysteria. In J. Strachey (Ed.), *Standard Edition* (Vol. II, pp. 1–319). London: Hogarth Press. (Original work published in 1893–1895).

Camus, A. (1958). Caligula. In A. Camus, *Caligula and 3 other plays* (S. Gilbert, Trans.) (pp. 1–74). New York: Vintage Books. (Original work published in 1944).

Camus, A. (1989). *The stranger* (M. Ward, Trans.). New York: Vintage Books. (Original work published in 1942).
Camus, A. (1991). The myth of Sisyphus. In A. Camus, *The myth of Sisyphus and other essays* (J. O'Brien, Trans.) (pp. 3–138). New York: Vintage Books. (Original work published in 1942).
Christakis, N. A., & Fowler, J. H. (2009). *Connected: The surprising power of our social networks and how they shape our lives*. New York: Little, Brown and Company.
Cooper, S. H. (2017). The analyst's "use" of theory or theories: The play of theory. *Journal of the American Psychoanalytic Association, 65*, 859–882.
Derrida, J. (1991). Différance. In P. Kamuf (Ed.), *A Derrida reader: Between the blinds* (pp. 59–79). New York: Columbia University Press. (Original work published in 1972).
Engelman, E. (1976). *Bergasse 19 Sigmund Freud's home and offices, Vienna 1938: The photographs of Edmund Engelman*. New York: Basic Books.
Erikson, E. (1963). *Childhood and society* (2nd edn). New York: W.W. Norton & Co. (Original work published in 1950).
Foucault, M. (1972). *The archeology of knowledge & The discourse on language* (A. M. S. Smith, Trans.). New York: Pantheon. (Original work published in 1969 & 1971).
Freud, S. (1961). Civilization and its discontents. In J. Strachey (Ed.), *Standard Edition* (Vol. XXI, pp. 64–145). London: Hogarth Press. (Original work published in 1930).
Heidegger, M. (1982). *The basic problems of phenomenology* (A. Hofstadter, Trans. Rev. ed.). Bloomington: Indiana University Press. (Original work published in 1975).
Heidegger, M. (2010). *Being and time* (J. Stambaugh & D. J. Schmidt, Trans.). Albany: State University of New York. (Original work published in 1927).
Husserl, E. (2001). *Logical investigations* (J. M. Findlay, Trans.). London: Routledge. (Original work published in 1913).
Idhe, D. (2012). *Experimental phenomenology* (2nd edn) *Multistabilities*. Albany: SUNY Press.
Janik, A., & Toulmin, S. (1996). *Wittgenstein's Vienna*. Chicago: Ivar R. Dee. (Original work published in 1973).
Johnston, W. M. (1972). *The Austrian mind: An intellectual and social history 1848-1938*. Berkeley: University of California Press.
LaFarge, L. (2017). From "either/or" to "and": The analyst's use of multiple models in clinical work. *Journal of the American Psychoanalytic Association, 65*, 829–844.
Latour, B. (1999). *Pandora's hope: Essays on the reality of science studies*. Cambridge: Harvard University Press.
Leffert, M. (2010). *Contemporary psychoanalytic foundations*. London: Routledge.
Leffert, M. (2013). *The therapeutic situation in the 21st century*. New York: Routledge.
Leffert, M. (2016). *Phenomenology, uncertainty, and care in the therapeutic encounter*. New York: Routledge.
Leffert, M. (2017). *Positive psychoanalysis: Aesthetics, desire, and subjective well-being*. New York: Routledge.
Leffert, M. (2018). *Psychoanalysis and the birth of the self: A radical interdisciplinary approach*. London: Routledge.
Luft, S., & Overgaard, S. (Eds). (2012). *The Routledge companion to phenomenology*. New York: Routledge.
Lukes, S. (2005). *Power a radical view* (2nd edn). New York: Palgrave Macmillan.
May, R. (1958). The origins and significance of the existential movement in psychology. In R. May, E. Angel & H. F. Ellenberger (Eds), *Existence: A new dimension in psychiatry and psychology* (pp. 3–36). New York: Basic Books.

May, R., Angel, E., & Ellenberger, H. F. (Eds). (1958). *Existence: New directions in psychiatry and psychology*. New York: Simon & Schuster.

Panksepp, J. (1998). *Affective neuroscience: The foundations of human and animal emotions*. Oxford: Oxford University Press.

Rudden, M., & Bronstein, A. A. (2017). New educational approaches to the study of psychoanalysis. *The American Psychoanalyst: Quarterly Magazine of the American Psychoanalytic Association*,51.

Sartre, J.-P. (2003). *Being and nothingness* (H. Barnes, Trans.). London: Routledge. (Original work published in 1943).

Sartre, J.-P. (2007). *Existentialism is a humanism* (C. Macomber, Trans.). New Haven: Yale University Press. (Original work published in 1947).

Tuckett, D. (2008a). On difference, discussing differences and comparison. An introduction. In D. Tuckett, R. Basile, D. Birksted-Breen, T. Böhm, P. Denis, A. Ferro, H. Hinz, A. Jemstedt, P. Mariotti & J. Schubert (Eds), *Psychoanalysis comparable and incomparable: The evolution of a method to describe and compare psychoanalytic approaches* (pp. 5–37). London: Routledge.

Tuckett, D. (2008b). Reflection and evolution: Developing the two-step method. In D. Tuckett, R. Basile, D. Birksted-Breen, T. Böhm, P. Denis, A. Ferro, H. Hinz, A. Jemstedt, P. Mariotti & J. Schubert (Eds), *Psychoanalysis comparable and incomparable: The evolution of a method to describe and compare psychoanalytic approaches* (pp. 132–166). London: Routledge.

Tuckett, D., Basile, R., Birksted-Breen, D., Böhm, T., Denis, P., Ferro, A., Hinz, H., Jemstedt, A., Mariotti, P. & Schubert, J. (Eds). (2008). *Psychoanalysis comparable and incomparable: The evolution of a method to describe and compare psychoanalytic approaches*. London: Routledge.

Tulving, E. (2003). Memory and consciousness. In B. J. Baars, W. P. Banks & J. B. Newman (Eds), *Essential sources in the scientific study of consciousness* (pp. 575–591). Cambridge: MIT Press. (Original work published in 1985).

Tulving, E. (2005). Episodic memory and autonoesis: Uniquely human? In H. S. Terrace & J. Metcalfe (Eds), *The missing link in cognition: Origins of self-reflective consciousness* (pp. 3–56). Oxford: Oxford University Press.

Yalom, I. D. (1980). *Existential psychotherapy*. New York: Basic Books.

Zimmer, R. B. (2017). The analyst's use of multiple models in clinical work: Introduction. *Journal of the American Psychoanalytic Association, 65*, 819–827.

1 Psychoanalytic knowing

A *brief* history of Psychoanalysis and Psychotherapy

Introduction

For as long as Psychoanalysis has existed, clinicians have searched for *a* theory that could explain human psychology and psychopathology with a related theory of cure. We have been concerned with the psychoanalytic *knowing* of our patients and, more recently, ourselves. Theories of care have come much later (Leffert, 2016). Fifty years ago (Gill, 1976; Gill & Holtzman, 1976; Klein, 1969/1976), we began to realize that there were two sorts of theories out there: One was a very successful clinical theory and the other was a set of very unsuccessful—to borrow a term from the attachment theorist Mary Main (1991)—theory theories. These theories range in complexity from the simplicity of a dynamic unconscious separated from consciousness by a repression barrier to the elaborate mathematics-like complexity of the now highly popular theories of Wilfred Bion (1963/1984). Our term for this kind of theory is *metapsychology*. There tends to be confusion on this point, and Gill and Holtzman's work has largely been forgotten. Although there has been no shortage of metapsychologies, a century-and-a-quarter's work has failed to yield proof or to validate any of them. Despite a general awareness of this fact, we have been loath to give them up. I have elsewhere (Leffert, 2010, 2013) offered critiques of these theories and spoken of the impossibility of verifying them. Nonetheless, they somehow remain in use, the idea of doing without them remains disturbing to some clinicians who continue to cling to them, and there remains confusion between fact, opinion, and supposition. That they endure and are still taught suggests that they may *perhaps* serve some clinical purpose,[1] and we need to review them in a macro-historical way to try to better understand what that might be. We will look at this century and a quarter of theory building, the theory theories

---

1 If a psychotherapist successfully teaches a school of metapsychology to his patient and they both proceed to apply it to the patient's unhappinesses, there *will* be some amelioration of their symptoms through suggestion and as a result of giving the patient a system whereby they can bind anxiety. (Whether or not there is any *Meaning* to be had in such a process alone is another question.) We must try to be on guard against such theoretical enactments in our work.

and the clinical theories, from a macro perspective, a kind of flyover, if you will. Then we will look at how the two theories are used by clinicians today, from those adhering to a single theory to a large majority of Psychotherapists[2] who freely sample the theoretical buffet, at times without even knowing the antecedents of their choices. Indeed, Psychoanalysts are beginning to study these questions, a sort of meta-metapsychology, if you will. We will consider recent projects (Rudden & Bronstein, 2017; Tuckett, et al., 2008) aimed at studying the ways analysts work and the theoretical underpinnings of what they do. A section of a recent issue of the *Journal of the American Psychoanalytic Association* (Vol. 65, #5) was devoted to four papers (Blass, 2017; Cooper, 2017; LaFarge, 2017; Zimmer, 2017) on how analysts deal with theoretical plurality today.

We will want to explore the history of psychoanalytic theory from its inception (Breuer & Freud, (1893–1895)/1955) in the late 19th century until the 21st century present (Leffert, 2018). We will want to know about how and why new theories came into existence and what happened to them. Some will have passed away while others remain, but in unnamed forms. We will be looking through a wide-angle lens at macro-historical trends, not at details of psychoanalytic thought in the various schools of Psychoanalysis.[3]

Before proceeding with this inquiry, we should, however, ask the question: How many clinicians are there, and how many of those do actually cling to a single or multiple named theory theories? This is a very hard question to answer, and we can only offer supposition based on assumption—always a dicey proposition.

The International Psychoanalytic Association in 2018 boasts on its website of 12,700 members throughout the world, of which approximately 3000 are also members of the American Psychoanalytic Association. Membership in these organizations requires graduation from a psychoanalytic institute credentialed by these organizations and suggests a commitment to organized Psychoanalysis. It should be safe to assume that these clinicians have some commitment to psychoanalytic theory. Meanwhile, there are approximately 30,000 clinicians in the United States who identify themselves as Psychoanalysts (Kirsner, 2009). Although we know nothing about the theoretical proclivities of these clinicians, we can say that, by choosing to identify themselves as Psychoanalysts, they have *studied* psychoanalytic theory in some depth and with some formality.[4] The final question is how many clinicians in the United States identify themselves as

---

2 Many psychoanalysts see a sharp distinction between psychotherapy and Psychoanalysis and speak of converting the former into the latter. After much thought, I find myself unable to make such a clear distinction and see it as a quantitative rather than qualitative matter. I posit that Psychoanalysis sits under the umbrella of Psychotherapy. When I use the terms *psychotherapist* and *psychotherapy*, please take them to include *Psychoanalysis* and *Psychoanalyst* unless otherwise specified.
3 Schools can be named after some beloved father or mother—Freud and Klein are examples—or some fundamental theoretical idea—Self Psychology or Relational Psychoanalysis.
4 The questions of what a psychoanalytic education or a psychoanalytic practice consist of are highly contested with no certain evidence of superior validity or therapeutic efficacy of any of the differing parameters (beyond the strong opinions of members of the different groups) used to describe them.

Psychotherapists? According to the United States Department of Labor's Bureau of Labor Statistics there were, in 2011, 552,000 mental health professionals practicing in the U.S. We would be inclined to think that this is a highly diverse group including counselors, social workers, psychologists, psychiatrists, and some psychoanalysts who no longer self-signify themselves as such.[5] Members of this large group have almost certainly had some *exposure* to *named* psychoanalytic theory and theoreticians at some point during their education and, also, exposure to psychoanalytic ideas in contexts where they were not named as such. We have then four groups of Psychotherapists—the APsaA Psychoanalysts, the IPA Analysts, the self-signified Analysts, and the Psychotherapists—of whom we are going to want to talk about, their educational habits and habits of practice. This discussion can offer a background for a conversation concerning the current theory and practice in Psychoanalysis.

The broad sweep of Psychoanalytic history

A Surveille of Psychotherapy and Psychoanalysis from their rudimentary beginnings and up to the 21st century would certainly require at least an entire volume but would contain nothing that isn't readily available in the psychoanalytic literature. If this were an introductory text, one could argue for a need for such detail, but here it would be redundant. Metaphorically, I want to offer a history using a kind of time-lapse photography that enhances movement. It is a phenomenologically based inquiry in that it describes what was and what is, what existed in conceptual terms: It does not argue for one point over another, and does not worry about attribution. In our contentious discipline, we can't get into detail without engendering conflict and uncertainty, and our approach here dispenses with these theory wars. It leaves a lot out, details, names in particular, that can be filled in by any student of Psychotherapy or found in any of the histories of Psychoanalysis. We will end up instead with a rather messy braid of different threads, threads that often oppose each other: What we will then have is a sheaf of *différance* (Derrida, 1982),[6] a Post-Structural narrative that more accurately describes the state of things compared to any attempt at a linear account.

Psychotherapy evolved very gradually out of traditions of folk medicine and folk healing, almost certainly going back to prehistoric times, whereas Psychoanalysis appeared over the span of a few decades, initially out of medical roots.

---

5 Increasing numbers of committed Psychoanalysts market themselves, particularly on their personal websites, as Psychotherapists—an implicit acknowledgement of how the former term is viewed by the lay community of potential consumers of mental health services.
6 The idea behind the term *différance* is that a thing may be best described by a number of ideas, here threads, often in conflict with or opposition to each other, maintained in a tension that best describes its meaning. The tension persists between signs; there *is* no final meaning. One-person and two-person psychologies are examples of such threads held in tension in the therapeutic situation. We will have more to say about *différance* later in the chapter.

The preeminent history of these developments is to be found in Henri Ellenberger's *The Discovery of the Unconscious* (1970). Although he writes about an evolution of dynamic *psychiatry*, in itself an implied slight of non-medical psychotherapists common at the time, it is as relevant for the latter group as for the physicians.

Ellenberger (1970) recognized the development of the healing professions out of aboriginal and undoubtedly prehistoric roots. The study of these aboriginal healers revealed that they used many of the techniques of modern psychotherapy albeit in different, at times subtly different, forms. He posited, "The study of primitive healing thus is of interest as being the root from which, after a long evolution, psychotherapy developed" (p. 3). We know that the healing arts were practiced in pharaonic times in Egypt dating back to the first Dynasty (3000 B.C.E.) with extant written records going back to 1700 B.C.E. (Nunn, 1996). Healing was practiced by physicians (*swnw*), priests (*wab*), and magicians (*sau*). It involved many of the elements present in modern psychotherapy[7] that would be effective for the treatment of what we would call nervous and mental diseases. For our purposes, *swnw* listened to their patients, took a history, and examined them. (The medical papyri also use the term *swnw* in connection with the laying on of hands.) Treatment involved, in addition to the laying on of hands, the use of the placebo effect and of suggestion (Leffert, 2016); all were consistent with Freud's early proto-psychoanalytic practice. Better documentation survives concerning the healing practices of ancient Greece (beginning ca. 800 B.C.E.). There were two kinds of health practitioners: the *iatroi*, the healers, and the *medici*, the early physicians. As I've previously written (Leffert, 2016, chapter 6), both threads were interested in healing, but the *iatroi* in particular focused on care of the patient and relief of pain and suffering. They practiced amicably together, side by side, through Roman times. After the fall of the Roman Empire, conflicts over market share and power resulted, with the Catholic Church,[8] facilitating the depreciation of the latter by the former. The healers were, in effect, outlawed and forbidden to practice, an edict frequently enforced by charges of heresy. "Witchcraft" was, in effect, a power relations term. Healers were at best tolerated and were *permitted* to treat the poor.

These trends persisted into premodern times (1500–1800) but with a twist. Folk medicine remained as the purview of healers and apothecaries but pastoral counseling appeared, sanctioned by the Church and becoming a part of the job description of the parish priest or minister. A readily identifiable feature

---

7 An active pharmacopeia and effective surgical procedures (including obstetrical and gynecological practice) existed in pharonic Egypt that offered successful treatment of some medical illnesses and physical trauma.
8 This was a power struggle that persisted into modern times. It was complicated by the fact that medicine, until the 20th century, had, on average, less to offer patients than the healers and, in many instances, did more harm than good.

of these various practices was the way they accomplished healing through suggestion.

Psychoanalysts have often depreciated the clinical use suggestion. They have seen fit to ignore the reality that *any* intervention constitutes a suggestion to do or think something else. Suggestion falls along two axes. One is the explicit/implicit axis and the other is the advertent/inadvertent axis. Implicit/inadvertent suggestions account for much of what we unknowingly do in the Therapeutic Situation. I have argued (Leffert, 2013, 2017) that suggestion remains a significant salutary part of therapeutic practice.

During this same period, physicians became involved in the treatment of the mentally ill. In his magisterial work, *The History of Madness*, Foucault (1961/2006) described the care of the insane, the *déraisonnés*, during what he designated as the Classical Age dating from 1650–1800. The *déraisonnés* were defined by power considerations as much as illness and included individuals deemed moral reprobates (classified as individuals living at the margins of society and constituting a threat to society) as well as the insane. In Paris, 5000–6000 people, roughly 1% of the population, were institutionalized, to protect society from social and infectious contagion, over a period of a very few years: This *Great Confinement*, to use Foucault's term, ushered in the Classical Age. In the Asylums where these people were confined, the role of the physician was to direct the efforts of what might be termed a treatment team comprised of "empirics," nuns, monks, charlatans, druggists, and herbalists. The latter administered nostrums, potions, and herbs. Guards were also present in the asylums and at times dispensed "therapeutic" punishment. Prominent among the drugs dispensed were mercury, antimony, and opium. But what was most sought after, sadly without success, was a universal *panacea* that would return individuals suffering from any number of conditions to a state of normal function.

The asylums with their medical directors persisted through the 19th century (the organization that would become the American Psychiatric Association was founded in 1844 by a group of 14 superintendents of such asylums who met to discuss administrative and logistical rather than therapeutic issues in the running of their institutions). Asylums existed for the care of the poor and the insane, while sanitaria and spas, where wealthy individuals could "take the cure," appeared in the 18th and 19th centuries. A moment's thought reveals that the treatments provided in each were often quite similar; only the luxury of the surroundings differed greatly (what else is new?). As the *fin de siècle* approached, an amalgam formed of residential treatment, the academic study of mental illness, and neurology, that began to resemble modern psychiatry.

By the mid-19th century, at least in Europe, large numbers of patients[9] presented at their physicians' offices suffering from messy concoctions of physical,

---

9 I stay with the term *patient* rather than *client* to emphasize that people come to us who are suffering and are seeking healing and cure to the extent possible and relief of their suffering. They usually do not, at least not initially, come to us seeking to understand themselves.

psychological and neurological symptoms for which no physical causes could be found. They were quite distinct from patients who, for lack of a better term, were suffering from Madness and whose treatment was provided in asylums and sanitaria, much as it had been in centuries past. These illnesses were often thought of as degenerative conditions. People, mostly physicians, some calling themselves psycho-analysts, appeared around the *fin de siècle* to serve this marketplace. (This is an important point because, for the last few decades, this marketplace has grown progressively smaller.) Freud, then a busy young neurologist bent on establishing a practice and raising a young family, has remained historically the most prominent member of this group, while many others, whose names we don't remember, fell by the wayside.[10] His original effort was based on an attempt to derive a complete theory of psychopathology and cure out of the vicissitudes of adult patients' sexuality, their childhood sexual histories, and the putatively derivative symptoms and defenses they manifested. Early in his practice, he made use of a couch, initially to do hypnosis and later to relieve himself from the pressure he experienced as a result of being looked at by his patients. He made house calls and, in the early years, massaged his patients on a daily basis (Leffert, 2017). In his early correspondence with Fliess, his colleague cum transference object, he makes reference to many patients dropping out after what sounds like a session or two. He subsequently put forth two theories of psychic structure—the Topographic and the Ego-Psychological. Although they were described as growing out of clinical practice, this did not constitute any sort of proof, nor, despite efforts to the contrary (e.g., Solms, 2013) has any convincing proof for them subsequently appeared (Leffert, 2010).

Adopting the broadest possible perspective, clinical theory was based on a number of observations. If patients were seen several times a week and encouraged to talk freely about whatever they wished, their associations (really only another word for talking) would tend, like a compass, to spontaneously point at what was psychologically important to them. (A patient came to see me due to his inability to form a satisfying relationship with a woman. After about a month, he noted with great surprise that he had been talking almost exclusively about his parents.) A Therapeutic Discourse (what *this* consisted of was and is highly controversial) would then develop between the two participants. It was observed that, as a result of these procedures, some patients felt better; when they did not, the failure was ascribed to either the patients' "resistance" or to failures in the theory.

There were two linked therapeutic goals. One involved the pursuit of an understanding of an adult patient's symptoms in terms of the vicissitudes of their repressed childhood experiences or their childhood fantasies of such experiences. The second followed from the clinical theory that the relationships that patients develop with significant figures in their early lives become

---

10 Pierre Janet (Ellenberger, 1970) for example, was at least as well known in those times but is forgotten today.

templates that shape how subsequent relationships are experienced (Freud, 1912/1958). These templates become ways in which present relationships are misunderstood, and these misunderstandings occur through the psychic mechanisms of displacement or projection. Psychoanalysts were and are particularly interested when such misunderstandings occur in the Therapeutic Situation with the Patient misunderstanding the Analyst. (The Analysts' misunderstandings of their Patients would have to wait another half-century (Tower, 1956) to become interesting.) The *transference* relationships that thus formed were seen as freestanding things, discrete from other ways of experiencing the therapist. (Eventually (Laplanche & Pontalis, 1967/1973), it was understood that transference was a much more complex and dynamic entity that was quite inseparable, for other than heuristic purposes, from the wider relationships that *Homo sapiens* have with each other.) The named tools of therapeutic action employed by psychoanalysts to accomplish these dual ends were limited to offering interpretations and new narratives (reconstructions) of the patient's early life history (there was disagreement during this period about just how early). Other psychotherapists, however, continued to employ a much larger pallet of tools, including suggestion, advice, and support. So here we are. Although many other details were added over the ensuing half-century, clinical practice remained unchanged, and again, despite a sense to the contrary, what was added could not actually be proven.

Historically, where exactly had we gotten to since? Again taking a macro view, we learned: 1) that nervous and mental diseases were psychological in origin (the biological component would have to wait another half-century to be considered; 2) that it was possible to understand their meaning, but that there were many possible understandings; 3) that whatever the understanding, patients' early lives and their recall figured prominently in that meaning; 4) that some degree of cure was possible through "talk therapy," although ideas about who did the talking, what they talked about, and what did the curing, differed considerably; and 5) that, rather disquietingly, the nature and specifics of theory theory did not seem to matter very much. Contemporary clinical psychotherapy, as opposed to Psychoanalysis as we know it, evolved from a combination of this package with its earlier roots.

Starting in the 1950s, there was an explosion in psychoanalytic theory building, both of clinical theory and of theory theory. During the Second World War, young physicians in the United States military had great success in treating what we now call Post-Traumatic Stress Disorder (PTSD)[11] in men overwhelmed by their combat experiences. We would now call this treatment brief psychoanalytic psychotherapy. The therapeutic excitement and optimism that these young doctors felt in their work led them to swell the postwar classes at American psychoanalytic institutes. However, as the 1950s progressed, there was a realization by many individual psychotherapists, some of whom clustered in small groups, that the theory and practice that evolved largely out of the

---

11 Called shell shock in WW I and battle fatigue in WW II.

successful brief therapies and Freudian ego-psychology either didn't do the job at all, or did only a part of it. A similar realization occurred in some, albeit a minority, of established psychoanalysts who learned their discipline before the war. As Rollo May (1958) summed it up in the opening chapter of the so aptly titled book (May, Angel, & Ellenberger, 1958) *Existence: New Dimensions in Psychiatry and Psychology*,

> Many psychiatrists and psychologists in Europe and others in this country have been asking themselves disquieting questions, and others are aware of gnawing doubts which arise from the same half-suppressed and unasked questions. Can we be sure, one such question goes, that we are seeing the patient as he really is, knowing him in his own reality; or are we seeing merely a projection of our own theories about him?
>
> (p. 3)

This concern received interdisciplinary support two decades later from the work of Kahneman and Tversky (Kahneman, Slovic, & Tversky, 1982) on judgments made under uncertainty. They found that, in trying to navigate an uncertain world, we make use of strategies called Heuristics and Biases. They consist of different kinds of shortcuts for navigating this uncertain world with insufficient data. The most important kind of shortcut is the Representativeness Heuristic. Therapists (that is, us) as a class of individuals functioning in an uncertain world make use of it. Let's say we are listening to a patient. We think that we discern a pattern in what they are saying and that it is consistent with a theory we subscribe to. The first problem is that we are certain of the theory even though we have no basis for that certainty. The second is whether or not the patient's associations are consistent, *representative*, of that theory. What's interesting is that while we have some ability to doubt the representativeness of the patient's associations, we have no ability to doubt the validity of the theory; hence it becomes a projection onto the patient. Another fallacy in our position that Kahneman and Tversky write about is that, in our psychoanalytic thinking drawn from out practice, we are forced to rely on small samples of patients from which to reach conclusions. We expect these small samples to accurately reflect the behaviour of very large samples drawn from the same population. We experience our conclusions drawn from them (the small samples in our practice) as valid and revelatory when they are neither, and cling to them with great conviction.

As I will argue throughout the course of this book, the full answers to these questions lead inevitably to *an* Existential Psychotherapy. However, the more immediate responses of psychoanalytic theoreticians were quite different. Let's list them, trying to stay in roughly chronological order. First we have the Interpersonal School (e.g., Sullivan, 1953/1997; Thompson, 1964) and the British Middle School (e.g., Guntrip, 1971; Winnicott, 1972, 1975). Then came the Existentialists, who came and went (not the fully realized Existentialist psychology I am aiming for here) and the Self Psychologists who continued to evolve. Finally, at the end of the century, the Relational and Intersubjective Schools, founded by a handful of theorists, made their appearance. Through all of this, the Freudian-Kleinian conflict remained and a growing number of clinicians began to pick and choose at will pieces of each of these schools that seemed to most accurately reflect their clinical experience. Beginning in the last quarter of the 20th century, philosophy (Existentialism/Phenomenology and Post Modernism) and Neuroscience were added unevenly by psychoanalytic alchemists intent on making therapeutic gold. This is the tradition in which I find my own work. Attachment Theory (Bowlby, 1958, 1969) was a prominent early and successful example of this late 20th century trend. At the very end of the century, a small identified and named group, the Boston Change Process Study Group, and a far larger and disparate collection of Psychotherapists concluded that something more, something *beyond* what *any* of these schools could offer, was needed to produce Therapeutic Action. The something more was *a human and caring attitude* that a therapist conveys to their patient, *even if they remain unaware that they are doing so*.

Freud and Klein (and their descendants) maintained a focus on anxiety derived from sex and aggression whereas these other schools focused instead on the Self, or relationality (the Interpersonal, Intersubjective, or Relational Schools), or meaninglessness and death. These groups, particularly the Freudians and Kleinians and the mid-century Existentialists tended to view the focus of each other as defensive byproducts of "the truth." I would accept the Existentialist critique but argue for striking out *defensive* and instead trying to see how these pieces might fit together, albeit in unexpected ways.

There are two controversial points to be made here. The first is what I have *not* said. In offering a psychoanalytic history, I have offered no critical or opprobrious comments about *any* of these schools. This is not because it is a history and historians must present their material in a neutral or measured way. It *is* because it cannot be said that one theory is better than any of the others, makes meaning better than the others, or, for that matter, can claim more interdisciplinary verification than the others. They have their foibles, of course. Classical Kleinian Theory, for example, asserted and continues to assert that an infant at age 4 months or, even in utero, is capable of cogent thought and fantasy, that that thought is accessible and can be remembered by the adult patient when the analyst interprets it. For a treatment to be successful, the *something more* is always required of the analyst, but, since that something more can be delivered without the therapist's awareness, OK, unconsciously, it cannot follow that the ideas present in any named school are necessary let alone sufficient for therapeutic success.

In contrast, the oral (as opposed to the textual) history of the development of psychoanalytic theory as taught in our psychoanalytic institutes has had, at times, a mythic quality. In its first half-century, it was driven by putative discoveries made from subjective observations of patient behavior and theory-based clinical impasses. It was the stuff of drive theories and one-person psychologies. The full meaning of the theoretical shifts that ensued from its failings often did not become clear for decades after they had occurred.

The second point I want to make is that our history, for the moment, has paused here. After the millennium, with the exception of the interdisciplinary consideration of neuroscience, *no major innovations have so far been added to the canon of Psychoanalysis.*[12] To take a bit of the sting out of this observation, let's talk about the contributions of Martin Bergmann (1993). Bergmann described three sorts of psychoanalytic innovators, both clinical and metapsychological: Extenders, Modifiers, and Heretics. As I described this in 2003,

> Extenders take current theory into unexplored areas but do not demand a modification of theory, theory of technique, or means of validation. Modifiers present a revision or reformulation of theory or technique but do so without leaving the framework of current theory or its methodology for the validation of hypotheses. Heretics formally break with the standard theory and methodology of the times, whether or not they remain organizationally under the umbrella of Psychoanalysis. Heretics also define new criteria for validating the efficacy of their views or approach.
>
> (p. 127)

What I mean, then, when I say that there have been no major innovations in Psychoanalysis since roughly the millennium is that *there have been no new heresies since then.* Heresies would be things like, in their day, Self-Psychology or Relational Psychology. There *have* been extensions and modifications to clinical theory and at least extensions to theory theory since the millennium.

Although I hesitate to say it, the exception to this statement is my own work. I would classify the Telephone Analysis paper I wrote in 2003 as a modification, although an important one. However, since 2007 and now stretching over five books, the current volume, and a half-dozen or so papers, I have been offering a radical critique of standard psychoanalytic theories and have constructed instead an interdisciplinary theory grounded in neuroscience, general psychology, and Existentialist philosophy. The jury is still out on the ultimate success of these efforts.

How is Existentialism different from all these other theories? Whereas other psychological theories content themselves with discussing etiologies of psychopathology, treatment, normal development, perception, and motivation (an all-inclusive list would be larger), Existentialism takes up the Psychology of Being. As a named theory, it rose to prominence in the United States in the 1960s and then sort of disappeared in the 70s as the spirit of the 60s waned. It entailed an integration of philosophy and psychology that was novel for the times, although its roots could, arguably, be traced back to *The Metaphysics* (Aristotle, 1998). As a mostly implicit psychological theory, we will find that it has continued to exist in the work of Irwin Yalom (1980, 1989/2012) and as an unnamed part of other theories—Self Psychology

---

12 This is not to say that considerable tinkering hasn't taken place. Analysts are, after all, great tinkerers.

(Kohut, 1977) and the British Middle School (Guntrip, 1971; Winnicott, 1975). Its phenomenological cousin (Boss, 1963) has been recently revived in the work of the Intersubjective School (Stolorow, 2011). (We will discuss the relationship of Existentialism and Phenomenology in Chapter 3.) In this and my previous works (Leffert, 2016, 2018), I aim to redraw an Existentialist position (as opposed to a theory) on a much wider interdisciplinary canvas. This entails an integration of psychology, philosophy, and physiology (to offer a larger umbrella than does neuroscience). It allows for Interdisciplinary Studies to make a *clinical* entrance and render Psychoanalysis as a special case of the wider understanding of Human Being. To accomplish this, I will posit, we will have to take positions in ontology and epistemology (the studies of Being and of Knowing).

Have Psychotherapists and Psychoanalysts engaged this material at all, and, if so, how have they done it?

The educational and practice traditions of Psychotherapists

If we look at the different disciplines that produce (among other things) Psychotherapists—Counseling, Medicine, Nursing, Psychiatry, Psychoanalysis, and Psychiatry—we find that they manifest dramatically different educational and clinical practices. So we return to a consideration of these various groups of Psychotherapists and the way they came by their interests in clinical theory and metapsychology. Psychotherapists and Psychoanalysts differ in their education and modes of practice from the other healing professions in an at times problematic fashion. Disciplines like medicine or nursing, for example, are taught didactically and ahistorically. They are clinically practiced entirely in the present; how they *were* practiced is seen as largely irrelevant (except for a rare history course that appears now and again). They are also professions focused on patient care.

In contrast, the *history* of the way we (Psychotherapists and Psychoanalysts) work is taught to us, some would say over-taught, both didactically and clinically. Here's the problem. Some concepts and understandings that developed in the past, in our history as a profession, are relevant to and useful in our practice as clinicians today. They involve teachings of clinical theory, not theory theory, and are often associated with the names of the clinicians who developed them. The problem, *the problem*, is that some of them are not currently relevant, are only arcane historical artifacts, and we clinicians are sometimes *unable to tell the difference*. For those concepts that remain of clinical utility, there is a danger of confusing their history with their contemporary usage and then employing them in arcane ways. The distinction between idea and artifact is at times hard to define (and, once defined, to maintain); a particular source of that difficulty can be found in the works of Freud and, in the Kleinian institutes, those of Melanie Klein. Freud, over his long career, gave birth to many psychoanalytic concepts that subsequently became indispensable, however, his writings on them are not indispensable and indeed sometimes serve to obfuscate contemporary *connaissance* (knowings) of them. It is true, however, that Psychotherapists are taught much less history of their disciplines than are Psychoanalysts and, as a result, are less burdened by the problem. *This* situation is changing. If one looks at the *current* curriculum taught at a range of psychoanalytic Institutes—from the William Alanson White to the New York Psychoanalytic to the New Center for Psychoanalysis—one finds that much less history is taught now than was taught even a decade ago and that instead we find that a large number of short diverse courses appearing in a positive attempt to ground our students more fully in the wide range of our discipline.

The idea that Human Beings (of which patients are a sub-class) can be unconscious of things guiding their thoughts and behavior and that we need to deploy clinical theory based on this idea is an example of an ancient but still clinically relevant idea.[13] On the other hand, the idea (now a century old) that the mental apparatus, Mind or whatever, can be divided up into three boxes—Ego, Id, and Superego—with mental activity falling into one, or another, or the conflicts between them has no *empirical* standing in the present. In other words, it is a construct. Some significant number of Psychoanalysts still, however, relies on them to guide their clinical work and their thinking. To the extent that they represent a kind of taxonomic shorthand they do little harm, but to the extent that they are employed as tools for theory-based Therapeutic Action they lead to incomplete therapies and analyses.

We have not yet talked specifically about how therapist education plays out across the disciplines of Psychotherapy and Psychoanalysis: Let's turn to this task now.

The Psychotherapists

So let's begin with the roughly half million clinicians whose varying education and degrees make them so hard to classify. I know of *no* attempts to study *or* classify this group as a whole, and attempting to do so is a bit like trying to describe the proverbial elephant: What you perceive depends on your tools and your perspective. I'm going to use broad strokes to draw on this very large canvas to see what we can actually say about them.

Psychotherapists have graduate degrees (masters level or doctorate) in Counseling, Nursing, Psychiatry, Psychology, or Social Work. Psychology as a discipline led to Psychotherapy through roots grounded in client *assessment and research*. It has been argued that Modern Psychology appeared on the scene in 1879 (Hunt, 2007). That was the year in which Wilhelm Wundt performed the first psychological experiment at a university. It was designed to collect data for a PhD thesis. But speaking to psychology's schizophrenic-like origins, the most important psychologists of the late 19th and early 20th centuries were

---

13 Please note the language: I am *not* describing a dynamic system Unconscious separated from consciousness by a repression barrier with our therapeutic task being to perforate that barrier.

undoubtedly the neurologist Sigmund Freud and the philosopher and physician Pierre Janet. In contrast, Social Work evolved out of a discipline grounded in *care*, tending directly to clients' needs in hospitals and in the World:[14] the physical world and the world of relationships. Psychotherapy appeared later in the teaching and practice of Social Work. Psychologists thus approached the field from the direction of observation and measurement, while Social Workers came from a discipline that prioritized care of the patient. Psychiatry, a *medical* specialty, grew principally out of the *supervision of the care* of psychotic or gravely disabled, usually hospitalized patients (Foucault, 1961/2006) and only much later added talking therapy to its treatment armamentarium for dealing with less disabled outpatients. It is fair to say that the advent of modern psychopharmacology eventually took most, but by no means all, Psychiatrists out of the Psychotherapy marketplace. Today's graduate education of all of these groups would likely include some number of classes (varying greatly from institution to institution and program to program as do all of these descriptions) on named psychoanalytic theories and theory theories. They would have been added to eclectic curricula on the practice of psychotherapy. Courses on child development and neuroscience also appear in contemporary curricula in some fashion. Attachment theory and functional neuroscience are (as they should be) of great pedagogic interest right now.

Psychotherapists encounter psychoanalytic teachers in different ways. One involves psychoanalysts who may teach a course in a graduate program involving clinical theory, theory theory or group supervision. The other includes continuing education courses in psychoanalytic ideas concerning theory or practice that psychotherapists (students or practitioners) choose to attend.

The other parallel path is more interesting. It involves teachers of clinical and theoretical psychodynamic psychotherapy who are themselves Psychotherapists, not Psychoanalysts. It can be assumed that these teachers, in both their own training and subsequent to graduation, have encountered psychoanalytic ideas in the manner described above. But what they teach is psychotherapy, teachings that they themselves have absorbed as part of *their* education. This involves the intergenerational transmission of a unique body of knowledge, one that includes psychoanalytic teachings as an *integrated part of a wider whole*. I know very little about just what this process looks like over the generations[15] and just what kinds of things are passed on in this way.

Recently, however, I came upon a blog posting by Harry Butler (2018), a past Dean of the San Diego State University School of Social Work, entitled "The Healing Power of Clinical Social Work." What better place to see how Social Workers teach their discipline? As Butler puts it, "people come to therapy for three reasons: to heal, to problem solve, and to grow." He awards Attachment

---

14 I capitalize *World* to indicate that it is World in a Phenomenological sense, inhabited by Selves, where needs *at hand* are taken up and ministered to in a state of Everydayness.
15 We know a great deal about what transgenerational transmission looks like in Psychoanalysis.

Theory pride of place in normal and pathological development and as a tool of therapeutic action. He rejects the split in Social Work between systems practitioners (hospitals, nursing homes, etc.) and psychotherapists, positing instead what I would describe as a deconstruction of the term *Social Work* into *work on the social*, which continues to join the two. Clinical Social Workers, in Butler's view, thus bring a particular skillset to the study and treatment of their patients. He finds a place for psychoanalytic ideas in his teachings and also describes some of the power struggles unique to the field. We can't generalize from a sample of one, but we at least have a window into the field.

We know little or nothing about how Psychotherapists continued to educate themselves, after they graduated from their training programs, prior to mid-century. The 1960s saw an explosion of interest in self-understanding and self-actualization that brought with it exploratory psychotherapies aimed at putting a patient in touch with early affects and traumas (for example, so called primal scream therapies), improving interpersonal skills and experience (sensitivity training, encounter groups, and group therapy), and improving relationships (couples therapy and family therapy). Psychotherapists also began to more frequently seek out Psychotherapy and Psychoanalysis for themselves. As these disciplines appeared on the scene, psychotherapists made use of the burgeoning new literature to educate themselves in them. The appearance of continuing education requirements for licensure facilitated this process for all mental health professionals.

The Psychoanalysts

Psychoanalysts, psychoanalytic literature, and psychoanalytic education have been known for their conservatism and resistance to change. For the first 20 or even 30 years or so of its existence, this reputation was certainly not merited. An atmosphere analogous to that of the Wild West pertained with the term *psychoanalyst* being a kind of self-signifier used by individuals who had availed themselves of whatever study, clinical supervision, or personal analysis seemed good to them. For the next 50 years or so, its reputation for rigidity, orthodoxy, and resistance to change in either its theories or its clinical practice was certainly merited but, with the waning of the century, at least for some analysts, it became less warranted. This trend accelerated in the new millennium. Organizational politics grounded in power dynamics (Leffert, 2010, 2013) was certainly a factor in this struggle, played out in the pluralistic but rigid International Psychoanalytic Association (IPA) and in the more rigid American Psychoanalytic Association (APsaA). In the United States, these factors expressed themselves in the then well-known[16] 50-year battle to medicalize

---

16 I suspect that, a generation later, the memory of this struggle has faded and am offering this brief narrative as a kind of reminder that knowledge and power/politics, as Foucault (2000) stated, are impossible to separate.

Psychoanalysis that was lost in 1985 (Pear, 1992)[17] when four psychologists supported by the American Psychological Association brought suit against APsaA charging that it and several of its institutes had conspired to establish a monopoly and stifle competition. While the lawsuit was successful in that it forced APsaA to integrate (in practice, APsaA remained a largely medical organization until the opening decades of the new millennium), it could *not* force it to change the rigidity with which it regulated the creation or dissemination of psychoanalytic knowledge. I suspect that, for most readers, the idea that politics could so control the creation and dissemination of knowledge is an unfamiliar one, although it is well-known in postmodern thought (see Leffert, 2010, for a discussion of this issue).

APsaA implemented its policies of orthodoxy and control in two ways. A certification process directed at individual members provided a required ticket for faculty advancement in local institutes, particularly to reach the esteemed rank of training analyst and the patient referrals that flowed from it. Phenomenologically speaking, despite claims to the contrary, certification never translated into any measure of clinical competence, but it did require its applicants to demonstrate a thorough knowledge of orthodox clinical theory and theory theory. At the same time, APsaA maintained control of institute curricula (that is, the dissemination of what is defined as psychoanalytic knowledge) through a process of institute site visits and continued institutional re-accreditation. This state of affairs could not, however, continue indefinitely.

The success of The Lawsuit, and the enormous loss of face suffered by the then orthodox leadership of APsaA that ensued, planted seeds that flowered into a challenge to that leadership that led to open civil war.[18] As a result, APsaA's regulatory functions have begun to disintegrate and it is (as of 2018) becoming a largely scientific and facilitating organization. No one has as yet made any connection between these political events and the growing eclecticism of institute curricula, but such a connection would certainly seem warranted.

But there is more. As I have posited earlier, although interdisciplinary studies, particularly neuroscience, are becoming a part of Psychoanalysis, we have seen no theoretical advances beyond the relational and intersubjective thought of the late 20th century. What *has* appeared is an increasing interest in theoretical plurality and in trying to figure out what exactly analysts *do* as opposed to what they write and talk about.

---

17 In describing what came to be known as "The Lawsuit" I have chosen to cite an article that appeared in *The New York Times* to illustrate just how public the arguments over orthodoxy had become.

18 An unnoticed effect of the lawsuit and the resulting increase in psychologist membership in APsaA were the advent of increasing concerns about validity and replicability. These concerns highlighted the role of certification, not as a replicable measure of competence but as a rite of passage, and contributed to its downfall.

Theoretical plurality

If one wants to date the origins of Psychoanalysis to the publication of *Studies in Hysteria* in 1893–1895, within 15 years there were major theoretical if not clinical disagreements among Freud and his small band of followers. In branding these disagreements heresies punishable by expulsion, Freud established a tradition whereby theoretical disagreements were handled within Psychoanalysis until roughly the latter part of the 20th century.[19] (I have argued repeatedly that these disagreements are matters of belief, not fact, and that none of the theory theories at least has ever been proven, either clinically or interdisciplinarily.) Whereas the heretics had heretofore been comfortably expelled, beginning with the Self-Psychologists and moving on to the Relational and Intersubjective theorists, a secular change occurred: *they refused to leave*. Indeed, in institutes such as Chicago's Institute for Psychoanalysis, they even retained a significant share of power. Meanwhile, the Intersubjectivists founded their own institute in Los Angeles, the Institute for Contemporary Psychoanalysis, while their senior members maintained their seats at the table of the four somewhat orthodox institutes situated in the area. Meanwhile, Relational analysts rose to prominence in an Interpersonal and Existentialist institute (Rollo May was an important member) in New York: the William Alanson White (WAW). The Post-Doctoral Program at New York University that had formerly been a site of advanced studies in Ego Psychology also became a center of Relational Psychoanalysis. Analysts still had theoretical fights all the time, but nothing happened as a result, and, eventually, most of us got tired. It was in this atmosphere that theoretical plurality was eventually born. It involved an acknowledgement that different analysts subscribed to different theories, mostly theory theories, and that, in order to exist in institute or society life, they would have to at least tolerate one another. I would stress that many of us went beyond that minimum to maintain collegial relationships with, well, *our colleagues*.

But this trend has gone farther still. As analysts and psychotherapists read and communicated with each other, exclusive orthodoxy gave way to theoretical eclecticism. Such eclecticism is now taught to candidates in most institutes, and our candidates grow up into eclectic analysts. Individuals simultaneously kept multiple theoretical points of view in their heads in the clinical situation and employed one or another as circumstances required. These practices were even encouraged during training when candidates were required to present clinical material (either in written or oral form) and then discuss it from the perspective of different metapsychological theories. Rather than maintain these separate theories, many of us began talking and thinking in terms of theoretical hybrids. We did this with a variable recognition that these theories were sometimes in

---

19 Again, although this history was well known in the past I have no idea whether it is still common knowledge or has been largely lost to memory or significance.

conflict or even mutually exclusive. Those of us who thought about this state of affairs used to reach the conclusion (as I did before abandoning metapsychology altogether in the new millennium) that we lacked an over-arching theory but would develop one sometime in the future. In the meantime, lacking this *über*-theory, we would make use of the discontinuous theory fragments that we had developed.

So, today, what exactly is plurality, or as it is also referred to, the use of multiple models? A recent issue of the *Journal of the American Psychoanalytic Association* (Volume 65 #5, October 2017) contains a section of four papers on the subject. The four authors (Blass, 2017; Cooper, 2017; LaFarge, 2017; Zimmer, 2017) manifest diverse opinions on plurality, and Zimmer is politically careful to respect their diversity. My purpose in accessing their work is not to seek truth about these complex issues but rather to simply take a look at contemporary psychoanalytic thinking on the subject. As more Psychoanalysts and Psychotherapists find themselves thinking and speaking in multiple psychoanalytic languages, they are implicitly using Postmodern tools (Leffert, 2010) to do so. Certainty seems to have given way to Uncertainty, Subjectivity, and Unknowability. The concept of multiple threads of ideas existing braided into an inter-referential sheaf of *différance* (Derrida, 1982) in which conflicting hypotheses are given equal standing and maintained in connection with each other (a *multilectic* constructivism) is widely although largely unknowingly employed by psychoanalytic clinicians. Hoffman (1998), however, enunciates this position with great clarity in what he describes as a *dialectical constructivist* point of view. I believe this is what Zimmer, perhaps unknowingly, is talking about when he refers to us being in a *post-pluralistic state*.

Zimmer (2017) draws a distinction between abstract theoretical discourse such as prevails in classrooms and scientific meetings and what he terms *"crisis management"* (p. 820, italics retained) and I would term simply as the normative therapeutic discourse that takes place in the clinical situation. Here, the analyst must act "before all the data are in and fully processed" (p. 820). He goes on to argue that what we have called clinical theory is much more useful than theory theory. Indeed, contemporary study of clinical material by small groups of analysts has come, more and more, to focus on important *clinical* moments, irrespective of the theoretical orientation of the participants. There are two problematic premises inherent in Zimmer's position. The first of these is that the uncertainty of the clinical situation would be resolvable if only the analyst had time to think about it. I have argued for some time (Leffert, 2016) that this is not the case, that uncertainty is an inherent part of the human condition in general and human discourse in particular. This is, in effect, an ontological critique. The second is that none of these authors consider the possibility of a world without theory theory and that, apparently, no thought was given to including a contributor who holds this position in the discussion as a fifth participant.

Although I want to talk individually about the contributions of all of these authors (Blass, 2017; Cooper, 2017; LaFarge, 2017; Zimmer, 2017), there are some general points that I want to make first. Each of them harbors some kind of *core theoretical model* that organizes both their thinking and their clinical work. My own reading of this concept is that it involves a significant dilution of theory theory with clinical theory (the content of which varies with the author) in their work with patients. As Zimmer describes them, Blass remains committed to the model she was taught in training, whereas Cooper has completely separated from his, with La Farge lying somewhere in between. I have reached the conclusion in my own work that there is no place for theory theory as it has been constituted beyond something that analysts like to think about and somewhat arbitrarily apply to their patients. Indeed, Tversky and Kahneman (1974/1982) draw similar conclusions about the wider world encompassing any judgments made under uncertainty, positing that we devise subjective, *but not necessarily valid* ways of navigating this territory. This argument led me to remember that I didn't always think clinically in the way I do now. In the 1960s, 70s, and early 80s, I was a committed Freudian, making use of psychosexual developmental theory and ego psychology. I saw the goal of analysis as facilitating the development of patients' transference neuroses, the working through of which would enable a final separation from their infantile objects. It was a one-person psychology. My development as a Psychotherapist, which, I'm happy to say, continues into the present, does not seem to have involved a renunciation of these beliefs so much as a gradual realization that I was no longer using them. In saying this, I do not mean to deny that my origins, as those of any analyst's, have shaped and flavored my development as a clinician and a philosopher.[20] So has the knowledge of the multiple theories I have studied since. Instead, I slipped into a phenomenological form of therapeutic discourse, although it was only some years later (Leffert, 2007a, 2007b) that I acquired the language to be able to speak and write about it (Leffert, 2016).

LaFarge (2017) makes points about clinical theory as well as theory theory. Her model is that of the analyst's possessing a personal core theory to which elements of other theories can be imported in the clinical moment, albeit with considerable risk. In offering us a rich and intricate paper, she raises issues involving levels of Existential complexity beyond the points she recognizes. She first cites and introduces us to two concepts of, interestingly, Kleinian origin. The first has to do with Bion's (1962/1984) clinical idea of the *selected fact*. He posits that the analyst's listening with free-floating attention is suddenly interrupted by the coming into awareness of some idea about what the patient is saying. The idea is conscious; the process of its selection is not. Neuroscientists studying consciousness and memory have defined a conscious Workspace Theory in which elements appear after selection by a parallel distributed processing network. The analyst then pursues the selected fact in her own reflections and with the patient in whatever manner seems most appropriate

---

20 The unstated premise here is that in fully describing our work, we need to talk philosophy rather than metapsychology.

to her. Britton and Steiner (1994), however, warn that it may be impossible to distinguish between the configuration that emerges from a selected fact and "the crystallization of delusional certainty from an 'overvalued idea'" (p. 1069). Indeed, their concern mirrors my own in that I would equate the *overvalued idea* with Tversky and Kahneman's (1974/1982) Representativeness Heuristic, in which the listener grasps some similarity, either actual or imagined, between what they are hearing and a particular pattern of meaning that they have constructed in the past.

LaFarge (2017) describes her *personal core theory* as placing "unconscious fantasy at the center of [her] view of mental life, as the point of articulation of historical experience, trauma and wish, of internal and external reality" (p. 833). She stresses that Discourse (my word) must always occupy the analytic foreground while, for the analyst to listen analytically, theory must also present, albeit in the background. For our purposes here, I am most interested in the fact that, by introducing the concept with the possessive personal pronoun, she is asserting that other analysts can have other personal core theories with none given pride of place. The personal core theory, then, is a manifestation of the Psychotherapist's *irreducible subjectivity*. In this vein, she introduces a clinical vignette of a patient in analysis for a year and a half with the parens "(The analysis was conducted on the couch at a frequency of four times a week.)" (p. 834). In doing so, she again suggests that an analysis can take place at other frequencies and not necessarily involve a couch. Whether in saying this she is acknowledging that this is true of the work of *other* analysts or whether she means to include some of her own work here as well remains uncertain.

LaFarge (2017) uses a case vignette to illustrate how an analyst can move from their core personal theory to *importing* elements of other theories (in the case, she gives up her focus on the patient's unconscious fantasy, shifting to his traumatic affects). She considers this procedure to be somewhat perilous, embodying a risk of the move being made defensively, as a sign of the analyst's countertransference resistance. In positing this, she ignores the other possibility: that clutching the core theory, an overvalued idea, can also be motivated by the same kind of defensive reasons. She believes that following the course of the analysis will reveal the accuracy of either position, but the assumed objectivity of the necessary observations seems unfounded. LaFarge sees similar dangers in what she describes as a "less integrated personal theory, in which multiple models with contradictory clinical indications coexist side by side [facilitating] a defensive shifting between models in the analyst's formation of the selected fact" (p. 842). Such an assertion seems more of an opinion than a truth. Indeed, many Psychotherapists might be more comfortable with the post-structural viewpoint in which, in the face of an arbitrary certainty, a dialectical constructivist position is more likely to yield therapeutic success.

Despite the differences touted by Zimmer (2017), at the end of the day, a hard day I might add, Blass's (2017) views turn out to be very similar to LaFarge's (2017). Again, there are interesting complexities that remain unaddressed. According to Blass, we Psychotherapists each have a uniquely personal analytic model that LaFarge would call a personal core theory and I would call a theory of personality, psychopathology, and cure. Both authors talk about these models shifting to *incorporate* new or different clinical or theoretical ideas; these change the single model. Although this process may involve a transitional phase in which multiple models are taken in, the process ultimately leads back to a single model. Like opinions, everyone has a model, but they may sometimes, for multiple reasons, refuse to admit that they do.

Blass (2017) seems to find it in no way problematic that some models are in conflict with others; by seeing a model as limited to a single slice of the pie, involving what she calls *restrictions*, there is no problem with what goes on in any of the other slices. By referring to herself as a "Kleinian," Blass tells us that what she means by a model involves a particular metapsychological space. Speaking for myself, I don't find such restrictions tolerable or clinically effective, and I will tell you something else: *Neither does Blass*. In spite of the Kleinian self-signifier, she elsewhere defines models as

> Not merely formulations of objective findings regarding the workings of the mind or the sources of pathology or what kinds of interventions bring about change most effectively. Rather, they offer conceptions of the person, of health and disorder, and of what it means to bring about effective and meaningful psychoanalytic change.
>
> (pp. 846–847)

This *phenomenological* (Leffert, 2016) definition exists on a much higher ontological level than does the signifier "Kleinian," it adequately contains *all* the pieces of psychoanalytic thought that exist on this level. It also accepts and metabolizes questions and conflicts about what comprises truth that cannot be tolerated at lower ontological levels (the Anna Freudians vs. the Melanie Kleinians, for example).

Cooper (2017) goes down his own different road entailing multiple models. Like LaFarge (2017) and Blass (2017), he sees Psychoanalysis as a quest to elucidate a patient's *unconscious fantasy*. In contrast to their positions, he clinically employs multiple metapsychologies to "expand the metaphorical language with which the analyst tries to make contact with the patient's unconscious life" (p. 859). He extends this position when he says, "I think of our relationship to theory as a type of object relationship in which we aim to work and play in thoughtful and supple ways within and between our theories—an interplay of theories, as it were" (p. 860). For Cooper, multiple theories promote the analyst's degrees of freedom for self-reflection. In accepting multiple theories, he is not promoting theoretical integration (about which he remains doubtful) but rather pragmatically employing one or more of them when needed in a given therapeutic situation. For Cooper (2017),

> Theory is our best construction of that workable path (or our best route back to it) and our use of one theory or multiple theories is to some

extent the result of our personal, pragmatic discovery about what has been most useful to us in understanding and helping our patients.

(p. 862)

I would rephrase this slightly to "…our best construction *at the time*…" to reflect our analytic adaptability. We are (hopefully) vibrant human beings who must be open to change, as our patients must be if an analysis or psychotherapy has any chance of success.

Cooper (2017) offers a case vignette to illustrate what he is talking about. A patient, Mark, repeatedly asks him questions about Psychoanalysis, asks him to explain the process to him. Cooper, over time, discovers that these questions have many meanings, mostly having to do with differing facets (Cooper calls them surfaces) of Mark's relationship with his mother. He deploys a changing series of metapsychologies in order to understand his patient. In following him, I can see how each of the metapsychologies applies, but I cannot connect them to one another; the manner of Cooper's doing so seems arbitrary to me. And this, perhaps implicitly, is his point: That we use metapsychology individually, perhaps idiosyncratically, not only as it pertains to us as analysts, but rather, uniquely, as it pertains to each therapeutic couple. To go further still, even those therapists who *believe* they are subjectively adhering to some single theory in rigorous isolation may be doing the same thing.

I cannot, in all honesty leave the subject of multiple models, of plurality, without some statement of my own views on the subject. I must first acknowledge that I find myself on the horns of a dilemma. As a phenomenologist, I have come to find that there is very little ontological standing to be had in any of the metapsychologies, and yet, *and yet*, the context of this position is that I am very well-educated in all of them. So I am left with the question: [Is the latter necessary for the former?] To rephrase the question: [Do I maintain an unconscious understanding of these theories that is necessary for me to do my work?] Although I *can* envision a psychoanalytic education without metapsychology (drawing on interdisciplinary studies and philosophy, and clinical theory), I'm not yet prepared to say what people coming out of such a program would look like as analysts. My solution to the dilemma, for the present, has been to bracket[21] the questions. It may well be that they will answer themselves over time in response to the gradual evolution of institute curricula.

There is a further problem in the use of psychoanalytic theories. Implicit in the work of these authors (Blass, 2017; Cooper, 2017; LaFarge, 2017; Zimmer, 2017) is a premise that I believe to be widely held. Briefly, it is that the clinician's examination of his own work while immersed in the clinical situation can lead to observations that in themselves have *evidential value* in defining the

---

21 Brackets were used phenomenologically by Husserl (1937/1970, 1913/1983) to acknowledge and state a point but to *defer* (half of Derrida's (1982) *différance*, the other half being to *differ*) it until more information became available.

Psychoanalytic Situation. Further, if one is to view psychoanalytic theory theory or metapsychology as [scientific], then one *must* hold our observations to at least approach validity.[22]

Theory, then, is a construction (Cooper, 2017) with very fuzzy boundaries, which places it implicitly (whether the authors realize it or not) in the post-structural camp; we also understand that constructions can operate consciously and/or unconsciously. Constructions (Hoffman, 1998) are just that; they are often temporary structures that help us to explore meaning. Ego psychology is an example of a very long-lived construction that leads some analysts to great meaning while others find little to be had there. If one does not try to prove that some people are right and others wrong (Psychoanalysts have attempted to prove things like this since the turn of the century, the *20th century*, with no demonstrable success), then theories became *everyday* tools, kept *at hand* for use as needed. The construct of tools is particularly valuable, many of them are handy, they accomplish work, and all can be useful. Their everydayness, their *Alltäglichkeit*, to bring Heidegger (1927/2010) into the conversation and get ahead of ourselves by a chapter or two, refers to usefulness, capable of accomplishing the work at hand. It involves neither the creativity, the *thrownness*, that many analysts ascribe to theory, nor the broken, useless, *fallen* status that a nihilist would ascribe to it.

What I have wanted to convey in this section about theory and plurality is that there are no final answers here but that a phenomenological approach, such as we will be discussing, offers a path to grasping the issues here (perhaps a theory theory theory?) without asking more of us than we can deliver.

What do psychoanalysts and psychotherapists actually do with their patients?

This is an extremely difficult question to answer, and, until recently, few true attempts have been made to do so. An interesting attempt *is* currently being made and will bring us into the present and the future. I believe, and have written about it a number of times, that there are differences, sometimes large differences, between what Psychoanalysts and Psychotherapists say or write about what they do, what they believe that they do, and what they actually do. There are also differences in what analysts think *other* analysts are doing and what they are doing. The same differences apply to therapists. There are also serious questions concerning the extent to which what goes on in an analysis is even knowable and, more heretical still, whether these limits on knowability are necessarily a bad thing.

---

22 By saying this, I am not taking a position in the old fight about whether Psychoanalysis is or isn't a science but rather that although metapsychology lies outside of [science] the same need not be true about the rest of Psychoanalysis. (I am again using brackets here because the whole question of what exactly is science, what ontological properties distinguish it, and how one navigates its geography is so exceedingly complex.)

There has been a sea change in the ways in which clinical material has been handled at conferences and in small group study groups. The discussions of plurality we have looked at have grown out of an exhaustion with clinical seminars in which the participants offer the presenter unsolicited supervisory advice and fight amongst themselves over the primacy of their preferred theories. This approach lies far away from studying what analysts actually *do*. Instead, formal and informal study groups have been forming, studying things like *selected facts* (Bion, 1962/1984) and *clinical moments* in which these groups single out agreed upon points of clinical urgency (my own term) in a clinical process and discuss them mostly in the absence of theory.

With this as background, a more organized, *somewhat* free-from-theory approach to studying clinical Psychoanalysis has been developing into the millennium. It has led to the formation of the Comparative Clinical Methods (CCM) project (Rudden & Bronstein, 2017; Tuckett, et al., 2008) that offers a kind of bridge between the Psychoanalysis past and present we have been discussing and Psychoanalysis future that we will be considering. Interestingly, the CCM project began in Europe with its roots going back to 2001 and was brought to North America via an International Psychoanalytic Association grant in 2008. The aim of the project is to develop "ways to describe and compare different methods of practicing as a psychoanalyst" (Tuckett, 2008a, p. 5).

The CCM method consists of a three-step approach. Groups of 8–15 members, led by a trained moderator, meet to study a case presented by one of its members. Their aim is to "examine each interpretation, prolonged silence or statement uttered by the presenting analyst during three or four analytic sessions with the same patient" (Rudden & Bronstein, 2017, p. 21). There are two ground rules: It is taken as a given that the case presented is analysis and the presenter a psychoanalyst and that the work was to be studied, not crypto-supervised. The discussions are structured to be experience-near and free of theoretical terminology. The rules removed most of the negative verbiage that plagues case presentations.[23] They looked at the clinical material along two dimensions: what was the analyst *doing* at a given point (step 1) and what is the analyst's understanding of the patient and the process that leads to these clinical actions (step 2). Lastly, the moderators of several groups meet to discuss what has taken place in them. Over the course of several rounds of such meetings, the authors (Tuckett, et al., 2008) decided (Tuckett, 2008b) that the things analysts do could fit into six categories, and that the analysts' understanding of the patient and the process, the theories they were using, could best be described in terms of five elements. The six categories are:

---

23 The two questions which are not dealt with and which we must bracket are [the degree to which the material present is an accurate rendition of events in the sessions] and [the question of how much the analyst's preparing a record of the sessions (taking detailed notes) alters the sessions, mostly by affecting the activity levels of the analyst].

1 Maintaining the analytic frame;
2 Adding something to facilitate unconscious process;
3 Questions and clarifications aimed at making things conscious;
4 Identifying emotion and fantasy in the here and now relationship with the analyst;
5 Interpretations or constructions that expand meaning;
6 Sudden reactions beyond the analyst's usual way of operating.

The five elements are:

1 What the analyst thinks is wrong with their patient;
2 The analyst's idea of what a psychoanalytic process is (what does the analyst listen for) and how it will transform their patient;
3 How does the analyst think analysis will help the patient (theory of therapeutic action)?[24]
4 What does the analyst feel they must do, step by step, to address the patient's problem, to further the process (theory of technique), and bring about change;
5 How does the analyst think about the therapeutic relationship (theory of transference)?

I have to return to the "*somewhat* free from theory" description that I suggested a few paragraphs back. The authors (Rudden & Bronstein, 2017; Tuckett, 2008a) variously describe limiting the group discourse to what is descriptively going on, without recourse to "theoretical language" or "jargon." Well and good. But they also want to take it as a given that every analyst *must* have a theory, that it serves as an analytic third, and that, along with the analyst and patient, it configures an oedipal triangle. They of course recognize that analysts have different theories, but they must have *some* theory. I see no problem with their wanting to assert these points; the problem I see is in their being taken as givens. They are actually hypotheses that are being posited: They need to be proved and could easily be explored within the confines of the study.

Another problem with the "six and five" is that they make an implicit assumption of knowability and dismissal of uncertainty that is on epistemological shaky ground. If they are treated as simply Post-Structural knowledges, this is not so much of a problem.

These objections aside, what unfolds here over the three steps is a rich and complex process, taking place consciously *and* unconsciously among the participants. It cannot help but change who they are as psychoanalysts and how they think about their work. There is also a selection process at work here. CCM groups meet over two days. This is a significant time commitment. Those participating in the groups must be open to studying diversity in the theory and practice

---

24 This is Rudden and Abbott's (2017) third element, Tuckett's (2008b) is how does the analyst listen to the patient's unconscious? The fact that there is a difference is of interest.

of Psychoanalysis and are already likely to be agents of change. Two important things take place beyond the boundaries of these meetings. The first is that anyone reading this material (I offer myself as an example) finds themselves thinking, or perhaps rethinking is better, about what they do in new ways. In other words, even if these ideas are used only in self-reflection, they can be of considerable value, sparking changes in how we work. It offers a way of thinking about what we are doing *in the session* in greater conscious depth. The second has to do with what happens when the participants in the CCM groups return to their respective psychoanalytic communities. My hypothesis here is that they serve as agents of change and that they gradually effect how communities think about theory and practice. The likelihood that this will happen is affirmed by Birksted-Breen's (2008) observation that it "was reflected in the enthusiasm of many participants who joined the workshops in increasing numbers and who took a version of [their] comparative method back to their own country to use with their colleagues" (p. 2). One might dismiss this idea with the thought that there is no possible way to know or quantify this. But there is a way, and it is to be found in Social Network Theory (Christakis & Fowler, 2009).

I have already (Leffert, 2013, 2016) written about the uses of Social Network Theory in understanding the behavior of psychoanalytic groups and the transfer of information (called contagion) both consciously and, more importantly, unconsciously between individual group members (called nodes). It provides a perspective on both psychotherapist and patient who, in addition to being members of their own group of two, are also members of multiple social networks through which contagion travels. One looks at the construction of groups in terms of degrees of separation; the limit for group cohesion and contagion is three degrees of separation. Psychoanalytic groups, institutes and societies manifest one and two degrees of separation. This means that they cohere tightly and are ideally structured for the transfer of contagion. Another factor at play here (that Christakis and Fowler, 2009, have not studied) is what I call *receptivity*. It involves the degree to which an individual is willing, consciously or otherwise, to accept a piece of information. In Social Network language, a lack of willingness might be termed *immunity*. Relatively high levels of immunity have historically characterized psychoanalytic groups, but their tight organization also offers a potential for change.

Agents of change, members returning from national or international meetings, speakers recruited externally to address local groups, and, now, members returning from CCM groups all serve as disrupters that break down immunity and promulgate new ideas. In the past, orthodox group members attended orthodox national meetings and very little actually *happened*. The situation is radically different now, and that difference may already be self-sustaining.

Metapsychology and *différance*

Metapsychology exists as a phenomenon. It used to exist as a group of adversarial ontologies. It currently exists in a state of plurality with the great majority of

Psychotherapists relying on some form or forms of metapsychology. It is unclear whether this is an intermediate state or what place, if any, metapsychology will have in the future. We are left to explore its meaning in the present. Perhaps what we come back to, for lack of a better term, is an inquiry into a theory theory theory, a theory of theory theories.

You will recall that a given of the CCM (Rudden & Bronstein, 2017; Tuckett, 2008a) project is that every analyst must have a theory, and by theory they mean metapsychology. They have nothing to say about the correctness of any theory beyond that of an Oedipus Complex (Birksted-Breen, 2008).[25] This serves as simply a repetition of Freud's position that the Oedipus complex is the foundational structure of modern Western society. The authors' position is further weakened by what I would infer to be their ignorance of the expanding body of writing on Queer Theory (Giffney & Watson, 2017) that views Freud's position on infantile sexuality as a power-laden lie. Tuckett observes that the CCM project is about studying the psychoanalytic process by looking at analyst's work, beliefs and ideas from the related perspectives of difference, differentiation, and comparison.

So where do metapsychologies come from anyway? Metapsychologies have grown out of a clinical process: clinicians trying to abstract and understand what was going on with their patients, how to construct theories of psychopathology and cure. These then developed by processes that can, in Bergmann's (1993), terms, broadly be described as extension, modification or heresy. With the exceptions of child observation and, more recently, neuroscience, they did not arise out of efforts to apply the world (the *Mitwelt* and *Umwelt*) to the clinical situation.

My own idea of what Psychoanalysis is differs considerably from the above. I was first educated in Freudian theory and subsequently learned the other metapsychologies. Although I no longer think of my work in terms of metapsychologies, I realize that they remain latently present within me, potentially as a perspective serving as an essential *Counterpath* (Malabou & Derrida, 1999/2004)[26] to the way I see things. I view the psychoanalytic situation as a therapeutic conversation, taking place in a physically and temporally defined space. Conversation should be understood in its widest sense to denote a rich and elaborate process that takes place simultaneously on conscious and unconscious levels, verbally and nonverbally. *It is atheoretical.* The analyst's role is to collaborate with their patient in seeking out or maintaining a focus on whatever points of urgency seem relevant to the patient and their life. The goal is to help patients seek out meaning in their lives; they mostly come to us because they have *fallen* (Heidegger, 1975/1982) out of meaning; they are in what

---

25 A child's relationship to their parents is certainly of immense importance but I would posit that it is impossible to reduce it to its psychosexual elements.
26 Malabou and Derrida posit that any path or idea exists in relationship to an opposite that it brings into Being.

I characterize as Crises of Being. An equally important goal is the relief of the pain and suffering attendant on this condition.

I am not trying to convert anyone to this position. I do hope that if readers follow these ideas through the coming chapters, they will reconsider, if not necessarily change, their ideas about the theories they cleave to.

To return to those metapsychologies that, irrespective of my views, do currently exist and even flourish in today's psychoanalytic world: Can we say more about their relationship to each other beyond their being plural or different? Post-structuralism (Leffert, 2010; McGowan, 1991) offers a tool for dealing with statements about the world that cannot be simultaneously or exclusively true; it has to do with *différance* (Derrida, 1982). Différance is a constructed term, a signifier that is derived from the French verb *différer*, which can mean "to differ" *and* "to defer."[27] Derrida inserts the final "a" in place of an "e" to signify what he is about. The first refers here to differing iterations of the same concept; different theories of neurosis or transference, for example. The second says that we will defer the question of which one might be correct or whether it is even possible to single out a concept. It includes the possibility or even likelihood that the question is undecidable. If we go back to the Greeks, it becomes clear that we are talking about *aporia*, referring to a group of concepts that, while individually plausible, are contradictory when taken together. This part also relates to Husserl's (1937/1970) concept of bracketing a term: retaining it for the present without considering its existence. This permits us to keep in the present concepts that conflict or even exist in either/or relationship to one another. They constitute dialectical relationships and, if created, dialectical-constructivist (Hoffman, 1998) relationships. So if we have a group of differing metapsychologies, we can, metaphorically, braid them into a *sheaf of différance* that allows multiple concepts drawn from differing strands to, in total, describe some point on the threads. In so doing, we are treating metapsychologies not as meta-knowledges but simply as knowledges.

We cannot say that any thread, any metapsychology, is true. Nor can we say that the braid of metapsychology, however interesting, tells us any truths about the world (the *Umwelt*). What we can say, and this is the interesting point, is that this braid does manifest a *social* truth, it tells us things about psychoanalysts and how they think about what they do at different points in time. It does not offer, however much we might wish it, reliable truths about our patients (a subset of the *Mitwelt*). Although I reject metapsychology as a successful ontology, we cannot reject its social truth. If you have followed my arguments about Post-Structuralism at all (in keeping with the chapter title, I have made them *brief*, perhaps too brief), then it should be emerging that I am offering an

---

27 Unlike in English, in French, there is no noun that has been formed to signify deferral and/or deferment. Derrida creates a neologism by changing out the "e" in the usual French noun *différence* and substituting an "a," creating *différance*, a noun, now adopted into common usage, that signifies both difference and deferment.

interdisciplinary epistemology of Psychoanalysis that is at the very least a supplement to metapsychology.

In this roundabout way, I am trying to suggest a way forward for Psychoanalysis present, acknowledging its social reality. To further understand the meaning of this term, I would add still another piece to the epistemology I have now been developing over several volumes (particularly, Leffert, 2010). This has to do with the work of Bruno Latour (1991/1993) who, to briefly summarize his position, posits and offers a proof that in *science* (not just *social* science), the "science" can never be separated from the "social." Latour's position in his aptly titled classic, *We Have Never Been Modern*, is that knowledge, scientific knowledge if you will, cannot be separated from the social circumstances of its discovery, maintenance, and deployment. The way that Latour describes this ontological situation is that knowledge exists in the form of very large, branched chain phenomenological hybrids that have social and "scientific" elements. The full extent of these branched chains may not at first be obvious. The psychoanalytic hybrid was composed of historical chains of theory and chains of clinical experience, to which, over the years, neuroscience chains and philosophical chains have been added. I have, over the years, gone about identifying other chains, such as those dealing with Social Networks (Leffert, 2013) and the nature and origins of the Self (Leffert, 2018). Through all of this, I have maintained an Existentialist/Phenomenological position that we will elaborate in the coming chapters.

References

Aristotle (1998). *The metaphysics* (H. Lawson-Tancred, Trans.). London: Penguin Books.
Bergmann, M. S. (1993). Reflections on the history of psychoanalysis. *Journal of the American Psychoanalytic Association*, 41, 929–955.
Bion, W. R. (1984a). *Learning from experience*. London: Karnac Books Ltd. (Original work published in 1962).
Bion, W. R. (1984b). *Elements of psychoanalysis*. London: Maresfield Library. (Original work published in 1963).
Birksted-Breen, D. (2008). Introductory forward. In D. Tuckett, R. Basile, D. Birksted-Breen, T. Böhm, P. Denis, A. Ferro, H. Hinz, A. Jemstedt, P. Mariotti, & J. Schubert (Eds), *Psychoanalysis comparable and incomparable: The evolution of a method to describe and compare psychoanalytic approaches* (pp. 1–4). London: Routledge.
Blass, R. B. (2017). Committed to a single model and open to reality. *Journal of the American Psychoanalytic Association*, 65, 845–858.
Boss, M. (1963). *Psychoanalysis and Daseinanalysis*. New York: Basic Books.
Bowlby, J. (1958). The nature of the child's tie to his mother. *International Journal of Psychoanalysis*, 39, 350–373.
Bowlby, J. (1969). *Attachment and loss*. Volume 1: *Attachment*. New York: Basic Books.
Breuer, J., & Freud, S. (1955). Studies in hysteria. In J. Strachey (Ed.), *Standard Edition* (Vol. II, pp. 1–319). London: Hogarth Press. (Original work published in 1893–1895).
Britton, R., & Steiner, J. (1994). Interpretation: Selected fact or overvalued idea? *International Journal of Psychoanalysis*, 75, 1069–1078.

Butler, H. (2018). The healing power of clinical social work. On "In Situ" – the Blog of the SDSU School of Social Work, April 2.
Christakis, N. A., & Fowler, J. H. (2009). *Connected: The surprising power of our social networks and how they shape our lives*. New York: Little, Brown and Company.
Cooper, S. H. (2017). The analyst's "use" of theory or theories: The play of theory. *Journal of the American Psychoanalytic Association, 65*, 859–882.
Derrida, J. (1982). Différance (A. Bass, Trans.). In J. Derrida, *Margins of philosophy* (pp. 1–27). Chicago: University of Chicago Press.
Ellenberger, H. F. (1970). *The discovery of the unconscious*. New York: Basic Books.
Foucault, M. (2000). *Power* (R. Hurley & others, Trans.). New York: The New Press.
Foucault, M. (2006). *History of madness* (J. Murphy & J. Khalfa, Trans.). London: Routledge. (Original work published in 1961).
Freud, S. (1958). The dynamics of transference. In J. Strachey (Ed.), *Standard Edition* (Vol. XII, pp. 97–108). London: Hogarth Press. (Original work published in 1912).
Giffney, N., & Watson, E. (Eds) (2017). *Clinical encounters in sexuality: Psychoanalytic practice and queer theory*. London: Punctum Books.
Gill, M. M. (1976). Metapsychology is not psychology. In M. M. Gill & P. S. Holtzman (Eds), *Psychology verses metapsychology: Essays in honor of George S. Klein* (pp. 71–105). New York: International Universities Press.
Gill, M. M., & Holtzman, P. S. (Eds) (1976). *Psychology verses metapsychology: Essays in honor of George S. Klein*. New York: International Universities Press.
Guntrip, H. (1971). *Psychoanalytic theory, therapy and the self: A basic guide to human personality in Freud, Erikson, Klein, Sullivan, Fairbairn, Hartman, Jacobson, and Winnicott*. New York: Basic Books.
Heidegger, M. (1982). *The basic problems of phenomenology* (A. Hofstadter, Trans. Rev. ed.). Bloomington: Indiana University Press. (Original work published in 1975).
Heidegger, M. (2010). *Being and time* (J. Stambaugh & D. J. Schmidt, Trans.). Albany: State University of New York. (Original work published in 1927).
Hoffman, I. Z. (1998). *Ritual and spontaneity in the psychoanalytic process*. Hillsdale: The Analytic Press.
Hunt, M. (2007). *The story of psychology*. New York: Anchor Books.
Husserl, E. (1970). *The crisis of European sciences and transcendental phenomenology* (D. Cairns, Trans.). Evanston: Northwestern University Press. (Original work published in 1937).
Husserl, E. (1983). *Ideas pertaining to a pure phenomenology and to a phenomenological philosophy. Book 1: General introduction to a pure phenomenology* (F. Kersten, Trans.). New York: Springer. (Original work published in 1913).
Kahneman, D., Slovic, P., & Tversky, A. (Eds) (1982). *Judgement under uncertainty: Heuristics and biases*. Cambridge: Cambridge University Press.
Kirsner, D. (2009). *Unfree associations: Inside psychoanalytic institutes updated edition*. Lanham: Jason Aronson.
Klein, G. S. (1976). Freud's two theories of sexuality. In M. M. Gill & P. S. Holtzman (Eds), *Psychology verses Metapsychology: Psychoanalytic Essays in honor of George S. Klein* (pp. 14–70). New York: International Universities Press (Original work published in 1969).
Kohut, H. (1977). *The restoration of the self*. New York: International Universities Press.
LaFarge, L. (2017). From "either/or" to "and": The analyst's use of multiple models in clinical work. *Journal of the American Psychoanalytic Association, 65*, 829–844.
Laplanche, J., & Pontalis, J. B. (1973). *The language of psycho-analysis* (D. Nicholson-Smith, Trans.). New York: W.W. Norton & Co. (Original work published in 1967).

Latour, B. (1993). *We have never been modern* (C. Porter, Trans.). Cambridge: Harvard University Press. (Original work published in 1991).
Leffert, M. (2003). Analysis and psychotherapy by telephone: Twenty years of clinical experience. *Journal of the American Psychoanalytic Association, 51*, 101–130.
Leffert, M. (2007a). A contemporary integration of modern and postmodern trends in psychoanalysis. *Journal of the American Psychoanalytic Association, 55*, 177–197.
Leffert, M. (2007b). Postmodernism and its impact on psychoanalysis. *Bulletin of the Menninger Clinic, 71*, 15–34.
Leffert, M. (2010). *Contemporary psychoanalytic foundations*. London: Routledge.
Leffert, M. (2013). *The therapeutic situation in the 21st century*. New York: Routledge.
Leffert, M. (2016). *Phenomenology, uncertainty, and care in the therapeutic encounter*. New York: Routledge.
Leffert, M. (2017). *Positive psychoanalysis: Aesthetics, desire, and subjective well-being*. New York: Routledge.
Leffert, M. (2018). *Psychoanalysis and the birth of the self: A radical interdisciplinary approach*. London: Routledge.
Main, M. (1991). Metacognitive knowledge, metacognitive monitoring, and singular (coherent) vs. multiple (incoherent) model of attachment. In C. M. Parkes, J. Stevenson-Hinde, & P. Marris (Eds), *Attachment across the life cycle* (pp. 126–159). London: Routledge.
Malabou, C., & Derrida, J. (2004). *Counterpath* (D. Wills, Trans.). Stanford: Stanford University Press. (Original work published in 1999).
May, R. (1958). The origins and significance of the existential movement in psychology. In R. May, E. Angel, & H. F. Ellenberger (Eds), *Existence: A new dimension in psychiatry and psychology* (pp. 3–36). New York: Basic Books.
May, R., Angel, E., & Ellenberger, H. F. (Eds). (1958). *Existence: New directions in psychiatry and psychology*. New York: Simon & Schuster.
McGowan, J. (1991). *Postmodernism and its critics*. Ithaca: Cornell University Press.
Nunn, J. N. (1996). *Ancient Egyptian medicine*. Norman, Oklahoma: University of Oklahoma Press.
Pear, R. (1992). M.D.'s make room for others in the ranks of psychoanalysts. *The New York Times*, August19.
Rudden, M., & Bronstein, A. A. (2017). New educational approaches to the study of psychoanalysis. *The American Psychoanalyst: Quarterly Magazine of the American Psychoanalytic Association, 51*.
Solms, M. (2013). The conscious id. *Neuropsychoanalysis, 15*, 5–19.
Stolorow, R. D. (2011). *World, affectivity, trauma*. New York: Routledge.
Sullivan, H. S. (1997). *The interpersonal theory of psychiatry*. New York: W.W. Norton & Co. (Original work published in 1953).
Thompson, C. M. (1964). *Interpersonal psychoanalysis: The selected papers of Clara*. New York: Basic Books.
Tower, L. (1956). Countertransference. *Journal of the American Psychoanalytic Association, 4*, 224–255.
Tuckett, D. (2008a). On difference, discussing differences and comparison. An introduction. In D. Tuckett, R. Basile, D. Birksted-Breen, T. Böhm, P. Denis, A. Ferro, H. Hinz, A. Jemstedt, P. Mariotti, & J. Schubert (Eds), *Psychoanalysis comparable and incomparable: The evolution of a method to describe and compare psychoanalytic approaches* (pp. 5–37). London: Routledge.

Tuckett, D. (2008b). Reflection and evolution: Developing the two-step method. In D. Tuckett, R. Basile, D. Birksted-Breen, T. Böhm, P. Denis, A. Ferro, H. Hinz, A. Jemstedt, P. Mariotti, & J. Schubert (Eds), *Psychoanalysis comparable and incomparable: The evolution of a method to describe and compare psychoanalytic approaches* (pp. 132–166). London: Routledge.

Tuckett, D., Basile, R., Birksted-Breen, D., Böhm, T., Denis, P., Ferro, A., et al.(Eds) (2008). *Psychoanalysis comparable and incomparable: The evolution of a method to describe and compare psychoanalytic approaches*. London: Routledge.

Tversky, A., & Kahneman, D. (1982). Judgment under uncertainty: Heuristics and biases. In D. Kahneman, P. Slovic, & A. Tversky (Eds), *Judgment under uncertainty: Heuristics and biases* (pp. 3–20). Cambridge: Cambridge University Press. (Original work published in 1974).

Winnicott, D. W. (1972). *Holding and interpretation: Fragment of analysis*. New York: Grove Press.

Winnicott, D. W. (1975). *Through paediatrics to psycho-analysis*. New York: Basic Books.

Yalom, I. D. (1980). *Existential psychotherapy*. New York: Basic Books.

Yalom, I. D. (2012). *Love's executioner: And other tails of psychotherapy*. New York: Basic Books. (Original work published in 1989).

Zimmer, R. B. (2017). The analyst's use of multiple models in clinical work: Introduction. *Journal of the American Psychoanalytic Association*, 65, 819–827.

2 Existentialism

The cafés of Vienna and Paris and beyond

Introduction

This chapter and the two that follow will set out the central thesis of this book: a discussion of the Existentialist enterprise and its application to Psychotherapy and Psychoanalysis. This, the first of these chapters, will offer a kind of philosophical history of the Existentialist movement beginning with Kierkegaard and reaching to the mid-20th century. I qualify the term *history* because what I am offering is non-linear—more of a family tree, really—and because it will include elements not usually considered a part of the existentialist story. It involves a *vast* literature that is impossible to describe in any comprehensive way, and I am certainly not proposing to do so here. Similarly, I can only describe the work of a select few of the players in the Existentialist game; to do otherwise would be to, in effect, offer the reader a data dump that would obfuscate the story I am trying to tell. What I *am* proposing is to offer a story of the evolution of several fundamental ideas as part of the central narrative of this book, the development of what I call the Psychoanalysis of the Absurd. I am offering a narrative, a telling of a story that makes a number of arguments. I do not claim any ontic standing for it; it is an interpretation and many others are possible. The second of these chapters will offer an account of Existentialist Psychotherapy. It will describe how Existentialist and Phenomenological ideas were introduced into Psychotherapy and Psychoanalysis from their origins in Europe and transmitted to America in the post-World War II period through to the present day. We will look at what actually happened to Existentialist Psychotherapy, because you don't read about it much anymore. The third chapter lays out my own modifications and elaborations of Existentialist therapy into a novel amalgamation of theory and practice that I have come to describe as the Psychoanalysis of the Absurd. Included among those modifications drawn from Interdisciplinary Studies are Affective Neuroscience, Network Studies, Studies of Subjective Well-Being, and Studies of Uncertainty. I will offer clinical illustrations in these last two chapters that will serve to show the differences between conducting a psychotherapy from an Existentialist perspective and from what I have come to call an Absurdist perspective. I am provisionally going to try to run a single thread through all of these: the axis of human Meaning and Meaninglessness. I would posit that meaning in its globalist of senses; the quest for it, achieving of it, and the potential failure to achieve it is an umbrella topic under which the multiple issues of Existentialism can fit.

So why is this chapter necessary? The literature on Existentialism is readily available in piecemeal form, including even some literature discussing conflicts among the ideas of this disparate group. Its volume does not permit a comprehensive text and no Existentialist would ever want to write it. We certainly can't cover it all. I do, however, want to offer you my own reading of the story including some passages, like *fin de siècle* Vienna that aren't usually treated as a part of it. Let me start with a family tree, or, really, a very rough sketch of a family tree

These elements fit together in different ways. There are some linear connections, such as the Existentialists starting off from Kierkegaard, of whom they were rightly critical. But other things were happening in parallel, such as the way American Existentialist Psychotherapy was being fed not only by the French Existentialists but also by Boss and Binswanger bringing Phenomenological Psychotherapy directly to America. There are also instances of simultaneous occurrence; we have all observed that when "society seems ready"—whatever "ready" means—innovation appears in a number of places and originates in a number of individuals.

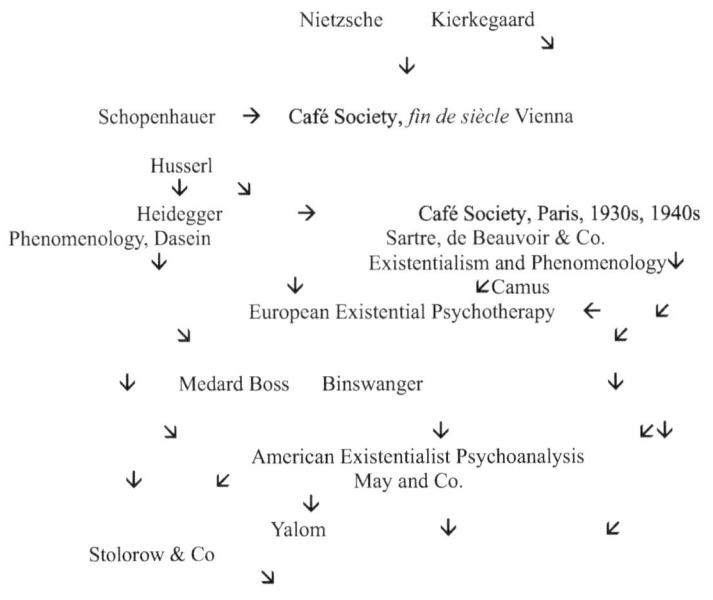

Figure 2.1 The Psychoanalysis of the Absurd: A family tree of Existentialism, Phenomenology, and Absurdity

We have to say something about the two terms: Existentialism and Phenomenology. Unfortunately, in spite of what one might read, there *is* no widespread agreement on their definitions. In contrast to whatever claims may have been made, usages are more often than not overlapping, fluid, and idiosyncratic. Heidegger, for example, called himself a Phenomenologist during his Husserlian years. When he broke with Husserl, he called himself nothing, but the World mostly retained the term or called him an Existential Phenomenologist. Since I have to take a position, I would stress the ambiguity of the distinction between the two terms. I have said that I would use "Existentialism" to refer to both, but in practice I often still use both terms together: "Existentialism and Phenomenology." For *myself*, Phenomenology has more of an ontological feel, offering a geography of World and Self, while Existentialism refers more to the *human* literary and psychological events that follow from that geography. I know this is inconsistent with the usage of many authors. What I can say is that there is no active fight going on and no body of literature that focuses on conflicts between the terms (unlike, for example, psychoanalytic literature focusing on definitions of transference).

Walter Kaufmann (1956/1975) offered, if not a definition of Existentialism, then at least a *description* of the terrain it covers:

> The refusal to belong to any school of thought, the repudiation of the adequacy of any body of beliefs whatever, and especially of systems, and a marked dissatisfaction with traditional philosophy as superficial, academic, and remote from life—that is the heart of existentialism.
>
> (p. 12)

Existentialism, Kaufman tells us, is not so much a philosophy as it is a *series of revolts*.

If we are really going to talk about Existentialist and Phenomenological Psychotherapy, their appearance, their subsequent apparent disappearance, and their end-of-century reappearance, then we need to begin with the difficult story of the birth and development of Existentialism itself—to borrow famously from Husserl: a return to the things themselves. There has been a tendency to gloss over this difficult material in the psychoanalytic literature. It is necessary for us to first spend some time with it if I am going to be able to offer a presentation of the ideas that I want to add to Existentialist Psychotherapy (in Bergmann's (1993) terms, modifications) to render it more contemporarily useful.

If we look at global accounts of the history of Existentialism and Phenomenology, we usually (e.g., Barrett, 1962/1990) find a reductionist chronological listing of the "Big Four": Kierkegaard, Nietzsche, Heidegger, and Sartre. I am not entirely out of sympathy with their approach. While I would add Schopenhauer, Husserl, and Camus to this short list, if one were to argue that this is reductionist thinking and open things up, the list grows quickly to include perhaps 50 names[1] and it becomes impossible to offer an integrated discussion of their individual work. Even so, we are faced with an unmanageable volume of material. The big four (particularly numbers one and four) were *vastly* prolific, with their output measured in thousands of pages, often peculiarly titled, and resulting in whole schools of descendants who arose to study them. There is really no way to cover this material in the space we have: we are going to have to pick and choose.

A further problem is that if we were to focus solely on a series of individuals, even if we were to make some effort to connect them, we would be ignoring the profound influence of the social on the work of the individual, in this case going beyond the list of four. A sequential individual focus would offer a seemingly discontinuous narrative where in fact more integration can be had. Again, *this* sociology of Existentialism is a vast subject but one that we can, for our purposes, reduce to two [Daseins][2]: *fin de siècle* Vienna and 1930s Paris.[3] These socio-cultural places of Being (Being theres) served as incubators for what we came to know as Existentialism and Phenomenology. Although the role of Parisian café society in the evolution of Existentialism has been recognized (Bakewell, 2016) and *fin de siècle* Vienna has been well described (Janik & Toulmin, 1973/1996; Johnston, 1972; Leffert, 2013; Schorske, 1980) in other contexts, they have not been made a part of a single narrative such as I am describing here. All of these events unfolded across a broad social canvas of Europe in turmoil: the liberal Peoples' Revolutions of the "European Spring" of 1848 and the 30 years of liberality that they introduced into European culture, the Franco-Prussian War of 1870 and the Paris Commune, the return of repressive and anti-Semitic trends to European Society, the First World War and *its* sequelae, and, finally, the Second World War.

I am going to posit that the work of all of these authors, working during a period beginning in the mid-19th century and continuing into the mid-20th, was at least implicitly psychological and offered a bridge between psychology and philosophy that had been lost. This period drew to an end as Existential philosophy became *clinically* psychological. Prior to this time, if psychoanalysts recognized this oeuvre (for lack of a better term) as psychological at all, it was as an *object* of analysis (the analyzed): it/they became *subjects* of analysis (the analyzers) only beginning in the post-World War two years.

---

1 Johnston (1972) writing about Vienna, posits a number of 70 men and women who were responsible for defining 20th century thought.
2 The epoché in this case is temporary; we will discuss the unwieldy concept of Dasein and Being There, *Da-sein*, below.
3 If this were a philosophy text, we would discuss the *archaeology of knowledge* (Foucault, 1969 and 1971/1972) of these periods, the rules of knowledge and discourse that pertained to them, but, for our purposes, it represents an unneeded complexity.

In French philosophy, the Existentialism of the mid-20th century gave way to Structuralism, Post-Structuralism, and the wider disciplines of Postmodernism. This displacement did not take place in psychoanalysis, where all of these schools seemingly maintained only a limited relevance. I have previously (Leffert, 2007a, 2010, 2013) written about them in some detail.

Kierkegaard

If we are not to go back to Plato and Augustine, the story of the origins of Existentialism begins with an unlikely and unhappy Dane, Søren Kierkegaard, and takes place in what philosophers of the time termed the "present age": the mid-19th century. Kierkegaard could best be described non-diagnostically as a very strange man. He coyly brought out much of his prodigious opus under a variety of pseudonyms, Johannes Climacus, Anti-Climacus, and Inter et Inter among them (these *seemed* to reflect differing issues related to Christianity). He engaged in a lifelong love-hate relationship with Christianity and the Church; he hated Hegel (mostly); and he was ambivalent about and ultimately refused to marry his muse, Regine Olsen. This latter decision somehow became a *cause célèbre* among Existentialists of the present age and subsequent Kierkegaard scholars. In spite of, or perhaps because of, his pained unhappiness, he managed to *Surveille* the range of concepts—matters of Being, really—that would occupy Existentialists and Phenomenologists even into the present. His preoccupation with religion earned him the enmity and contempt (but the continued interest) of the Existentialists who followed him in the 20th century.

Kierkegaard began what would be called Existentialism with the insight that *Human Beings had a special kind of existence* for which he used the term *existenz* (Danish and German). (Heidegger would later spend his career delving into the existence of Human Beings, for which he would create the complex term Dasein.) This *existenz* was different from the ways in which animals and the surrounding World existed. It abandoned the false cleavage of subject and object and, for the first time, reformulated *truth* as *relational truth* (Kierkegaard, 1846/1992).[4] Lest this should be imagined to be unscientific, it presaged Heisenberg's Uncertainty principle, the ultimate formulation of the concept of the inevitability of subjective observation, by a century.[5] He himself appears to have spent his life in a sort of chronic crisis of Being, very much of a piece with the patients whom the British Middle Group would write about a century later, a concept that Boss

---

4 Freud, in fact, maintained this cleavage in his use of psychoanalysis as a tool to get at the objective truths of his patients' lives; it was only with the advent of the Existentialist and later the Relational and Intersubjectivist schools that psychoanalysis took a different turn. Psychoanalysis did, ultimately, return to Heisenberg's concept of the *participant-observer*.
5 In their discipline, theoretical physics, Heisenberg and Bohr replaced Copernicus and Newton.

(1963) and Binswanger (1958) would describe in Existentialist terms and transport to America at roughly the same time.

Reading Kierkegaard, it is sometimes difficult to unravel what I would call his significant philosophy from his—I hate to say it—anxious and self-lacerating ditherings about Christianity and the Church. (My position here, albeit somewhat baldly stated, is not much different from that of Camus and Sartre.) This is perhaps unkind. If one does believe in, if one subjectively *knows*, a system of religion that includes an all-knowing, paternal God, a path of behaviour leading to Grace, and some kind of eternal life—OK, eternal *existenz*—then one is all set. One's problems with Being, dread, nothingness, meaninglessness, and Death (all posited by Kierkegaard) fall away. Sadly, Kierkegaard was not up to the task of such belief, unlike Martin Luther who, facing a similar problem in his fear of eternal damnation was able to create a new religious system that satisfied the needs that grew out of his beliefs.

In perhaps the strangest of Kierkegaard's works, *Concluding Unscientific Postscript's to Unscientific Fragments* (1846/1992), brought out under the pseudonym Johannes Climacus, he offers up a discussion of subjectivity upon which, stripped of what I would call his multiple obfuscations, the Existentialist and Phenomenological movement was based. Subjectivity, according to Kierkegaard (Climacus!), simply involves what it means to exist humanly. The task of being a subject is a lifelong task of becoming (as we would later say, Being *towards*). One can thus already see in the Present Age the formulation of issues that are applicable to our contemporary patients.

Kierkegaard (1844/2014) defines anxiety (*Angst*) as the possibility that comes from freedom (by which he means "free will"). (Sartre, a century later, would term this condition Nausea (1938/2013).). Possibility means that anything is possible ("good" and "evil") and can lead to "the terrible as well as the cheerful." What follows from the above is that anxiety is a property of human subjectivity and that the danger can come from within as well as without. (This, after all, is the premise upon which psychoanalysis was founded a short time later.)

For our purposes, the most important of Kierkegaard's *psychological* works with contemporary relevance is *The Sickness unto Death* (1849/1980). This sickness in Kierkegaard's language is despair; in its extreme, it is the wish to die when we cannot die. He is, of course, talking about what we have talked about for at least two centuries under the rubric of depression and 2½ millennia as melancholia. More importantly he describes despair as an *illness of the Self*. The Self, he tells us, relates *itself to itself*, and this is a complex proposition. What Kierkegaard is defining here is the *nature* of Human Being, what Heidegger will come to call Dasein. In 1849, we already find ourselves solidly in Existentialist territory.

Kierkegaard (1849/1980) offers us a kind of bimodal theory of despair: "If only the abstract idea of despair, *without any thought of someone in despair*, it must be regarded as a surpassing excellence" (pp. 14–15, italics added). Further, "the *possibility* of this sickness is man's superiority over the animal" (p.

15, italics added). However, while "to be able to despair is an infinite advantage…to be in despair is not only the worst misfortune and misery—no, it is ruination" (p. 15). We are dealing with the relation between possibility and actuality, the requirements for Being a Human Being. If we feel able to edit out the religious, as it appears, for example, in *The Concept of Anxiety* (Kierkegaard, 1844/2014), we see just how much Kierkegaard has to offer.

Nietzsche

Both Kierkegaard and Nietzsche, who called themselves and can be considered early psychologists, were taken up with the problem of Man [sic] and his need to constantly search for meaning. This is, of course, a statement of what we might call *the* Existentialist Problem. If for Kierkegaard this meant a return to Christianity, for Nietzsche, his paganism, his lack of systematization, and his frequent contradictory ideas played out across the lifetime of his poor health.[6,7] This ill health figured mythologically in his work as Dionysus, the god of ecstasy and tragedy, being torn to pieces for what he brought to Man. Both authors struggled with what might be called the animal nature of Man, often in equally obscure ways, a struggle taken up by Freud, particularly in *Civilization and Its Discontents* (1930/1961). Freud (1925/1959), alas, dismisses Nietzsche as merely "another philosopher whose guesses and intuitions often agree in the most astonishing way with the laborious findings of psycho-analysis" and he (Freud) avoided Nietzsche "on that very account; [He] was less concerned with the question of priority [Freud tells us] than with keeping [his] mind unembarrassed" (p. 60). Sadly, this comment's appearance in his *Autobiographical Study* (1925/1959), preceding *Civilization* by 5 years as it did, is just one example of Freud's failure to properly cite his ideas. Nietzsche also offered theories of psychic energy, a dual instinct theory, and a turbulent impulse-filled unconscious that preceded and bore more than a passing resemblance to Freud's. Again, one can argue that these were simply ideas whose time had come and that multiple individuals working across *fin de siècle* Europe were discovering and formulating simultaneously. In this vein it is important to remember that, whoever we imagine Freud to be, he and the others were simply turn-of-the-century European psychologists. In any event, attributions of discovery are often dubious and unstable things.

---

6 Sadly, obscurity is often prized by its readers. The struggle to attain a sometimes-arbitrary understanding of an author's work may bring with it a sense of superior understanding that is often unwarranted. Instead, it is perhaps better to simply factor out what doesn't hold together and then assess what is left. That is the stance I have been taking with these two authors.

7 Nietzsche's life was terrible. He was plagued by ill-health, perhaps syphilis, later insanity, delusions of grandeur, and early death. His writings (particularly the superman business), perverted by his sister who survived him as his executor, were adopted by the Nazis, poisoning Nietzsche's work for a generation.

How much they actually matter is another question we have never fully considered; certainly, in a *macro-history*, they do not.

In *Thus Spoke Zarathustra* (1883/2016), Nietzsche posits that we (Man) in the end only experience ourselves. This was his version of irreducible subjectivity, a building block of Existentialism, presented nihilistically by him, as if to say nothing is real. Lacking here is the way in which World impacts the Self. Zarathrustra lives alone on the top of a mountain and decides to "go down among men." The mountain represents the superior solitude of the spirit, while the lowlands are the home of ordinary men. *These* themes foreshadow Heidegger's[8] concepts of the *thrown* and the *everyday*. Nietzsche struggles here with his personal experience of aloneness, meaninglessness, and emptiness: whether he will get the better of it (achieve a rebirth) or it will get the better of him. This, in essence, is *the* Existential Problem writ large that must wait a half-century for Sartre, Camus & Company to engage more fully.

As a psychologist, Nietzsche also talked about uncovering or unmaking the hidden and the secret, later part of a phenomenological critique of the Freudian concept of an unconscious. Hidden and secret were outcomes of a process that he called *inhibition* (Hemmung in the German)[9] foreshadowing repression but without the sense that the state of being of the inhibited contents had changed. He and Kierkegaard "were much more concerned with understanding *man as the being who represses*, the being who surrenders self-awareness as a protection against reality and then suffers the neurotic consequences" (May, 1958, p. 23). Kierkegaard and Nietzsche foreshadow Camus and Sartre in their questioning the "sickness of man:" how exactly can Man give up his consciousness, his existence and his consciousness that he exists, when blocking off this consciousness results in suffering anxiety and despair?

Barrett (1962/1990), in slightly different terms, describes Zarathustra's (Nietzsche's) problem as the loneliness, emptiness, and power of the mountaintop versus being a whole and individual human being, no longer alone, but no longer a superman: "Once we set ourselves to reclaim that portion of human nature that traditional morality rejected—man's devil to put it symbolically—we face the immense problem of socializing and taming those impulses" (p. 191). Zarathrustra fails to come to terms with his devils in the book while Nietzsche fails to do so in his life.

To restate this: The problem in *Zarathrustra*, a superman who fades when he goes down to dwell among Men, is whether a rebirth, a resurrection, a new fusion of spirit and body, is possible. This is Nietzsche's own struggle

---

8 Heidegger was not only familiar with Nietzsche and his work, but also lectured and wrote extensively about him. It is thus not surprising that we find in the latter's work concepts in rudimentary form that will be developed and expanded on by Heidegger.

9 This theme was again picked up by Freud in one of his most important works, *Inhibition, Symptom, and Anxiety* (Freud, 1926/1959), titled in the original German *Hemmung und Angst*.

with the wreckage of his body and his oncoming madness: Again, in Heidegger's terms, Nietzsche is, in the end, a *fallen* Man unable to recover his thrownness. Nietzsche's struggle proved particularly attractive in the cafes of *fin de siècle* Vienna (Janik & Toulmin, 1973/1996; Johnston, 1972)

Schopenhauer

Although he predates Existentialism by a generation, we must still consider Schopenhauer's work. In addition to influencing Nietzsche and the philosophical discussions of *fin de siècle* Viennese café society, his ideas prefigured some of the Existentialists' and contributed to the interdisciplinary basis of Absurdism. Although he doesn't claim the term and others have not claimed it for him, he can be considered an early ontologist, focused on the phenomenology of Being. Much of this is to be found in his first major work, *The World as Will and Representation* (Schopenhauer, 1844/1969a, 1844/1969b). Schopenhauer's oeuvre is both large and dense, with *Will and Representation* requiring some 1300 pages. There is no way that I can summarize either it or the arguments he makes in it, and I will not pretend to do so. What we must also remember is that, while *we* are interested in how his work prefigures particular issues of later 19th and 20th century philosophy, this was not Schopenhauer's intent. He was rather a working philosopher of the first half of the 19th century who was interested in setting out his views about Existence as they were consistent with or in opposition to the philosophy of the 18th century and *its* roots. *Schopenhauer's* context was the philosophy of Hegel, Kant, and Berkeley. What I want to do instead is to pull out the few ideas that are a part of the story of Existentialism that I want to tell you.

Schopenhauer (1844/1969a, 1844/1969b) asserts that the World must be viewed as representation (*Vorstellung*); it is what presents itself in a *subject's* experience. In this idealist position, World depends for its order on the existence of a *knowing subject*, governed, with a bow to Kant, by the rules of space, time, and causality. Without the subject, all is randomness;[10] *individual* things (e.g., *my* desk as opposed to the world of desks) do not exist as such. We individuate things by applying the criteria of space and time to them. Schopenhauer's corollary to this is that individuation does not exist on the thing itself side of things but rather on the Subject side of things. Schopenhauer was a radical subjectivist whose ontological views would play out over the following century.

---

10 Some studies of perception do in fact support this. Von Senden (1932/1960), for example, studied the appearance of vision in individuals who had their congenital cataracts removed and became sighted for the first time. While those in early adolescence or younger developed normal vision, older subjects saw only streams of shapeless color that were highly dysphoric. This is fully consistent with World, absent the visually knowing subject.

This same World, however, must also be viewed in another way: as Will (Schopenhauer, 1844/1969a). We think that this, after all, is not so hard, and expect Will to have to do with Desire, and we are, to a degree, correct. Schopenhauer, in *Will and Representation*, then makes this rather strange statement (according to Janaway, 1989/1999): While *Vorstellung*, as *appearance*, involves World as Representation, this second aspect of World, *Will*, involves *the Thing Itself*. The Thing Itself would seem to prefigure the phenomenology of Husserl (1913/1983) and the path to Existentialism, but how does Desire figure into this path? Let's try to unpack Schopenhauer's position and see if this helps us.

Schopenhauer looks at the world through the twin lenses of idealism and skepticism and creates a conundrum for himself. Idealism means that the world of space-time only exists within consciousness, whereas, if this collapses, we are left with skepticism: The World exists, but it exists outside of consciousness and we cannot know it. *This* position had legs in Viennese Café society: "We are aware of ourselves as knowers or thinkers and as actors or agents" (Janik & Toulmin, 1973/1996, p. 151). Schopenhauer's separation of World into representation and the thing itself resonated with a skepticism in these Viennese circles that fit with their ideas of decadence and death.

Fin de siècle Vienna

Vienna is only one center of a socio-cultural-psychological-philosophical movement or way of Being (*episteme* is a better if less familiar term for the entirety of this) that encompassed all of Europe at the turn of the 20th century. Ellenberger (1970) describes a sea-change in European thought occurring in about 1885 with the term for it, *fin de siècle*, bursting on the scene in Paris in 1886). It was a reaction to 19th century naturalistic science and the Industrial Revolution that existed side-by-side with both rather than superseding them. The general movement in the arts and literature was called Neo-Romanticism and prized two major elements: a worship of the individual-in-isolation that involved a narcissistic over-valuation of the Self and a proclamation of the decadence of western civilization. The West had reached its high point, so this story went, and was in a state of decline that would lead to its dissolution. (We are perhaps, a century and a half later, dealing with this very problem.) The social backdrop for these themes was the decadence of the thousand-year-old *Reich*, the Austro-Hungarian Empire (as the saying goes, it was neither Austrian, nor Hungarian, nor an Empire) of the Hapsburgs, and the senescent 60-year reign of its Emperor Franz Joseph. There was a parallel in French society following its humiliating defeat in the Franco-Prussian War of 1870, the siege of Paris and the socialist uprising of the Paris commune. Neo-Romantics identified (fancifully rather than historically) the *fin de siècle* with other historical periods of decline, such as that of Rome and of Byzantium. Decadence had also acquired a particular meaning, that of a rich, seductive, and alluring corruptness leading to death.[11]

> In the educated world of *fin de siècle* Vienna, everyone discussed philosophy and all things were culturally interreferential. The Viennese intellectual community viewed the central issues of post-Kantian thought as relevant to their own individual concerns, be they art, science, law, or politics. Everyone worked in this wider literary and cultural milieu and was in turn influenced by it.
>
> (Leffert, 2013, p. 163)

The pessimism of the period was wrapped in the philosophy of Schopenhauer, something of little interest today. The 18th century "noble savage" was replaced by the corruption of the "civilized" man. Mysticism was much prized. "The deep-reaching affinity between the new, incipient dynamic psychiatry and the spirit of the times is revealed by the similarity between patients described by the psychiatrists and by the novelists and playwrights" (Ellenberger, 1970, p. 283). The Viennese playwright Arthur Schnitzler, whose works were known for their psychological insights, developed a stream of consciousness style of writing in which the work contained only the subject's thoughts without action of any kind. This trope became important both in clinical psychoanalysis and in the writing of the Existentialist years.

Viewed from a distance of 125 years,

> *fin de siècle* Vienna at first appears to be a place of café society: brilliant intellectuals, grand public architecture, all-night civic balls, quaint uniforms, Strauss *Waltzer*, and *Schlag* (whipped cream) that suggests nothing so much as a glorious empire at the height of its powers.
>
> (Leffert, 2013, p. 161)

It seemed to truly be a *City of Dreams*. In reality, it was a society on the brink of dissolution and the intellectual inhabitants of its cafés were aware of it. It would die in the final spasm of World War I. Much went on beneath its glittering surface. It was pervaded by a gritty strangeness (Janik & Toulmin, 1973/1996), a darkness that brought with it the rot of decay and the seductive, decadent sensuality of *Les Fleurs du Mal* (Baudelaire, 1857/2008).

The reason the Viennese cafés bustled all day was in part due to the city's housing shortage. Small, dark, unheated rooms were the norm for the intellectual class; warmth and light as much as spirited discussion drove them to the cafés. Meanwhile, if the intellectuals were ensconced in their cafés and the nobility in their palaces, the working classes were left to a life of grim

---

11 The course of European history would lead to a recurrence of these themes at several points, including, it would seem, in our contemporary world.

misery (Maderthaner & Musner, 2008) seething with political unrest. In 1911, this culminated in a general uprising in the Ottakring suburb of Vienna in which the Austrian army opened fire on the populace for the first time since the "Spring of the Peoples" rebellions of 1848. Buildings and streetcars were set ablaze and violence spread to adjacent quarters of the city. This was an uprising of the proletariat in response to the wage levels that were lower and prices that were higher in Austria as compared to the rest of Western Europe. Inflated food prices and bad housing led to this social breakdown that was closely monitored by the young Austro-Marxists who haunted Vienna's Café Central. The oppressed working class, following the further devastation of the First World War provided fertile soil in which, a generation later, communism and Nazism would take root.

The generation reaching 20 to 30 years of age in 1890 in Paris and called *Jung Wien* in Vienna was the most gifted that France and Austria had produced. As Schorske (1980) described them, "Not only Vienna's finest writers, but its painters and psychologists, even its art historians, were preoccupied with the problem of the nature of the individual in a disintegrating society" (p. 4). "It was in Austria and its successor states that many, perhaps even most, of the seminal thinkers of the twentieth century emerged" (Johnston, 1972, p. 1). Seventy of them, mostly men, lived and worked in the City of Dreams for at least part of their careers, where they formed a vibrant *social network* (Christakis & Fowler, 2009) through which all sorts of information was rapidly exchanged via a social process described, a century later, as *contagion* (Christakis & Fowler, 2009).[12] The issue of dissolution produced, for individuals, regardless of social position, a crisis of Being without a *fin de siècle* path to a solution, a subject that Heidegger and the French Existentialists would take up and document a generation later.

They created a *fin de siècle* worldview known as *Viennese Impressionism* (Johnston, 1972) that prized ephemerality, aestheticism, and nostalgia while remaining committed to positivistic science. This love of science sustained the belief that *anything* could be explained scientifically. The view from the tables of Vienna's Café Central was markedly influenced by three philosophers we have already spoken about: Schopenhauer, Kierkegaard, and Nietzsche.

Nietzsche was particularly prized for his "vehement attacks against the current ideologies, the social order, established religion, and conventional morality" (Ellenberger, 1970, p. 272). *Thus Spoke Zarathrustra* (Nietzsche, 1883/2016), the story of a prophet told in soaring myths and allegories was particularly moving to Vienna's troubled intellectual youth. Nietzsche's nihilistic attacks on existing social order and religion fit well with their views of the

---

12 Undoubtedly, these individuals connected with probably some hundreds of other intellectuals, making up interlocking social networks. Contrary to his assertions of solitary creativity, Freud was fully integrated into this system (Timms, 1986/1989).

senility and decadence of the Austro-Hungarian Empire. He asserted that civilization was in decline because it was incompatible with the true nature of Man, that of the solitary prophet.

For the jobless sons (and it was mostly sons) of the Viennese upper, middle, and professional classes with no prospects in the dying Hapsburg Empire, life was a burden and there was a fascination in seeking out empirical and philosophical causes for the circumstances in which they found themselves. Death was to be found in the wasting cases of tuberculosis, cancer and venereal disease and in suicide: It offered a psychological as well as a physical conclusion to life.

For these young intellectuals, Kierkegaard (1849/1980) offered insights into the causes of their misery. He was a vibrant social critic whose social commentaries were taken up by the biting *fin de siècle* satirist Karl Kraus[13] (Timms, 1986/1989). The Existentialist authors of the 1930s (e.g., Camus, 1942/1989) would later pick up these criticisms. On a different note, his ideas about existence and misery in the abstract would speak to the romantization of death. Despair, for Kierkegaard, is the "sickness onto death." It is despair in the abstract, without someone in particular suffering from it, that was of surpassing value. The capacity for despair, its *possibility*, is what separates man from animals. What Kierkegaard is about is "the leap into the absurd" by which he means a leap of faith through which a finite personality commits itself to the infinite (Janik & Toulmin, 1973/1996). The *infinite* can only be death and what comes after it.

Enter Schopenhauer. Schopenhauer begins the second volume of *The World as Will and Representation* (1844/1969b) by offering a Representation of World, absent Will, deeply resonant to the Existentialism of *Jung Wien*, a society of *fin de siècle* writers who met in Vienna's coffeehouses.

> In endless space countless luminous spheres, round each of which some dozen smaller illuminated ones revolve hot at the core and covered over with a hard cold crust; on this crust a moldy [sic] film has produced living and knowing beings: this is the empirical truth, the real, the world. Yet for a being who thinks it is a precarious position to stand on one of those numberless spheres freely floating in boundless space, without knowing whence or whither, and to be only one of innumerable similar beings that throng, press, and toil, restlessly and rapidly arising and passing away in beginningless and endless time.
>
> (p. 3)

---

13 Unfortunately, Kraus' work has not been translated into English. He owned, edited, and wrote the bi-monthly journal *Die Fackel* (The Torch). However, to grasp Kraus' work it is only necessary to summarize the "personal information" he included in its first quarterly report:
  Anonymous reviling letters 236
  Anonymous threatening letters 83
  Assaults 1
  (Janik & Toulmin, 1973/1996, p. 69).

This paragraph and the cold emptiness of the objective World it describes foreshadow both the struggles of *fin de siècle* intellectuals and the following Existentialist enterprise. World hangs on the *"consciousness* in which it exists"; without it, there is nothing.

If one looks at the literature, Schopenhauer is *mentioned* in connection with many of "the seventy" and probably influenced all of them at least indirectly. His effect on the young Wittgenstein, for example, is well documented (Janaway, 1989/1999). Being clear about their stated takeaways, however, is not so easy, and there is little writing on the subject. What proved of most interest in the *fin de siècle* cafés had to do with Schopenhauer's approach to death. Again, I could find little on the subject with Jacquette (1999) and Janaway (2002) offering brief exceptions. Schopenhauer spoke directly to the fascination with which these young Viennese intellectuals beheld or even longed for death. "At bottom," he tells us, "we are something that ought not to be; therefore we cease to be" (Schopenhauer, 1844/1969b, p. 507) and "Death is the great opportunity to no longer be" (p. 507). He argues that the fear of death is irrational; *subjectively* it is annihilation but, if we cease to exist, there is no subject, no "I" to experience it. Objectively, in the *phenomenological* world, we exist in a defined space and time with "birth" and "death" signifying its endpoints, that's all.[14]

Schopenhauer (1844/1969a) goes on to assert that "constant suffering is essential to all life" (p. 283) but that we can nevertheless find satisfaction and take delight in it. Death for him is an affirmation of the will, not its denial, and suicide follows from it when satisfaction is no longer available and only suffering and misery remains. Ending one's life when pain and suffering become too great is, according to Schopenhauer, an affirmation of life. "To die willingly, to die gladly, to die cheerfully, is the prerogative of the resigned, of him who gives up and denies the will-to-live" (Schopenhauer, 1844/1969b, p. 508). We see threads here of something that, under Heidegger, will become *thrownness*.

In the *fin de siècle*, Austrians were in love with death (Johnston, 1972). As Johnston observed, three aspects of Viennese thought, aestheticism, therapeutic nihilism, and impressionism fueled the affair. Death and the subsequent funeral and internment were aesthetic experiences for all the participants, planned to offer a Baroque vision of death as the fulfillment and consummation of life. An interaction between positivism and impressionism drove the cultural creativity of many of the "seventy." The circle of writers and playwrights, *Jung Wien*, were much taken up with it. There was an intellectual fascination with life's inevitable end and its meaning alongside of attempting to portray it with broad symbolic strokes. Impressionism was an expression of the changeable, the ephemeral, and the constantly fluctuating aspects of

---

14 These arguments held a significance for the *fin de siècle* episteme that, with our greater emphasis on subjectivity, would carry less weight today.

Vienna city life. It involved an evanescence in which life itself was volatile and easily lost in death both for the dying and the mourners. Therapeutic nihilism was an attitude prominent in the latter half of the 19th century. Medicines and cures did little to heal (and conceivably harmed) the body or the mind, so it went; they were best avoided and body and mind left alone to heal for themselves.[15] The physician turned playwright Arthur Schnitzler was the best known of the circle with his ideas of repression, and an epiphanic return to consciousness paralleling Freud's own; both these unique individuals were imbedded in the Viennese episteme.[16] Vienna was the source of Freud's writing on the death instinct, which was exactly what he meant it to be, not an aggressive drive as it was reformulated to be by subsequent generations of psychoanalysts.

Johnston (1972) tells us "Viennese literati who around 1900 frequented coffeehouses and wrote feuilletons shared a preoccupation with evanescence, especially with its definitive form—death" (p. 169). If death was the definitive form of evanescence, then its ultimate means of expression was suicide. "Between 1860 and 1938 an astonishing number of Austrian intellectuals committed suicide" (p. 174). The most celebrated of these suicides was that of Crown Prince Rudolf of Austria, the only son of Emperor Franz Joseph and heir to the Austrian throne. He died in a suicide pact with Baroness Mary Vetsera, his mistress, at Myerling, a hunting lodge owned by the crown prince. The romantic preoccupation with the event cannot be overstated. It remains the subject of film, art, and literature across the world into the 21st century. It is still the subject of dark political speculations. The children of famous parents were particularly vulnerable to suicide. They felt they could not approach their parents' creativity. Epidemiologically, the seeming desirability of death, which spread within Viennese society via contagion, was not understood at the time.

Psychoanalysis of the late 19th and early 20th century had little to offer this ailment. Conflict theory, reaction formations, and analysis of guilt did not provide tools with which to effectively stem this epidemic and Freud ultimately punted by positing the existence of a Death Instinct drawn from the times and obviating the need to search for a cure.

Untreatable in the fin de siècle, we for some time now have had psychotherapeutic and psychopharmacological tools with which to help such suffering Human Beings. These severely disturbed, non-psychotic, patients were understood by the British Middle Group and Analysts and Therapists in the United States who worked with them, often in hospital settings. Much later,

---

15 Nineteenth century medicine being what it was, this was by no means an indefensible position.
16 Despite Freud's assertions that he acted alone, there is solid evidence that he was embedded in Viennese café society. Timms (1986/1989), in his biography of the satirist Karl Kraus offers a partial map of the Viennese Social Network (p. 8). He shows Freud as having a major circle of influence reciprocally embedding him in the Network.

the work of empathic and courageous therapists with these patients, who were often suffering with Major Depressive Disorder and Bipolar Disorder, would be supplemented by the use of anti-depressants, anti-psychotics, and mood-stabilizers. However, by mid-century, a group of clinicians began developing new therapeutic tools derived from an understanding of Existentialism and Phenomenology. These patients could be understood, could be *known*, to be suffering from illnesses of Being (Leffert, 2018), and with that *knowing* would come different, more effective ways of treating them.

Simply put, what is Phenomenology? Luft and Overgaard, the editors of *The Routledge Companion to Phenomenology* (2012), describe Phenomenology as defined by three central paradigms.[17] The first that it is about the "I" and what *I* experience; that is, *it is a first-person ontology* (Husserl) including the subjects and objects *I* experience. Experience is irreducibly Subjective, but there is objectivity in it if it is intersubjectively validated. It is about Human Beings (see Kierkegaard). The second is that Phenomenology describes first-person experience; it attempts to hold in abeyance historicities (see Husserl), but cannot always do so. It tries to avoid prior theories or beliefs. The third is that there is a directedness of consciousness (and unconsciousness as well); Intentionality is central to Phenomenology (Husserl).

This last concept, Intentionality, was developed and explored by Franz Brentano (1874/1995) who resurrected the term from the scholasticism of the middle ages. Simply put, thought is always intentional; it manifests an *aboutness*. Brentano argues that *all* psychological phenomena are intentional and *only* psychological phenomena are intentional. To believe is to believe *something*, to desire is to desire *something*, and so on. The presence or absence of intentionality can also be used to distinguish psychological from non-psychological phenomena. Husserl was deeply influenced by the idea of intentionality and its ontological implications.

Husserl

If the *story* of Existentialism begins with Kierkegaard, its *father*, from whom the Existentialists and Phenomenologists of the 20th century are descended, was Husserl. The single most important thing that Husserl did was to break with the search for underlying meaning that had preoccupied philosophers forever with his celebrated battle cry, a "return to the things themselves" (in Carman, 2006, pp. 98–99). (If the search for generic meaning was meaningless, the meaning of *particular things* was a subject for significant inquiry.) Phenomena are the ways things *present themselves to us* (not some external thing) and Phenomenology is the science of describing Phenomena. Phenomena may sometimes manifest considerable distortion; this can produce clinical problems. According to Husserl (1913/2001), psychology is an empirical

---

17 This description follows that which can be found in Leffert (2013, p. 36).

science that studies the factual nature of consciousness[18] manifesting some degrees of vagueness and probability rather than certainty. A Pure Phenomenology is without presuppositions, it simply means to describe psychological processes *as they are* and, when unable to do so, brackets the offending content in an *epoché* [], reserving it for future consideration.

Husserl posited a crisis in the science of the 20th century: that objective science had grown so much that it overshadowed *everyday* science, which concerns itself not with the existence of the objective but rather with the "science" of the Being of Human Beings. Husserl resurrected the term *intersubjectivity* from the scholastics of the middle ages to signify the fact that "*my* perceptions present me with intersubjectively accessible being, that is, being that does not exist for me alone, but for everybody. I *experience* objects, events, and actions as public, not as private" (Zahavi, 2003, p. 110, italics added). There is, then, *my* subjectivity and a second, public subjectivity; for the relation of the two, Husserl applies the term *transcendental intersubjectivity*.

If Husserl was the father of Phenomenology, Heidegger was his prodigal son. Husserl was Heidegger's teacher who led him into Phenomenology and to whom *Being and Time* is dedicated (Heidegger, 1927/2010). Heidegger later broke with him over two points: the assertion that a thing's *history* is an essential part of its Being and cannot be left out of its description and Husserl's continued commitment to 17th and 18th century philosophers such as Descartes. He subsequently refused to call himself a phenomenologist although his work remained solidly in that vein.

Heidegger

If the *fin de siècle* Viennese intellectuals saw death as the consummation of life, Heidegger saw it as the inevitable end to life that *demanded* it be lived to the fullest. Heidegger is difficult. But he is worth the trouble in ways that some authors are not. An argument can be made that Heidegger is the most important philosopher of the 20th century.

An initial difficulty has to do with Heidegger's relationship to Nazism and the related argument that, if he was an active Nazi participant, it must also condemn his work. Many of us (e.g., Boss, 1963; Leffert, 2016) who have studied him, have seen it as morally necessary to take up this question. Briefly, the facts. Heidegger joined the Nazi party in the mid-1930s. During this period, he was Rector of the University of Freiburg where he expressed Nazi views. He saw the error of his ways and resigned the Rectorship but he never resigned his party membership (perhaps he was understandably afraid to

---

18 The repudiation of unconsciousness by the phenomenologists is actually a repudiation of a Freudian unconscious, of an unrealized, dynamic unconsciousness separated from consciousness by repression as opposed to a kind of psychological activity manifesting various existential properties, among them that of not being conscious.

do so).[19] In some of his seminars he also expressed Nazi ideas (Gordon, 2010.03.12) as he did as well in one or two of his journals. No evidence has emerged over the past *80 years* that he did anything else. The conclusion others and I have reached is that he was, for some few years, a fellow traveler of the Nazis, nothing more. Some have condemned him for this, while others are more forgiving. I find myself unable to do either, but I *am* understanding. Like Boss (1963) I can value Heidegger's work, but feel I have to also keep the thread of his Nazism in mind, perhaps as a *counterpath* (Malabou & Derrida, 1999/2004), part of a sheaf of *différance* in his ideas.

Bear with me for just a bit. Heidegger's seminal work is *Being and Time* (Heidegger, 1927/2010), but it is unfinished; Heidegger refers to it as "half-complete." For Anglophone speakers in particular, *The Basic Problems of Phenomenology* (Heidegger, 1975/1982) is an important supplemental text; it is a better translation and takes up some of the material that should have appeared in *B&T*. Heidegger asserts that *"being is the proper and sole theme of philosophy"* (1975/1982, p. 11). In doing so he breaks with Kant, and the dual projects of science and epistemology (knowledge). *Philosophy* is the study of *ontology*. It is not about human beings per se, but it is about the Being of Human Beings, for which he coined the very complex term *Dasein*. Dasein means existence, particularly the unique existence of human beings. Heidegger *at the same time* splits the term into *Da*-sein or a Human Being Being-*there*, by which he means to locate the Self in the World, in space (and in time). It is Dasein who asks the question: What is the Being of Human Beings?

Heidegger defines Dasein's world as consisting of three places (Idhe, 2012): The World of things and animals that are *at hand* (*Die Umwelt*), the World of other human beings *with whom* Daseins relate (*Die Mitwelt*), and the World of Dasein's inner self and inner reflections (*Die Eigenwelt*). Dasein exists relationally (intersubjectively, transcendentally) in World in three different ways, and this formulation is at the center of Existentialist psychotherapy or as Boss (Boss, 1963; Heidegger, 1987/2001) describes it, *Daseinanalysis*. The first of these is in a state of everydayness (*athandedness*), in which Dasein is working with and caring for the things (and animals) that are *at hand*. It is not a conscious state. If, for example, we need to hammer a nail, we pick up the hammer *that is at hand*; we do not *think* of the hammer as being a tool or a member of the class of hammers. Care in general and husbandry, caring for animals, and caring for people (again not consciously and not thinking about the person) fall into this category. The second way of Being is in a state of *thrownness*. In this state one is literally and consciously *thrown* into life. We are aware that life must lead to death and this must lead us to reflect on where we have gotten to in life and

---

19 In his exploration of everydayness in *Being and Time* (1927/2010), *prior to the advent of Nazism*, Heidegger developed the principle of the folk-leader, the *Führer* principle. When Hitler appeared with *his* Führer principle a few years later, Heidegger was easily seduced and remained seduced, for a time.

to live every moment fully engaged. Care in this way of being is Care for another Human Being known to us (understood as) as a person. The final state occurs if both everydayness and thrownness should fail; it is *fallenness*. (I have come to separate fallenness from everydayness where Heidegger does not; fallenness does not make sense to me as an inevitable part of everydayness or athandedness.) Fallenness is falling away from the Self, from the *authentic* Self. It is a being in the world of "they" as the impersonal motivator, a world of relating to others in a state of idle chatter. In a fallen state Dasein's life becomes meaningless. Fallenness involves a terror of death, a subset of what we will normatively term *Death Anxiety*, with the linked thought that it is avoidable, a denial of death. Attempts at imagining that aging can be avoided and fantasies that death can be endlessly postponed (so that the way one lives in the moment is no longer important) always fail. Such inauthenticity inevitably breaks down into terror. It is very present in our 21st century world. The clash of these two ways of Being, thrownness and fallenness is mirrored in the work of Erikson (1950/1963). First, there are the psychoanalytic alternatives of Human Development and Fixation or Regression. Erikson goes on to famously posit eight ages of Man [sic]. Each poses a developmental task that can be met or failed; one can remain thrown and go on or fall back. The later stages have in part the task of assessing one's life and preparing to meet death, the ultimate Phenomenological task. Erikson suggests this series of Existential/Developmental tasks with engaging End-of-Life usually left for the later Developmental stages (more about Erikson in the next chapter).

There is one last piece of Heidegger's ontology that we must discuss and that is temporality. Unfortunately, despite the title, *Being and Time* (1927/2010), Heidegger never developed his thinking on the subject of time. (It was supposed to be taken up in subsequent volumes of Being ant Time that were never written.) Time's proposed importance is contained in the statement: "What has to be shown is this: temporality is the condition of the possibility of all understanding of being; *being is understood and conceptually comprehended by means of time*" (Heidegger, 1975/1982, p. 274). To put it differently, Dasein must also be understood in terms of the *history* of its Being. None of this involves theory or the plumbing of any depths. It is rather a description of things as they are, of their Being. (Other descriptions are certainly possible.) There is no depth in the conscious and unconscious elements of our Being; both are fully present, fully deployed, although one may be secret from the other (as the neuroscientists, Risse & Gazzaniga, 1978, describe in the functioning of the left and right cerebral hemispheres). The close relatives of depth, historicity of cognition and historicity of development, do exist, but we must keep this distinction in mind. What we remain with are Husserl's "The Things Themselves," and, despite Heidegger's break with Husserl, they are straight Phenomenology. They can go awry in different ways and can, as we will see, be healed with Existential tools.

The complexity of the neuropsychology of Consciousness was not available to the early Phenomenologists and Existentialists and was largely not taken up by the later ones. Briefly, Tulving (1985/2003, 2005) posited three kinds of Consciousness—Anoetic, the *unknowing* lower brain consciousness of animals, Noetic, the knowing cerebral cortical consciousness of facts and procedures of higher animals, and Autonoetic, the cortical, narrative, self-reflective consciousness (that most of us mean by the term) that may (opinions differ) be restricted to Human Beings. Autonoetic consciousness is the province of the thrown or the fallen while, I would posit, the Noetic and the Anoetic are the province of the Everyday. (I have discussed Consciousness more fully in a previous volume (Leffert 2010) and will discuss it again in a subsequent one.)

Paris between the wars and beyond

If in *fin de siècle* Vienna we were interested in how its inhabitants, those disparate intellectuals, were *applying* the Existentialist philosophy of the 19th century to their work and their problems in living, in Paris between the Wars we want to talk instead about how *its* inhabitants were *doing* philosophy, creating a new, 20th century Existentialism. Unfortunately, while there is a lot of literature on Paris between the Wars, it is a literature that describes the writers and artists who lived and worked there, and how they interacted with each other and the intellectuals of the "Lost Generation." That literature, although fascinating, does not include the philosophers. While these groups interacted, no one seems to have been interested in globally documenting these interactions and one is left to do one's own research on a case-by-case basis. However, a single, recent volume, *At the Existentialist Café: Freedom, Being, and Apricot Cocktails* (Bakewell, 2016), does offer a convincing narrative of the lives and work of these philosophers.

If we cannot speak of the birth of Existentialism in Paris, we can speak of its conception. That occurred sometime in December of 1932 (Bakewell, 2016) when three young philosophers were sitting in the Bec-de-Gaz Bar on the rue du Montparnasse in Paris, drinking the house specialty, apricot cocktails (apricot sours?). There was Simone de Beauvoir, 25, who wrote most about it, her boyfriend, Jean-Paul Sartre, 27, and Sartre's old school friend, Raymond Aron, also 27. Where de Beauvoir and Sartre were in town for their winter break from teaching in the French provinces (work they detested), Aron had come from Berlin, and he brought with him a new philosophy that went by the name of Phenomenology. It was compounded in equal parts of Husserl's cry of "return to the things themselves" and Heidegger's central focus on Dasein, the Being of Human Beings. In truth, de Beauvoir and Sartre had seen a French translation of Heidegger's paper "What is Metaphysics?" that had appeared in 1931 but had been unable to understand it. With the benefit of Aron's descriptions, they now saw Phenomenology as reconnecting philosophy with normal, lived human experience. Sartre made his own trip to "Lourdes" (that is, Berlin) the following fall. He was to combine the ideas of the German Phenomenologists with Kierkegaard's interest in the unique Being of Humans. To this he added an idea of his own, that literature could be a vehicle in which to do philosophy; giving birth in the process to French Existentialism.

If French Existentialism percolated through the cafés of 1930s Paris, its first major writings (e.g., Camus, 1942/1989, 1942/1991; Sartre, 1943/2003) were published during the German occupation years of World War II, somehow slipping past the collaborationist Vichy censors.[20] It was, however, in the postwar years of the 1940s and 1950s that Existentialist writings truly exploded on the scene.

Sartre turned Phenomenology into a philosophy of the full range of human experience, of human feelings (moods and emotions) and the sensations (perceptions) that went along with them. The fundamental issue of Human Being, for Sartre, was not thrownness but Human Freedom. It was Freedom that set Humans apart from all other objects; we define ourselves by our experience. He wrote about this like the novelist (1938/2013) and playwright (1946/1989) that he was. In its latency years (Paris between the wars), Existentialism was conflated with rebellion and much was made of the fact that Sartre & Co. were Marxist and supporters of communism.[21] Meanwhile, Sartre and de Beauvoir lived in the cafés and cheap hotels of the Left Bank where they worked and hung out, a part of the café and club scene of post-war (WWI) Paris.

Both de Beauvoir and Sartre believed that philosophy was *lived*, not simply written about; their refusal to seek academic posts, to accept awards (both refused the Legion of Honor and Sartre the Nobel Prize for literature), and their refusal to marry but instead to maintain a sexually and intellectually free, open relationship were all manifestations of this dictum. Sartre and the freedom and rebellion he was seen as preaching became famous in post-war Paris. In the process, Existentialism became a cultural movement in a way that Phenomenology never could or did.

Others soon joined Sartre and De Beauvoir in their Existentialist project. One was a friend from de Beauvoir's teenage years, Maurice Merleau-Ponty (1948/1964, 1945/2012), who was to focus his work on perception and cognitive science. Another was Albert Camus. Although they were familiar with and had written about each other's work, it was not until 1943 that the Algerian philosopher, journalist, and writer introduced himself to Sartre at a rehearsal of the latter's play, *The Flies* (Sartre, 1947/1989). Camus had by then finished and published what he was to call his "Three Absurds:" *The Stranger* (1942/1989), *The Myth of Sisyphus* (1942/1991), and *Caligula* (1944/

---

20 *Nausea* (Sartre, 1938/2013) and its anti-hero Roquentin actually appeared shortly before the war.
21 By and large, their Communist Party membership did not survive Stalin's non-aggression pact with Hitler in 1938 and the former's demands that they cease their opposition to fascism and Nazi Germany.

1958). In these three works, later supplemented by *The Plague* (1948/1991) and *The Rebel* (1956/1991), he would lay down the tenets of Absurdism, one of the threads that I will draw into what I call the Psychotherapy of the Absurd (Chapter 4, below). To imagine they formed a tightknit and likeminded group of philosophers could not be farther from the truth either socially or philosophically. With the exception of Sartre and de Beauvoir, friendships and hatreds shifted with volatility, as did philosophical disagreements. Again, the Nazi occupation and its Russian roulette quality in which people were there one day but might disappear randomly and without notice the next could have fueled this instability.

Unlike the German Phenomenologists, the French Existentialists believed that their philosophy could be just as well (if not better) expressed in fiction, plays, and works of art. As we will see, they really used these works as case illustrations that were often clearer than their lengthy and at times arcane philosophical tomes. This is what Camus had in mind when he observed in his *Notebooks* (1962/1963) that if you wanted to do philosophy, you should write novels, and *The Stranger* (1942/1989) must be read with that in mind. Similarly, Sartre (Barrett, 1962/1990) sees "literature [as] a mode of action an act of the writer's freedom that seeks to appeal to the freedom of other individuals and eventually to the total free collective of mankind" (p. 250).

Like the *fin de siècle* Viennese, the French Existentialists were drawn to cafés such as Café de Flore and Les Deux Magots because they were warmer than the cheap hotels in which most of them lived. There they became part of the expanding, cross-pollinating social circles that included writers Ernest Hemingway, James Joyce, and Jean Genet, and artists Pablo Picasso and Alberto Giacometti among others. In particular, the Existentialists, writing as novelists, were profoundly influenced by Faulkner, Hemingway, and the hard-boiled American detective fiction writers of the 1930s.

On October 29, 1945 Sartre gave a lecture under the auspices of *Club Maintenant* (Club Now) at the Salle de Centraux on Paris' Left Bank entitled "Is Existentialism a Humanism" (Judaken, 2012). This was two months after the United States ended World War II by dropping atomic bombs on and obliterating the Japanese cities of Hiroshima and Nagasaki, six months after Hitler's suicide and the German surrender, the emergence of the photographs and newsreels of the concentration camps, and shortly after the first anniversary of the liberation of Paris and the end of the "dark years" of its occupation: 1940–1944. Hundreds of people squeezed into the hall to hear Sartre proclaim on Existentialism; thousands were turned away. The lecture "consecrated him as the high priest of existentialism" (p. 90). According to Annie Cohen-Solal, it "became one of the mythical moments of the postwar era, the first media event of its time, giving rise to the 'Sartre phenomenon'" (p. 90). He and de Beauvoir became a golden couple, pursued by photographers and reporters, the embodiment of the Existentialism described in the talk.

Sartre

We cannot talk about Sartre's 70 published works. Among the three kinds of writing, texts, novels and plays, the best known are *Being and Nothingness* (1943/2003), the novel with the pretentious title *Nausea* (1938/2013), and the play *No Exit* (1946/1989). *Being and Nothingness* is, however, problematic. The result of years of Sartre's note-taking, the 665 page tome was, as Bakewell (2016, p. 152), quoting Barrett in his 1946 review of its English translation, "a first draft for a good book of 300 pages."[22] Alas, this was a trend that would intensify over the course of Sartre's career and fame. He would eventually write drafts and publish them without a second look (Bakewell) and one has to wonder if he had fallen into the trope of other famous male philosophers (and it is mostly men) who used the obscurity of their writing to extend their fame. One could argue, indeed, that Sartre worked at being precious. *Being and Nothingness* is not fully realized; the crisp assertion "existence precedes essence" must wait for the 1945 lecture, and the subsequent slim, but tightly coherent (perhaps Sartre's most coherent) volume, *Existentialism is a Humanism* (Sartre, 1947/2007), containing it would only appear two years after that.

Being and no-thing-ness

Freedom, particularly Freedom in Nazi-occupied France was *the* great subject of Sartre's (and de Beauvoir's) written and lived philosophy; it is curious indeed that his masterwork on the subject, *Being and Nothingness* (1943/2003), written when France was not free, somehow got by the censors. But it is a book whose semiotics is idiosyncratic. The account gets a bit dicey. *Being, en-soi*, is a quality of objects, of the animals and things that make up Heidegger's *Umwelt*. Human Beings do not, according to Sartre, *Be*; they are defined only by the fact that they are Free and they exist through being conscious (a reformulation of Husserl's first principle), they are *pour-soi*. We Human Beings are, according to Sartre a kind of *Nothingness*; it is a specific not an amorphous Nothingness, a *No-thing-ness*. An old Existentialist joke (Bakewell, 2016) will illustrate this. Jean-Paul Sartre walks into a café and orders coffee with sugar and no cream. The waiter returns shortly and says, "I'm sorry M. Sartre, we are all out of cream; will milk do instead?" The point is that it is a specific nothingness; a "cream nothingness" and the waiter can only supply a "milk nothingness." But on a dark, horrible note (Bakewell) de Beauvoir writes of two attractive Czech women who appear daily at the Café Flore during the Nazi occupation. Then one day they are gone. "They never came back. It was unbearable to see their empty places: it was, precisely, a *nothingness*" (p. 146).

---

22 In fairness, Sartre & Co. would argue that this is simply the *essence* of Existentialist writing, to offer a multiply divergent text from which the reader could then *freely* assemble a personal meta-account.

As Existential Psychotherapists (and I will argue later that most of us are that, whether we so label ourselves or not), freedom and its lack are as much our concern as they are Sartre's, but the translation of Ontology into Being and Nothingness, if we are even able to accomplish it, is not of much use to us. We usually don't think about freedom in this way, but we should. On its simplest level our lives seem tightly constrained, we wake at a certain time, wash and breakfast (or not) at a certain time, arrive at the office at a certain time, return home, and so on. We feel tied down, prisoners of these rules. We are not *free*. Sartre points out that we are no such thing, that these are in fact choices we are constantly making and remaking and we are only pretending that we are not free. But there are also more subtle and far-reaching kinds of entanglements: *obligations, commitments* to programs of activities, to relationships, to a particular kind of life. Our patients come to us all of the time with lives ruined by such constraints. Indeed, much of what we do, explicitly or otherwise, is to teach them that these are in fact choices they have made, help them to understand how and why they made them, and enable them see how to free themselves from them. At the same time, a meaningful life for Sartre requires choice (Heidegger would argue, I think that a life without choice is a life lived in *fallenness*) but choice requires a constraint of freedom. What we are also interested in (and even an orthodox Freudian would agree) is a life governed by conscious not unconscious choices.

Existentialism is a Humanism

Sartre begins *Existentialism is a Humanism* (1947/2007) "by saying that what we mean by 'existentialism' is a doctrine that makes human life possible and also affirms that every truth and every action imply an environment and a human subjectivity" (p. 18). What he wants to say (or to shout, really) by this is *his* call to arms: that Existentialism is "simply the belief" that "*existence precedes essence*" (p. 22, italics added). By this he means that, through a variety of random circumstances—not the least being which of roughly 20 million spermatocytes wins the contest to fertilize a particular ovum, through no thought or action of his own—Man is first *thrown into existence* and must then proceed to *define and construct his essence*. (Man is also randomly thrown into time, body, race, place, and social class.) I have (2018) offered a fuller account of *existence* in a previous volume. A corollary to this is that Man is responsible for who he is, for his essence. *Creation* exists in the constant making and remaking of choices; however we imagine our situation, our essence is composed in part of choices (including choosing not to choose), that are freely made. The compelling issue of our Being is then to determine how we can best use these freely made choices.

Sartre (1947/2007) describes two kinds of Existentialism: a religious strand founded by Kierkegaard and continued by Karl Jaspers and Gabriel Marcel, and an atheistic strand, present in the works of Nietzsche, Heidegger, the French Existentialists, and himself. The former use God as a key to the system: if God creates *men* (and women), God must have *what he is creating in mind before he does so*, hence, for the religious Existentialist *essence must precede existence*. Essence, for the religious Existentialist, provides outside meaning *from the start*. The atheistic existentialists viewed this as Absurd, seeing meaning as something individual Man must create for himself. However, for all of that, Sartre did particularly appreciate how Kierkegaard was a socially difficult and confrontive man writing his strangely titled books and always freely seeking to shock his circle of acquaintances. He saw this as an expression of living freely. A lifelong atheist, he, like de Beauvoir, did not accept Kierkegaard's turning to God to heal his anguish, seeing it instead as a flight into the Absurd.

Man manifests an irreducible subjectivity (as Psychoanalysts we have, following our own fraught path, reached the same conclusion). What *Sartre* means is that, as individual essences, we project ourselves (and other selves) into the future and are *conscious* of doing so. This is the unique property of the Being of Human Beings. *No Exit* (1946/1989) and *Nausea* (1938/2013) serve as illustrations of what he is talking about.

No Exit

In *No Exit*, Sartre's (1946/1989) short play, three characters, Garcin, Estelle, and Inez, are individually led by a "Room-Valet" into a room, furnished in the manner of the Second Empire[23] with a "massive bronze ornament standing on the mantelpiece" along with a paper knife, but lacking mirrors or windows. The room has a door that cannot be opened and a doorbell that doesn't ring. We are given to understand very quickly that the three characters are dead, that this is a room in Hell, and that they are expecting, despite a lack of evidence, to be physically tortured.

They dislike the term *dead*; Estelle prefers *absent*, and the dead, then, are absentees. She says that death doesn't mean much and that they've never been so alive as now (when they are dead). They begin to talk about how hot it is. Estelle feels "queer"; she observes that when she can't see herself (in a Mirror; there are no mirrors in the room), she wonders if she truly exists. Inez counters that *she* is always conscious of herself, painfully conscious. In this room without mirrors, they can only see themselves through one another's eyes (complete intersubjectivity). They exist as little more than their physical appearance to an other.

It emerges that Garcin, Inez, and Estelle are locked together for eternity, that even when the door "flies open" none can leave, and that they are their own torturers, famously, in Sartre's words, *L'enfer, c'est les autres*, Hell is other people. In it, they can only see themselves as objects of the other's consciousness. (Consciousness and the other are central themes for Sartre.) To exist, to

---

23 The reign of Napoleon III, 1852–1870.

Be, occurs only through the *look*, the *gaze*, and never as a subject. The characters' struggle for salvation is to become subjects; interestingly, they try sex and attempted murder to bring this about, but they fail.

We are left with the play's two themes: Being and Death. It neatly solves the Existential problem of death, Heidegger's fallen state, by telling a story in which because one is dead, one does not cease to be and by a particular *nothingness*: If there is a Hell, then there can also be an unmentioned Heaven (But is Heaven *necessary*? A joke at Kierkegaard's expense) in which, if one hasn't sinned, one can hope to exist forever. Then again, the Existentialists and the Phenomenologists would argue that to exist forever is its own Hell. The play is as important for what it does not say as for what it does.

Nausea

Nausea (Sartre, 1938/2013) is a more complex matter. It is a novel and a first draft of Sartre's Existentialism that would emerge more fully formed if not fully realized in *Being and Nothingness* (Sartre, 1943/2003). Freedom is the central issue for both works.

Sartre was influenced by the American writer John Dos Passos (Barrett, 1962/1990) in his view that what the writer should do is to struggle with Man's problems in his time and milieu. Barrett thought that *Nausea* "might well be" Sartre's best book in that it comes closest to joining the philosopher and the creative artist. His fiction, like that of the other Existentialists, comprises philosophical texts in literary form.

In the beginning of *Nausea*, its protagonist Antoine Roquentin does not recognize the objects we find in the world, Sartre's objects of Being that, in *Being and Nothingness*, make up the *en-soi*. It is only later, in the famous scene where he confronts the bark of a chestnut tree as an object and recognizes that *absurdity* is a property of all *en-soi* objects *in that they exist independently of any way that humans might relate to them*. To exist, objects must simply "be there"; they have no meaning except that which humans bestow on them.

The first thing you must understand about Roquentin is that he is *free*. He has enough money and has no need to work. He can wander as he likes (or, for our purposes here, doesn't like), observing as he likes, being with people or acting as a loner; he is existentially free. Freedom is inescapable, and he is left to make his own meaning. As the story unfolds, he is unable to do so and experiences only meaninglessness. These are all solid Existentialist themes.

Roquentin has come to a dull seaside town, not unlike Le Havre where Sartre was forced to teach for a number of years, to research the papers of the Marquis de Rollebon whose life was a series of swashbuckling adventures. Roquentin plans to write his biography but is unable to: *If someone is dead, they no longer exist* and there is nothing to write. Life is nothing like these adventures and, without moorings of any kind, he simply wanders through the town, noting down what he sees. Life is characterized only by contingency, everything resembles a featureless blob, and there *is* no necessity; Roquentin pines for it. With this realization, he experiences what he calls the "sweetish sickness," *nausea*, a disease of existence, more specifically, a disease that grows out of his nearly complete detachment from other people. He feels relief for a few moments in his favorite café when they play a bluesy record of a woman singing "Some of These Days" in which each note *must* follow the preceding one, in other words, for that moment, Roquentin experiences *necessity*. It is through art, then, that he rescues himself, leaving for Paris to write, not the impossible biography, but a book about existence. In life, Roquentin's dilemmas about writing and finishing a book were Sartre's own.

Why *Nausea*? Sartre, somewhat autobiographically, is proposing that we all suffer from nausea; it arises from Man's existential condition in which there is only contingency. It is a symptom that results from a state of total detachment. Interestingly, Sartre does not consider it an illness; we all have suffered degrees of detachment and alienation. However, most of us *would* consider Roquentin to be depressed and perhaps schizoid, to use an old and half-forgotten term (Guntrip, 1971). (I would consider it an illness of Being that lies within the purview of the Psychotherapy of the Absurd.) Indeed, Sartre's working title for the book was "Melancholia"; *Nausea* was later suggested by his publisher. For our purposes, Nausea is an illness that people suffer from, an illness that mainstream therapists (that is, us) often don't consider. It is an illness of *despair*. According to Sartre and most other Existentialists, *Roquentin is experiencing the inherent meaninglessness of the World; he is suffering because of it*. The problem can be solved or the illness cured through the *self-construction of personal meaning*. This is the central tenet of the Existentialist project. Roquentin was the kind of patient that Rollo May and his colleagues discovered in the 1950s. Unfortunately, with the exception of the British Middle School, their work seemed to have largely fallen out of favor, and one of our tasks is to figure out just what happened to it. For now, let's turn to Absurdity and its principal proponent: Albert Camus.

Camus and the "Three Absurds"

Absurdism at its most basic is about a fundamental discrepancy between Self and World. World here would include Heidegger's world of objects inanimate and animate, the *Umwelt*, and the world of Human Beings, the *Mitwelt*. The Existentialists would see the latter as somewhat (and I choose the term carefully) more important than the former. The discrepancy occurs in two ontological properties involving value and emotion: Meaning and Desire (Leffert, 2017). A failure to find Meaning, or its gradual or sudden loss, involves a state of meaninglessness, while a failure of Desire as a tool for successful living occurs when it parts company with the possible. In these circumstances, life becomes Absurd. It is a school of Existentialism that has since fallen out of philosophical favor (one could, however, argue that Neo-Pragmatism (Rorty, 1979, 1982) is not unrelated to it) and clinical favor (one could argue that it never was in clinical favor). I like Stoltzfus' (2003) definition best:

The absurd describes the state of mind of individuals who are *conscious* of a discrepancy between desire and reality: the desire for freedom, happiness, and immortality, and the knowledge that life imposes limits on desire even as death announces finitude.

(p. 1, italics added)

We are dealing here with issues that are fully deployed in consciousness "rather than metapsychologically conceived of as things rooted in an unavailable unconscious concealed by repression" (Leffert, 2018, p. 133). Psychoanalysis sadly gives consciousness short shrift, mostly focusing on trying to see past it in search of putatively deeper meanings, whereas it (Autonoetic Consciousness actually) is seen by Existentialist thought as the peak in Evo-Devo attained by Human Beings (Donald, 2001; Humphrey, 1992/1999, 2011).

In what he referred to as his "Three Absurds"—a novel, *The Stranger* (1942/1989), an essay, *The Myth of Sisyphus* (1942/1991), and a play, *Caligula* (1944/1958)—Camus sets out his theory of Absurdism. Although *The Stranger* is still considered one of the most important novels of the 20th century, it is not much treated as the essential philosophical text it is.

The Stranger

As Camus acknowledged, *The Stranger* is written in a style influenced by American detective fiction of the 1930s and, specifically, the work of Faulkner and Hemingway[24] (Stoltzfus, 2003). He drew his characters from life and offered a narrative in short, punchy, sentences in which what was left out is as important as what is said. In Faulkner's style, the second part of the book offers multiple narratives of the same events, something similar to what we see when our patients at various times offer up differing accounts of the same event. The book opens with the famous sentence: Mamma (or mommy) died today, or yesterday, Meursault doesn't know. This vague, dissociative account contrasts with the next sentence: a punching account that comes next in the telegram he received, Mother dead. Funeral tomorrow. Faithfully yours. The periods pummel us. Camus divides the book into two parts, although really there are three. The first is the story of Meursault's trip to the nursing home and his mother's funeral under the blazing Algerian sun. The second is a narrative of his life afterwards culminating in his senseless shooting of an Arab at the beach, again under the blazing sun. Finally, there is the story of the trial with its multiple tellings by the witnesses. *The Stranger* ends with

---

24 I have written about *The Stranger* before (Leffert, 2018, chapter 5), but my emphasis here is somewhat different. I would repeat, however, that the book was written for a 1942 French audience in Nazi-occupied Paris, that the Algerian setting is a kind of code for the meaninglessness and brutality of life under the Nazis, and that Meursault's miscellaneous shooting of the Arab must be understood in that light, not as the subject for some post-colonial narrative (e.g., Daoud, 2013/2015).

Meursault's being sentenced to death with the execution to be carried out by guillotine in the public square. The death sentence, its public execution, and the hope he will be hated make Meursault happy for the first time in the book. They give him a sense of *meaning*.

Meursault tells us (and why, given his listless connection to World, he even bothers to tell us, is unclear) that he lives life at one remove from people and things, a loner, in a state of perpetual Depersonalization and Derealization. This state is akin to the "sweetish sickness," Nausea, that Sartre (1938/2013) describes Roquentin as suffering from. While the latter solves the problem by returning to Paris and reconstructing a personal meaning for himself, Meursault can find meaning only in his death sentence, carried out in an atmosphere of hatred.

The third part, the trial, is again a different matter. Meursault's guilt (in the legal, not the moral sense) is a given from the outset. The prosecutor instead calls a series of witnesses that describe Meursault's behavior at the vigil over his mother's body and the funeral the following day. They all describe him as without feeling, without *grief*, and it turns out that he is being tried for these disassociations, as a rebel against societal norms. (This, of course, is the position that Camus uses *The Stranger* to convey.) Meursault can only speak of the *physical* discomfort, the heat of the sun, at her funeral. He is unable to say or feel *anything* about her death. As the prosecutor sums up, Meursault lacks a *soul* and any feelings to put inside it. The guillotine is his avid solution; we know that Camus had read Heidegger and Meursault will be *thrown* into his death.

Camus later tells us more about what he meant *The Stranger* to be about. In the introduction to a 1955 English language translation (Carroll, 2008), he tells us that he had once quipped that any man who does not weep at his mother's funeral runs the risk of a death sentence. What he tells us he meant is that *Meursault is condemned because he refuses to play the game*. Camus takes the opportunity to offer a critique of bourgeois societal values, but he also suggests that Meursault is capable of making a *choice* to disassociate, something entirely beyond the power of the man Camus has described for us. We are left with our absurd anti-hero alive in an absurd world (Nazi-occupied France) where the specters of death and meaninglessness overshadow everything.

The Myth of Sisyphus

I read *The Myth of Sisyphus* as a sort of companion volume, even a study guide, to *The Stranger*. In it, Camus (1942/1991) is concerned with the fundamental question of Existence: Why do we go on living? *Camus sees "Is life worth living?" as the fundamental question facing philosophy* and, as psychologists (which all therapists and analysts are), we are interested in how each Human Being answers this question. To plug the *Myth* into the question, we must use Camus' reading of it. Sisyphus, the King of Corinth, lived the life he pleased, making fun of the gods and in defiance of them. Of interest to us is that he put Death[25] in chains, emptying the underworld. Pluto, god of the underworld, could not bear to be alone and dispatched Ares, the *God of War* (this is relevant to occupied France in World War II), who freed Death from *her* chains. Sisyphus died but convinced Pluto to send him back to life for a time, where he again led a life of excess. He refused to return to the Underworld at the end of his allotted time and, ultimately, a decree of the gods was necessary. Mercury seized him from his joys and returned him to it where "his rock was ready for him." Ultimately, he was condemned by the gods for his deceitfulness and arrogance to endlessly roll a boulder up a hill only to have it slip from his grasp, just before reaching the top, and roll back to the bottom where he had to repeat the process. Camus sees Sisyphus as representative of Heidegger's Fallenness: How do you decide to keep going when, ultimately, life has no objective meaning and ends in death?

Camus casts Sisyphus as the Absurd Hero, a stand-in for all Men. Sisyphus faces a profound dilemma as he roles his rock up the mountain only to lose his grip on it at the very end and watch as it rolls down the mountain. He then walks down the mountainside so he can start again. Camus (1942/1991) is writing about the absurdity of Man's position, the conflict between his wish for meaning and significance on the one hand and the silent, cold universe of stars and galaxies and atoms in which he lives on the other. In the face of absurdity, Camus suggests three possible ways forward.

The first is that if life is truly meaningless and not worth living, and that these are simply facts about life in general as well as a life in particular, then the only sensible response is suicide. Suicide is the way out of Absurdity. Put another way, the choice is to end the Self. In the Preface to the 1955 English translation, Camus rejects the premise of this argument. He argues that even within nihilism it is possible to find the means for moving beyond it. Even, *Sisyphus*, written in 1940 and much influenced by the European and French "disaster" of World War II, follows from this premise. If we reject suicide as the solution to the dilemma, what alternatives are there? More than any of the other Existential writers, a superficial reading of Camus as a psychologist of despair has been used to justify suicide as the only logical response to an absurd world (a friend told me of a relative, a college student in the late 1950s whose studies of Existentialism led him to end his life). Camus touched on the ideas that *Jung Wien* struggled with in *fin de siècle* Vienna that also not infrequently led to romantically committed suicide.

The next option, in Kierkegaard's terms is to make "a leap of faith" (Ferreira, 1998). This leap, according to the latter, lies at the root of all life. If Camus did not draw religion from Kierkegaard's work, he was nevertheless profoundly influenced by the latter's Absurdism. In *Fear and Trembling* (1843/

---

25 Recall that the acceptance or denial of Death is a central issue to Existentialists and Phenomenologists alike.

1983), Kierkegaard retells the story of Abraham and Isaac in which an angel appears and commands, in God's name, that Abraham travel to Mount Moriah and sacrifice his son Isaac to him rather than the customary sheep or goat. Abraham with a strange matter-of-factness agrees, only to have a messenger from God stop him at the very last moment and provide a ram as a substitute. Kierkegaard is not struck by either the command or the reprieve. What astonishes him is that the two must travel for three days and the better part of a fourth to reach Moriah, the one knowing what he will do and the other in ignorance and then, after the aborted sacrifice, traveling together again and taking up their lives with Abraham still convinced of his love for his son. "Abraham resigned everything and then took everything back on the strength of the Absurd" (p. 42). This is the impossible leap necessary to continue life with its fatal flaws (Bakewell, 2016). The idea here is that God gives life meaning and we fill in the blank with our belief in Him [sic]. In effect, God knows what he is doing and that *we* are doing what he has in mind for us. Indeed, this works for many people. It does offer some ontological difficulties, however, in that it reverses our premise: If we buy the package of God, then essence precedes existence and we have seen that this doesn't work. But if Sisyphus wished to make the leap of faith, then who are we to gainsay him?

Kierkegaard thought of this leap as doing the job while Camus saw Absurdity instead, something Man must do for himself. (For Camus, this represented life and work amid the nihilism of the French defeat and the Nazi occupation.) The leap of faith replaces human experience with abstraction. It also escapes rationality and may require a suspension of the ethical in favor of the religious. Interestingly, Sartre (1947/2007) comes at the problem from an entirely different angle: Man's subjectivity. If he were to tell the story, Sartre would ask, "How does Abraham know that the angel comes from God (as opposed to, say, the Devil)?" How does he know that it is even an angel and, for that matter, how does Abraham know that he *is* Abraham? Any of the above should stop Abraham from setting off for Mount Moriah.

The third path is to embrace the Absurd condition, an acceptance of the subjective that is an acknowledgement of the limitations of the objective. Camus returns to Sisyphus to define this path. When the boulder slips from his hands, he must go back down the mountain. He walks heavily down to the plain and the torment he must face. That "hour" walking down the mountain is a breathing space. It is also an hour of consciousness. The descent is a time of sorrow but also a time of joy. Sisyphus accepts his task in the same way that working people throughout the world do, claiming for themselves as well a time of freedom and reflection.

What Camus is arguing for is his view that, by its very nature, life is Absurd and we must live in it Sisyphus-like. Sartre and de Beauvoir did not accept Camus' ideas on Absurdity, and, for that matter, Camus did not consider himself to be an Existentialist. Life, for Sartre, *has* meaning, experience comes to us *with* significance, and it is the task of the individual to freely seek out (construct) their own subjective meaning. Sartre views Absurdism as a collapse into a pathological state, and the problem is for the individual to regain meaning, while Camus posits that there are things in life that cannot be changed and it is our task to, like Sisyphus, find meaning *in* them. As a practicing Psychotherapist, I have been arguing for both *clinical* positions in a rudimentary way for some time. (The Serenity prayer with which Alcoholics Anonymous meetings are begun does the same thing.) It is our task as Psychotherapists, as I will suggest in the next two chapters, to help a patient to find or regain meaning by first correctly identifying in which of these so different situations they find themselves. And yet there is a problem to be found in Everydayness. All this may be fine for Philosophers and Psychotherapists, but what about the worker at MacDonald's who spends her life endlessly preparing Big Macs? Heidegger would argue that, unlike Sisyphus, she is productive in an Everydayness of Care (Leffert, 2016) and *her* problem is to somehow get to thrownness. A more complete answer is to say that one's life must be considered as a whole, and like so many things about Human Beings, the whole is both different from and greater than the sum of its parts. To put it another way, it is a different world in which Sisyphus gets to leave work at 5 and go home to his wife and family. We come, then, in this roundabout way, to *Caligula* (Camus, 1944/1958).

Caligula

The emperor Caligula (Camus, 1944/1958) offers us his own solution to an Absurd life. Caligula is *Homo absurdus* (Foley, 2008), a figure in history, as opposed to the mythical heroes of *Sisyphus* or *The Stranger* in a novel or play.[26] Unlike Sisyphus, Caligula fails in his recognition of Absurdity and in his concept of what it means to live free. (For Caligula, living free involves having and using the power to *capriciously* exert sexual or life and death control over the lives of his subjects.) What is Absurdity and what does it mean to be free, are the major questions that the play addresses. Caligula will contemptuously reject the gods, that is, he rejects a leap of faith, and an embrace of the Absurd condition, that is, an ability to find meaning in it. That leaves only the one alternative and Camus ends the play, and Caligula his life, via assisted suicide.

The play begins shortly after Drusilla's (Caligula's sister and mistress) death. Prior to it, Caligula is described as a just man, opposed to suffering in any of its forms. Caligula vanishes for three days. He returns to say that he has been seeking the moon because he wants it but has been unsuccessful in his quest. He says he is less affected by Drucilla's death than the simple truth it reveals —that we are helpless to affect a changing world. He says he now knows that *nothing lasts* (the basis of the Existentialist condition). In the face of these

---

26 For that matter, one could write a similar history of a contemporary figure such as Hitler or Stalin.

two failures to change the world, he decides to seek freedom through larceny, rape, and murder. Caligula believes that he can only be free at someone else's expense. He ultimately realizes that he is practicing *the wrong kind of freedom*. It is relevant that the nobles surrounding him adjust to the situation and this is reminiscent of the French people having to deal with the Nazis. *They* see, however, that he is draining their lives of meaning and that a man cannot live without some reason for doing so. Without that reason, one's life has no more meaning than a speck of dust.

Caligula, the anti-hero, has set out "rationally" using his power as emperor to force the whole world to discover the Absurd. (On a much lighter note with a much happier outcome, *The Taming of the Shrew* has been coming to mind as I write this.) In Cherea, Caligula's chief adversary, Camus introduces a voice of reason that speaks to the community's ethical solidarity in the face of Absurdity. Camus considers the assassination of Caligula as morally necessary as opposed to Meursault's execution for his failure to publicly mourn his mother rather than his shooting the Arab, which is Absurd.

Caligula addresses the question: Does Absurdism entail Nihilism? His sought-after assassination by his subjects who finally reassert control of their lives at play's end suggests that it does not. Camus does mean to describe how the absurd "may force itself onto the stage of history with more sinister and bloody consequences than might have been imagined in *The Myth of Sisyphus*" (Foley, 2008, p. 23).

Whatever happened to Existentialism?

The Phenomenologists and the Existentialists have been interested in a particular subset of ontology: the Being of Human Beings. The interests of contemporary philosophers shifted gradually in the latter half of the 20th century to epistemology, the study of the various groups of rules governing knowledge and knowability. Epistemology had been bracketed by the Phenomenologists and the Existentialists. The Postmoderns, as they came to be called—the Neo-Marxists, the Post-Structuralists, and the Neo-Pragmatists—were, in effect, returning to a consideration of the contents of those brackets. This is not to say that a vibrant contemporary discourse on the Existential and the beginnings of a re-consideration of the largely-ignored Absurd is not taking place, because it is. What it does say is that people of the stature discussed in this chapter have not continued to be present and turning over new ground in the field. In a kind of reverse order, I had first taken up Postmodernism (Leffert, 2007a, 2007b) and how it informed Psychotherapy and Psychoanalysis before only now (Leffert, 2016, 2018, and the present volume) coming to consider these earlier disciplines and how they *must* inform our work. If what happened to Phenomenology and Existentialism is not problematic to philosophers, the question of whatever happened to Existential Psychotherapy is of importance to us as clinicians. We will, however, first turn to the question of how Existential Philosophy led to Existential Psychotherapy and what, exactly, that consists of.

References

Bakewell, S. (2016). *At the existentialist café: Freedom, being and apricot cocktails.* New York: Other Press.
Barrett, W. (1946). Talent and career of Jean-Paul Sartre. *Partisan Review, 13,* 237–246.
Barrett, W. (1990). *Irrational man: A study in existential philosophy.* New York: Anchor Books. (Original work published in 1962).
Baudelaire, C. (2008). *The flowers of evil* (Oxford World's Classics, English and French Edition) (J. McGowan, Trans.). Oxford: Oxford University Press. (Original work published in 1857).
Bergmann, M. S. (1993). Reflections on the history of psychoanalysis. *Journal of the American Psychoanalytic Association, 41,* 929–955.
Binswanger, L. (1958). The case of Ellen West. In R. May, E. Angel, & H. F. Ellenberger (Eds), *Existence* (pp. 237–364). New York: Simon & Schuster.
Boss, M. (1963). *Psychoanalysis and Daseinanalysis.* New York: Basic Books.
Brentano, F. (1995). *Psychology from an empirical standpoint* (L. L. McCalister, Trans.). London: Routledge. (Original work published in 1874).
Camus, A. (1958). Caligula (S. Gilbert, Trans.). In A. Camus, *Caligula and 3 other plays* (pp. 1–74). New York: Vintage Books. (Original work published in 1944).
Camus, A. (1963). *Notebooks 1935–1942* (P. Thody, Trans.). Chicago: Ivan R. Dee. (Original work published in 1962).
Camus, A. (1989). *The stranger* (M. Ward, Trans.). New York: Vintage Books. (Original work published in 1942).
Camus, A. (1991). The myth of Sisyphus (J. O'Brien, Trans.). In A. Camus, *The myth of Sisyphus and other essays* (pp. 3–138). New York: Vintage Books. (Original work published in 1942).
Camus, A. (1991). *The plague.* New York: Vintage Books. (Original work published in 1948).
Camus, A. (1991). *The rebel.* New York: Vintage Books. (Original work published in 1956).
Carman, T. (2006). The principle of phenomenology. In C. B. Guignon (Ed.), *The Cambridge companion to Heidegger* (pp. 97–119). Cambridge: Cambridge University Press.
Carroll, D. (2008). *Albert Camus the Algerian: Colonialism, terrorism, and justice.* New York: Columbia University Press.
Christakis, N. A., & Fowler, J. H. (2009). *Connected: The surprising power of our social networks and how they shape our lives.* New York: Little, Brown and Company.
Daoud, K. (2015). *The Meursault investigation: A novel* (J. Cullen, Trans.). New York: Other Press. (Original work published in 2013).
Donald, M. (2001). *A mind so rare: The evolution of human consciousness.* New York: W. W. Norton & Co.
Ellenberger, H. F. (1970). *The discovery of the unconscious.* New York: Basic Books.
Erikson, E. (1963). *Childhood and society* (2nd edn). New York: W.W. Norton & Co (Original work published in 1950).
Ferreira, M. J. (1998). Faith and the Kierkegaardian leap. In A. Hannay & G. D. Marino (Eds), *The Cambridge companion to Kierkegaard* (pp. 207–234). Cambridge: Cambridge University Press.
Foley, J. (2008). *Albert Camus: From the absurd to revolt.* Montreal: McGill-Queen's University Press.

Foucault, M. (1972). *The archeology of knowledge & The discourse on language* (A. M. S. Smith, Trans.). New York: Pantheon. (Original works published in 1969 and 1971).
Freud, S. (1959). An autobiographical study. In J. Strachey (Ed.), *Standard Edition* (Vol. XX, pp. 7–74). London: Hogarth Press. (Original work published in 1925).
Freud, S. (1959). Inhibition, symptom, and anxiety. In J. Strachey (Ed.), *Standard Edition* (pp. 87–178). London: Hogarth Press. (Original work published in 1926).
Freud, S. (1961). Civilization and its discontents. In J. Strachey (Ed.), *Standard Edition* (Vol. XXI, pp. 64–145). London: Hogarth Press. (Original work published in 1930).
Gordon, P. E. (2010). Emmanuel Faye; Heidegger: The introduction of Nazism into philosophy in light of the unpublished seminars of 1933–1935. *Notre Dame Philosophical Reviews*, 3 December.
Guntrip, H. (1971). *Psychoanalytic theory, therapy and the self: A basic guide to human personality in Freud, Erikson, Klein, Sullivan, Fairbairn, Hartman, Jacobson, and Winnicott.* New York: Basic Books.
Heidegger, M. (1982). *The basic problems of phenomenology* (A. Hofstadter, Trans. Rev. ed.). Bloomington: Indiana University Press. (Original work published in 1975).
Heidegger, M. (2001). *Zollikon seminars: Protocols-conversations-letters* (F. Mayr & R. Askay, Trans.). Evanston: Northwestern University Press. (Original work published in 1987).
Heidegger, M. (2010). *Being and time* (J. Stambaugh & D. J. Schmidt, Trans.). Albany: State University of New York. (Original work published in 1927).
Humphrey, N. (1999). *A history of the mind: Evolution and the birth of consciousness.* New York: Springer. (Original work published in 1992).
Humphrey, N. (2011). *Soul dust: The magic of consciousness.* Princeton: Princeton University Press.
Husserl, E. (1983). *Ideas pertaining to a pure phenomenology and to a phenomenological philosophy: Book one: General introduction to a pure phenomenology* (F. Kersten, Trans.). New York: Springer (Original work published in 1913).
Husserl, E. (2001). *Logical investigations* (J. M. Findlay, Trans.). London: Routledge. (Original work published in 1913).
Idhe, D. (2012). *Experimental phenomenology* (2nd edn.). *Multistabilities.* Albany: SUNY Press.
Jacquette, D. (1999). Schopenhauer on death. In C. Janaway (Ed.), *The Cambridge companion to Schopenhauer* (pp. 293–317). Cambridge: Cambridge University Press.
Janaway, C. (1999). *Self and world in Schopenhauer's philosophy.* Oxford: Clarendon Press. (Original work published in 1989).
Janaway, C. (2002). *Schopenhauer: A very short introduction.* Oxford: Oxford University Press.
Janik, A., & Toulmin, S. (1996). *Wittgenstein's Vienna.* Chicago: Ivar R. Dee. (Original work published in 1973).
Johnston, W. M. (1972). *The Austrian mind: An intellectual and social history 1848–1938.* Berkeley: University of California Press.
Judaken, J. (2012). Sisyphus's progeny: Existentialism in France. In J. Judaken & R. Bernasconi (Eds), *Situating existentialism: Key texts in context* (pp. 89–122). New York: Columbia University Press.
Kaufmann, W. (1975). *Existentialism from Dostoevsky to Sartre.* New York: Plume Books. (Original work published in 1956).

Kierkegaard, S. (1980). *The sickness onto death* (H. V. Hong & E. H. Hong, Trans.). Princeton: Princeton University Press. (Original work published in 1849).
Kierkegaard, S. (1983). Fear and trembling (H. V. Hong & E. H. Hong, Trans.). In H. V. Hong & E. H. Hong (Eds), *Fear and trembling/Repetition*. Princeton: Princeton University Press. (Original work published in 1843).
Kierkegaard, S. (1992). *Concluding unscientific postscripts to unscientific fragments* (H. V. Hong & E. H. Hong, Trans. Vol. II). Princeton: Princeton University Press. (Original work published in 1846).
Kierkegaard, S. (2014). *The concept of anxiety: A simple psychologically oriented deliberation in view of the dogmatic problem of heredity sin* (A. Hannay, Trans.). New York: Liveright. (Original work published in 1844).
Leffert, M. (2007a). A contemporary integration of modern and postmodern trends in psychoanalysis. *Journal of the American Psychoanalytic Association, 55*, 177–197.
Leffert, M. (2007b). Postmodernism and its impact on psychoanalysis. *Bulletin of the Menninger Clinic, 71*, 15–34.
Leffert, M. (2010). *Contemporary psychoanalytic foundations*. London: Routledge.
Leffert, M. (2013). *The therapeutic situation in the 21st century*. New York: Routledge.
Leffert, M. (2016). *Phenomenology, uncertainty, and care in the therapeutic encounter*. New York: Routledge.
Leffert, M. (2017). *Positive psychoanalysis: Aesthetics, desire, and subjective well-being*. New York: Routledge.
Leffert, M. (2018). *Psychoanalysis and the birth of the self: A radical interdisciplinary approach*. London: Routledge.
Luft, S., & Overgaard, S. (Eds). (2012). *The Routledge companion to phenomenology*. New York: Routledge.
Maderthaner, W., & Musner, L. (2008). *Unruly masses: The other side of fin de siècle Vienna*. New York: Berghahn Books.
Malabou, C., & Derrida, J. (2004). *Counterpath* (D. Wills, Trans.). Stanford: Stanford University Press. (Original work published in 1999).
May, R. (1958). The origins and significance of the existential movement in psychology. In R. May, E. Angel & H. F. Ellenberger (Eds), *Existence: A new dimension in psychiatry and psychology* (pp. 3–36). New York: Basic Books.
Merleau-Ponty, M. (1964). *Sense and non-sense*(H. L. Dreyfus & P. A. Dreyfus, Trans.). (Original work published in 1948).
Merleau-Ponty, M. (2012). *Phenomenology of perception* (D. A. Landes, Trans.). London: Routledge. (Original work published in 1945).
Nietzsche, F. (2016). *Thus spoke Zarathustra* (T. Common, Trans.). New York: Digireads.com. (Original work published in 1883).
Risse, G. L., & Gazzaniga, M. S. (1978). Well-kept secrets of the right hemisphere: a carotid amytal study of restricted memory transfer. *Neurology, 28*, 487–495.
Rorty, R. (1979). *Philosophy and the mirror of nature*. Princeton: Princeton University Press.
Rorty, R. (1982). *Consequences of pragmatism: Essays 1972–1980*. Minneapolis: University of Minnesota Press.
Sartre, J.-P. (1989). *The flies*. In J.-P. Sartre, *No exit and three other plays* (pp. 47–124). New York: Vintage Books. (Original work published in 1947).
Sartre, J.-P. (1989). *No exit*. In J.-P. Sartre, *No exit and three other plays* (pp. 1–46). New York: Vintage Books. (Original work published in 1946).

Sartre, J.-P. (2003). *Being and nothingness* (H. Barnes, Trans.). London: Routledge. (Original work published in 1943).
Sartre, J.-P. (2007). *Existentialism is a humanism* (C. Macomber, Trans.). New Haven: Yale University Press. (Original work published in 1947).
Sartre, J.-P. (2013). *Nausea* (L. Alexander, Trans.). New York: New Directions. (Original work published in 1938).
Schopenhauer, A. (1969a). *The world as will and representation* (E. F. J. Payne, Trans. Vol. 1). New York: Dover Press. (Original work published in 1844).
Schopenhauer, A. (1969b). *The world as will and representation* (E. F. J. Payne, Trans. Vol. 2). New York: Dover Press. (Original work published in 1844).
Schorske, C. E. (1980). *Fin-de-siècle Vienna*. New York: Alfred A. Knopf.
Stoltzfus, B. (2003). Camus and Hemingway: The solidarity of rebellion. *The International Fiction Review, 30(1)*.
Timms, E. (1989). *Karl Kraus apocalyptical satirist: Culture and catastrophe in Hapsburg Vienna*. New Haven: Yale University Press. (Original work published in 1986).
Tulving, E. (2003). Memory and consciousness. In B. J. Baars, W. P. Banks & J. B. Newman (Eds), *Essential sources in the scientific study of consciousness* (pp. 575–591). Cambridge: MIT Press. (Original work published in 1985).
Tulving, E. (2005). Episodic memory and autonoesis: Uniquely human? In H. S. Terrace & J. Metcalfe (Eds), *The missing link in cognition: Origins of self-reflective consciousness* (pp. 3–56). Oxford: Oxford University Press.
von Senden, M. (1960). *Space and sight: The perception of space and shape in the congenitally blind before and after operation* (S. Schweppe, Trans.). London: Methuen & Co. (Original work published in 1932).
Zahavi, D. (2003). *Husserl's phenomenology*. Stanford: Stanford University Press.

3 Existentialist Psychoanalysis and Psychotherapy

If I am not for myself, then who will be for me?
If I am for myself only, then what am I?
If not now—*when?*

Hillel

Introduction

Although Existentialism and Phenomenology made their way into American Psychotherapy and Psychoanalysis (May, Angel, & Ellenberger, 1958) in the 1950s, they did not, with the partial exceptions of Heidegger's influence on the Intersubjectivists (Stolorow, 2011; Stolorow & Atwood, 1992) and in the work of Irwin Yalom (1980), persist as a widely known school much beyond the 1970s.[1] As we speculated on in the previous chapter, this did not necessarily mean that they ceased to find their way into the teaching and practice of eclectic Psychotherapy (the boundaries of orthodox Psychoanalysis were much harder to breach). In addition to exploring the appearance and development of Existentialism as a *clinical theory* of care and practice, we will also explore its role in current practice. Where is it now when no one *seems* to be talking about it? It seems to have been passed down for two generations both explicitly in teaching and clinical supervision and as uncited theories of practice and technique but also implicitly in the *character* of our teachers' and supervisors' approach to patients and the therapeutic situation. Do we also, however, encounter a Contemporary Existential literature?

This has been a difficult chapter to write. In it, I describe a major thread of psychology, Existential Psychology, and look at its appearance and clinical use in the present. But in doing so I am also holding something back: the additions I have made to Existentialism that fold it into the interdisciplinary contemporary psychology around which I organize my clinical work. I call this the Psychology of the Absurd, the title of the book; it will be fully taken

---

1 While reading this present chapter, it will be useful to keep the previous one open to refer back to.

up in the next chapter. This renders the present chapter, in my eyes at least, as a bit historical; I ask you to bear with me for heuristic purposes, and accept the case illustrations that appear later in that light.

The story of Existential Psychotherapy is an unusual one. New metapsychologies arose largely out of clinical failures that led Psychotherapists to look *within* the therapeutic situation and its accompanying theories for new answers to old problems. They sought (and continue to seek, for that matter) what they would term "scientific" answers to what *I* would term questions pertaining to discourse and Existence arising both inside and outside of the therapeutic relationship. Similarly, by mid-century, a number of clinicians—Binswanger (1958a, 1958b), Boss (1963) and Frankl (1959/2006, 1969/2014) in Europe, May and his colleagues (May, 1958b; May, et al., 1958) in the United States—had recognized a failure of standard theories and techniques to adequately address symptoms such as anxiety and depression and a wider problem of subjective meaninglessness and anhedonia. Although many may disagree with their observations, these "Existential" therapists then identified circular elements in standard theory and technique that represented hermeneutics at its worst: theory concerned with substantiating theory rather than offering clinical paths leading to healing and happiness (Leffert, 2017). What was new was that these Existentialists, in searching for solutions to these problems, turned *outside* of Psychoanalysis and Psychology, seeking answers in philosophy, particularly Existentialism and Phenomenology. It goes without saying that what the Existentialists viewed gently as new tools for human observation, the organized schools of Psychoanalysis saw as heresies (Bergmann, 1993; Leffert, 2010). *Their* response to Existentialism was simply to not talk about it in their Institutes or Societies.

The discovery that these clinicians made in mid-century Europe and America was that what the Existential movement in philosophy was about could be characterized as a *psychopathology of Human Being*, a failure to successfully engage the developmental tasks of life. These were the tasks that Sartre, Camus, and Heidegger had been describing, albeit using different terminology. These clinicians also studied the 19th century Existentialists, Kierkegaard and Nietzsche, and the relationship of their work to that of Freud (May, et al., 1958). Both Kierkegaard and Nietzsche described a fragmented Man in a fragmented World with anxiety and depression as a response to this condition (Kierkegaard, 1844/1968, 1849/1980, 1844/2014; Nietzsche, 1883/2016). (Freud, for much of *his* career took a different path, turning away from World and Self and studying Man as a series of broken fragments—id, ego, superego, etc.—isolated from each other via the posited process of repression.^{2}) The corollary to these Existentialist discoveries was that there were therapeutic tools available to treat problems of anxiety, depression, meaninglessness and

---

2 Anna Freud (1936/1966) observed that, in the absence of conflict, no such fragments existed.

depersonalization that were distinct from those that we were accustomed to wield in order to treat conflict-based psychopathology.[3]

Origins

It is difficult to document and date the appearance and development of Existentialist Psychology[4] and the subsequent development of Existentialism-based Psychoanalysis and Psychotherapy. As May (1958b) describes it, the movement appeared in Europe in the 1940s and 50s. Unusually, it did not derive from the work of a single founding father or mother but rather it grew out of the more-or-less simultaneous empirical discoveries made by multiple clinicians working across the continent. (These spontaneous multiple births lent weight to the conclusion that they were onto something important about their patients.) They made a number of crucial observations. They encountered patients whose anxiety or depression was not relieved by the application of any of the theoretical models, the metapsychologies, or the accompanying standard techniques existing at that time. These clinicians found that they were often unable to ascertain whether they were actually seeing something in their patients or projecting their own existing theories onto them—a distinction that mostly went unconsidered. When a patient did get well, these Existential Psychologists were honest enough to realize that they truly had no basis for attributing the cure to any particular piece of theory. Although they recognized that Psychoanalysis could prove a successful clinical technique for some patients, they refused to accept it as a *Theory of Man*. They rejected unverifiable psychic constructs such as that of a dynamic unconscious separated from consciousness by a repression barrier (Leffert, 2010) or the structural theories of ego-psychology, opting instead for the observation that unconscious ideas attributed to a patient might originate in the *conscious* ideas of the therapist. Finally, instead of returning to existing theories and polishing them in the hope that something new would be seen in their reflection, *they went back to simply studying the patient as a Human Being in the World* and to studying her suffering not as a neurosis or a psychosis but as a state of Being, a painful deviation from a healthy Human Condition. This was and is crucial. They studied a patient's life history and the psychopathology found therein, not in terms of Metapsychology but as "modifications of the total structure of the patient's being-in-the-world" (May, 1958b, p. 5).[5] Their formulations

---

3 The Existentialists continued to assign a central role to repression, one that I have previously criticized (Leffert, 2010).
4 In choosing the term *Psychology* I do not mean to emphasize a particular discipline over another but rather to signify the study of the minds of Human Beings.
5 It remains curious that although the leaders of the Relational Movement "grew up" in the later years of Existentialist discourse, they fail to mention it as influencing their development as clinicians and therapists. The intersubjectivists did come to Phenomenology, but only top down, some years *after* they developed their theories.

thus came to represent something very similar to how we might understand the characters Sartre and Camus had written about in their novels. Their study was initially informed by the Phenomenology of Martin Heidegger (1975/1982, 1987/2001, 1927/2010), which made its way to the United States in the 1950s and was only subsequently influenced by the French Existential Philosophers (as English translations of their work became available). These studies yielded new ways of looking at patients and new tools for engaging them and their problems.

Looking at the case reports of these European Existentialists (e.g. Binswanger's (1958a) "Ellen West" and Boss' (1963) "Dr. Cobling") brought to North America in the 1950s, we find that they involve inpatients or severely disturbed outpatients. These were the kinds of patients reminiscent of the work of some of the British Middle Group:[6] Guntrip, Fairbairn, Khan, and Winnicott, for example. (Indeed, I would suggest that members of this Middle Group were unsung Existentialists.) It is possible that the initial bloom of European Existentialism included therapists in outpatient practice who developed this approach independently but simply didn't record their work. Be that as it may, the patients described in their literature were very sick, dysfunctional people, and classical psychoanalytic approaches of whatever theoretical ilk had proved, publicized claims of theoretical success to the contrary, strikingly ineffective in achieving healing or cure (Leffert, 2017).[7]

As it first appeared in Europe, or at least in Switzerland and Germany, Existential analysis was called *Daseinanalysis*, reflecting its Phenomenological roots. The term, to demystify it, variously translates as the analysis of Dasein, Human Beings' Being there (*da*) in World, or of the Existence [of Human Beings]. Its basis was an insistence that Man be understood through observing and understanding the way he is, *not in terms of a theory*. A fundamental point of Existentialism and of Existentialist Psychology was that Man could not be considered in isolation (as they often were in psychoanalysis). The corollary to this point was that, prior to Existentialism, the study of Man isolated from World had involved a *cleavage between subject and object* that led to a failure of understanding. (The Post-Structuralists, particularly Derrida and Foucault, continued to develop a critique of this cleavage and the founders of the Interpersonal and Relational Movements within Psychoanalysis have taken it as a starting point for the development of their theories.) As an introduction to

---

6 Within the British Psycho-analytic Institute, a bitter internecine war between two factions, the Melanie Kleinians and the Anna Freudians, was resolved by the formation of two independent educational tracks within the British Psycho-Analytical Society. For those people who didn't feel a part of either group there was a third track aptly named the Middle Group.

7 Despite the availability of appropriate treatments with psychotropic medications, Freudian psychoanalytic theories of the origins and treatment of schizophrenia continued to be taught in residency programs at least through the 1970s, and Kleinian approaches are still in widespread global use (indeed, the work of Bion is currently experiencing a Renaissance in the United States).

Daseinanalysis,[8] let me describe Boss' work with his patient "Dr. Cobling," a gifted, but deeply troubled British psychiatrist.

"Dr. Cobling" grew up, Boss (1963) tells us, in "the rigorously ascetic atmosphere of a sectarian [that is, religious] community, characterized by its inordinate zeal for mortification of the flesh"; the community demanded "unremitting self-denial and sacrifice to duty" (p. 5). Her intelligence and indomitable will led her to becoming a psychiatrist; with unstinting personal sacrifice, she worked her way up to being the director of a sanitarium where her sacrifice was "richly enjoyed" by others. (It is clear from the start of his narrative that Boss both liked and admired her.) When he first saw her, she had worked herself into such a state of exhaustion that she stood on the brink of emotional collapse. She suffered from a compulsion to suicide. It emerged that she had, throughout her life, suffered from periodic depressive episodes that were never diagnosed or treated. The death of her father, a year before she consulted Boss, began the downward spiral that led to this emotional and intellectual breakdown.

Boss' (1963) first action was to break this descending spiral by telling his patient that she needed to rest and to allow herself to not work. As he expected, he tells us, psychotic symptoms[9] were then free to manifest themselves. She experienced visual hallucinations of the faces of the church women from her childhood, auditory hallucinations telling her she was a prostitute and paranoid delusions of the world ending with Boss somehow involved in the plot and its concealment. Her hallucinations went on to appear in her drawings. His response was to first attempt to logically discuss her symptoms with her as a colleague, refuting and then offering biological explanations for them. Dr. Cobling dismissed his explanations with contempt, as she did his interpretations of her symptoms as projections from the Unconscious. Similar attempts to apply other psychologies failed, all of which rested upon assumptions of psychological meaning that we make but cannot prove. To get anywhere at all, Boss had (shades of Husserl) to return to the patient herself and where she existed in the world (a return to Dasein). In keeping with this Phenomenological position, he suggested to her that she try to allow her thoughts, including what might be described as hallucinations or delusions to simply *be* and to see what happened. (This can be a powerful clinical technique even when applied to disturbing but more mundane matters.) Dr. Cobling felt profoundly understood as a result of his suggestion and was able to seek direct meaning in her thoughts and dreams rather than the symbolic constructions of Metapsychology.

Healthy little children's faces began to appear in her dreams, and Dr. Cobling felt able to play, with Boss' assistance and permissive acceptance, at *being* the

---

8 Boss chooses this term, he tells us (1963), because the terms *existential* and *existentialism* have been so broadly applied that they have lost all meaning.
9 "Psychotic" should not be construed as schizophrenic per se but rather understood descriptively as a break with reality.

child her mother and aunts never allowed her to be. Meaning was worked through in cycles of healthy regression interspersed with delusional episodes that ultimately led to the emergence of adult artistic creativity as a replacement for the patient's pseudo-vocation in Psychiatry.

A foundational observation at the heart of the Existentialist approach to Psychotherapy and Psychoanalysis (May, 1958b) that goes back to Husserl (1913/1983) is the singular importance of the analysis of the real, living relationship of patient and therapist in the conscious present. This is, in effect, the opposite of a dictum of psychoanalytic orthodoxy in which the analyst strives to reduce the psychoanalytic situation to a transference[10]-countertransference relationship that the therapist then attempts to maximize by forcing a regression away from the real present relationship to an unreal infantile one.

It is important to discuss the often-overlooked role of abstract and impressionist artists in the Existentialist movement. They broke art out of a prettified and petrified photographic phase in which it had, for millennia, filled a decorative role and recast it in a discursive position that considered the fragmentation of World and Self.[11] Artists such as Van Gogh in his later works portrayed fragmentation of Self and World decades before the Existential writers appeared. *Guernica*, Picasso's now iconic mural, painted in 1937 to show the destruction and suffering caused by the bombing of this sleepy Basque village by Spanish and Italian fascist aircraft, portrayed the social circumstances that drove Sartre's and Camus' writing.

This brings us to an often-forgotten issue that confronted the early American Existential Psychologists: the absence of translations, let alone good translations, of the standard European works we now take for granted.[12] (You will remember that in their early years, Sartre and de Beauvoir initially had similar problems accessing Heidegger's work that led them to at first dismiss it.) May in 1958 describes Heidegger as impossible to translate, with only a few of his essays available at the time. This is why he has so much more to say about Kierkegaard and Nietzsche; translations of *their* work were readily available by the 1950s. Boss and Binswanger travelled to North America in 1961, conducting seminars as they went with therapeutically "left-leaning" Psychotherapists and Psychoanalysts. They were of particular importance in that they orally transmitted their phenomenological approach to patients based on the work of Heidegger. (Binswanger's account of his work with his patient "Ellen West" (1958a) appears as a chapter in *Existence* (May, et al., 1958).)

---

10 Transference-countertransference exists to be sure, but such an accentuation of it was seen by the Existentialists as a distortion of the here-and-now reality rather than an invaluable technical tool.
11 Sadly, such discourse was not economically viable, and it is only now, when this art has *become* decorative, that it commands vast prices.
12 With the *Standard Edition* then only just beginning to appear a volume at a time, a milder version of this problem existed with respect to the works of Freud.

By 1958, May and his colleagues were thus able to lay out a viable Existentialist Psychology that could be applied to therapy and analysis. May remains throughout highly respectful of Freud and his "genius." He either didn't realize or, more likely, refused to say that Existential Psychology mounted radical critiques of Freudian Psychoanalysis (back to Bergmann's *heresy*) that would have required thoughtful theoretical and clinical modifications to answer. (One could argue that Interpersonalism, Relationalism, and Intersubjectivism eventually offered those modifications.) He is, however, clear about a fundamental distinction between Freudian Psychoanalysis and Existential Psychology. Psychoanalysis sets out to apply science and technique to understand how a Man with a particular group of symptoms has gone awry and to use the recovering ability to work and to love (Freud's famous dictum: *Arbeiten und Lieben*) in conjunction with achieved insight as a measure of success. Existential Psychotherapy looks at how an Ill Man has ceased to be a Human Being and seeks to help him recover both his Humanness and his Being.

An important piece of the story of the appearance of the Existentialist Therapies, at least in North America, was the social milieu in which they arose. And, as it was profitable to explore two previous social settings, *fin de siècle* Vienna and the café scene of Paris between the wars, it is important to look at the social setting in which Existentialism first flourished: the 1960s.

The sixties

If the 1960s was a decade like no other, its *anno mirabilis* was 1968. If the end-of-century and between-the-wars decades were times when Western civilization attempted to creatively engage existential collapse, the sixties was, initially, a time of hope and possibility. For those of us who came of age then, it was a time like no other, a time in which the social institutions of power—race, gender, politics, and freedom—in the postwar years were being deconstructed. It was the age of *la pilule* (contraceptive) and *la bombe* (atomic). The individual's right to freedom, to psychological change and to personal growth were asserted—sometimes with success, sometimes in abject failure—by the postwar generation and a surprising number of its elders. If Freudian psychoanalysis and its lengthy recipes for insight and everyday unhappiness had flowered in the 1950s,[13] the 1960s saw a rise of what we would now call a belief in the Self, its meaningful connections to other selves, and its entitlement to a fulfilling life.

If the cafés of Vienna and Paris were the centers of the social movements of the *fin de siècle* and the *interbellum*, the 1960s was centered in the University, be

---

13 We psychoanalysts, regardless of orientation, have continued to view ourselves as *the* singularly important part of the therapeutic "show," even though, as we saw in Chapter 1, the therapeutic statistics tell quite a different story. (Reading psychoanalytic journals, of whatever ilk, conveys no such impression.)

it the Sorbonne, Columbia, or Berkeley, and, for lack of a better term, in the streets. The first two began in the cafés as elitist, intellectual movements that only later moved into the streets with the labor riots of Austro-Hungary in the early 20th century (Maderthaner & Musner, 2008) and the French Resistance to the Nazi occupation. In contrast, the 1960s was and began as a people's movement. It manifested two major thrusts: civil rights and social activism. The Civil Rights Movement was led by mature groups such as the NAACP (Roy Wilkins), the Southern Christian Leadership Conference (SCLC) (Martin Luther King, Jr.), and the Conference on Racial Equality (CORE) (James Farmer, Jr.), and radical, younger groups such as the Student Nonviolent Coordinating Committee (SNCC) (Stokely Carmichael) and the Black Panthers (Huey Newton). In contrast, the social activist movement was staffed by university youth. Although it involved spontaneous local movements and uprisings—the Berkeley free speech movement of 1965 and the sympathetic protests at UCLA, the Columbia riots and sit-ins of 1968 focusing on both the Viet Nam War and Race—the *national* organization for change in the universities was the Students for a Democratic Society (SDS). Founded in 1960, in 1962 it held a convention in Michigan that produced the Port Huron Statement, a manifesto advocating widespread social change that was mostly written by Tom Hayden. The situation in France in May of 1968 was more complex. What began as a student uprising at the Sorbonne University in Paris, much like the protests arising in American Universities, quickly spread to a series of general strikes taking place across France and threatening the government itself. Their themes —first anti-imperial, anti-capitalist, anti-American, then pro-labor and pro-social freedom—epitomized, broadly speaking, left-leaning populist social critiques and impassioned pleas for change.[14]

If the 1960s embodied a *populist* movement advocating social change, the arts had a unique place in it as the *voice* of social change. Among the singer-song writer-poets, Bob Dylan comes to mind along with a number of related performers. Dylan spoke to a generation, the Baby Boomers, about their aspirations, the changing world they lived in, and how they were different from their parents. The Beatles were of similar importance. They were the most influential, best-selling band in music history. They reached a broader audience, offering popular songs with strong rhythms and melodies that resonated unconsciously with its listeners and are still relevant (as is Dylan) a half-century later. Implicitly, as Dylan did explicitly, they offered social messages about emotional freedom and sexuality that would have been impossible to say out loud a decade earlier. In privileging their work in the 1960s we are doing no more than following Camus' recommendations that if you want to do philosophy, write novels. In other words, these artists were crypto-philosophers.

---

14 Sartre participated in and was briefly arrested for civil disobedience during the student revolts.

This is not to say that it was a time of unmitigated optimism. It was a time of promise and tragedy. Then, as now, we Americans were engaged in a war that drained the very meaning out of life and the decade saw three assassinations—the Kennedys and Martin Luther King, Jr.— that, taken together, suggested that the promise of the 1960s would never be fulfilled. We, as a country have never really recovered from these events, and we find ourselves struggling with similar issues of societal failure today. These are best understood as problems Being in World—Existentialist problems.

So, what does all this have to do with our Existentialist project? If there was a single philosopher, other than Jean-Paul Sartre, who captured the hearts and minds of the university students of the 1960s, it was certainly Herbert Marcuse (1964/1991, 2007). In particular, Marcuse's synthesis of Marx and Freud, of Labor and Eros, had widespread appeal. He posited that the irrational values of the then current social world led Man astray, pointing him at false needs. He called this process "repressive desublimation."

The 1960s, in contrast to the earlier periods we have discussed that began in the heads (the *Eigenwelt*) of their participants, began in the world: the social world, the *Mitwelt* of Marcuse's *One-Dimensional Man* (1964/1991), and the physical world, the *Umwelt*, of Rachel Carson's *Silent Spring* (1962/2002). It is by inference that we can see that this generation *as a whole* was struggling with the issues that Existential and Phenomenological psychologists were writing about and trying to treat in their individual patients. The 1960s were *about* a search for Meaning, first in the group but then *personal* Meaning in the individual. It has remained a subject of personal search ever since. Anxiety and depression were beginning to be understood as terms in the language of folk psychology, and folk psychopharmacology—marijuana and the hallucinogens— was being used to treat these problems, often, as encountered by those of us on the psychiatric front lines, with harmful or even disastrous results. The hallucinogens were sometimes being used, with dubious results, *in* psychotherapy to facilitate the process.

If Existentialism as a philosophy had long since become mainstream, Existentialism as a *psychology* was relatively new to North America. Where mainstream psychoanalysis was centered along an axis connecting metropolitan New York, Boston, and Washington, the Existential psychotherapies and the attendant Encounter and Sensitivity Training movements (Bradford, Gibb, & Benne, 1964) came to fruition in California, centered on a shorter axis connecting San Francisco and Big Sur.

The Existentialist approach to the therapeutic situation

We should perhaps begin this discussion by asking the question how, in a general way, do the Existentialist Psychotherapies (I include Psychoanalysis here) differ from the more usual Metapsychologies that most of us are familiar with. Some might think that they lead the patient to places where these usual (I can't think of a better word) Intensive Psychotherapies do not. I don't think this is the case. What differentiates all of the Psychotherapies, including those with a claim to eclecticism is simply *what we choose, consciously but mostly otherwise, to talk to our patients about.* (In the next chapter I will try to answer the questions of what I talk to my patients about and how that has changed over the decades.) How relevant this often-unconscious choice is to a particular patient's needs determines the success or failure of the therapy.

May (1958a), in his foundational work (about what he talks to his patients about) on the advent of Existential Psychology in North America, is very careful to state that, while the Existential Psychotherapist is first, uniquely interested in Man as a Human Being, this interest "does not deny the validity of dynamisms and the study of specific behavior patterns in their rightful places" (p. 37). That is to say, he does not mean to repudiate the psychoanalytic formulations of neurosis and character but only to insist that they live *within* the Existence of the person who has consulted us—a person with a lot more going on psychologically and ontologically.

This is fine as far as it goes, but it glosses over what is a major shift in the Existentialist position. Within the domains of most psychoanalytic metapsychologies, we would approach the *patient* (here a creature of a particular and unique ilk) with free-floating attention, waiting for things to strike us about the *unconscious* origins of what she is telling us. While today we would still adhere theoretically to May's position, the "dynamisms" we now accept and even base our work on are very different from those of modern Psychoanalysis and (May does not consider this point) vary significantly from therapist to therapist.[15]

Karen, a patient in her 50s who I have seen in analysis for some years, approached life and her relationships with those close to her in a rigid controlling fashion; the way she thought things *should* be was the best way for them *to* be, for others as well as herself. One could trace this position, using a psychoanalytic theory of psychosexual Development, back to her close relationship with a constantly critical father whom she wished to please oedipally, and then dealt with her failures to do so by a regression to an anal-sadistic position. But what proved far more meaningful was to highlight how her father's critical rejection of her, supported by the rest of the family, threatened her very *existence* and required her constant defense against what felt like obliteration.

As Existentialist Psychotherapists, we discover a suffering Human Being, Karen is a fine example, instead of a patient, in our office. We are interested in what strikes us about this Human Being, this Dasein, how we engage each other, and care about the collection of symptoms she brings as a source of suffering that impacts and detracts from her life rather than as an entry into

---

15 My own dynamisms are probably best described in terms of the work of the French Postmoderns (Leffert, 2010) that superseded the Existentialists in the 1970s, the dialectic constructivist approach as described by Hoffman (1998), and, where possible, to follow an injunction of my own *to think neuroscientifically.*

some putative Metapsychological venue. We understand that her approach to the World is what, ultimately, makes her unhappy. We are interested in knowing her, in grasping her; both are intimate, non-sexual kinds of knowing (I prefer the French, *connaissance*, here). Further, this knowing comes to us in part in a nonverbal way, *a non-verbal sensing of the person*. We have unfortunately been taught to suppress that kind of knowing in favor of verbal and diagnostic knowing (here, the French *savoir*, with its power implications, is a better match). The latter is what Foucault (1973/1994) termed—critically I might add, in *The Birth of the Clinic: An Archealogy of Medical Perception*—the *regard médicale* of the clinic, which turns a Human Being into a specimen, an *object* of teaching and learning to be acted *upon* rather than a subject in pain to be engaged. We must teach ourselves instead to return in part to our pre-therapist days, with the particular ability to grasp people that goes with it. It is an encounter with a new Person first, and an information gathering session second. We grasp her Being quite differently from grasping any particular information about her, consciously avoiding the *regard médicale* that may serve as a defensive abstraction on our part. The latter causes a distortion of reality as seen in the highly artificial and stylized setting of orthodox psychoanalysis in which neither patient or therapist is fully seen or known. This approach may suit a secretive patient (all patients keep *some* secrets) or a therapist suffering from social phobia very well, but it serves to provide only limited insight rather than therapy. (I am well aware that, in these few sentences, I am mounting a powerful criticism of standard psychoanalytic and psychotherapeutic theory and practice. It is my intent to do precisely that, and I will argue for it over this and the following chapters. It is consistent with the criticisms of standard theory and technique I have been developing since 2007.)

The problem with talking about Existentialism and Phenomenology in a way that the broad spectrum of therapists can find meaningful is one of language. On the one hand these terms and others—Being, Human Being, Human, Existentialist—have been used so broadly and used by people who have not immersed themselves in these disciplines, that they have, in effect, become meaningless. In order to counteract this, it is necessary to actively refocus on the words and remind ourselves of what they mean. Then there are the arcane-sounding terms in German (no worse than psychoanalytic terms, but *they* at least have been with us for a century)—Dasein, *Eigenwelt, Mitwelt, Umwelt*—that most of us have had to start from scratch on, and, as a result, tend to simply not bother with. Topics of Being and Meaning have largely been discarded by materialistic, Western societies, while retaining their importance in the East—India, China, Japan—forcing us to struggle to reclaim *their* meaning. It also must be admitted that defining all these terms is very hard work and requires us to accept a plurality and inexactness of meaning.

Let me again offer a definition of Dasein as part of a series of attempts on my part to make the term meaningful and more user-friendly. Dasein signifies Woman/Man, the Human Being, as the Being who is There (*da*) where *there* is their location, *physical and temporal*, in World. Dasein is the *located* Human Being. Dasein incorporates the capacities for self-consciousness and for choosing, where Man is the only creature or thing that manifests such properties (Leffert, 2018). Being, it should be remembered, is a verb form, the participle of *to be*, and it means both *being something* and *being towards* or *be-*coming something. The term *Self*, I have posited (Leffert, 2010), encompasses all of these considerations; it refers to a truly Bio-Psycho-Social Self. Man manifests a being-for-himself that is also unique, but can all too easily be inhibited or damaged, problems that bring *Human Beings* to consult us.

The inevitable corollary to Being, to Being *there*, is *not-*Being, Nothingness. This involves the Self's unique ability to apprehend the state of its no-longer-Being—that is, its death and the death of other selves. As Sartre (1943/2003) wrote, it is a specific, not a general, nothingness in which something or *someone* in particular is gone (Sartre, 1943/2018). Although Being-towards involves Being towards many things, ultimately it involves Being-towards death. Human Beings are unique among the species in that we apprehend the inevitability of our own Death. For us it is a Being-towards-not-Being. This Being towards Death should not be confused with Freud's poorly reasoned concept of a Death *Instinct*, a Death *Drive*, which, as we saw in the last chapter, was derived from the concept of Death as it was formulated in the cafés of *fin de siècle* Vienna. The role of Death in Being-towards is determined by whether the Self spends its life running away from Death and in speaking of it uses impersonal pronouns or, instead, uses an awareness of Death and the finitude of life to render each *moment* as precious and as meaningful as possible. Two of Heidegger's three states of being, *thrown* and *fallen*, signify the two different ways of dealing with Death. In a less extreme ontology, the two states are differentiated by whether or not Dasein remains individual and reflective or allows itself to be engulfed into a collective "they" that is Soul-numbing and Soul-killing.

If May and his colleagues (May, 1958a, 1958b; May, et al., 1958) are to be faulted for anything in their sweeping introduction to Existential Psychology and treatment, it would only be their largely uncritical attempts to retain Freudian psychoanalytic orthodoxy in their view of Human Beings and their sufferings. Contemporary Existentialists are similarly uncritical. I have, over the course of several works, offered radical critiques of classical positions along with Cotemporary reformulations of some that I have found indispensable.[16]

What May & Co., and the authors who came after them, proposed was the application of the philosophy discussed in the preceding chapter (with the exception of Absurdity, which I privilege and they have little to say about) to

---

16 These critiques and reformulations, beginning in 2007 and now spanning five volumes and several papers, are beyond the scope of this chapter. I would suggest *Contemporary Psychoanalytic Foundations* (Leffert, 2010) for a general introduction to them.

the therapeutic situation. We should remember that while May and his colleagues Ellenberger, Angel, and Binswanger were at work, other Existential authors—Frankl (1959/2006, 1969/2014), Reik (1941/1957), Fromm (1947/ 1990, 1941/1994), to name but a few— were also writing and treating patients. Consistent with May's observations to the effect that classical therapeutic approaches had little to offer people psychotherapeutically (classically oriented clinicians are often *clinically* successful but there is no evidence that it is that orientation that actually produces their clinical success), I believe that what we have to contend with therapeutically can be subsumed (with only a little shoehorning) by the three states of Being and four ontological problems: Anxiety, Despair, Meaninglessness, and an internal lack of Freedom. This involves a sharp distinction between states of Being and states of neurosis. We are, for example, talking about Existential Anxiety, anxiety about the state of our being, not Neurotic Anxiety growing out of some putative conflict (the latter can, however, lead to the former). Along the same lines, Guilt would be first of all Existential Guilt, not making the most of life, rather than neurotic guilt over one's impulses. The first thing to remember is that we *are* these things, we don't *have* these things. The second is that these terms, although they seem simple, are complex and manifest a degree of uncertainty. The third is that they are inseparable; meaninglessness can cause either anxiety or despair, and they can precipitate each other.

Although classical theories do offer some useful tools (the redevelopment of personal narrative (Leffert, 2010) that is called Reconstruction is but one example) for releasing an individual from neurotic compulsion and replacing it with personal freedom, these theories fail to provide therapeutic tools for relieving anxiety and depression or despair (I have written about these failures for much longer than I have written about Existentialism). The Relational and Intersubjective Schools can be successful in these areas, but they lack a clear description or engagement of the Existential problems that, associated with these ontological states, they are trying to address. How to explain this? Unlike the Freudian and Kleinian Schools, the Relational and Intersubjective Schools developed *after* Existentialism appeared on the therapeutic scene, with the latter being present at their births. Although neither the Relationalists nor the Intersubjectivists cite Existentialist sources, I think we can understand their success in Existential and Phenomenological terms. I would posit that we might think of them in part as crypto-Existentialists—likely to be an unpopular position.

We are left to consider the meaning/meaninglessness dilemma. Many of the Existential Psychologists wrote of the human condition in the postwar years (e.g., Frankl, 1959/2006; Fromm, 1947/1990, 1941/1994), under the shadow of the Nazi crimes against humanity. (As we will discuss in Chapter 5, there have been other shadows since: nuclear war, the cold war, Vietnam, 9/11, and now, perhaps, the Trump presidency, the effects of which will be much clearer when you read this than it is as I write about it in late 2018.) Under this postwar shadow, Man found himself psychologically in an empty world with no sense of how to proceed or even what to *expect* in life. The

Existentialist Psychotherapists described the Existentially Displaced Person, first the victims of the war and the soldiers returning home from it (who were its victims too), then those in the postwar years, and, then, gradually becoming clear (in the 1960s) that their descriptions applied to a large swath of the population.

These authors came at the problem from two directions. Frankl (1972, 1959/2006, 1969/2014) begins his narrative as an inmate in Auschwitz[17], describing an existence without meaning other than an animal instinct to survive, and his own search for meaning in the shadow of abuse and death. He originally titled this first section of *Man's Search for Meaning* (1959/1992) as *From Death Camp to Existentialism*. Camp life for the inmate quickly devolved into a harsh Existential struggle, a struggle to continue to exist. Frankl kept his focus on *human experience*, the provender of Existentialism—he was interested in "facts," Phenomenological facts, as they were processed into that experience. This Existential setting of World was unique to the camps. Upon admission, all identifying papers and all possessions were taken away and replaced with a *number*, tattooed on the inmate's arm and written on his clothes; the system set out to take an inmate's humanity and his identity from him and turn him into a unit of work.[18] This procedure immediately set out the principle requirement for the *possibility* of survival in a concentration camp: that one in whatever way possible holds on to his individual spark of humanity (Human Beingness) maintained along with self respect and separateness. The alternative was to sink into the fallen mass of the group in which one becomes a robot, welded to other robots, or, worse, an animal. A loss of Self that inevitably leads to death. He writes about how it is possible, even in such extreme conditions, to search out actions and experiences that celebrate one's humanity, that make life meaningful. The key to survival in such a bleak, devastating world was one's own inner world of memory, fantasy, and intellectual activity; the memories of love and loved ones that accompanied it. These thoughts and feelings involved an inner experience of beauty intensified by the blasted landscape of the world of the Camps. "Psychological observations of the prisoners have shown that only the men who allowed their inner hold on their moral and spiritual selves to subside eventually fell victim to the camp's degenerating influences" (Frankl, 1959/2006, p. 69). One also holds on to personal meaning by being able to ignore rather than focus on the possibility of catastrophe; as a random act, for

---

17 Although there is considerable controversy over the veracity of Frankl's narratives of his concentration camp experiences, it does not bear on the usefulness of his personal accounts of Meaning and the search for it.
18 An inmate's body represented to the Nazi state some number of harvestable Calories. It was a resource that could be utilized in slave labor until, supplemented by a sub-human diet (inmates were fed roughly 1300 Cal per day and forced to do hard labor that required 4,000 Cal to perform), it was used up and the inmate, now barely more than a skeleton covered by skin, died on his own or was sent to the gas chambers.

example, a guard might draw a pistol, bringing sudden death. Death was always a possibility, but Frankl learned to approach it much as a professional gambler would. Had it happened to Frankl it would have made his every act even more human and meaningful; we simply would not have gotten to read about them.

Obviously, there will be gradations of Experience and Being determining what an individual is capable of and what they will walk away with at the end of any ordeal. The camps became a kind of Existential laboratory in which inmates developed or failed to develop ways of Being. Inmates survived *physically* but not necessarily psychologically from their experiences. I do not believe that they were ever studied in the postwar years with these Existential issues in mind.

A central problem—perhaps beyond survival, *the* central problem—facing concentration camp inmates was how they would face death if they knew it to be inevitable. This involves, according to Frankl (1959/2006), the capacity to make death into a transcendent experience, meaningful in its own right. The question of Frankl's awareness of the work of the Existentialist philosophers, Heidegger and Sartre & Co., is unanswerable. He does not cite them anywhere, yet they all came at the problem of death vs. absurdity in the same way. A particular problem facing Human Beings forced to live in such circumstances arises out of what should have been a uniquely Human asset: the capacity to predict (accurately or not) or plan for the future, what Schacter (Schacter, Addis, & Buckner, 2008) called a capacity for mental time travel. The fact that a future itself was taken away, to be replaced by a state of absolute uncertainty, was overwhelming.[19]

Frankl the Psychotherapist practiced what he called Logotherapy (although we rarely hear this term today outside of Logotherapy circles). I prefer the term Meaning Therapy for what we do, out of a wish to avoid cluttering up the Ontology with still more jargon (Dasein is enough!) and to make it feel more approachable to a wider psychotherapeutic audience. The focus of the therapy is fundamentally identical to that of the other branded Existential and Phenomenological therapies: a search for personal meaning and freedom in the present that will go forward into the future.

Fromm (1947/1990, 1941/1994) went at this problem differently. He wrote about people who were unsuccessful in their search for meaning after finding— having it thrust upon them, really—personal freedom, lives in which they could do whatever they chose. Freedom became impossible in the face of an internal emptiness offering no clues as to how to exist (Sartre's Roquentin suffered from this condition). For them, this freedom imposed its own

---

19 Soldiers experience similar feelings when in situations of extreme, protracted combat. Eugene Sledge's (1981) remarkable and haunting memoir of his combat experiences in the Pacific Island campaigns of WW II illustrate this, along with universal, sometimes life-threatening, PTSD in the survivors.

tyranny, was, in its own way dehumanizing, and a strictly regulated life brought with it relief.

Existentialist Psychology today

Contemporary Existential Psychotherapists posit that the problems in Being that bring patients to consult us are emotional: anxiety, depression, loneliness, despair, and general emotional suffering. A corollary to this observation (May, et al., 1958) is that standard psychoanalytic theory and technique often do not provide symptomatic relief from the suffering connected with these feeling states. Overshadowing these emotional states is a profound sense that their lives lack meaning although it can sometimes require considerable therapeutic work for patients to become aware of this lack. They exist as responses to external objective and internal subjective events, with the two being hard if not impossible to separate. These problems are mitigated by the found presence of a sense of personal meaning. Existential theorists believe that finding personal meaning is the central task, the reason for Being, of Human Beings, and that our task as Psychotherapists is to help them with their search and separate out distractions as they arise. Among Existentialists, there is a generally held belief that although explorations of psychic conflict can be useful when such conflict is visibly present rather than simply posited, they do not constitute a major form of therapeutic action. The Existentialists tend to limit but not do away with explorations of patients' pasts, that is, the use of personal narrative, and the explorations of unconscious memories or fantasies.

From our perspective as Psychoanalysts and Psychotherapists who define ourselves as either members of the well-known theoretical and clinical schools—Freudian, Kleinian, Relational, Intersubjective, etc.—or as drawing ideas eclectically from some combination of them, Existential Psychology, after bursting on the North American scene in the late 1950s, appeared to have largely waned by 1980. (I have written from that perspective and asked: Whatever happened to Existentialism anyway?) It turns out that we were all very much mistaken. Existentialist psychotherapy and its relatives are alive and well in Europe and, to a lesser extent, in North America. There are multiple Logotherapy Institutes in Europe, if not in the United States. The two Existential Schools prominent in Europe are Logotherapy and *Daseinanalysis*. There is a *Journal of the British Society of Phenomenology* and a *Journal of the Society for Existential Analysis*. There is an Existential Psychotherapy Center of Southern California, located in Los Angeles. It would appear that these are functionally active disciplines not much known by the wider world of Psychoanalysts and Psychotherapists, even more so than, for example, the Jungians and the Lacanians. There is a large Contemporary literature devoted to Existentially and Phenomenologically based Psychotherapy (e.g., Schnell, 2010; van Deurzen, 2006, 2012a; van Deurzen & Adams, 2016; van Deurzen & Kenward, 2005; Wong, 2012; Yalom, 2009). The classic Existential literature continues to sell well in reprint editions. (My 2006 edition of Frankl's

Man's Search for Meaning bears a sticker on the cover that says, "More Than 12 Million Copies in Print Worldwide.") Irwin Yalom's *Existential Psychotherapy* (1980) has a high sales ranking on Amazon. If we are interested in what could be called the contemporary Existential psychotherapy scene, we are even more interested in how it continues to appear in modern Psychotherapy and particularly interested in its presence, overt or covert, in Psychotherapy in North America.

Barnett and Madison (2012) describe three strands of contemporary Existential Psychology: a North American strand, a British strand, and a European strand best described as Daseinanalysis and Logotherapy. They subtitle their book with terms —Legacy, Vibrancy, and Dialogue— that also characterize the contemporary Existential project as it is practiced in Psychotherapy. *Legacy* involves the root concepts of Existential Psychotherapy as set down in the foundational work *Existence* (May, et al., 1958) that we have already discussed and are still applicable today. We think of our patients as having their own personal legacies that often constrain them and from which we try to free them (this freedom is a goal that is common to most psychotherapies, however it may be conceptualized by them). *Vibrancy* refers to the potential of the Existential situation that we as Human Beings encounter—Existence, thrownness, and death—and the way Psychotherapy and Psychoanalysis can help our patients to achieve it. For what they call *Dialogue* I would choose the more powerful term *Discourse*. I have written about Therapeutic Discourse (Leffert, 2010, 2013) for some time as the final reorganization of a therapeutic process that began over a century ago with a patient who spoke and an analyst who listened and occasionally interpreted. Discourse takes place all the time on many levels: between patients and therapists, patients and the *others* in their lives, between clinicians, and between clinicians and the texts they choose to read.

Another fundamental goal unique to the Existential project involves Human Beings' (our patients') search for meaning. This embodies the dichotomy between meaning and meaninglessness and relates them to the poles of Sartre's (1943/2018) title *Being and Nothingness* where meaninglessness and nothingness refer to specific *somethings* that are not present, not simply to a void.

Our *Essence* is grounded in our *Existence* (Sartre, 1943/2018). What we as existentialists aim to teach our patients is that their (and our) Beingness, their Human Beingness, follows from our history and context and is always contingent. This speaks to one sharp difference between Existentialism and formal Psychoanalysis: Existentialism is most concerned with *ontology*, Psychoanalysis is concerned with a species of metaphysics, Metapsychology. Ontology is approached through Phenomenological inquiry: Instead of studying unsubstantiated theories, the Existential analyst follows Husserl's dictum to "return to the things themselves" (1913/2001), in this case, our patients as Human Beings. A further difference between the two is that, as Phenomenological therapists we maintain an absolute insistence on therapeutic results whereas

Two cases

We can easily see the difference in approaches, the Phenomenological and the Metapsychological, when a patient begins talking about or manifesting affectionate feelings for us. Many years ago, I treated a severely depressed woman, we'll call her Constance, whose life circumstances, her existence, were, at the time, terrible. An accomplished baker, she brought me a box of expertly baked and elaborate Christmas cookies for the first several years of our work together. I of course[20] accepted them. Phenomenologically, I saw this gift, *in the present*, as part of our relationship, an expression of gratitude and appreciation of my care of her (Leffert, 2016). I thanked her (and later told her I had enjoyed the cookies) without further comment; I felt that the transaction was healing for Constance and that it worked best Right Brain to Right Brain, Unconscious to Unconscious. Over the years the cookies became less elaborate and then stopped altogether; Constance was too busy in her new life to have time for baking. Would I deny that childhood longings could also be involved here? Certainly not, but I did not see them as relevant to this Therapeutic Situation.

Some years later, I had cause to treat another woman who was similarly alone and miserable;[21] we can call her Diana. She brought with her a history of sexual and physical abuse beginning in childhood and progressing into her adult years. She arrived in a flurry of action, announcing that I was *her* analyst and that she expected to be special to me. She spent much time gazing silently at me; when she did speak she described me as a combination of father and lover, with a "little pee-pee." My failures to live up to whatever expectations of perfect treatment she had were met with rage and incorporated a depreciating contempt for men. Early on in the treatment she had plopped herself down on my couch where she at first lay gazing at me and then, eventually, used in the usual manner. She would say nothing about what this behavior meant to her. Initially taken aback, bowled over really, I *was* clear, Phenomenologically, *not* Metapsychologically, that I was dealing with a highly disturbed little girl lacking any adult modulations of her sexual and aggressive impulses. At the time, all I knew to do was to interpret Diana's behavior for her and to work with her in piecing together a narrative

---

20 At the time I called myself (whether I was or was not is, however, a tale for another time) an orthodox Freudian, but I knew, as many of my colleagues did not (see, for example, Casement, 1982) that to have refused this gift, or "analyzed" it would have been destructive to Constance, even soul-killing.
21 I choose terms like *miserable* because they are affect-laden and highly descriptive rather than experience distant and clinical, recognizing that we tend to be more comfortable with the latter (dysphoria, anhedonia) but need to engage the former.

of her disastrous early childhood; she often responded with verbal outbursts like those of a really nasty child. After some years of this, years in which interpretations, reconstructions, questions, and empathic sounds produced no discernable changes in Diana's emotions and behavior, a day came in which I told her to sit up. She did. I then told her that she needed to stop all of this and get busy doing therapy. She asked me what I would do if she didn't comply (indicating that she knew perfectly well what she had been doing); I told her I wasn't going there. This proved a turning point in a treatment that yielded significant results. Diana became more involved in her life and her work and her behavior in the sessions went from infantile-explosive to something modulated that we were able to work with and understand.

The first question one might ask is why I chose that moment to intervene. I have no answer; it had occurred to me in the moment and suddenly made sense. Could I have acted a year earlier? Certainly, but it didn't occur to me to do so. Would it have worked then? Possibly, I just can't say. In circumstances like this, my act has come out of my unconscious; I was ready to say it and Diana was ready to hear it. In favor of such action's validity I can say that I have done this perhaps a half-dozen times over my half-century of practice and that the interventions *have always been successful*. I can also think of a few instances where it "should" have but didn't occur to me to intervene and the treatments ultimately failed.

Let me conclude this case illustration by saying something about transference in the general, if not the particular. Transference has been and remains an uncertain subject; indeed, even in 1973, Laplanche and Pontalis (1967/1973) saw it as so uncertain that they left it to individual clinicians to describe it for themselves. I am not about to make pronouncements about it. My own view is that the term involves the unique and specific transfer of infantile wishes and relationships onto the person of the analyst or therapist. These relationships are the starting point for *all* relationships, although they evolve in different and complex ways. When I treated Diana, I thought I was seeing some sort of intense, primitive, highly ambivalent and eroticized paternal transference. Now, I don't think so. I think that what I was seeing was simply how Diana related to men *in the present*—something that had a history, had developed over time, and that she often concealed. This was how Diana behaved with any man in her life who was not abusing her (she was extremely passive in those situations). Her position needs to be understood Existentially, as a part of what it meant to her to be a Human Being with a past, not as a projected holdover of something that had lived in an earlier time. Let's now look at some of the schools of Existential Psychology and how they differ.

Daseinanalysis

Contemporary *Daseinanalysis* is a species of Existential Psychology owing its origins to Heidegger (1975/1982, 1987/2001), Boss (1963, 1975/1977), and

Binswanger (1958a, 1958b). Boss followed Heidegger's post-Cartesian stance (the distinction is one between Dasein, being-in-the-world, and the Cartesian subject) that mind and body are inseparable and hence the treatment of a "mental" problem could not take place in the absence of a regard for the physical body. The origins of this position lie in the Medical Model, that we must treat the whole Human Being, something that today is often forgotten by mainstream therapists, particularly those lacking formal medical training. Boss viewed the cause of human suffering as constraint, external and internal constraint, constraint of functions, of wishes, actions, emotions, whatever, and that what treatment we offered involved freeing a Human Being from constraint. If we looked at the question of what is the most important constraint, it must be a constraint of meaning, either an inability to find it in life or an inability to find a hidden meaning that one is keeping secret from oneself, which brings us back to Existential Psychotherapy and Logotherapy (Frankl, 1959/2006, 1969/2014). *Daseinanalysis* is no more unified than is any other discipline of psychotherapy. There is both an objective Dasein-analytic and a subjective Dasein-hermeneutic. This brings us back to Kierkegaard's quasi-contradictory observation that suffering in the abstract is to be prized because, after all, it is what makes us uniquely Human but in particular, when experienced, it is to be deplored indeed. (This terminology is difficult to get one's head around and I suggest taking it slowly and referring back to the previous chapters.)

What is sought after is *openness* to the world and freedom to explore it. The issues that patients struggle with are at once individual but also universal aspects of the human condition (Holzhey-Kunz & Fazekas, 2012). The *Daseinanalyst* continues to privilege the therapeutic relationship as a central feature of therapeutic action; that is to say *Daseinanalysis* is a Relational therapy. This position follows from Heidegger's Successful Being-in-the-world; for the *Daseinanalyst* it involves the ability to live *within* possibility, a concept that bridges the internal and external worlds.

So how does what the Contemporary Daseinanalyst does differ from what the Existential Psychotherapist (or Psychoanalyst) of North America or Britain, or the Logotherapist of Vienna do? The answer is that they privilege differing elements of therapeutic action but ultimately end up, therapeutically, in the same place. (This is also true for some but not all of the standard metapsychological theories). Early Heidegger (1927/2010) involved seeking out the different kinds of Being and the patient's (Dasein's) place in World. It dichotomizes authentic and inauthentic and seeks to differentiate fallen from thrown Being (this was subsequently seen as more of a *range* of Being). Later *Daseinanalysts* were more interested in Dasein as a subject and its Relational Being. This would eventually get them to individual freedom and the quest for meaning that the Existentialists and Logotherapists were working on.

So, what do *Daseinanalysts* talk to their patient about? Initially, I think, the way the patient lives and has lived historically, subjectively, in the world of people (*Mitwelt*) and things (*Umwelt*), then looking at problems of inauthenticity and fallenness, finally coming around to Meaning. The first category would include what Boss' "Dr. Cobling" (1963) brought to the therapy, the second had to do with the inauthentic and fallen life she had lived, and the last with her search for meaning as a creative artist. But a moment's thought will reveal that these are the same things that most[22] exploratory-psychodynamic psychotherapists would talk to their patients about. It is rather that the Daseinanalyst would understand them very differently.

The North Americans and the British

When one prioritizes Meaning in Human Existence (or *Existenz*) a number of things happen. The most important perhaps is that one parts company from the other schools of Psychotherapy that retain a focus on the Biological needs of sex and survival and look at their primary, secondary, and tertiary affective derivatives (Panksepp & Biven, 2012). This is not to dismiss these components of our Being but rather to stress that it is our search for meaning and our capacity for reflection (here, actually, the tertiary affective derivatives come into play) that make us uniquely *Human*.

In the Therapeutic Situation, "Attending to *our own* ways of making meaning at different levels helps us to recognize our therapeutic bias" (van Deurzen, 2012b, p. 172, italics added). Van Deurzen describes this essential process aptly as "cleansing the lenses through which we look at the world" (p. 172). We must also be constantly aware of our own values and beliefs and their potential for impact, both salutarily and deleteriously, on the patient and their therapy or analysis. The goal here is for us to be able to locate a point from which one can see the World as it is rather than the subjective World we spend most of our time in. To say a word about myself, my personal values are consistent with those espoused by the Existentialists and Phenomenologists that I have been describing over the course of this book. Before I knew of this body of work I already embraced these ideas in rudimentary form. Even as a beginning Freudian Psychoanalyst I deployed a discursive approach to Being-with patients and maintained a conviction that I should view my ideas about therapeutic action as open and subject to a creative uncertainty that allows them to evolve. I find that a therapist who has fixed beliefs (knows) about what they're doing is subject to problems succeeding (that is, curing and healing patients) in their work.

---

22 I have to exclude the orthodox Freudian analyst who will prioritize listening and offering occasional putatively depth interpretations and the Kleinian analyst who would, with minimal listening, launch into a string of deep transference interpretations and reconstructions. (Some decades ago, a prominent Kleinian analyst giving the Plenary Address at a meeting of the American Psychoanalytic Association described a case in which the patient came in for his first session, lay down on the couch and sighed deeply. The analyst interpreted, "It must have been a difficult birth.")

Turning to the patient, we have to recognize their authentic personal values and beliefs as something distinct from the dysfunctional ways in which they relate to Mitwelt and Umwelt. This is tricky because those values may only emerge after some time (e.g., "Dr. Cobling," Boss, 1963, whose career we would, initially, have "approved" of) and we must be alert to their appearance and their difference from earlier psychic organizers.

All schools of Psychotherapy rest on the basic assumption that, to a greater or lesser extent, accurately or inaccurately, we can understand another person (van Deurzen, 2012a). Beyond that, different schools of therapy rest on different assumptions. Psychoanalysis, for example rests on the premise that discovering unconscious wishes, fears, defenses, and impulses (to name but a few categories) will make the patient *well*, however well is defined. Relational therapy adds the premise that these things must be worked out through discourse in the relationship between patient and therapist, and Interpersonal therapy focuses entirely on the relationships, including the therapeutic one, that the patient engages in. A person's existence, the Interpersonal therapist believes, cannot be separated from the web of relationships in which she dwells. We must first ask of any premise: Can it be true? Can it be partly true? Can it be individually true or can it be universally true? If none of these questions can be answered affirmatively, recognizing that there are intense disagreements about the answers to them, then a premise cannot be recommended. If there is an affirmative answer, then we must ask if it suits a particular patient and their disorder, and that asked, does the patient have any interest at all in achieving the goals of a particular therapy? If the patient is in an acute state of dysfunction it may be difficult to answer this question. John, for example, came in wanting the obsessional behavior that haunted his life to cease. He wanted to know nothing about the symptoms; he expressed no interest in finding out what the symptoms meant or how they came into being. John would not benefit from seeing any of the therapists embracing these schools, but he might well benefit from a course of CBT. Jean, for most of her life, had one unsuccessful relationship after another. In addition to wanting to marry and have children, she felt that she had to know *why* she failed so consistently with these relationships because change was tied up with the knowing.[23] Jean would gain some benefit from therapy in any of these schools.

Existential Psychotherapy is aimed at people who feel like they are unable to make sense out of their lives or life in general and cannot find meaning in their existence. What I am calling the Psychoanalysis of the Absurd adds the considerations of how meaning can be found in Absurd Existence and the search for Subjective Well Being (SWB) (Diener, 1984). These issues of Absurdity have taken on urgent meaning in the early 21st century America that most of us live in.

---

23 These are simple and very partial stories, I know, but they do make the point I want to make very clearly.

Although there continues to be a group of practitioners who practice in an Existential vein, there has been, for *some* of them, a slippage away from intensive psychotherapy towards counselling. Van Deurzen (2012a), for example, talks about a philosophical investigation rather than a medical or psychological one, with an inherent lessening of the former with respect to the latter. This, unfortunately, comes off as intellectual and superficial rather than healing and curing and, in treating Existentialism as exclusively a philosophical school, ignores it's also being, as I have insisted, a Psychology. This is by no means the universal approach to Existential Psychotherapy (e.g., Barnett & Madison, 2012); we can turn now to the work of Irvin Yalom to see how it is not.

Yalom on Death

Irvin Yalom, who started out his professional life as a psychiatrist and group therapist, became an active writer in the later 1960s, just as the wave of Existential Psychology begun by its founding mothers and fathers in the 1950s (e.g., Boss, 1963; May, et al., 1958) was beginning to peak. He describes four givens of the Human Condition: isolation, meaninglessness, mortality, and freedom, to which a Human Being can respond in a functional or dysfunctional fashion. They constitute four existential challenges that we must all face and overcome (freedom, although sounding so obviously positive, is, as we shall see, just such a challenge (Fromm, 1941/1994) to be surmounted). Yalom (1980), in *Existential Psychotherapy,* will divide his discussion of these into four parts taking up each of these givens.

Through metaphor, Yalom (1980) introduces his now classic text with the observation that, while most of our literature of theory and technique attempts to portray what we should do in a precise way, "when no one is looking the [successful] therapist throws in [a handful of] the 'real thing'" (p. 3).[24] Such ingredients are difficult to describe, and the therapist is not necessarily aware that she is using them. This is not per se an Existentialist position, but Existentialist Psychotherapy probably allows itself more leeway in admitting it than the staider therapeutic disciplines (although I have believed this about therapy for some time, I have never seen it written elsewhere). This observation is at odds with the high value that most therapists assign to their often elaborate theoretical orientations.

Yalom (1980) sees the therapy as focused on an individual's Existence, her search for personal meaning, and her coming to grips with the finiteness of life. In contrast to what van Deurzen (2006) posits, he sees the therapy as focused on *healing*, healing that takes place through the therapeutic relationship. Existential Psychotherapy is a Psychodynamic Psychotherapy but, if Freudian therapy focuses on conflicts between the ego and the id, and

---

24 It should be obvious that the "real thing" is precisely what the Boston Change Process Study Group (2005) "discovered" 25 years later and evocatively referred to as "the something more."

interpersonal therapies focus on conflicts between a child's strivings and the demands of the adults (and, later, their introjects) around her, then Existential therapy focuses on an individual's confrontations with the givens of Being (the term that I would use to roll up all of the Existential challenges).

Consistent with this Existential/Phenomenological approach is that a therapy *takes place in the present*. As we have already considered, this does not mean that we would put aside what I would call historicity and Development (we have already disposed of the rather seductive concept of non-historical psychological depth in the present) but simply that these elements are not by definition privileged, a position that puts us at odds with the classical schools of Psychoanalysis.

Some Existential therapists and many clinicians who knowingly or unknowingly incorporate Existential ideas in their work fail to see Death per se and patients' fears of it as coming up in everyday clinical work. This is particularly true of the wider range of Psychoanalysts and Psychodynamic Psychotherapists. They fail to take note of the fact that death is a psychological issue that is all around them and their patients. Instead they immediately take the death of the other into issues of grief, mourning, and, yes, depression, and death of the Self into anxiety and loss. These are displacements that serve to bypass Death as a singularly important, developmental issue in its own right. Yalom (1980, 2009), in contrast, is particularly good in his discussions of death and I am going to focus on this dimension of his work. He examines it as an Existential issue affecting both adults and children; his work with the latter seems to be unique. He begins with two premises: "1) Life and death are interdependent; they exist simultaneously not consecutively; death whirs continuously beneath the membrane of life and exerts a vast influence upon experience and conduct and 2) Death is a primordial source of anxiety and as such, is the primary fount of psychopathology" (1980, p. 29) (and, of necessity, *should* be a focus of any therapy). To these premises, I would add the corollary that the perception and presentation of death differ significantly across the life cycle.

As Psychotherapists we seem to prefer to think of Death as something with which children are not overly concerned, except when they stumble upon it under unusual circumstances, and we tend to not bring it up much with our youngish adult patients. As Yalom (1980, Chapter 3) describes, children, if given the chance, talk and ask about death all of the time; we just don't like it very much. Indeed, we prefer to confine such concerns to older patients or those who are chronically or terminally ill.[25] These biases also relate to the great difficulty that therapists have in dealing with their own illness or mortality as it pertains to closing their practices. We, all of us, encounter death *all of the time*. As therapists, we often tend to disavow it or take it into the psychological depths of conflict-based rather than Existential meaning. Surprisingly,

---

25 Dementia falls into this category as well.

if we listen for it, we hear our patients talking about death as Death, and our task is to guide them in exploring it as a subject in its own right, not something that only has meaning as the death *of* some*thing* or some*one*.

Yalom (1980) writes about helping patients to shift from what he calls "forgetfulness of being" to "mindfulness of being," more accessible language than Heidegger's difficult terms *everydayness* and *thrownness*. Yalom, like Heidegger, does not make the clear ontological distinction between fallen and everydayness that I do; both their arguments suffer, I think, as a result. It is the acceptance versus the denial of death (or, to put it another way, the acceptance of the finiteness of life) that thrusts us into a state of meaningfulness/thrownness/authenticity. This is something of a hard sell, as is Heidegger's concept that the acknowledgement of death enhances the meaning of life. If we turn to folk psychology, we find two differing positions. Most of us can grasp the intellectual argument that immortality would make life meaningless, in fact that it would make of life an empty horror. At the same time, however, if we are reasonably healthy, it is hard to see how we wouldn't feel like we could use another ten years or so. The relevant Existential point here is that we don't get to choose.

At the same time, we are, in different ways, preoccupied with speculations about death. Our literature, cinema, and poetry are much taken up with it; without the presence or risk of death, few of these works are meaningful. The fact that some consideration of death is what renders these works meaningful to us tells us we are taken up with death all across our own life cycle. This is true regardless of the social or educational identity of the reader or viewer. Tolstoy's *War and Peace* describes how Pierre, the protagonist's, life is changed when he faces random death and a random reprieve from it, while in *Star Wars* death is meted out and avoided around much simpler and impersonal themes that are nonetheless meaningful to an audience numbering in the hundreds of millions. If we turn to children, we have *Grimm's Fairytales* that risk death and mutilation and *Harry Potter*, where death is rare, grief real, and life is sacred and honored. No religion exists that does not address death in some fashion and, often, attempts to mitigate it with an afterlife.

We tend to view death as a terrible evil, in part, I think, because the last century has brought with it so many ways of extending life that we have come to feel that it is an avoidable exception. In earlier times, in the face of the frequent inadequacy of medical cures, the immediacy of death at all points in the life cycle made for its more-ready acceptance as a part of life. There is also a distinction between death as something that happens to others, sometimes beloved others, the death of the object, and something that happens to ourselves, the death of the subject. The latter may be considered something of a developmental achievement. A brush with death at whatever point in the lifecycle it might occur or being given a terminal diagnosis pretty uniformly leads to a reappraisal and a reassessment of life and an alteration in one's priorities.

Then there is humor that mitigates a helplessness in the face of staving off death. John goes to see his physician for a routine physical examination and lab work. Two days later, the doctor calls with the results and informs his patient that he has some good news and some bad news. Taken aback, John asks for the good news; his doctor tells him that the tests results showed that he has 24 hours to live. John replies, "My god, if that's the good news, what's the bad news?" His doctor replies, "I got the results yesterday." Then there is the ancient Mesopotamian tale, "An Appointment in Samarra." A merchant sends his servant on an errand to the marketplace in the morning where he encounters Death. Death stares at him. Terrified, he flees home and borrows the merchant's horse, racing off to Samarra where he thinks he can hide from Death. Later that day, the merchant encounters death in the marketplace and asks him why he tried to frighten his servant. Death replies that he wasn't trying to frighten the servant but his look was one of surprise at finding him there because he had an appointment with the servant, that afternoon, in Samarra.

Yalom (1980) describes Death as appearing in life (and hence in Psychotherapy) in two ways: as an enhanced "boundary situation" and as a primary source of anxiety. In the former someone experiences a kind of Existential shift in their life. It may be a brush with a serious illness or a life change like retirement or a last child's going off to college. What these events have in common is a lesson about the finitude of life, increased death-awareness and a push towards figuring out how to make the most of the time one has. Susan had suffered an acute bout of hepatitis that was never adequately diagnosed but was at one time thought to be terminal. After her recovery, she began to question the compromises she had made to keep a 25-year marriage afloat; when she came to see me, she wanted to either figure out how to make the marriage work or to move on.

Death Anxiety tends, unless Death is imminent, to be hidden[26] and accessible mostly through its displacements. We are all afraid of and/or anxious[27] about Death, but to be regularly aware of Death anxiety in the absence of immediate and realistic threats, however broadly defined, leads to a dysfunctional life. All of us have occasionally encountered such patients. Hypochondria represents, arguably, a subset of them manifesting minimal displacement. We cannot seek to *cure* Death Anxiety (as we might its displacements); it is, after all, an Existential emotion. We can expect that we should be able to mitigate it to a degree that renders it functionally *useful*. Death Anxiety is a complex emotion and, as a way of Being, it does not dictate a universal

---

26 I prefer the term *hidden*, which is Existentially descriptive, to *repressed*, which is Metapsychological-Psychodynamic and cannot necessarily be assumed.

27 I have not found the distinctions between fear and anxiety to be consistent enough across clinicians to be meaningful. Instead, we tend to have our own ideas about how to define the two; in a situation of this kind it is probably best to consider their meanings plural and interreferential.

therapeutic response. It requires instead the same kind of multifaceted clinical decision making that other aspects of our patients require. In some patients, it may require intensive exploration, while in others, PTSD patients come to mind, excessive exploration can lead to destructive repetitive thinking. In none of these situations, however, is the patient well served by anything other than the therapist's understanding of the subject. It is part of the wider Existential frame of reference that I have been arguing for as an essential part of what we do.

Annette, a successful, married businesswoman in her 50s, had been in analysis with me for ten years. She presented with the feeling that, although her life seemed to be fulfilling on all fronts, some vague something was nevertheless missing. Over the course of our work, it only very gradually emerged that the ideal, loving family she claimed to have been raised in was, indeed, a sadistic household manifesting frequent nudity, in which she was disliked by both her parents and her siblings. As I interpreted fairly early on, she had brought this upon herself by taking the role of Cassandra, voicing truths no one wanted to hear and repeating them until someone eventually struck her. The bright spot in Annette's childhood was her beloved grandmother, who preferred her to her siblings and provided a loving refuge for her. (The grandmother reminded me of Miss Daisy from the play and film of the same name.) The grandmother appreciated Annette's piercing intelligence and curiosity that drove her parents to angry distraction. When she was 13, the grandmother collapsed and was taken to the hospital where she died a day or two later. Annette was not allowed to visit her, and her parents subsequently suppressed her attempts to mourn or to talk about the loss. Annette was convinced then and now that the hospital and the doctors had allowed her grandmother to die needlessly; I was the first person to encourage her to talk about these ideas and to investigate the reality of her accusations (they proved false).

Annette began to mention in passing how she would attend memorial services at the large Congregational church where she and her husband were members. She would attend alone and, when I asked specifically, told me it was usually a twice-weekly practice of hers. She saw this as a simple expression of community, what people did for each other. She saw nothing unusual in her behavior and had little interest in discussing it.

My first theory was that this was Annette's attempt to deal with her inability to mourn for her grandmother by acting it out. This was a fine theory but it led us nowhere. She had a fixed narrative of her relationship with her grandmother and the grandmother's death that she periodically recycled verbatim and never went beyond. Annette was not depressed, never had been, and was capable of warm, loving relationships. She even maintained, for her part, loving relationships with her parents and siblings, denying their dislike of her; I was gradually able to piece that denial together and to draw her attention to it. It was around this period that I had begun to explore Existential Psychology as a supplement to my clinical work. It occurred to me that Annette was simply dealing with death, her failure to comprehend it, her *hidden* terror of it, and the way it exerted an ongoing influence on her life. Her fear of Death was being expressed in multiple displaced phobias and counter-phobic interests in dangerous sports. She would warmly imagine life after death as a way of being reunited with her grandmother, only to reject it because it meant that she would also have to be reunited with her husband's first wife. I was able to suggest to her that the missing piece was the finitude of life and the ultimate failure of attempts to cling to it by memorializing it for herself or for others. The only solution to the inevitability of death was a dedication to living life to the fullest, something, oddly enough, that Annette was already doing, without an awareness of its significance. Her attendance at funerals declined at about this time; she found that she had become so busy with her life that she didn't have time for them (much as Constance had found with her Christmas baking).

If we find it difficult talking to adults about death, we find doing it with children even harder. Yalom (1980) notes the paucity of literature, Developmental or psychopathological, concerning how children perceive and deal with Death in contrast with how taken up they are with the issue. My experience has been the same. To the incomprehensible sexual mysteries of childhood must be added the mystery of death—what is it, how does it happen, what happens afterwards. The presence of mystery, however, if anything, increases interest and investigation. To study children and ask them how they think and feel about Death we have to act in the face of our own biology, the operation of the CARE system that Panksepp (Panksepp & Biven, 2012) described which would push us to cooperate with their denial and not frighten them. Denial, of course, makes fear worse.

I want to consider two affective states, Anxiety and Despair, from an Existential rather than a Metapsychological perspective. Looked at in this way they tell a very different story.

Anxiety

The first of these, Anxiety, illustrates the difference. Anglophone authors first point out that there are two words, Anxiety and Fear, and then work on finding a distinction between the two. There are a number of possibilities. One (which one?) is more powerful than the other. One is internal, that is, intrapsychic, and the other involves the external world. Perhaps one is subjective and the other is objective. One may come in both small and large servings that are ontologically different. Finally, maybe one involves conflict and, maybe, one involves Existence. Even though I can find contradictory examples of any of these possibilities (how can something be external if it is only subjectively known, for instance?), most American therapists have fairly definite ideas about what they think about these various possibilities.

If we look at Freud's (1926/1959) theories of anxiety (as described in the Strachey translation) we find a number of attempts to describe or explain it that evolved over the course of Freud's career. His earliest ideas defined anxiety as transformed, dammed-up libido and anxiety as a response to the trauma of birth. He later (Freud, 1926/1959) distinguished anxiety in small doses, "signal anxiety," a warning that anxiety in larger doses, traumatic anxiety, was on the way, and posited that anxiety arose in situations of intra-psychic conflict and that it was actually a fear of impending castration. Freud dealt with the anxiety that we now see as a facet of PTSD as a "real" as opposed to an intra-psychically generated anxiety and, early on, coined the term *Actual Neurosis* to describe the situations in which it arose. A major contribution of the Existentialists was to bell the cat so to speak, insisting that none of this was really of any use in understanding or treating the anxiety that their patients sought help with. Instead, they employed the Existential approach we have been describing relating anxiety to PTSD involving both past and present Traumas.

Perhaps a better place to start is with folk psychology.[28] English-speaking people generally distinguish anxiety and fear on the basis of intensity, with the latter being the more intense of the two. There is also a less well enunciated sense that anxiety takes place within the person, while fear has to do with some objective (whatever that might mean) external threat. (This is akin to the folk psychological experience of a cleavage between mind and body with mind residing in the head, looking out the windows of the eyes.)

The problem with *all* of these theories is that they require cleavages of whatever sort between Self and World or subject and object. Furthermore, whenever one tries to invoke any sort of cleavage—anxiety vs. fear, external vs. internal— it fails to hold up if we question it a bit. The Existentialists recognized the problems inherent in cleavages, but they did not think to apply that recognition to their theories of anxiety. The way around these problems is by a return to the German, where we find the single word, *Angst*, which refers to both anxiety *and* fear. (In English, *anxiety* is derived from the Latin *anxius* while *fear*, as *faer* traces its Old-English roots back to Beowulf (*The* Oxford English Dictionary, 1989).) The German language, making no distinction between the two, allows the various properties we have been trying to apportion above to all refer to the one term. In support of this choice, *Angst* made its way into the intellectual language of the 20th century, where it denotes a kind of Existential anxiety, anxiety related to existence, again, different from garden variety anxiety or fear.

If we try not to be too systematic about it, keep in mind the ideas we already possess about anxiety, and try not to worry too much about any contradictions in our beliefs that we may uncover, there are some useful things we can say about the state of being anxious. A majority of the time, anxiety is objectless but not causeless (we *can* also be anxious about *something*). Its diffuseness threatens our Being as anxiety about something does not. Some years ago, on a weekend, I was overwhelmed by a terrible feeling, a painful tension, within me and a restlessness that would not go away. It was so bad

---

28 Folk psychology might be defined as what the person-on-the-street thinks goes on in their head.

that I could hardly concentrate, let alone think. It took me hours to realize that what I was feeling was severe objectless anxiety. I had no sense of anything in particular disturbing me, nothing to be anxious about. With the realization that this was anxiety I began to take small doses of valium, which took the edge off of it. This relief restored my ability to think. I remembered that my internist had prescribed a new medication to help with gastric motility: I had taken two daily doses of it. Looking it up in the PDR, I found that, sure enough, one of its potential side effects was severe akathisia. I discontinued the medication and the anxiety was slowly extinguished over the next 48 hours. I learned a lot from this experience. It was a pure culture of anxiety, clearly different from fear, being diffuse and internal rather than focused and external. By my own experience, it is impossible to live with such a thing (although people do). But such pure cultures are rare in nature. External threats do involve fear, but it is hard not to tease out components of anxiety that go along with it. It is best to try and think of all this in terms of *Angst*.

You would be remiss if you did not ask me about the nature and origins of these anxious feelings. First, they are Existential, threatening some dimension of one's existence in any of the three Phenomenological "Worlds" of Being—the *Eigenwelt*, the *Mitwelt*, the *Umwelt*. They may involve some near or distant connection with a threat of death. Both fear and anxiety can (usually? often? always?) harken back to past experiences, traumas if you will. All of these elements must be subject to therapeutic exploration. This is really all that can be said. There are, of course, various metapsychologically driven theories and, while some therapists base their interpretations on them, there is no evidence that they actually have anything to do with relieving anxiety as it is encountered in the therapeutic situation. Indeed, as May (1958b) noted, it was this very failure that led to the widespread birth of Existentialist Psychotherapy and Psychoanalysis.

The Existential position about anxiety is that it fundamentally has to do with fear of death (Yalom, 2009); Erikson sees it as Yalom does as appearing in present or displaced form throughout the life cycle. Freud's position was that since Death is unknowable in the unconscious, the fear of Death must be a displacement from other forms of anxiety. For the orthodox therapist or analyst there is no ontological place for Death in metapsychology.

Anxiety offers a useful illustration of the distinction between Existential and Metapsychological understandings of patients in the Therapeutic Situation (Leffert, 2013). Let's consider the first session with a patient. (It is probably more accurate to consider the initial telephone contact(s) as a part of the first session.) Both the Existential and the Metapsychological frames of reference would find a place for a patient's being anxious in their first contact with the therapist. A therapist or analyst operating from some metapsychological frame of reference would look for that anxiety as arising in a patient's core issues and conflicts: the uncertain outcome of a struggle for control with this new person (the therapist) as a representative of old objects, or a competition with a fear of loss and retaliation. A Freudian or Kleinian analyst would be interested in getting to the patient's unconscious fantasies while a Relational or Intersubjective analyst would be interested in a patient's fundamental *relatedness*. (At some point an Existential analyst could very well be interested in these issues as well.) The Existential frame of reference recognizes that a first contact with someone expert or more powerful whom one is turning to for help is *inherently anxiety provoking*, regardless of what the patient brings to the table. In both frames of reference what the therapist actually *does* (or should do), how she *acts*, depends on the same kinds of issues of understanding, tact, and timing that govern all of a therapist's actions. Holding to the Metapsychological or Existential frames of reference, a therapist might mostly listen at the start, but the latter would lead them to act in some way to put their new patient at ease. (I nearly always, at some point in a first session, ask a patient how it is feeling to them and, early in the *second* session, I ask for their thoughts and feelings about the first session.)

Despair

Existential Psychologists use the term Despair in much the same way as they use other terms signifying negative emotional states of Being such as meaninglessness, hopelessness, aloneness. It is not necessarily of special concern to them. It is, as are all these terms, an object of therapy. Merriam Webster (Merriam-Webster's Dictionary, 2004) defines the noun *Despair* as a state of having lost all hope and the adjective, *despondent*, as what it means to suffer from this state of hopelessness. I am after bigger game here and would define despair as a particular state of Existential Being. This discussion has a place in the next chapter, "The Psychotherapy and the Psychoanalysis of the Absurd," but it will play out across the other chapters that follow. I only want to begin this conversation here. I have chosen to name this particular negative state of Being *Despair* although other terms might appear at first glance to work descriptively. The more obvious, well-used choice would have been *Depression*; let me tell you why I *didn't* choose it. Depression carries with it Metapsychological connotations; all therapists approaching a patient in this way cleave to fundamental theories concerning its origins that they then attempt to apply in order to mobilize therapeutic action. (As I have argued for some time, whether or not a patient experiences relief from a symptom or group of symptoms through their therapy, there is no actual evidence that the relief has come as a *result* of the therapist's applying some posited theory.) A second issue is that the term *Depression* carries with it neurobiological meaning and with that at least the consideration of adjunctive psychopharmacological treatment. In other words, Depression is an entirely different entity than what we are talking about. It differs from Despair but Despair can lead to it. We will deal with these considerations in the next chapter as well.

Despair is a state of mind, composed of emotional and cognitive elements, that has to do with hopelessness, a hopelessness about personal meaning lost or about whether meaning can ever be found. It can occur at any point in the life cycle, but it is a particular sequela of the physical and mental declines that normally or pathologically accompany aging. As an extreme reaction, it can follow regret over lost time or the realization that points in the life cycle at which certain accomplishments were possible have passed. Despair can, for a time, be denied; Heidegger, as we saw, described fallen states in which someone attempts actually or symbolically to live out an immortality in which all things remain possible.

The hopelessness of Despair may or may not seem merited by one's life situation but can in any event become an object of therapy. It is a problem in Being, an ontological rather than a metapsychological problem, that has uniquely to do with Dasein. Keeping to Phenomenological language, Despair is a response to experienced severe problems in Dasein's location and historicity in the *Eigenwelt, Mitwelt,* and *Umwelt* (Heidegger, 1975/1982). (These would relate to failings of the biology and psychology of the Self, relational failings, and failings in the wider *physical* world respectively.) This implies an objective issue or issues where, strictly speaking, it is not. Despair is certainly *about* objective problems in Existence, but *significant numbers of people who suffer from these problems do not experience Despair*. Sudden onset of failings in Being can result in trauma or depression, but that is not Despair; we are dealing here instead with a particular *subjective* response.

The beginning of a long case

After keeping you waiting for more than two chapters it is past time to offer you a lengthier case illustration[29] of just what beginning an Existentialist Psychotherapy might look like. Please read it as an Existential narrative; the "history," that is, the *objective facts*, could be summarized in a couple of paragraphs but the *meaning* would be lost.

A man called my voice mail on a Monday morning, leaving his name, Russell S., asking if I was taking new patients, and wanting to make an appointment. He had a slightly high-pitched, tentative voice. When I returned his call later that morning he sounded relieved and happy to hear from me, calling me Dr. Leffert. I asked him what was "going on," why he felt he needed to see me. He told me that his wife had left him (a slight non-sequitur,

---

29 Clinical material when presented in scientific papers or books is too often either implicitly or explicitly offered as *proof* of what the author(s) is talking about. In fact, the limits of knowability inherent in such efforts mean that these are simply illustrations of the point the author(s) is making, illustrations that, while of explanatory value are, per se, lacking in probity. For reasons of confidentiality, the case *illustrations* I present are composites drawn from multiple disguised cases. The case composite I am presenting here reflects an Existential approach to diagnosis and treatment, reflective of my work in the first decade of this new century, prior to the Absurdist approach I will describe in the next chapter.

stressing his passivity in the matter). This was all he said and, rather than starting a therapeutic conversation on the phone, I gave him an appointment.

Russell was a tall, thin man wearing a loosely-fitting grey suit who *looked* tentative as I ushered him into my consulting room. What first struck me was that his face was a bit rabbit-like; a more careful observation was that his upper lip was trembling, whether from being on the edge of anxiety, or tears, or both, I couldn't say. So, after un-reflectively making these observations to myself and moving onto the purpose of his visit, I asked him, as I usually do, how I could be of help to him. (I had stressed need in the phone call and help here, communicating to him that I saw them as the reasons one would seek out therapy.) He told me that he didn't know. A colleague of his who understood the effect of his wife's leaving had had on him had suggested he see me. She, the colleague, and perhaps the only partner in the firm where he had spent his career whom he felt comfortable with, ran into him browsing listlessly in a bookstore and told him she was worried about him. He could only tell me that he didn't feel "right." I asked him to "tell me about it," starting then to *be* the therapist in what I hoped would become a therapeutic situation.

I felt that a psychodynamic-deconstructivist approach,[30] appropriate for some patients, however tactfully deployed could have, at least at this point, caused a psychological collapse in this particular human being. So, I simply told him that I thought he was struggling and in pain (he found the naming of this very settling) and that I wanted to see him frequently so I could help him. What I did was to ask him questions about himself, asking follow-on questions to encourage him to tell me more. I pursued the things he seemed to find disturbing by again asking him to tell me more about them. I did not push him to tell me about the painful areas of his life but encouraged him instead to talk further about the things he spontaneously brought up. I maintained my concentrated attention on what he was telling me, lapsing only briefly into periods of free association. I aimed for a Subject-to-Subject discourse with both of us in the room as real people all of the time. I learned that he lived his life once removed from it; his wife was never a person to him, only a motherlike figure he had nurturant fantasies about (he never attempted real emotional contact with her in order to actualize his wishes for closeness). In adopting this stance in the initial hours, I was both gathering information and communicating my intense interest in the patient as a Human Being, what I would call in contrast to a *regard médicale* a *regard thérapeutique* (Foucault, 1973/1994 would, I think, approve of the change).

---

30 This would have entailed a discourse about his life and his problems as he saw them, with my looking for the fault lines, where pieces of his narrative discourse didn't quite fit together, drawing his attention to them and thinking with him about their origins. Most therapies get to this at some point (even though therapists might describe them using different language) but if the timing and tact of these interventions are not right, they can cause severe iatrogenic (as opposed to therapeutic) regressions or lead the patient to (wisely) discontinue the "treatment."

I have found (Leffert, 2013) that a number of things happen as a result of positioning myself vis-á-vis a patient in this way. I would call it a position of *empathic interest* (as opposed to a *benign skepticism*) residing in a created therapeutic space[31] embodying a dialectic interaction of field and frame: It is something most patients have never experienced as adults and have only sometimes experienced as young children. Such therapeutic positioning is, in its own right, a potent tool for healing and relief of pain and suffering. Support and containment are also important parts of the developing therapeutic relationship, but they should not be dismissed as something less than: They are very much tied to the *content* of the therapeutic encounter, the subjects of its discourse, and our early attempts to seek out meaning.

So what came of this? I learned that Russell was a 75-year-old retired attorney, and that he was coming to see me a few weeks after Sara, his wife of 37 years, seemingly (to him) without warning, announced (as he put it) that she was divorcing him and immediately (that day) moved out of their home. Six years before this, she had returned to school, seeking and receiving a doctorate in clinical psychology. She had since opened a practice. During those years, she had been largely absent from the home; Russell had been unhappy with this; he could not say why; he always meant to speak to her about it, but, somehow, he never did. He was crushed and his repeated attempts to affect a reconciliation or even to get her to talk with him about it failed. She would only say that they had grown apart. She did not seem angry and, indeed sounded happy. They had two married daughters, living with their families on the East Coast, who claimed to be as surprised by their mother's departure as he was. He had not asked them to intercede and they had not offered to do so. Russell's relationship with his daughters was best described as cordial but distant. They seemed *to him* interested in nothing more but their prompt responses to him suggested that it was perhaps his flatness that had kept them at arm's length. I held that thought for the present.

Symptomatically, what had been lifelong periodic attacks of mild anxiety at times of stress had now become severe and were accompanied by insomnia. He obtained moderate relief from the Ativan prescribed by his primary care physician but preferred not to take it because of a fear of dependency. It emerged that fears of dependency had been prominent throughout his life (we learned much later that they had also been operative in his marriage).

Russell was, had been, a successful attorney, highly paid for his work in mergers and acquisitions. He had treated his work, just like his marriage, as a given, not thinking at all about how meaningful it was or wasn't and, after retirement, was left only with golf. While he had enjoyed the game on weekends, he found it boring now that he could play it as often as he wished. The loss of work and the accompanying increased freedom brought with it the

---

31 I have written previously about therapeutic space (Leffert, 2010), drawing on Bachelard's (1958/1994) concept of the subjective experience of space that he described in *The Poetics of Space*.

meaninglessness, the feelings of being alone and alienated, that Fromm (1941/1994) wrote about in *Escape from Freedom*.

The only child of a busy surgeon father and an equally busy litigator mother, Russell had grown up in Manhattan where he had been largely left to fend for himself. He barely saw his father and his mother always had a criticism to offer when he did not live up to her exacting standards (which was most of the time). He had no idea why he had followed her into the law if not into litigation, saying it was the only work he could imagine doing. (He initially presented himself as an unreflective Human Being, but this turned out to be a disguise, initially a defense he maintained against his dangerous mother, a defense that had served his so poorly in his marriage.) He'd always felt at least a little frightened of his parents and, only when I asked, described a childhood without verbal or physical closeness (again only when asked, he told me that there had been little physical affection in his marriage and wondered why his wife had not initiated it). He suffered from agonizing undiagnosed and untreated childhood migraines that were only picked up on a college physical; prophylactic treatment with β-blockers then promptly cured them. (I took this as a measure of his parents' indifference to him and preoccupation with their own lives.)

My metapsychological formulation was that he had suffered a massive traumatic injury in his wife's leaving him and had regressed in the face of it to the chronic, fearful isolation of his childhood. My preliminary Existential formulation was, however, a very different animal. He manifested a dual defense of passivity, particularly when it came to relationships, and an inability to recognize his feelings. As a result, he had no ability to distinguish what was meaningful from what was not and was afraid to grasp the extent of his loneliness. I suggested to him that this was a kind of defensive unknowing (they were Heideggerian secrets, not the products of repression) that we would eventually find our way through. His marriage, from what I could make of it, had been a sham that his wife had endured for decades before figuring this out for herself. *He* eventually found out that she had moved in with a woman whom she married a year later; *I* got the feeling that this relationship, with another psychologist she had met in graduate school, had been going on for some years. He described himself as shocked by his wife's actions but could not say any more about his feelings. As I began to talk to him, I was reminded of both Roquentin, Sartre's protagonist in *Nausea* (1938/2013) and a hypothetical *Sisyphus* (Camus, 1942/1991) deprived of his rock. Taken all together, he was a poster-child for Existentialist psychopathology, manifesting all of the problems in Being we have been talking about. (He did not, however, manifest any of the severe regressions seen in some of the patients described in the early Existentialist literature.) What, then, were we to do?

I have come to expect symptomatic improvement as a result of this kind of early work combining history-taking (more accurately, *narrative*-taking) and empathic interest; indeed, Russell's anxiety decreased from severe chronicity to occasional brief bouts. He visibly perked up and was overtly happy to see me. I expected it would take a considerable time (years in the low single digits) for him to understand what a Human Being was and what this particular Human Being's (that is, Russell himself) life was all about. Only at that point would it be possible to make contact with him around the dysfunction we have been talking about. We will continue the story of that process in the next chapter.

Existentialist Psychology offered a new path to clinical work, a new approach founded on Being rather than Metapsychology. While having had (and still having) much to offer, it could, by the end of the millennium, have justifiably been accused of becoming somewhat shopworn. Broadly speaking, there were two sorts of problems. Its therapeutic approach was based on facilitating a patient's discovery of new ways of Being-in-the-World that would bring new meaning with them. This confused an at least partly subjective problem with an objective one. The founding American Existential therapists and analysts derived their therapeutic stance from Heideggerian Daseinanalysis and the Existentialism of Sartre, Merleau-Ponty, de Beauvoir, & Co. They did not much consider the work of Camus. He had suffered an untimely death in 1960, relatively early on, and they may have found his novels, the center of his philosophical works, uncongenial as a source of clinical ideas. What Camus (1942/1989, 1942/1991, 1948/1991) did pioneer was the study of the psychology of the Absurd. (It remained, unfortunately, a subject primarily of philosophical inquiry.) Broadly speaking, he addressed the question of how one could find meaning in an inhospitable and *unchanging* world. Frankl (1959/2006) would later address this question in his own way. The Psychoanalysis of the Absurd is a subject that I particularly wanted to address in the current volume.

The second problem the Existentialists faced was the same as the one faced by the mid-century Metapsychologists: A failure to incorporate Interdisciplinary Studies into their theorizing and clinical work. I have been writing about this much-needed integration for some years now but a reappraisal is necessary because they bear on Existential ideas in a very particular way. We will turn to both of these areas in the next chapter.

References

Bachelard, G. (1994). *The poetics of space* (M. Jolas, Trans.). Boston: Beacon Press. (Original work published in 1958).
Barnett, L., & Madison, G. (2012). *Existential therapy: Legacy, vibrancy, and dialogue.* London: Routledge.
Bergmann, M. S. (1993). Reflections on the history of psychoanalysis. *Journal of the American Psychoanalytic Association, 41,* 929–955.
Binswanger, L. (1958a). The case of Ellen West. In R. May, E. Angel, & H. F. Ellenberger (Eds), *Existence* (pp. 237–364). New York: Simon & Schuster.
Binswanger, L. (1958b). The existential analysis school of thought (E. Angel, Trans.). In R. May, E. Angel, & H. F. Ellenberger (Eds), *Existence* (pp. 191–213). New York: Simon & Schuster.
Boss, M. (1963). *Psychoanalysis and Daseinanalysis.* New York: Basic Books.

Boss, M. (1977). *Existential foundations of medicine and psychology*. New York: Jason Aronson. (Original work published in 1975).
Boston Change Process Study Group (2005). The "something more" than interpretation revisited: sloppiness and co-creativity in the psychoanalytic encounter. *Journal of the American Psychoanalytic Association*, *53*, 693–729.
Bradford, L. P., Gibb, J. R., & Benne, K. D. (1964). *T-group theory and laboratory method: Innovation and re-education*. New York: John Wiley & Sons.
Camus, A. (1989). *The stranger* (M. Ward, Trans.). New York: Vintage Books. (Original work published in 1942).
Camus, A. (1991a). The myth of Sisyphus. In A. Camus, *The myth of Sisyphus and other essays* (J. O'Brien, Trans.) (pp. 3–138). New York: Vintage Books. (Original work published in 1942).
Camus, A. (1991b). *The plague* (S. Gilbert, Trans). New York: Vintage Books. (Original work published in 1948).
Carson, R. (2002). *Silent spring*. New York: Houghton Mifflin Company. (Original work published in 1962).
Casement, P. J. (1982). Some pressures on the analyst for physical contact during the re-living of an early trauma. *International Review of Psychoanalysis*, *9*, 279–286.
Diener, E. (1984). Subjective well-being. *Psychological Bulletin*, *95*, 542–575.
Foucault, M. (1994). *The birth of the clinic: An archeology of medical perception* (A. M. Sheridan Smith, Trans.). New York: Vintage Books. (Original work published in 1973).
Frankl, V. E. (1972). The feeling of meaninglessness: A challenge to psychotherapy. *American Journal of Psychoanalysis*, *32*, 85–89.
Frankl, V. E. (2006). *Man's search for meaning* (I. Lasch, Trans.). Boston: Beacon Press. (Original work published in 1959).
Frankl, V. E. (2014). *The will to meaning: Foundations and applications of logotherapy*. New York: Plume Books. (Original work published in 1969).
Freud, A. (1966). *The ego and the mechanisms of defense* (revised edn). New York: International Universities Press. (Original work published in 1936).
Freud, S. (1959). Inhibition, symptom, and anxiety. In J. Strachey (Ed.), *Standard Edition* (pp. 87–178). London: Hogarth Press. (Original work published in 1926).
Fromm, E. (1990). *Man for himself: An inquiry into the psychology of ethics*. New York: H.R. Holt and Company. (Original work published in 1947).
Fromm, E. (1994). *Escape from freedom*. New York: H.R. Holt and Company. (Original work published in 1941).
Heidegger, M. (1982). *The basic problems of phenomenology* (A. Hofstadter, Trans. Rev. ed.). Bloomington: Indiana University Press. (Original work published in 1975).
Heidegger, M. (2001). *Zollikon seminars: Protocols-conversations-letters* (F. Mayr & R. Askay, Trans.). Evanston: Northwestern University Press. (Original work published in 1987).
Heidegger, M. (2010). *Being and time* (J. Stambaugh & D. J. Schmidt, Trans.). Albany: State University of New York. (Original work published in 1927).
Hoffman, I. Z. (1998). *Ritual and spontaneity in the psychoanalytic process*. Hillsdale: The Analytic Press.
Holzhey-Kunz, A., & Fazekas, T. (2012). Daseinanalysis: A dialogue. In L. Barnett & G. Madison (Eds), *Existential therapy: Legacy, vibrancy, and dialogue* (pp. 35–51). London: Routledge.

Husserl, E. (1983). *Ideas pertaining to a pure phenomenology and to a phenomenological philosophy: Book one: General introduction to a pure phenomenology* (F. Kersten, Trans.). New York: Springer (Original work published in 1913).

Husserl, E. (2001). *Logical investigations* (J. M. Findlay, Trans.). London: Routledge. (Original work published in 1913).

Kierkegaard, S. (1968). *The concept of dread* (W. Lowrie, Trans.). Princeton: Princeton University Press. (Original work published in 1844).

Kierkegaard, S. (1980). *The sickness onto death* (H. V. Hong & E. H. Hong, Trans.). Princeton: Princeton University Press. (Original work published in 1849).

Kierkegaard, S. (2014). *The concept of anxiety: A simple psychologically oriented deliberation in view of the dogmatic problem of heredity sin* (A. Hannay, Trans.). New York: Liveright. (Original work published in 1844).

Laplanche, J., & Pontalis, J. B. (1973). *The language of psycho-analysis* (D. Nicholson-Smith, Trans.). New York: W.W. Norton & Co. (Original work published in 1967).

Leffert, M. (2010). *Contemporary psychoanalytic foundations*. London: Routledge.

Leffert, M. (2013). *The therapeutic situation in the 21st century*. New York: Routledge.

Leffert, M. (2016). *Phenomenology, uncertainty, and care in the therapeutic encounter*. New York: Routledge.

Leffert, M. (2017). *Positive psychoanalysis: Aesthetics, desire, and subjective well-being*. New York: Routledge.

Leffert, M. (2018). *Psychoanalysis and the birth of the self: A radical interdisciplinary approach*. London: Routledge.

Maderthaner, W., & Musner, L. (2008). *Unruly masses: The other side of fin de siècle Vienna*. New York: Berghahn Books.

Marcuse, H. (1991). *One-Dimensional Man* (2nd edn). Boston: Beacon Press. (Original work published in 1964).

Marcuse, H. (2007). *The essential Marcuse: Selected writings of philosopher and social critic Herbert Marcuse*. Boston: Beacon Press.

May, R. (1958a). Contributions of existential psychotherapy. In R. May, E. Angel, & H. F. Ellenberger (Eds), *Existence* (pp. 37–91). New York: Simon & Schuster.

May, R. (1958b). The origins and significance of the existential movement in psychology. In R. May, E. Angel, & H. F. Ellenberger (Eds), *Existence: A new dimension in psychiatry and psychology* (pp. 3–36). New York: Basic Books.

May, R., Angel, E., & Ellenberger, H. F. (Eds). (1958). *Existence: New directions in psychiatry and psychology*. New York: Simon & Schuster.

Merriam Webster's Dictionary (2004) (11th edn). Springfield: Merriam-Webster Inc.

Nietzsche, F. (2016). *Thus spoke Zarathustra* (T. Common, Trans.). New York: Digireads.com. (Original work published in 1883).

The Oxford English Dictionary (1989) (2nd edn). Oxford: Clarendon Press.

Panksepp, J., & Biven, L. (2012). *The archaeology of mind: Neuroevolutionary origins of human emotions*. New York: W.W. Norton & Co.

Reik, T. (1957). *Of love and lust: On the psychoanalysis of romantic love and lust*. New York: Grove Press. (Original work published in 1941).

Sartre, J.-P. (2003). *Being and nothingness* (H. Barnes, Trans.). London: Routledge. (Original work published in 1943).

Sartre, J.-P. (2013). *Nausea* (L. Alexander, Trans.). New York: New Directions. (Original work published in 1938).

Sartre, J.-P. (2018). *Being and Nothingness: An essay in phenomenological ontology* (S. Richmond, Trans.). (Original work published in 1943).

Schacter, D. L., Addis, D. R., & Buckner, R. L. (2008). Episodic simulation of future events concepts, data, and applications. *Annals of the New York Academy of Science, 1124*, 39–60.

Schnell, T. (2010). Existential indifference: Another quality of meaning in life. *Journal of Humanistic Psychology, 50*, 351–373.

Sledge, E. B. (1981). *With the old breed at Pelelui and Okinawa*. Oxford: Oxford University Press.

Stolorow, R. D. (2011). *World, affectivity, trauma*. New York: Routledge.

Stolorow, R. D., & Atwood, G. E. (1992). *Contexts of being*. Hillsdale: The Analytic Press.

van Deurzen, E. (2006). *Everyday mysteries: Existential dimensions of psychotherapy* (2nd edn). London: Routledge.

van Deurzen, E. (2012a). *Existential counselling & psychotherapy in practice* (3rd edn). London: Sage Publications.

van Deurzen, E. (2012b). Reasons for living: Existential therapy and spirituality. In L. Barnett & G. Madison (Eds), *Existential therapy: Legacy, vibrancy, and dialogue* (pp. 171–182). London: Routledge.

van Deurzen, E., & Adams, M. (2016). *Skills in existential counselling and psychotherapy* (2nd edn). London: Sage Publications.

van Deurzen, E., & Kenward, R. (Eds). (2005). *Existential perspectives on human issues: A handbook for practice* (2nd edn). London: Palgrave Macmillan.

Wong, P. T. P. (Ed.). (2012). *The human quest for meaning: Theories, research, and applications* (2nd edn). London: Routledge.

Yalom, I. D. (1980). *Existential psychotherapy*. New York: Basic Books.

Yalom, I. D. (2009). *Staring at the sun: Overcoming the terror of death*. New York: Jossey-Bass.

4 The Psychotherapy and Psychoanalysis of the Absurd

Introduction

Although we have been speaking now for several chapters in what may still seem a new and strange language, dealing with problems of Existence and Essence (Sartre, 1947/2007) is the central task that we have always faced as Psychotherapists.

May et al. (1958) began by critiquing standard psychoanalytic techniques for the relief of anxiety and depression (these critiques have remained largely unanswered by the psychoanalytic establishment here or in Europe). These standard techniques offer history- and narrative-based therapies informed by an understanding of normal and pathological development. Patients have sick pasts, but are they any different from everybody else (i.e., people who do not seek out Psychotherapy) and, if not, are they different symptomatically? What exactly is a good enough childhood? My patients have disturbed childhoods but so do my friends, colleagues, and, arguably, so do I. What is really going on here?

As we saw in the preceding two chapters, Existential Psychotherapy and Psychoanalysis address problems unique to the Being of Human Beings: problems having to do with the search for personal Meaning in the face of Meaninglessness, Loneliness, and Despair, and giving rise to symptoms of anxiety and depression as they play out in a world of irreducible subjectivity. The pursuit of personal Meaning and a meaningful life is what makes us uniquely human (Leffert, 2017). The relationship of that subjective world to the objective one is complex and not much explored by these therapies.

An area of Existentialist thought that has largely failed to make the leap from Philosophy to Psychology and its clinical applications, has to do with the idea that the Self dwells in an *Absurd* World and is, at times, overwhelmed by it. I would posit that one of the things we do clinically, in whatever manner we do it, and with whatever language we use to describe it, is to access and treat that Absurdity and the way a patient unknowingly replicates it. Stoltzfus (2003) offers us a working definition:

> The absurd describes the state of mind of individuals who are conscious of a discrepancy between desire and reality: the desire for freedom,

happiness, and immortality, and the knowledge that life imposes limits on desire even as death announces finitude.

(p. 1)[1]

To this I would add a second broad category of Absurdity that can be applied independently or in concert with the above. It has to do with what happens when the world does not behave or respond as Dasein expects.

If we look for the philosophical roots of the Absurd in the Existentialist movement, we find them in the work of Albert Camus (1942/1989, 1942/1991) and his focus on life and death in an Absurd world. Camus was one of the French Existentialists but saw his ideas as very different from those of his colleagues (Sartre, de Beauvoir & Co.). In a movement known for its personal animosities and bitter internecine warfare—like Psychoanalysis for that matter—his relationships with them remained cordial. This, however, does not mean that they either accepted his ideas or agreed with them; they did not. This, along with Camus' untimely death in a car crash at 47 in 1960 and his bringing out his ideas in only a few short novels (rather than Sartre's 70+ books), may account for his work not being taken up by Existential and Phenomenological Psychologists.

Metapsychologically based treatments also fail to address the Absurd. They work to increase personal freedom, most broadly defined, in response to inhibition (Freud, 1926/1959), allowing a patient to try out new [ways of Being][2] that bring with them [Meaning] and satisfaction. They also do not consider the Existential problem that Freedom can sometimes also be meaningless (Fromm, 1941/1994). These approaches all acknowledge the presence of [the Absurd as defined by Stoltzfus], but their approach to the problem is contained in Freud's very old advice: Change your situation or replace "neurotic misery with everyday unhappiness." They do not, as the Existentialists and the Daseinanalysts do not, attempt to seek out the alchemy of changing the Absurd into Meaningful experience. Frankl (1959/2006) addresses this necessity of dealing with the Absurd:

> The way in which a man accepts his fate and all the suffering it entails, the way in which he takes up his cross, gives him ample opportunity—even under the most difficult circumstances—to add a deeper meaning to his life. It may remain brave, dignified and unselfish. Or in the bitter fight for self-preservation he may forget his human dignity and become no more than an animal. Here lies the chance for a man either to make use of or to forgo the opportunities of attaining the moral values that a difficult situation may afford him and this decides whether he is worthy of his sufferings or not.

(p. 67)[3]

---

1 This statement includes an implied "fallen" that owes an unmentioned debt to Heidegger.
2 The brackets denote this as Existential language that is closer to meaning and jargon-free.
3 Frankl's description here bears an uncanny (and uncited) resemblance to the conclusions reached by Camus in *The Myth of Sisyphus* (1942/1991) that will be discussed below.

Setting a patient on a road from Absurdity to Meaning needs to be an essential tenet of Existential therapy and analysis. As applies to so much of this, many (but not all) of us implicitly work with our patients in this way but remain unaware of it.

If this were 1960 or thereabouts, addressing Absurdity, the Existential concept, and folding it into the clinical applications of Existential Psychology would put paid to the task, but it does not. In 2020, we exist in and must navigate a clinically and theoretically different, diverse world. In brief, it is an Interdisciplinary world in which we must take notice of Neurobiology, Psychopharmacology, Epistemology, Social Connectivity, and Uncertainty. We also have to address the great lapse in Existential Psychology: the failure to study Development.

We must somehow reconcile all of this with the Heideggerian dimensions of Being. Think of these as existing along three axes. One involves three *ways* of Being: the Everyday, the Thrown, and the Fallen. Another involves the three *locations* of Being: the *Eigenwelt*, the *Mitwelt*, and the *Umwelt*. The final axis is that of *temporality*: how Existence plays out (Developmentally) over the life cycle. We will have to refer back to these axes as we go. Describing how Absurdity is expressed along each of them is more than we can smoothly accomplish in a single chapter: we will separate the task across two. In this chapter we will deal with the ways of Being and the temporal-developmental axis on which they lie. We will take up Absurdity as it is faced developmentally across the life cycle and how it relates to the *Eigenwelt*: the hardware and software with which the Self is endowed. Much of the task of explaining Absurdity involves the way Self engages World (the location of Being, *Mitwelt* and *Umwelt*), a large enough task to fill the next chapter. Here, the Self has to deal with the social and physical environment in which it finds itself: the interplay of its irreducible subjectivity and the objective World in which it must operate.

I have been writing on Interdisciplinary Topics (Leffert, 2013, 2016, 2017, 2018) for the past decade, integrating them into a broadly defined, clinically based Psychoanalytic perspective. Applying them to the Existentialist enterprise is a complex business in that the early authors (Heidegger, 1975/1982, 1927/2010; Husserl, 1937/1970, 1913/1983; Sartre, 1943/2003) and the later clinicians (Boss, 1963; Frankl, 1969/2014; May, 1983; May, et al., 1958; Yalom, 1980) either ignored or explicitly excluded them.

So far, we will need a broad-based study of the Absurd in clinical practice and the way Interdisciplinary studies must contribute to our understanding of it. There is, however, a third area that must be taken up. Philosophy did not stop with the Existentialists; in fact, they came to be discarded in some quarters and considered passé in others. In any event, they were succeeded by the Postmoderns (Leffert, 2007a, 2007b, 2010): the Post-structuralists, the Neo-pragmatists, and the Neo-Marxists. These disciplines also shed light on Absurdity and bring us back to the clinical.

The problem we face here is twofold: We are dealing with a vast literature, beyond our ability to consider, and we must determine which parts of it are relevant or essential to our enterprise. Therapies grounded in Existentialism and engaging the problem of Absurdity rely on helping a patient to reflect on, well, their Existence and how to find meaning in it. It is an active and conscious process. This leaves us with two aspects of Existence unaddressed. The first involves the functioning of the Self that is not conscious and how it plays out *consciously*. Although many clinicians conflate this category with the operations of a dynamic Unconscious (and believe that if the Unconscious is not addressed, therapy or analysis has not taken place), I have argued repeatedly (e.g., Leffert, 2010, 2013, Chapter 1, this volume) that there is no evidence for the existence of such a discreet structure and that there is much more to unconsciousness, *all* of which bears on our understanding of Human Being. The second aspect has to do with the various systems we have developed that automate our ways of Being-in-World[4] and affect our search for meaning for good or ill. We seek to sometimes elevate these systems for purposes of conscious reflection.

Clinically, this is not the whole story. That is, addressing these Existential goals (including Absurdity) often requires performing the more familiar and standard *clinically* based therapeutic *praxes* (such as interpretation), preferably without referencing their supposedly metapsychological origins. In other words, a significant part of what we do is therapy as usual. We will begin here with a clinical discussion of Absurdity and then move on to how the concept informs discussions of Human Development. We will chart a course through those other disciplines necessary to the formation of a coherent Interdisciplinary narrative of Absurdity.

Absurdity and Meaning in the work of Camus and beyond

A *corollary* we might offer to *Existence precedes Essence* (Sartre, 1947/2007) is that *Existence is potentially Absurd*. Camus, however, is after bigger game— much bigger game. At the opening of *The Myth of Sisyphus*, (1942/1991) he defines the fundamental problem of philosophy as answering the question: Does life have meaning? The real question here is: Is life worth living? Subsidiary questions (Zaretsky, 2013) are: Need we ever have lived? and Will there be even the faintest shudder in the world when we die? If not, Suicide is the only action that makes logical sense in a life that lacks meaning. This resonates with suicide in *fin de siècle* Vienna where it was seen as a response to an individual's conclusion that their life could not have meaning. Unlike the *fin de siècle* position, which is a kind of passive submission to the inevitable, Camus' is a passionate claim growing out of an attempt to meet life head on. *Meaning is the antithesis of Absurdity*. He describes his conclusion in the book's introduction, written 15 years later in 1955, that *even within the*

---

4 They include such diverse systems as Semantic and Procedural Memory (Schacter, 1996), Heuristics and Biases (Kahneman, Slovic, & Tversky, 1982; Tversky & Kahneman, 1974/1982) and Social Connectedness (Christakis & Fowler, 2009).

limits of nihilism it is possible to find one's way beyond nihilism. (Frankl would later write the same thing) In a similar introduction to *The Stranger* (1942/1989), also written in 1955, Camus stresses that Meursault also retains the ability to choose which offers a path out of Absurdity. In both introductions, Camus stresses that his work was shaped by the defeat of the French Republic in 1940 and its occupation by the Nazis, destroyers of Worlds. If, however, none of this works, we are left with a second corollary: *Absurdity poisons Existence.*

Camus (1942/1991) offers us a narrative of *possibility*. It is a counterpoint to the reality that many Human Beings live lives of Absurdity; some realize it while many do not, projecting causality onto World, what we therapeutically term Externalization. When a patient comes to us, they have usually already taken the first steps on this road of self-reflection and -discovery but there are some who never do. Camus, in his description of Meursault, the protagonist in *The Stranger* (see Chapter 2 for the story) (Zaretsky, 2013), offers us a clinical narrative that is at once applicable to many of the patients we encounter.

Meursault is, first and foremost, a Human Being lacking in self-reflection. Even his sense at the end that his public execution before spectators who hate him will be restorative (healing?) lacks either reflection or self-knowing (autonoetic) consciousness (Tulving, 1985/2003, 2005). Lacking in these, there can be no meaning in Meursault's life. As Zaretsky (2013) describes his *absence* so precisely, he is a lover who cannot love, a mourner (for his mother) who cannot mourn, and a murderer without reason or motive. He lives almost entirely in the present with only a handful of references to past events and the single future event, his execution, that he so looks forward to. If one stays fixed in the present, nothing changes and again, without past or future, there can be no meaning. It is only towards the end of the final section of the book dealing with Meursault's trial that the imminence of his death by guillotine brings with it the development of self-reflection. Similarly, the advent in life of a potentially fatal illness, by bringing death into the picture, takes people from Everydayness to Thrown self-reflection.

Camus practiced what he preached. Living in a country, Nazi-occupied France, in which freedom was curtailed, human rights trampled, and anti-Semitism rampant, Camus struggled to find meaning for himself in this strange world. He quit his job at *Paris-Soir* (Zaretsky, 2013) because it had become an anti-Semitic propaganda sheet for the Nazi government, leaving himself with no income to support himself and his wife Francine; they returned to Oran where they lived in an apartment owned by her family. Early in 1942 he suffered a resurgence of his tuberculosis, this time in his previously unaffected lung. TB is, in part, a psychosomatic illness; its return was undoubtedly a response to his difficulty existing as a Human Being in a toxic and meaningless world. He was advised to spend the summer recuperating in the Cévennes Mountains of central France, staying in a farmhouse, again owned by his wife's family, because he could not afford a sanatorium. Camus was able to focus himself on the natural beauty of this rustic, thinly settled mountainous world in which he found himself, finding a "forgetfulness" that allowed him to put the outside world and his illness behind him (as a way of dealing with its Absurdity).

He was engaging in a kind of Existential Self-analysis, making use of the life tools available to him at the time to try to find meaning. Following the Allied landings in Africa in February, 1942, Camus found himself trapped in metropolitan France unable to return to Algeria and his family and friends; he had become again an Absurd man in an Absurd world (we will pursue these effects of World on Self, among them what it is like to live in early 21st century America, in the next chapter). His problems with Absurdity had returned to the *Mitwelt* and the *Umwelt*. However, *The Stranger* (1942/1989), having somehow passed the censors, was selling well and a second edition was called for.

If we think about Russell, the patient I introduced in the last chapter, we can see that he has lived his life just as Meursault lived his. He faces a meaningless existence and a blank emptiness in place of trying to think about himself. (We will return to Russell shortly.)

Before we can discuss the prevalence of Absurdity in Human Beings generally (a group that can too easily be skipped over) as opposed to hard-working philosophers, we have to talk about how it plays out across the three ways of Being, particularly Everydayness, and one of the locations of Being, the *Eigenwelt*, that is, a heuristically separated Self.

Everydayness (*Alltäglichkeit*) explained

We have already, in the preceding chapters, discussed what Heidegger (1975/1982) posited as three ways of Being—Throwness, Everydayness, and Fallenness. Where Heidegger allowed for some blurring of the Everyday and the Fallen, I have found it more meaningful to treat them as distinct categories. Fallenness is a failed way of Being for Human Beings. In it, they fail to accept life as contingent and inevitably finite; they fail to experience the *inevitability* of their own deaths and instead are terrified by them and seek an immortality they deem possible. By definition, *Fallenness is Absurd* and we seek, therapeutically, to address the irrationality of its desires with meaning. Similarly, Throwness is, also by definition, free of Absurdity; Meaning is contained in its very nature, its acknowledgement of finite life and inevitable death that must be made the most of. This leaves us with Everydayness, a way of Being that is at once more difficult to categorize.

Heidegger (1927/2010) describes what he calls the "average everydayness" of Being *at home* in the World. It is not a failed state; it is the original state (Leffert, 2018) of Being Human that takes us back to the Savannahs of Southern Africa around 200,000 years ago. Everydayness involves going about the usual business of living and differs to some degree from person to person. It involves an emersion in the everyday tasks of Production and Care. It is a non-reflective, non-narrating state, a state of Noetic (knowing) Consciousness (Leffert, 2010; Tulving, 1985/2003) as opposed to Autonoetic (Self-knowing)

Consciousness. In Everydayness the Self loses its separateness and individuality, it becomes *entangled* with other Selves; or, as Heidegger says, it is *dispersed*.

For the Everyday Dasein there is only the immediate surround with whatever useful things can be found "at hand;" there can be no experience of World as such. It instead involves Being-with (*Mitsein* and *Sein-bei*) and Caring-for (*Besorgen*). The latter includes things like food and clothing but is also part of social institutions such as nursing, teaching, and husbandry. It is allocentric where Thrownness is autocentric. For example, the presence of lumber and nails may lead Everyday Man to pick up a nearby hammer and begin constructing something. It does not involve the process or *recognition* that this implement is a member of the class of hammers and the various ways in which the class functions.

Everydayness is by its nature a meaningful state but not one in which *Everyday Man* can consciously reflect on its meaning. It would not seem to involve Absurdity. Heidegger's arguments (and mine so far) have not considered the role that Subjectivity plays in the categorization of what might reside in each of these states. Hence Sisyphus, Camus' (1942/1991) Sisyphus that is, is initially condemned to a "life" of Absurd (Fallen) immortality but is able to re-categorize it into Thrownness with its own reflective meaning. The converse is also possible. One can begin in Everydayness but Existence itself may change this. What starts out as the meaningful work of Care can, in the face of deteriorating social circumstances become Absurd and require a change in engagement (Development is an example of this kind of change). The way in which some psychoanalysts attempted to continue to practice as usual in Nazi Germany and Austria in the face of rising anti-Semitism could be cited as an illustration of this (we will delve further into social circumstances, past and present, in the next chapter).

Russell, the patient who was introduced in the last chapter, illustrates these trends. In law school and when he began to practice, he found his work in mergers and acquisitions fascinating; we would say he felt thrown into it. He was very good at it. As, over the years, he settled in, the work took on an Everyday quality; he found it pleasant, but not a subject of interest or reflection. These trends escaped his notice and it required discourse to reveal them. Later in his career, the work became mechanical, to be carried out by rote. Russell began to find it exhausting and of little interest. This was a Fallen state. He did not notice this change; I did, and I also wondered about a possible connection between his state of mind and his wife's decision to enter graduate school, the start of a path that would take her out of his life. I began by pulling together for him how his experience of work changed dramatically over the years, culminating in his empty retirement. This Existential approach "woke him up," and he became able to start thinking about himself again, an ability he had lost at about the time his life had become Absurd. Instead of his Desires being impossible in his World, Desire had vanished for Russell. This was a first step in his therapy.

The Self, Dasein, the *Eigenwelt*, and Absurdity

If the *Mitwelt* refers to one's relationships with other Human Beings and the *Umwelt* refers to our relationships with the physical World, the *Eigenwelt* refers to the world within the Self. And in 21st century Ontology, the best way we can talk about the Eigenwelt is to talk about the Bio-Psycho-Social Self, its Self-experience and Self-reflections. The Self has come, over the decades, to pose problems for Existentialism, Phenomenology, and Absurdism that simply did not exist when these philosophies and their psychotherapeutic counterparts were developed in the middle of the last century. Very much along the lines of quantum mechanics, when we consider the Self we are dealing with physical structures and functional processes that are irrevocably interreferential; the more we understand their relationship, the clearer it becomes that we are dealing with *differing aspects of the same thing* with neuroplasticity being the conceptual bridge between the two. In mid-century, the founders had two processes to deal with, Consciousness and Unconsciousness, and the earliest work on the functional neuroanatomy of the brain, explored mostly through the study of brain injury. From the birth of Phenomenology through mid-century, the Phenomenologists and Existential therapists rejected the relevance of Unconsciousness on almost religious grounds, positing that such a function and the areas of Mind in which they predominated were irrelevant to the aspects of Mind they were working with; perhaps even irrelevant to Mind itself.

It became impossible to ignore, however, that if we wanted to understand Being and meaning, we needed to explore the mechanisms through which the Self *existed* and *acted*, through which it *thought* and *felt*, and to do so we had to integrate our increasing knowledge and understanding of its structure/function.[5] In addition, what the Self had *become* over its history plays a fundamental role in determining what it finds to be meaningful, or desirous, or Absurd, in the present. (We will discuss the roles of the *Mitwelt* and *Umwelt* in the next chapter.)

I would posit that the 21st century Bio-Psycho-Social Self is the contemporary formulation of Dasein and that the *Eigenwelt* is the location—its *Da*— of Self-experience and Self-reflection. A component of this Self is the Reflective Self that deals with the Meaning and Absurdity we are interested in. We must remember that this Self is a Holistic System best understood through General Systems Theory (GST) (Laszlo, 1972/1996; von Bertalanffy, 1968) and governed by the rules of complexity (Leffert, 2008). The picture is further complicated by the fact that, as we shall see, these various elements of the complex system known as the Bio-Psycho-Social Self fall into qualitatively different categories: the social, the hard scientific and the psychological (Latour, 1991/1993). This moves us to a rather strange territory, a terra incognita for philosophers and most therapists that falls within the domain of Neurophilosophy.

---

5 I have been unable to find any evidence of such an attempted Existential integration before my own efforts (Leffert, 2010, 2016, 2017, 2018).

For our purposes, what we need to know about complex systems is that they are made up of components (or nested component sub-systems) such that the properties of the system are not discernable from the sum of the properties of its components—*the whole is not equal to the sum of its parts*. Further, the behavior of the system going forward cannot be entirely discerned from its behavior up to that point in time. The components of the system manifest attractions for each other (we call their sum total *attractor basins*) that resist changes in state and, when they do change, *tend* to change qualitatively (the snow covering of a mountain becomes an avalanche or a quiescent Self is flooded with emotion). Thus, when the system *does* change (unpredictably), it does so in massive qualitative rather than incremental quantitative ways. Complexity describes how massive systems such as earthquakes and hurricanes change but also how changes occur in the Self during therapy. All of this bears on how the sub-system we are calling the Reflective Self acts to consider Meaning—again, in ways quite at odds with the thinking of Existential Philosophers and Therapists. We can say that Absurdity changes; things that weren't Absurd become so, and things that were Absurd are no longer so (this will be important when we consider Development in a moment). The past sometimes induces stereotypy in the present. Another way of describing this is to say that the Self operates within a certain inherent level of Absurdity and must, consciously or not, make the best of it. All of this is but another way of describing ontologically what we contend with in therapy and analysis: frozen Selves that unexpectedly encounter changing situations and Selves that unexpectedly change in steady state situations. If we think about Russell, we can see that he remained frozen while his life dramatically changed and his adaptations to it became Absurd.

For Existentialism and Phenomenology, the relevant aspects of the Neuroscience of the Self can be understood today (I expect it to change over subsequent decades of research) as falling broadly within five categories. The first has to do with the neural hardware (Schore, 2003a, 2003b, 2009, 2011), the functional neuroanatomy of the Self. The second has to do with affective neuroscience (Panksepp & Biven, 2012; Panksepp & Watt, 2011), the neuroevolutionary origins and present functions of basic human emotions. The third has to do with the shaping of thought and action through acquired Heuristics and Biases (Kahneman, et al., 1982; Tversky & Kahneman, 1974/1982). The fourth has to do with the broad reach of Positive Psychology that drives our actions, particularly the way we try to define and manage our Subjective Well-Being (SWB) (Diener, 1984, 2009). The final fifth category, individual Connectedness in Social Networks (Christakis & Fowler, 2009) will fit into the next chapter's discussions of the *Mitwelt*. For Existentialism, a further complexity of the activities of the Self is that, while we *can* become conscious of these processes, they operate and evolved to operate unconsciously as parts of the Noetic and Anoetic Self. *Even though they are unconscious*, they profoundly shape Meaning and Desire and must be taken up as part of any Existential argument. The problem is that, for Existentialism and Absurdism (for convenience, I'll subsequently refer to them as E/A), Meaning and Desire arise out of a process of conscious reflection governed by serial logic, and now we must integrate the information from these other disciplines that insist that Meaning and Desire are also shaped by processes taking place outside of awareness that operate parallelly as Distributed Processing Systems (Baars, 1993/2003). I have written (Leffert, 2010, 2013, 2016, 2017, 2018) extensively on these subjects for the past decade and must offer enough of a reprise to integrate them with the E/A enterprise.

The neural hardware of the Self and its relationship to the Absurd and the Everyday

We must recognize that there is a basic relationship between Dasein, what makes us Human Beings, and our functional neuroanatomy. Our understanding of this neurofunctionality began in the mid-20th century with work on the anatomical location of points of cerebral function (Penfield & Penfield, 1954) and the exciting concept of cerebral laterality, described in the split-brain studies of Sperry and his colleagues (Sperry, 1969; Sperry, Gazzaniga, & Bogen, 1969). While *all* of the elements of neurofunctionality are relevant to the role of neural function outside of Consciousness in Existential processing, we only need to consider a sampling of the neuroanatomy to get us to the question we need to solve.

Although they weighted the importance of unconscious mental processes very differently, both orthodox Psychoanalysis and E/A saw auto-noetic, narrative, Self-knowing and Self-reflective consciousness as the final pathway, philosophically and psychologically, for Self-knowing. This form of consciousness was found to reside in the Left Cerebral Cortex or Left Brain (LB). The weight of the evidence is that this Self-knowing is a capacity exclusive to Dasein. There has been considerable disagreement concerning the state of affairs in the separate Right Brain but it made the most sense to me (Leffert, 2010) to define a parallelly organized RB Consciousness, a very different *kind* of consciousness quite separate from that of a LB that is *unconscious* (yes, *unbewusst*) of it. Mostly unconscious to the LB (Baars, 1993/2003), it operates via parallel distributed processing or PDP (Rumelhart & McClelland, 1986), whereas the LB is a serially organized system following the rules of formal logic. This is complicated, but both hemispheres also have (Baars, 1993/2003) their own processes that they are unconscious of. Although the LB is unaware of the RB, the RB nevertheless (Baars, 1988/2003) in part shapes its activity.

Allan Schore's (2003a, 2003b, 2009, 2011) work on the right cerebral hemisphere and particularly the right orbital pre-frontal cortex will get us into the problem. The serial-processing LB evaluates and judges things in seconds. It receives information from the parallel-processing RB about emotion and judgement that *it* has processed in milliseconds. That means that the

LB has only begun its deliberations when the RB is finished with its. The LB is unaware of how much its conclusions about meaning have been influenced by processes in the RB and unconsciously in the Self as a whole.

And here we face the first of our problems. If LB consciousness is the seat of E/A reflection and problem solving (which we would expect it to be), then does the *unconscious* influence of the rest of the Self (not just the RB) on its actions render it Everyday, Absurd, or Fallen? Can it make the whole E/A enterprise absurd? The answer, unfortunately is that, on the face of it, it is not immediately possible to say which it is and the question requires still more reflection. We certainly have to say: It depends. Again, this is a question that we have been bringing into therapy for some time but didn't know to name it as such. Higher level processing of emotions takes place in the Left Cerebral Cortex. It manifests autonoetic consciousness. We know from experience that the LB is capable of considerable distortion and of lying to itself and to other Human Beings. These cognitive behaviors are both Absurd and Fallen. It would be nice to be able to say that the RB is not capable of such behaviors but we know (Risse & Gazzaniga, 1978) that it does keep secrets from both the LB and from itself. Classifying this secret-keeping in E/A terms is difficult —it may sometimes be Everyday but at other times Fallen.

There is a final specimen of neural hardware that is essential to our understanding of the Self. Meaning is a Subject of Self-Reflection. That reflection requires a representation of the Self that can be reflected upon, and such representation(s) are the provenance of a unique area of the Brain: its Cortical Midline Structures (Leffert, 2013; Molnar-Szakacs & Arzy, 2009; Uddin, Iacoboni, Lange, & Keenan, 2007). These Self-Representations are dynamic, not static; they constitute Internal Working Models (Bowlby, 1973; Craik, 1943/1952) that are constantly being updated. They can also contain static distortions leading to pathological Self experience. Molnar-Szakacs and Arzy note that there is a *default mode* of Brain function that involves awareness of and contemplation of Self-Representation that is suspended during goal-oriented behavior. The Self is self-aware or engaged in action, not both. In Existential terms, it exists in a Thrown state involving contemplation of Meaning or an Everyday state of goal-directed action.

Panksepp (1998) argues that what he calls a Self (and I insist is a Self-*Representation*) has its early origins in the motor and sensory centers of the midbrain. I would argue that it is later co-opted in Human Beings by the cortical midline structures. They continue to draw on and provide feedback to the neurodynamics of sensory analysis in the thalamus (midbrain) and the cerebral cortex. Panksepp maintains "that the changing neurodynamics of the extended representations of SELF networks are essential for generating subjective emotional feelings in all mammalian brains" (p. 309). I want to maintain a distinction between the Self-Representation and the Bio-Psycho-Social Self in which the latter is, in its entirety, a complex system that observes itself, in part using the tools provided by the cortical midline structures. It is this complex entity that must contend with the Existential problems of living.

Affective neuroscience and the neuroevolutionary basis of human emotion

Our emotions are perhaps the major drivers of our thoughts and actions; they are the determinants of the things we find meaningful, gratifying, frightening, and enraging. They also bridge the Conscious and the Unconscious, the voluntary and the involuntary. In recent years, the neuroevolutionary origins and functioning of human emotion has essentially become synonymous with the integrative work of Jaak Panksepp (Panksepp, 1998, 2009; Panksepp & Biven, 2012).

Understanding emotions requires a neuroevolutionary perspective encompassing the observations that they are represented in different ways at different evolutionary levels of the brain: the older, sub-cortical reptilian and mammalian levels of brainstem and midbrain and the human levels of the neocortex. "It is clear that all mammalian brains inherit a variety of emotional dispositions as ancestral tools for living" (Panksepp, 2009, p. 1). Cross-mammalian and, in some cases, cross-vertebral studies reveal the presence of seven Primary[6] Emotional Systems—SEEKING, FEAR, RAGE, LUST, CARE, PANIC, and PLAY—that go on to higher level Secondary and Tertiary representations. In the event of affective dysregulation, cognition becomes indistinguishable from Primary Process Emotionality. These Primary systems are *anoetic* (Tulving, 1985/2003): They are intensely conscious but pre-propositional; they can only be reflected on by higher order Mind-Brain systems. We feel them but do not *know* that we feel: *feeling* without *knowing*. Is this state of affairs Absurd or Meaningful? Arguably, while it can be either or both, it is best classified, Phenomenologically, as *Everyday*.

Panksepp (2009) attaches particular importance to two of these systems, PLAY and CARE, that he sees as central to the positive emotional experiences of mammals generally and Human Beings in particular. They are of great importance in psychotherapy (Leffert, 2016); Panksepp emphasizes the role of shared play in therapeutic action. In conjunction with two of the other systems, SEEKING and LUST, they can be used therapeutically to restructure experience away from the systems FEAR, RAGE, and PANIC, moving from a dominance of Trauma to one of Subjective Well-Being (Leffert, 2017).

As Human Beings, we are endowed with this rich mammalian system of Primary Process Emotions that, however, must make it through possible defensive developmental constraints occurring in childhood to allow for its full expression in adulthood. Such damage is not immediately accessible to adult conscious Self-reflection, a situation that we can consider Absurd and seek to rectify in therapy or analysis. A major thread of therapeutic action involves helping a patient become conscious of such limitations and exaggerations on a path from Absurdity to Meaning.

---

6 To be distinguished from the psychoanalytic concept of primary process cognition.

If Primary Emotions are felt but not known, Secondary, *noetic* (known but not reflected upon) Emotions involve their control and Tertiary autonoetic emotions are *known*, complex, blended, and socially derived. Primary Process Emotions are much in control of the developing infant and young child. There is a developmental cascade from Primary, then on to Secondary and Tertiary. Unfortunately, as therapists, we have tended to spend much more time working with the higher-level emotions, shying away from the more powerful Primary Emotional States. We have, in the past, tended to work intellectually through interpretation. In Phenomenological terms, Primary and Secondary Process emotions are Everyday and play out experientially in therapeutic discourse while Tertiary Emotions involve Meaning or Absurdity.

In a Tertiary state, we are able to take pleasure in intense Primary Emotions: for example, enjoying scary or violent movies from what we feel to be a safe place. Annette, a successful married businesswoman in her 50s whose analysis was discussed in the last chapter, could only tolerate going to see comedies, children's movies, or dramas without even a hint of violence. Otherwise, she was terrified. I had not understood this and had limited myself to the suggestion that she might enjoy movies a little closer to the human condition if she tried it a bit at a time. As I better understood that she was still living in the dangerous, violent home of her childhood, I was able to first point out how unsafe she mostly felt then and how vigilant she needed to be. We then went on to talk about safety in the present and how the threats were all old threats. I observed to Annette that I could and did offer a safe place to talk about these threats. She was able to make a clean break with a borderline sibling she had felt tied to and to enjoy dramas that, inevitably, did contain a bit of violence.

So how are we to make Existential sense of emotions when we understand them in the wider neuroevolutionary and functional neuroanatomical world that is now open to us, and, I would posit, we are now *required* to make use of? We have found evidence of different emotional processes that draw on the Thrown and the Everyday, but also the Fallen, processes that are sometimes Meaningful and sometimes Absurd. We have to conclude that Meaning and Absurdity are, from this perspective, higher order appraisal functions pertaining to Tertiary and, perhaps, Secondary emotional states. Inevitably, they bring with them advanced socio-cultural perspectives.

Heuristics and Biases

As we continue to apply Interdisciplinary Studies to Existential Psychology, we have to integrate systems that operate outside of consciousness but can be brought into consciousness through directed Self-Reflection or Psychotherapy. We know that the bulk of processes in the brain-body operate unconsciously (Baars, 1993/2003). They all shape what goes on in the conscious cerebral hemispheres and hence must be considered if we are talking about Meaning and Absurdity. These unconscious systems should not be confused with the Freudian construct of a Dynamic Unconscious that I have been highly critical of (Leffert, 2010) in the past but lie outside the scope of these present arguments. Fundamental to questions of what actions produce Meaning and what actions lead to Absurdity is that we cannot, looking forward, entirely trust in outcomes. Charting this course between Meaning and Absurdity thus requires the making of judgments, judgments inevitably rendered under circumstances of Uncertainty. By Uncertainty, we mean being confronted with decisions for which no rule or axiom can guarantee a correct result. There is now a lot of information available about how we go about making these sorts of judgments.

In the past (Leffert, 2013, 2016), I have discussed decision-making under conditions of Uncertainty from the perspective of how Psychoanalysts and Psychotherapists decide on the meaning of what their patients are telling them and how they decide how they will comment on this putative meaning. This decision-making lies quite close to Kahneman and Tversky's (Tversky & Kahneman, 1974/1982) formulations of choices involving chances of success and risks of failure in situations like gambling, choosing among risky outcomes, and things like insurance. But here, in a wider context, we are looking beyond such choosing, not at choice as it pertains to therapeutic praxis but rather at how Uncertainty affects the way Human Beings make Existential and Phenomenological decisions.

Our story begins with Nisbett and Wilson's (1977) classic paper, "Telling More Than We Know: Verbal Reports on Mental Processes." Their "studies were designed to sample a wide range of behavioral domains, *including evaluations, judgements, choices, and predictions*" (p. 240, italics added). (These would include moral, ethical, and emotional decision-making.) The authors asked their subjects why they made the choices that they did. They found that although the subjects had ready explanations for their choices, questioning them further revealed that, indeed, they had no idea how and why they made these choices. As I observed in 2013, Nisbett and Wilson "proved empirically that mental processes, such as preferences, biases, and choices are not accessible to consciousness and that people's belief in their own introspective awareness (reported as introspective certainty) had no basis in fact" (p. 242n). We would have to say that these findings apply particularly well to the search for Meaning or the Fall into Absurdity. The choices made by Meursault (Camus, 1942/1989), Sisyphus (Camus, 1942/1991), and Roquentin (Sartre, 1938/2013) fit this pattern. Russell (remember Russell?), on the other hand, would readily admit that he had no idea why he made the choices or did the things that he did.

Classical theories of decision-making were first based on Expected Utility Theory and later, when complexity entered the picture, referred to Bounded Rationality (Simon, 1956). It was thought that all rational people would want to make decisions based on the likelihood of success. It was found, however, that "to the contrary, in making choices among outcomes involving risk, subject preferences systematically violated the axioms of expected utility theory" (Leffert, 2016, p. 104). This is where Kahneman and Tversky (1979/2000) entered the field with a ground-breaking paper on what they called Prospect

Theory. They developed the theory to account for decision-making in the face of varying degrees of *risk*. In decision-making under Uncertainty, Prospect Theory distinguishes a two-stage process, a framing stage and a valuation stage: "In the framing phase, the decision maker constructs a representation of the acts, contingencies, and outcomes that are relevant to the decision. In the valuation phase, the decision maker assesses the value of each prospect and chooses accordingly" (Tversky & Kahneman, 1986/2000, p. 46). These choices also manifest considerable variance. Although a rational theory of choice, one governed, for example, by Bounded Rationality, would assume an invariance in the framing process, in the real world we find a great deal of variance that can lead to very different preferences. Tversky and Kahneman have found "five major phenomena of choice, which violate the standard model and set a minimal challenge that must be met by *any* adequate descriptive theory of choice" (p. 45). They involve framing effects, nonlinear preferences, source dependence, risk seeking, and loss aversion.[7] As developmental psychologists we would conceptualize this variance in terms of multiple Internal Working Models. These models remain and shape the formation of other models that shape subsequent choices. Following the framing process, the decision maker formulates a *subjective* assessment of the value of each and then makes a decision.

Prospect Theory offers us tools powerful enough to understand Existential choices that lead to outcomes of either Meaning or Absurdity (e.g., Camus, 1944/1958; Sartre, 1946/1989). What Prospect Theory alone is *unable* to account for is the rapid and intuitive way in which many of these decisions are made (we also know that some of them are reached only after lengthy and agonizing reflection). We have already spoken of this in terms of the contributing functions of the left and right Cerebral Hemispheres, but we can also now say more *psychologically*. Enter Heuristics and Biases.

Decisions made under Uncertainty involve depending on data of limited validity; something more is required. Heuristics and Biases (Kahneman, et al., 1982) find two different kinds of shortcuts for decision-making under uncertainty. Biases are more simply understood. They decrease reliability: the probability of making a good choice. They are systematic ways of choosing whenever one is presented with some particular kind of choice. Biases are *context independent*, representing *tendencies* to choose in a particular way based on how one has come to experience the world, not a certainty of outcome. They are based on life experience leading to narrative and semantic memory (Schacter, 1996). They easily infuse decision-making with systematic errors and tend to interfere with the successful application of Heuristics.

Heuristics are decision-making shortcuts that select out some component of an uncertain situation upon which to base a decision. They are descended evolutionarily from the procedural knowledge of our ancestors and that which we

---

7 For a further discussion of these points, see Tversky and Kahneman (1986/2000).

acquired as developing individuals.⁸ People rely (Tversky & Kahneman, 1974/1982) on a limited number of heuristic principles in order to make uncertain decisions. Two of these principles are the Representativeness Heuristic and the Availability Heuristic. Representativeness involves identifying a choice with which one is faced as a member of a class of choices that have been successfully decided in a certain way. Availability refers to the tendency to identify a choice as being a member of a class of choices because one or more members of that class have recently appeared. Tversky and Kahneman focus on how Heuristics can be sources of systematic error (they can be) at the expense of also describing how they can be successful tools (if they were *regularly* unsuccessful they would extinguish themselves fairly quickly). Existential Representativeness serves to determine whether a particular choice is a member of a group of Existential choices: Thrown or Fallen choices, for example. Errors can occur here if the nature of the offered choice is misperceived or mis-experienced by the subject as being a part of some given class of events. Existential Availability is a dicey proposition. Recent repeated occurrences of some sort of choice do not provide a successful basis for *any* decision-making, let alone Existential decision-making. Let's move on to the Framing and Valuation phases of Existential decision-making.

Tversky and Kahneman (1986/2000) introduce the Framing problem with the proposition that the way a subject describes (to themselves) a situation or circumstance calling for a decision about how to move forward can vary. The corollary to this observation is that alternate descriptions give rise to different preferences and different choices. Expected Utility Theory based on Bounded Rationality does not apply to Existential decision-making. Framing and reframing are thus complex processes that involve a subject's careful consideration of their very Being and the meaning of the various ways they can go forward. Let's take Sisyphus, not the mythological Sisyphus but the Sisyphus of Camus' (1942/1991) eponymous oeuvre. Sisyphus is faced by a punishment that makes his life into an eternity of Absurdity.⁹ Rather than accept this Frame, Sisyphus/Camus *reframes* the situation from the Objective, which seeks an accessible outcome of the repeated task, to Sisyphus/Camus' Subjectivity: What *personal meaning* might he find in his "life" going forward? The Meaning he finds is in the experience of the boulder slipping out of his hands and in the hour of *consciousness* that he has as he trudges down the mountain to repeat his awful task. He is Thrown in this hour, and his consciousness involves both sorrow and joy: sorrow at the limitations the Gods have placed on his life, joy as he remains a Human Being who thinks and feels.

---

8 This brings us into the new combined field of Evolution and Development, christened *Evo-Devo*. See my earlier work *Psychoanalysis and the Birth of the Self* (Leffert, 2018) for a discussion of this exciting concept.
9 Camus (1942/1991) argues that in the face of unalterable Absurdity, suicide is the only choice that makes sense.

Valuing, the second part of the process, depends to a large extent on what an individual has learned about Meaning up to the point in life at which a decision must be made. It can lead to meaningful decisions about life or to absurd ones; decisions can be made intuitively and more or less unconsciously or as a result of reflection. Reflection can also lead to re-valuation. Russell, for example, had found golf enjoyable and to some extent meaningful (to the extent that Russell thought about meaning) while he continued his profession. When he retired, his expectations that golf would form a meaningful center to his life proved unfounded; a downward re-valuation had occurred. I suggested that he needed to find other things that would be meaningful to him. He remembered a wish from long ago to become a teacher. He came up with the idea that he could serve as a tutor and mentor to inner city high school students. It was a new experience to feel that he was getting so much for himself out of what he was doing for others.

Subjective Well-Being

On the face of it, any connection between feeling good, Subjective Well-Being (SWB), and personal Meaning or Absurdity might seem obscure. Not unlike Psychoanalysis, the field of Subjective Well-Being owes its origins and early development to the work of a single researcher—Ed Diener (e.g., 1984, 2009). Diener (1994) defines SWB as comprising peoples' longer-term levels of pleasant affect, lack of unpleasant affect, and life satisfaction. Surprisingly, research (Diener & Diener, 1995) has shown that life satisfaction and SWB are somewhat independent of environmental or social circumstances. Life satisfaction and personal Meaning turn out to be intimately tied up with each other.

Concerns about happiness and the good life probably date back to prehistoric times. As Diener (Kesebir & Diener, 2008/2009) observes two streams of thought arose in Greek philosophy as answers to the question of what constitutes happiness and the good life. Democritus insisted on a primary state of irreducible subjectivity and, following from it, happiness was the product of a state of mind rather than a particular set of external circumstances. Plato (1999), to the contrary, insisted that an *objective* happiness was achievable through the "secure enjoyment of what is good and beautiful" (p. 80) while Aristotle believed that it was to be achieved by living in harmony with the most highly esteemed virtues. Applied to our Existential explorations, happiness involves a subjective state of Being that is the outcome of an ability to act and to surround oneself with culturally-influenced values and objects whose worth can be externally and objectively determined. *Happiness* is one of a class of problematic terms that concern feelings. When we say we are happy or that we think someone else is happy, we are quite certain that we know what we mean (Kahneman, 1999/2003, describes this same problem). *Happiness* is here, then, a term drawn from Folk Psychology. If, however, we should ask the question, "What does it mean to be happy," an *objective* question, we find a scientific or philosophical term that is almost impossible to precisely define or offer a definition about which there would be some consensus. The Postmodern position (Leffert, 2007a) insists that some integration of the two is required. What I am positing is that happiness and Subjective Well-Being also require the outcome of a successful search for personal *Meaning*.

Subjective Well-Being is first of all a conscious assessment of how we experience life in general and our own lives in particular. The assessment has both an emotional hedonic and a cognitive judgmental component. We would expect the determination of Meaning to reside in the latter. Diener offers a cooking analogy: There is no single cause for SWB; some basic ingredients are necessary in large quantities while others in small quantities provide seasoning, producing desired flavors and qualities. Since the assessment of SWB involves judgments that, perforce, must be made under Uncertainty, it should not be a surprise that Kahneman was drawn to the work of Diener (Kahneman, Diener, & Schwartz, 1999/2003) and the world of hedonic psychology.

Kahneman (1999/2003) observed that we assess our SWB over the short-term and the long-term and that short-term assessments are made on the fly under conditions of Uncertainty. Those judgments would tend to be less conscious, dependent on the use of Heuristics, and *subject to error*. We are more interested in the long-term assessments that are slower, mostly conscious, usually reflective, and *not* dependent on Heuristics. Since SWB *is* Subjective, others might not agree with our assessment and, at some later point, we too might decide that our assessment was only partially correct, no longer correct, or the result of faulty values and reflections; that is, it was never correct. We might, then, conclude that our assessment of our SWB was invalid or that our sense of Well-Being at some point in the past was invalid. Let's apply this to the ongoing story of Russell.

When Russell first appeared in my office, my assessments of his SWB and happiness were solidly in negative territory. He felt that his life lacked Meaning. It should be obvious from what I've said about him in the last chapter and the beginning of this one that encouraging him to explore his feelings and motivations, to rekindle his Desire, would draw a blank. I tried instead to simply observe to him that he found himself in a terrible predicament. The fact that he teared up at the comment was a good sign that we had something going; that he could say nothing *about* the tears was only to be expected. As I adjusted my technique and theories of therapeutic action to fit Russell (as I believe we must do individually for every patient we see), I realized that I had to deal with my own frustrations whenever I tried to get him to explore his feelings or reflect on himself (this would, over some years, change, albeit at a snail's pace). This should not be taken to mean that Russell was incapable of analysis; while he tended not to pursue things, he continued to bring up live issues relevant to his problems. He told me two years or so into the therapy that after the previous evenings' session he had gone to dinner at a nearby Scandinavian restaurant known to both of us. He had enjoyed their Swedish meatballs. When I gave him space and just listened, he said, rather shyly, that he had thought of inviting me to have dinner with him. This was so historically foreign to him that it could only reflect a new (for Russell) level of emotional connectiveness. I considered this. If Russell did ask me to have dinner with him would I agree? I didn't know but also didn't rule it out (wondering what colleagues would think of such a thing). I considered how much I might successfully draw out of him if I said something about his wanting to be close to me: I thought, "not much." At the same time, if I said nothing, it would undoubtedly disappear. I contented myself with observing "that must have been really nice" which fell well within the boundaries of the necessary and the possible.

Russell was unusual only in the degree to which he was out of touch with himself and his resistance to altering that state of Being. I needed somehow to find a way past this if we were to ever talk about his wife and his marriage and his relationships with his daughters. I also wanted to talk to him about how his relationship with his mother had precluded intimacy with his wife. I decided that an entry into all of this might be to get Russell to think about his Subjective Well-Being. As Diener (1994) concluded from multiple studies, self-reporting scales offered a reliable assessment of SWB and I could adapt this tool to the Therapeutic Situation. Andrews and Withey (1976) used a one-item scale that began with the question "How do you feel about your life as a whole?" and asked subjects to frame their answers in terms of what has happened in the last year and what they expect will happen in the near future. The seven response items range from delighted to terrible; hence it is called the D-T scale. The scale was designed to reflect both affective and cognitive components of Well-Being; it has been shown to have a high validity co-efficient (0.77). For our purposes, it is not necessary to actually administer such a test but it tells us that if we ask a patient questions about their Well-Being the answers will be meaningful. Since I already had a good picture of Russell's Subjective past life, I asked him what he thought the future held for him. He said he didn't know. I then asked him what he *hoped* it might hold for him. *This* he thought about. He'd like to have something *really* [sic] interesting to do, he said, not just to make money (he had enough) and he'd like to be closer to his daughters. (Russell's relationship with his daughters had been confined to a couple of brief visits a year and semi-weekly phone calls that he thought was all they would want from him, although when he suggested a date for a visit they always promptly agreed.) He said nothing about his now ex-wife, the first concrete evidence that he had got past his empty wishes for a reconciliation.

So, four years into Russell's analysis, I responded with the suggestion that he might plan visits with his daughters and his grandchildren lasting more than part of a weekend. He was visibly flustered by this, doubting that he would be welcome. I pushed him, and he reported in the next session, with some surprise that they agreed and sounded pleased.

At this point, many of my colleagues and some of my readers will shake their heads dismissively, saying this is not and has nothing to do with psychoanalysis—and that is precisely why I have chosen to tell you this part of

Russell's story. Let me first observe that if I had said this to a patient I was seeing weekly for a few months, I would not consider it analysis but still good technique aimed at promoting change in a patient's life. But this was not Russell's situation and what I was aiming for was to get him to change the way he structured his thinking about people he was or could become close to. Such restructuring would include concepts that his daughters might have feelings for him, that they might actually think about him, and that he could *act* to influence their situation together. We already have a name for therapeutic tools that we employ to bring such things about: We call them *interpretations*. I would argue that what I am doing with Russell *is* an analytic therapy, but one conducted with Existential language based on Existential ideas. I had already studied (Leffert, 2017) how, with patients immersed in negativity, it was important to restructure feeling and cognition in a positive direction. Russell did not need to spend time acquainting himself with how angry he was at his daughters for not fixing things with his wife or his guess, an accurate one as it turned out, that they knew more about their mother than they had been willing to admit. He'd been *there* already.

What did Russell do with all of this? During his visits, he was surprised to discover that his daughters and grandchildren were interested in being with him. (He *was* interested in his grandchildren, had indeed established trust funds to pay for their college, but hadn't known how to be with them; now he read stories to them and they enjoyed it.) He talked to his daughters about how hurt he was when their mother had left him but that he had come to understand how little he had had to offer her. In many ways, the conversations served to summarize years of analytic work on the subject that he now found he wanted to include them in. He talked to his sons-in-law, really for the first time; he found Meaning in all of this that had been missing before and, for the first time, warmth.

The Absurdity of development across the life cycle (from uterus to grave)

Normal and pathological development are central to all forms of psychoanalytic understanding of Human Beings and their psychological treatment. Existential authors tend to ignore normative child development and, particularly, what I will call the presence of normative Absurdity as part of the passage from uterus to adulthood. Existentialist philosophers similarly do not address childhood and may well see children as not possessing the cognitive (particularly formal operational cognition) or emotional tools to participate Existentially in the World as Human Beings. Childhood truly can be described as what happens when we are thrown into existence and left to deal with it along with any help we can get. Often, such help is not forthcoming. If there is no writing on normative absurdity in childhood, there is writing on pathological absurdity in children. It comes from an unlikely source: D. W. Winnicott (1960, 1965, 1968, 1975). Winnicott, I want to posit, was actually an

Existentialist author, although neither he nor the usual Existentialist suspects ever thought of him as such. In the children and very disturbed adults that he wrote about, he described fundamental problems in Being and the emptiness and meaninglessness that went with it. Another linkage between Winnicott and the Existential psychologists (Boss, 1963; May, 1969; May, et al., 1958) is how central care and cure are to both; again, often unlabeled as such. Erikson (1950/1953, 1950/1963) offers us a bit of a paradox. In the first half of *Childhood and Society* he certainly appears as a card-carrying theorist of infantile sexuality as the organizing principle of developmental psychology. He then, however, moves on as a social theorist (the part of the book most therapists don't read) using the broad brushstrokes of Epigenesis to paint his work as a developmentalist, documented by observations of a number of American Indian tribes posing unique developmental challenges and solutions. (He does not consider how to use this material therapeutically.) We will also consider the question if any of the child development literature can be viewed through the Existentialist looking glass; that is, can it be considered phenomenologically as well as metapsychologically?

Development, from an Existentialist perspective, exists across the life cycle as a series of customized cycles of Absurdity and Meaning. As the child matures into an ever more complex world (and becomes growingly aware of that complexity), its set of life tools becomes ever more absurd and must be replaced with new tools that the individual child formulates to meaningfully master its world. Development is an interreferential interplay of the psychological and the biological with the latter being underestimated or misunderstood. I have summarized the biological component of the process in an earlier volume (Leffert, 2018, Chapter 4); its rapidity and complexity are almost beyond understanding. Since there seem to be no serious examinations of Child Development from an Existentialist perspective, what I am offering here is, of necessity, only a preliminary sketch and must be taken as such. I hope to pursue these ideas further in a subsequent volume.

The biology and the psychology of Development

The biology and psychology of Development are profoundly interreferential. For heuristic purposes only, it can be useful to separate the two as a way of generating two perspectives on the process that highlight the constant change in structure and function that the developing child must contend with. I am offering only the briefest of summaries of these perspectives to further our discussion of Absurdity. The biological statistics tell us just how complex the human brain is and how massive the changes in its hardware are during Development. At birth (Leffert, 2018), the Human brain[10] displaces 500 cm^3.

---

10 It should be taken as a given that although the brain is a discreet anatomical structure, it is functionally and structurally inseparable from the rest of the anatomy of the Bio-Psycho-Social Self, which is also changing dramatically.

At the end of the first year of life it has doubled in size to 1000 cm³ and ultimately reaches a displacement of 1300 cm³. The adult brain contains 86 billion neurons and 10- to 50-fold more glial cells (Herculano-Houzel, 2012) (although originally thought of as providing support functions to the brain's neurons which they surround, they are now also thought to participate in neuronal activity). Although accounting for only 2% of body mass, the brain uses 20% of the body's energy. Each neuron of the adult Cerebral Cortex has approximately 300,000 synapses (Doidge, 2007). By age 1–2 years (Huttenlocher, 1979), there are 50% more synapses and perhaps 20–25% more neurons than in the adult brain. The process known as *pruning* takes place as a late developmental event (Leffert, 2010) that reduces the number of (perhaps) redundant synaptical units.

If the hardware of the central nervous system is changing on a daily, even hourly basis as Development proceeds, the function of the system is similarly volatile. Laterality determines the functioning of the young Human brain. While the Right Cerebral Hemisphere (the RB)[11] is myelinated[12] and functional from birth, the LB does not begin to myelinate until the second half of the first year of life. For those first 18 months of life, the RB is running the show. It is a non-linear parallel processing system that reaches conclusions in milliseconds. Major structural developments include the right pre-orbital frontal cortex (Schore, 2009) that functions to establish attachment and intersubjectivity, and the cortical midline structures (Uddin, et al., 2007) and the mirror neuron system (MNS) that operate social cognition. They shape both self-image and internal working models (IWM). When the LB comes on line, it is a linear, serial system that operates slowly, taking seconds to reach a decision based on linear logic. This means that when both systems are up and running and separately processing information, the RB reaches its conclusions before the LB has barely started its work. The mature brain demonstrates this laterality (Sperry, 1969; Sperry, et al., 1969) with the LB being unconscious of the operation of the RB (this *may* fit the profile of the psychodynamic unconscious), while the RB seems to have at least some knowledge of the LB.

What can we say about psychological development in a couple of paragraphs that would be of any use at all, given how much has already been written on the subject? We can certainly say that the study of psychological development is inseparable from the development of the Self.

Memory is a good place to start. There are three sorts of memory (Schacter, 1996), Procedural Memory, Syntactical Memory, and Narrative Memory

---

11 Although not strictly true, we will for convention's sake refer to right-handed individuals as possessing a dominant Left Cerebral Hemisphere (LB).
12 Myelin makes up the fatty sheath that covers the long processes (axons) of mature cortical neurons. Unmyelinated axons conduct electrical impulses relatively slowly down their length while myelinated axons (the myelin sheath has a series of pinch marks or nodes) rapidly conduct impulses from node to node.

that in turn entail three sorts of consciousness (Tulving, 1985/2003), Anoetic Consciousness, Noetic Consciousness, and Autonoetic Consciousness. The familiar example of Procedural Memory is learning to ride a bicycle. I am going to use the term more broadly to signify the Self's operating memories of *how it works*. It is not conscious. It includes things like the regulatory abilities of the autonomic nervous system, the ability to organize sensory inputs into perceptions, and, yes, riding a bicycle or skiing too. Syntactical Memory is general information memory, the memory for facts about World and Self. It needs to be conscious *on demand* and relatively free of context. Finally, there is Narrative Memory, the memory of stories or events in which the Self is a participant-observer. Similarly, we have Anoetic Consciousness, a consciousness of action and existence that is found evolutionarily at least as far back as in the lower vertebrates. Then there is Noetic Consciousness, knowing in the moment and knowing what is taking place in the moment. This is at least present in mammals and birds. Finally, there is Autonoetic Consciousness, consciousness of a reflective Self that places itself in World, its history, and its future. This is the consciousness of Human Beings (who manifest all three): It *may* be present in higher primates, chimpanzees and gorillas, conceivably in elephants, and in a few birds, like the African Grey Parrot and the Kea Parrot of New Zealand, but this is uncertain. This possibility is gaining credence among current researchers.

How on earth *does* all this develop? As a metaphor imagine a large ship made up of many exceedingly small parts. It is navigating a river with multiple rapids and strong currents. During its trip, it is being extensively expanded and remodeled; many components must be changed out but some must remain unchanged. Much of this work involves wiring and rewiring. With this as a metaphor, how can development take place? The answer is that we are not talking about development in isolation: Development is inextricably wound up with and grew out of Evolution, offering up the combined process of *Evo-Devo* (Leffert, 2018). Development, well, developed, over time. It first appeared during the Cambrian Period 540–485 million years ago (mya). Prior to that, life was unicellular; it reproduced via budding or cell division, and the organisms then just existed and reproduced. Evolution occurred via changes in protein synthesis. Then, beginning about 540 mya and lasting 20–25 million years a period aptly called the Cambrian Explosion (Gould, 1989) occurred in which multicellular life forms appeared, and by its close the ancestors of *all* of the Phyla were represented. These multicellular organisms developed out of single embryological cells which meant that gradually more specialized cells had to appear as a result of cell division and then be moved around in the developing organism. The process *had to work* or else the adult organism would not exist and the complexity of the process had to evolve as new, more advanced organisms appeared. This is how the exquisitely orchestrated development of Human Beings (pre- and post-partum) first came to be.

We know some parts of the Self's memory systems like body regulation need to develop early (that is, before the LB is myelinated and comes on line), while others, like narrative memory, can only begin to appear when serial memory in the LB is possible. The mother is, if you will, an irreplaceable agent augmenting the development of the Self. For example, by making eye contact with her nursing infant, alternately constricting and dilating movements of her irises (Schore, 1994) serve to "burn in" the infant's autonomic nervous system (ANS), part of the procedural memory system. Some functions of the Brain-Self are broken apart as the young child grows in complexity, while others are essential (like those of the ANS) and are conserved. What is conserved are collections of neurons and their synaptic connections. Although not much talked about, it seems highly likely that Autonoetic Consciousness (what is generally meant by Consciousness) requires the functioning of both the LB and RB systems. It *has* been determined, however, that the extremely complex problem solving (Baars, 1993/2003) that only Humans can perform does require this mature, bilateral system to be in place.

It is important to remember that the life experience of the developing child shapes its brain and that shaping then also shapes subsequent life experience. I have not offered up the familiar psychoanalytic narratives of development; they are largely known to my readers and the material here could be readily applied to them. Let's instead apply them to what I will call Existential Development.

The Existential

In Existentialist terms, Development is the journey from Existence to Essence (Sartre, 1947/2007) that begins sometime *in utero* and ends in death. In order to talk about these Existential perspectives on development, we must recognize that we are talking about the infant's (pre- and post-natal) and child's experience of their World and their Selves in it. We are first of all *not* talking here about *conscious* experience but rather *the totality of the Self's experience and whatever historical record it is able to make and retain of it.*

The Self, throughout its life, is exposed to inner and outer experience beyond its abilities to master. During adult life, these experiences exist in the background and uncommonly come into the foreground. They are usually not beyond the adult's ability to cope with[13] and, indeed, solving them can (puzzles are a good example) be highly pleasurable. It is the experience of the infant and the child that we are interested in here. As the child ages and matures, it is exposed to a series of events and problems that it either lacks the capacity to master or possesses that capacity in only a partial or rudimentary form. At birth, the infant is totally helpless in World with its homeostasis being largely maintained by its parents. Its first developmental steps involve mastering the primitive vocalizations and bodily movements necessary for signaling its parents on how to fine tune their homeostatic support.

---

13 This is not true of natural or social disasters (Hurricane Maria, Hiroshima, Covid-19) that render people helpless.

If we are going to apply Existentialist psychology to an understanding of Development, we must say that the infant, and later the child, exists in a state of *Developmental Absurdity*. Its "Desire" for homeostasis completely exceeds its abilities to independently attain it. Homeostasis through communication, while effective, is also an Absurd state, recognizing as it does the *physical* Absurdity of the infant. If, in the adult, the opposite of a state of Absurdity is Meaningfulness, we have to adapt this thinking to the child. Meaning in adults is a cognitive event, occurring, to be sure, in a necessary emotional background. It requires *fully developed*, Auto-Noetic (Self-knowing), reflective Consciousness as it appears in Adolescence. This is not the same thing as Meaning is for the child, but just what is it, then? If we think of what children find meaningful, a number of things come readily to mind. Perhaps the first is Mastery. (Mastery is a part of Development that *has* been studied by Developmental Psychologists and Psychoanalysts alike and has been incorporated into Play Therapy.) In Mastery we include motor and later cognitive Mastery of both Self and World. What comes (fortunately) wired in the system is a constant Desire (or Drive if you prefer) to push on until challenges are met and Mastery achieved.

The next source of childhood (and some adult) Meaning is different kinds of problem-solving that lead to comprehension and understanding. Finally, I think, Meaning for the child (and again, later, for the adult) is contained in the *collection of narratives* about Self and World that the child develops out of its experiences that take place over the years.

The infant's and child's perceptions of body, World, and Self exceed its ability to act bodily or cognitively. She has, for example, a body that she cannot manage or control motorically; that is, *she finds herself in an Absurd situation*. In a good enough emotional and physical situation, she drives herself to master motor control and uses her musculature in ever more complex ways to engage world. Doing so also shapes neuroanatomical Development which moves the infant on to more complex behaviors and cognitions. (If, in conditions such as hospitalism (Spitz, 1965), an infant lacks adequate emotional and physical support, the drive to develop and master is retarded.) This description can serve as a template for the continued Existential Development of later childhood.

We are now in a position to ask the Existential question: How do Development and Evo-Devo play out in the Existence precedes Essence equation? Political and social considerations aside, Existence *begins* when an egg is fertilized,[14] *it is Essence that develops thereafter*. Existence is the product of Evo-Devo—Evolution, Development, and Epigenesis (Leffert, 2018). Sartre had the luxury of not having to consider embryology, child development, and their philosophical implications; we do not. However, the whole point of Sartre's (1947/2007) formulation was to repudiate Kierkegaard's position that

---

14 This is *not* the same thing as saying that sentient life begins at conception or that this *beginning* of Existence guarantees the development of a Human Being: only the possibility.

Essence comes first and is provided by God, and to assert that Existence comes first, the Essence of being Human only comes after.

The art of Existential interpretation

A last area of Existential concern is the role of interpretation in Psychotherapy and Psychoanalysis. Over the past century Psychoanalytic Psychotherapies have developed different understandings of the interpretive process beyond making the Unconscious (sic) Conscious. Auchincloss and Samberg (2012) still, however, rather narrowly construe it to be the analyst's verbal communication to the patient of her understanding of his unconscious mental life. Laplanche and Pontalis (1967/1973), although writing nearly a half-century earlier, offer a more expansive definition as the procedure that, via investigation, brings out the latent meaning of what the patient says and does. The reliance on meaning already has an Existential flavor. In both, the premise is that something *already there* is being made explicit. I take a much broader view of the process. I include the meanings of the word *interpretation* from common usage: to interpret as in offering a translation and to present a subjective rendition such as to play a piece of music, perform a play, or describe a painting. From an Existential point of view, there is a particular, even essential, place for interpretation in therapeutic *praxis*. It addresses situations in which there is an unrealistic or incomplete view of the Self, or of the relations of Self to World, or even of the relations between different parts of the Self. *Interpretations provide Meaning*; alongside the more orthodox views that Meaning is already present is the Contemporary view that *interpretation makes new Meaning*. Frequently, it also addresses the way that unreality grows out of a confusion between past and present Self and World and interpretation is the only way through such an ontological thicket.

Interpreting something that the therapist thinks already exists unconsciously in the patient, a fairly orthodox procedure, potentially has risks. How do we *really* know of this unconscious existence and, if not, are we actually offering a reconstruction? In doing so, we are potentiality creating a separate mental event rather than informing what already exists mentally. It also serves to treat the patient not as a Human Being but as a passive recipient. If instead we offer a construction (Hoffman, 1998) based on what we and the patient know about him, we add meaning to the process. An interpretation reframes the existence of Self in World. This is an Existentialist enterprise.

Existential Psychology differs from other theoretical frameworks in that it seeks out how we deal with the inevitability of our own eventual Death as a fundamental piece of the Human Condition. We have already discussed the way that responses to Death are either Thrown or Fallen. Patients do always make references to Death but we must listen for them and, at some point, respond to them interpretively. John, a man in his 70s, has been in analysis for several years. He has advanced heart failure, a condition he knows will eventually prove fatal. What he doesn't know is just when. He is frightened of dying and, indeed, this was the major reason he sought treatment. Instead of treating this as a displaced fear having to do with some past experience, I took it, Existentially, at face value. In exploring his fear, it first emerged that what he feared was the *experience of the moment of dying* and the complete loss of control it entailed. Dying unconsciously, in his sleep perhaps, did not trouble him at all. He was also frightened of what would happen to his body after he died; its being buried to decay or being burnt terrified him. I pointed out that for this to matter meant that he was envisioning death as a state in which he was, in some fashion, still alive, still present: a denial of death. Although still frightened he has, with help, come to see death's inevitability, and has struggled to find meaning in everything he does. After considerable further work, he came in on a Monday and described the weekend he has just spent with his son and daughter and their families. The son has a swimming pool, and they had spent the day around it. It was a perfect day. At one point, John was in the pool by himself, watching everyone. It struck him that there will be such perfect afternoons after he is gone. Everyone will be there, just as they are, but without him. And that will be fine because, for them, life will still exist. The realization makes him happy.

Let me offer an example of a more widely defined kind of interpretation. A patient in her 30s angrily describes a fight her mother picked with her that morning over who to include in the guest list for her party. She goes on about this at some length. It feels like something is missing. After several minutes I say with emphasis "Tell me how this makes you *feel*." She takes only a moment to say, "It makes me sad" and tears up. "Not how you would want a mother to act," I add and she nods. Most therapists might not want, as I would, to call the question an interpretation. I think of it as such because it leads to increasing meaning, offers the patient the opportunity to construct it, and does not add anything that I might have falsely construed.

In an Existential therapy, the singular focus is on interpreting the Absurd. In the examples above, the Absurdity was in imagining that death could be nullified or that the young woman was simply angry. Absurdity exists in false constructs of World or Self or Desire, sometimes derived from past traumas or conflicts, and these are the things that must be interpreted. Trauma itself is Absurd. It produces anxiety, depression, and meaninglessness. It is inevitably repetitive: All therapies run the risk of enhancing those repetitions through over-analysis: Existentialist approaches seek to treat Absurdity by restoring Meaning.

Some final thoughts about Absurdity

The replacement of Absurdity with Meaning is a contemporary restatement of the psychoanalytic premise of replacing neurotic misery with everyday unhappiness. It goes beyond the later premise of replacing immobilization and compulsion with internal freedom and autonomy. It seeks healing and change rather than insight and the lifting of repression. To rephrase the ideas of Loewald (1960) and the Shanes (Shane, Shane, & Gales, 1997): The Absurdity of the old relationship is replaced by the Authenticity of the new.

Some patients are ready for the new relationship at the start of a therapy while others must first work through the old.

In addition to finding meaning in life we seek out *Absurd Meaning*, the narrative memory of which it is a part, and the fantasies that go with it. We seek an emerging experience of our own Existence. It does not solve one's problems but is rather a *precondition* for their solution. This *I am* is not related to transference; indeed, transference involves Being only in the context of a particular other (an Absurd species of *Mitwelt*) as opposed to being in the context of World. The overarching question of existential Human Being, in whatever language has been used is how does one contend with the Absurdity of life, with its *inconsistencies of meaning*? The fact that this question does not appear in psychoanalytic thinking of whatever ilk (existential psychoanalysis, late intersubjectivity theory, and self-psychology come close) dooms them.

There is an inherent Absurdity to life that lies beyond our abilities to engage. It grows out of the fact that we have the potential for great control over the small events of life but that the larger, life-changing ones are often unpredictable. They are governed by Complexity and Chaos (Leffert, 2010). They do not, however render us helpless but rather define a space in which we can set out to make Meaning. Defining that space differently, in terms of how the Self makes its way in the outside and inside Worlds, we move on to the next chapter.

References

Andrews, F. M., & Withey, S. B. (1976). *Social indicators of well-being: America's perception of life quality*. New York: Plenum.

Auchincloss, E. L., & Samberg, E. (2012). *Psychoanalytic terms and concepts* (4th edn). New Haven: Yale University Press.

Baars, B. J. (2003). The fundamental role of context: Unconscious shaping of conscious information. In B. J. Baars, W. P. Banks & J. B. Newman (Eds), *Essential sources in the scientific study of consciousness* (pp. 761–775). Cambridge: MIT Press (Original work published in 1988).

Baars, B. J. (2003). How does a serial, integrated, and very limited stream of consciousness emerge from a nervous system that is mostly unconscious, distributed, parallel and of enormous capacity? In B. J. Baars, W. P. Banks, & J. B. Newman (Eds), *Essential sources in the scientific study of consciousness* (pp. 1123–1129). Cambridge: MIT Press (Original work published in 1993).

Boss, M. (1963). *Psychoanalysis and Daseinanalysis*. New York: Basic Books.

Bowlby, J. (1973). *Separation: Anxiety and anger, Attachment and loss* (Vol. 2). New York: Basic Books.

Camus, A. (1958). Caligula. In A. Camus, *Caligula and 3 other plays* (S. Gilbert, Trans.) (pp. 1–74). New York: Vintage Books. (Original work published in 1944).

Camus, A. (1989). *The stranger* (M. Ward, Trans.). New York: Vintage Books. (Original work published in 1942).

Camus, A. (1991). The myth of Sisyphus. In A. Camus, *The myth of Sisyphus and other essays* (J. O'Brien, Trans.) (pp. 3–138). New York: Vintage Books. (Original work published in 1942).

Christakis, N. A., & Fowler, J. H. (2009). *Connected: The surprising power of our social networks and how they shape our lives.* New York: Little, Brown and Company.

Craik, K. (1952). *The nature of explanation.* Cambridge: Cambridge University Press. (Original work published in 1943).

Diener, E. (1984). Subjective well-being. *Psychological Bulletin, 95*, 542–575.

Diener, E. (1994). Assessing Subjective Well-Being: Progress and opportunities. *Social Indicators Research, 31*, 103–157.

Diener, E. (Ed.). (2009). *The science of well being: The collected works of Ed Diener.* New York: Springer.

Diener, E., & Diener, M. (1995). Cross-cultural correlates of life satisfaction and self-esteem. *Journal of Personality and Social Psychology, 68*, 653–663.

Doidge, N. (2007). *The brain that changes itself.* New York: Viking.

Erikson, E. (1953). Growth and crisis of the healthy personality. In C. Kluckhohn & H. A. Murray (Eds), <i>Personality in nature, society, and culture (pp. 185–225). New York: Alfred A. Knopf. (Original work published in 1950).

Erikson, E. (1963). *Childhood and society* (2nd edn). New York: W.W. Norton & Co (Original work published in 1950).

Frankl, V. E. (2006). *Man's search for meaning* (I. Lasch, Trans.). Boston: Beacon Press. (Original work published in 1959).

Frankl, V. E. (2014). *The will to meaning: Foundations and applications of logotherapy.* New York: Plume Books. (Original work published in 1969).

Freud, S. (1959). Inhibition, symptom, and anxiety. In J. Strachey (Ed.), *Standard Edition* (pp. 87–178). London: Hogarth Press. (Original work published in 1926).

Fromm, E. (1994). *Escape from freedom.* New York: H.R. Holt and Company. (Original work published in 1941).

Gould, S. J. (1989). *Wonderful life: The Burgess Shale and the nature of history.* New York: W.W. Norton & Co.

Heidegger, M. (1982). *The basic problems of phenomenology* (A. Hofstadter, Trans. Rev. ed.). Bloomington: Indiana University Press. (Original work published in 1975).

Heidegger, M. (2010). *Being and time* (J. Stambaugh & D. J. Schmidt, Trans.). Albany: State University of New York. (Original work published in 1927).

Herculano-Houzel, S. (2012). The remarkable, yet not extraordinary, human brain as a scaled-up primate brain and its associated cost. *Proceedings of the National Academy of Science, 109*, 10661–10668.

Hoffman, I. Z. (1998). *Ritual and spontaneity in the psychoanalytic process.* Hillsdale: The Analytic Press.

Husserl, E. (1970). *The crisis of European sciences and transcendental phenomenology* (D. Cairns, Trans.). Evanston: Northwestern University Press. (Original work published in 1937).

Husserl, E. (1983). *Ideas pertaining to a pure phenomenology and to a phenomenological philosophy: Book one: General introduction to a pure phenomenology* (F. Kersten, Trans.). New York: Springer (Original work published in 1913).

Huttenlocher, P. R. (1979). Synaptic density in human frontal cortex—Developmental changes and effects of aging. *Brain Research, 163*, 195–205.

Kahneman, D. (2003). Objective happiness. In D. Kahneman, E. Diener, & N. Schwartz (Eds), *Well-being: The foundations of hedonic psychology* (pp. 3–25). New York: Russell Sage Foundation. (Original work published in 1999).

Kahneman, D., Diener, E., & Schwartz, N. (Eds). (2003). *Well-being: The foundations of hedonic psychology*. New York: Russell Sage Foundation. (Original work published in 1999).

Kahneman, D., Slovic, P., & Tversky, A. (Eds). (1982). *Judgement under uncertainty: Heuristics and biases*. Cambridge: Cambridge University Press.

Kahneman, D., & Tversky, A. (2000). Prospect theory: An analysis of decisions under risk. In D. Kahneman & A. Tversky (Eds), Choices, values, and frames (pp. 17–43). Cambridge: Cambridge University Press. (Original work published in 1979).

Kesebir, P., & Diener, E. (2009). In pursuit of happiness: Empirical answers to philosophical questions. In E. Diener (Ed.), *The science of Well-Being; The collected works of Ed Diener* (pp. 59–74). New York: Springer. (Original work published in 2008).

Laplanche, J., & Pontalis, J. B. (1973). *The language of psycho-analysis* (D. Nicholson-Smith, Trans.). New York: W.W. Norton & Co. (Original work published in 1967).

Laszlo, E. (1996). *The systems view of the world: A holistic vision for our time*. Cresskill: Hampton Press Inc. (Original work published in 1972).

Latour, B. (1993). *We have never been modern* (C. Porter, Trans.). Cambridge: Harvard University Press. (Original work published in 1991).

Leffert, M. (2007a). A contemporary integration of modern and postmodern trends in psychoanalysis. *Journal of the American Psychoanalytic Association, 55*, 177–197.

Leffert, M. (2007b). Postmodernism and its impact on psychoanalysis. *Bulletin of the Menninger Clinic, 71*, 15–34.

Leffert, M. (2008). Complexity and postmodernism in contemporary theory of psychoanalytic change. *Journal of the American Academy of Psychoanalysis and Dynamic Psychiatry, 36*, 517–542.

Leffert, M. (2010). *Contemporary psychoanalytic foundations*. London: Routledge.

Leffert, M. (2013). *The therapeutic situation in the 21st century*. New York: Routledge.

Leffert, M. (2016). *Phenomenology, uncertainty, and care in the therapeutic encounter*. New York: Routledge.

Leffert, M. (2017). *Positive psychoanalysis: Aesthetics, desire, and subjective well-being*. New York: Routledge.

Leffert, M. (2018). *Psychoanalysis and the birth of the self: A radical interdisciplinary approach*. London: Routledge.

Loewald, H. W. (1960). On the therapeutic action of psycho-analysis. *The International Journal of Psychoanalysis, 41*(16–33).

May, R. (1969). *Love and will*. New York: W.W. Norton & Co.

May, R. (1983). *The discovery of being*. New York: W.W. Norton & Co.

May, R., Angel, E., & Ellenberger, H. F. (Eds). (1958). *Existence: New directions in psychiatry and psychology*. New York: Simon & Schuster.

Molnar-Szakacs, I., & Arzy, S. (2009). Searching for an integrated self-representation. *Communicative and Integrative Biology, 2*, 365–367.

Nisbett, R. E., & Wilson, T. (1977). Telling more than we can know: Verbal reports on mental processes. *Psychological Review, 84*, 231–259.

Panksepp, J. (1998). *Affective neuroscience: The foundations of human and animal emotions*. Oxford: Oxford University Press.

Panksepp, J. (2009). Brain emotional systems and qualities of mental life: From animal models of affect to implications for psychotherapeutics. In D. Fosha, D. J. Siegal, & M. F. Solomon (Eds), *The healing power of emotion: Affective neuroscience, development, and clinical practice* (pp. 1–26). New York: W.W. Norton & Co.

Panksepp, J., & Biven, L. (2012). *The archaeology of mind: Neuroevolutionary origins of human emotions*. New York: W.W. Norton & Co.

Panksepp, J., & Watt, D. (2011). What is basic about basic emotions? Lasting lessons from affective neuroscience. *Emotion Review, 3*, 1–10.

Penfield, W., & Penfield, J. (1954). *Epilepsy and the functional anatomy of the human brain* (2 ed.). New York: Little, Brown and Company.

Plato (1999). *Symposium* (W. Hamilton, Trans.). London: Penguin Books.

Risse, G. L., & Gazzaniga, M. S. (1978). Well-kept secrets of the right hemisphere: A carotid amytal study of restricted memory transfer. *Neurology, 28*, 487–495.

Rumelhart, D. E., & McClelland, J. L. (1986). *Parallel distributed processing* (Vol. 1). Cambridge: MIT Press.

Sartre, J.-P. (1989). No exit. In J.-P. Sartre, *No exit and three other plays* (pp. 1–46). New York: Vintage Books. (Original work published in 1946).

Sartre, J.-P. (2003). *Being and nothingness* (H. Barnes, Trans.). London: Routledge. (Original work published in 1943).

Sartre, J.-P. (2007). *Existentialism is a humanism* (C. Macomber, Trans.). New Haven: Yale University Press. (Original work published in 1947).

Sartre, J.-P. (2013). *Nausea* (L. Alexander, Trans.). New York: New Directions. (Original work published in 1938).

Schacter, D. L. (1996). *Searching for memory*. New York: Basic Books.

Schore, A. N. (1994). *Affect regulation and the origin of the self*. Hillside: Lawrence Earlbaum Associates.

Schore, A. N. (2003a). *Affect dysregulation and disorders of the self*. New York: W.W. Norton & Co.

Schore, A. N. (2003b). *Affect regulation and the repair of the self*. New York: W.W. Norton & Co.

Schore, A. N. (2009). Right-brain affect regulation: An essential mechanism of development, trauma, dissociation, and psychotherapy. In D. Fosha, D. J. Siegal, & M. F. Solomon (Eds), *The healing power of emotion: Affective neuroscience, development, and clinical practice* (pp. 112–144). New York: W.W. Norton & Co.

Schore, A. N. (2011). The right brain implicit self lies at the core of psychoanalysis. *Psychoanalytic Dialogues, 21*, 75–100.

Shane, M., Shane, E., & Gales, M. (1997). *Intimate attachments: Towards a new self psychology*. New York: Guilford Press.

Simon, H. A. (1956). Rational choice and the structure of the environment. *Psychological Review, 63*, 129–138.

Sperry, R. W. (1969). A modified concept of consciousness. *Psychological Review, 76*, 532–536.

Sperry, R. W., Gazzaniga, M. S., & Bogen, J. E. (1969). The neocortical commissures: Syndromes of hemisphere disconnection. In P. J. Vinken & G. W. Bruyn (Eds), *Handbook of clinical neurology* (Vol. 4). Amsterdam: North Holland Publishing Company.

Spitz, R. (1965). *The first year of life*. New York: International Universities Press.

Stoltzfus, B. (2003). Camus and Hemingway: The solidarity of rebellion. *The International Fiction Review, 30(1)*.

Tulving, E. (2003). Memory and consciousness. In B. J. Baars, W. P. Banks, & J. B. Newman (Eds), *Essential sources in the scientific study of consciousness* (pp. 575–591). Cambridge: MIT Press. (Original work published in 1985).

Tulving, E. (2005). Episodic memory and autonoesis: Uniquely human? In H. S. Terrace & J. Metcalfe (Eds), *The missing link in cognition: Origins of self-reflective consciousness* (pp. 3–56). Oxford: Oxford University Press.
Tversky, A., & Kahneman, D. (1982). Judgment under uncertainty: Heuristics and biases. In D. Kahneman, P. Slovic, & A. Tversky (Eds), *Judgment under uncertainty: Heuristics and biases* (pp. 3–20). Cambridge: Cambridge University Press. (Original work published in 1974).
Tversky, A., & Kahneman, D. (2000). Rational choice and the framing of decisions. In D. Kahneman & A. Tversky (Eds), Choices, values, and frames (pp. 209–223). Cambridge: Cambridge University Press. (Original work published in 1986).
Uddin, L. Q., Iacoboni, M., Lange, C., & Keenan, J. P. (2007). The self and social cognition: The role of cortical midline structures and mirror neurons. *Trends in Cognitive Sciences, 11,* 153–157.
von Bertalanffy, L. (1968). *General systems theory: Foundations, development, applications.* New York: George Brazilier.
Winnicott, D. W. (1960). The theory of the parent-infant relationship. *The International Journal of Psychoanalysis, 41,* 585–595.
Winnicott, D. W. (1965). *The maturational processes and the facilitating environment: Studies in the theory of emotional development.* New York: International Universities Press.
Winnicott, D. W. (1968). Playing: Its theoretical status in the clinical situation. *International Journal of Psychoanalysis, 49,* 591–599.
Winnicott, D. W. (1975). *Through paediatrics to psycho-analysis.* New York: Basic Books.
Yalom, I. D. (1980). *Existential psychotherapy.* New York: Basic Books.
Zaretsky, R. (2013). *A life worth living: Albert Camus and the quest for meaning.* Cambridge: Belknap Press.

5 Culture and History
How Self engages World

Introduction

We have, over the preceding four chapters, been building an argument that the central and unique feature of the Being of Human Beings (this is already a reformulation of what would have been called even a decade or two ago, the Being of *Man*) is how our lives are centered on the quest for Meaning in the face of Absurdity. While a part of that quest can occur during a process of Self-reflection, most of it arises out of the Self's interactions with World, chosen or otherwise. In this chapter we are going to consider how Culture and History act to influence and define Meaning and how they can also present the individual with the Absurd. How the interactions of Self and World take place in the present is a product of an individual's Development and the unique Culture and History that they inhabit. Memory in its broadest sense, Developmental outcome, and the structure of the Self and its nervous system constitute a record of the impact of both History and Culture on the Self: its neurological and epigenetic memory (Leffert, 2018). These last two are defined narrowly as they shape the particular Self and broadly as they pertain to World as a whole. Finally, if we are going to consider the effect of World on Self, we are also going to have to consider the sometimes-disastrous effects of Self on World that have, for example, brought us to the climate crisis we now face. In taking this wider view of a Bio-Psycho-Social Self, we are going beyond what I would describe as the constrained understanding of the Self found in orthodox Existentialist thought.

Culture and History determine Being for the individual by *locating* them in very large groups of Human Beings that Christakis and Fowler (2009) call *Superorganisms*. As we shall see, such Superorganisms define Culture and exist in their own History; both are different in China, for example, from those in Western Europe.

In addressing the relations of Self and World, we have to consider what has been referred to topographically but really involves two linked ontological spaces: the one that practices conscious reflection and the one that does not. I think this terminology is necessary because Existential and Phenomenological authors have insisted on a clean break between the two with the former being the exclusive province of Human Beings. Consciousness, for them, is the singular aspect of the Existentialist enterprise. In insisting, to the contrary, on their relinkage (Leffert, 2016, present volume), one that goes beyond the standard linkages found in psychoanalytic theory (Leffert, 2010), I am positing that both influence the Being of Human Beings, that is, Dasein (Heidegger, 1927/2010).

When we are considering the parts of human behavior and reflection that go on outside of awareness we are again dealing with two sorts of processes that also influence each other. One has to do with operationally unconscious ways of engaging World, for example, the group of mental activities termed the Relational Unconsciousness (Gerson, 2004; Orange, 2000; Safran, 2006; Zeddies, 2000) while the other has to do with aspects of World that are perceived and processed outside of awareness, judgments made in the face of Uncertainty (Nisbett & Wilson, 1977; Tversky & Kahneman, 1986/2000), for example. Both of these involve considering the linked epistemological problems of Uncertainty and Unknowability.

In early 21st century America, we are dealing with unique and uncertain aspects of World. One is the particular political situation surrounding the Trump presidency that our Culture is currently struggling with (and *may* have resolved by the time you are reading this) and the *future-uncertainty* that it brings with it. The symptom of this Uncertainty, appearing regardless of the political and social orientation of the individual, is an intense, traumatic anxiety. We all see this daily in our practices although there is widespread disagreement about how to deal with it clinically (I will argue, perhaps controversially, for a particular therapeutic stance). The other aspect of World that is giving rise to at times crippling anxiety and depression is climate change: It has been termed *Eco-anxiety* (Nobel, 2007; Pihkala, 2018). It is not at all clear that the political and the meteorological are separable. Although these factors seem new and unique, they are not. Populations have often had to deal with catastrophic social and climactic change. If this chapter was being written in 1940 Britain, or 1942 America, or Germany (1938 if you were Jewish, 1945 if you weren't), populations would have faced similar crippling anxiety. Perhaps climate change is unique, or at least its ramifications are. But records of such climactic events are as old as the *Book of Genesis*, and Paleoclimatology documents climate change going back to prehistoric times with similar uncertainty concerning their final outcome for Human populations. In Phenomenological terms these various aspects of Being fall into two categories: the *Mitwelt* or the Social, and the *Umwelt*, the Physical.

Another category is also beginning to make its epistemological appearance: If we are considering how the Self relates to its outside, we will also have to consider how it relates to its *insides*. It has been recognized for some time that the human gastrointestinal tract is host to a kilogram or two of living bacteria. Beyond questions of GI health, the effects of antibiotics on them, and the strange practice known as "cleansing," not much thought has been given to them until quite recently. Now christened the *Microbiome* (Dinan,

Stilling, Stanton, & Cryan, 2015; Mayer, 2018), they have come to be seen as communicating with and influencing our Brain-Self in complex ways that include mood and dietary predilections. There is even tantalizing evidence that some bacteria actually live in our brains (Roberts, Farmer, & Walker, 2018). This is an area of intense research interest on which we can, at this time, only make some very preliminary and rudimentary observations.

It is best to proceed with inquiry into Self and World (*Eigenwelt* and *Mitwelt*) on two levels. First, we should discuss in Existential terms the ways in which Culture and History influence an individual's judgments of Meaning and Absurdity. This includes the way that present social forces, their history, and long-term societal structures and values impact the individual and, through Development, shape who they are and what they value. Then, we need to consider the *mechanisms* by which these forces act on the Self to shape identity and Meaning. Contrary to what might be termed classical Existentialist thinking, these socio-cultural mechanisms act on the Self mostly (but not entirely!) outside of its awareness. Before proceeding with this agenda, we need to refer back to a philosophical school that arose in part as a critique of Existentialism and Phenomenology and has, over the past three decades, also influenced Psychoanalysis. That school is Postmodernism (Leffert, 2007), particularly Post-Structuralism, and, for our purposes here, how it plays out ontologically in irreducible problems with knowability.

Unknowability and its post-structural effects on the ontology of the Self

In a previous introduction to Postmodernism (Leffert, 2010, Chapter 1), I took up a number of conditions of the postmodern project, all of which serve as qualifiers to a purely modernist Existentialist discourse based on the premise that some form of sustained inquiry would reveal at least a personal *truth*. Elliott and Spezzano (1996) identified three elements of a modernist/postmodernist debate: "an aesthetic debate over the nature of representation; philosophical and cultural issues of postmodernity; and the personal, cultural, and social issues found in a postmodern society" (Leffert, 2010, p. 3). All of these are relevant to our Existential concerns in addition to a fourth element: the need to characterize the very nature of discourse. McGowan (1991) adds that "within the configuration of postmodernism, two (or more) incompatible things are *desirable* and ... different strategies are involved in the effort to think these incompatibilities together" (p. 89, italics added). These considerations make Epistemology into a Dialectical-Constructivist project capable of simultaneously holding in mind conflicting representations of things (*choses*). It should be remembered that this constitutes a reformulation (not a critical disposal) of Husserl's (1913/1983) battle cry of a "Return to the things themselves!" It involves Derrida's organizing concept of *différance*: differing elements are arranged into *sheaves of différance* (Derrida, 1982) that exist in a state of dynamic tension and that for every way of proceeding, every *path*, there is also an opposite way, a *counterpath* (Malabou & Derrida, 1999/2004). These postmodern contentions all bear directly on *any* Discourse on Meaning.

A Postmodern position suggests multiple forms of unknowability that we must contend with. First, there is an infinite amount of information about and in the world, much of which is beyond our ability to know[1]; some of that which we might consider necessary if we could but know it. Then, there is a great deal about our Selves that we do not know; some of which we could find out through self-reflection, reflection on World, or discourse with another Self, others that we could not. There are also unknown (not unknow*able*) things about World and Self that we could ascertain through investigation. Finally, there is a problem with both for which the Heisenberg Uncertainty Principle serves as a *metaphor*. This is, simply put, that the act of reflection or discourse *changes* the nature of the thing that is being reflected upon or discussed so that the thing itself cannot be known "objectively" in isolation. A variant of this is interreferentiality, the process in which people or things cannot be known singly in isolation but only as part of a group or couple that constantly effect and modify each other.[2] We can see this problem facing Roquentin (Sartre, 1938/2013) and Meursault (Camus, 1942/1989) who are then irrevocably changed by their knowing: Their pasts then seem to fall away from them as unknowable. The Self is embedded in a socio-cultural matrix that it cannot fully know. A major mechanism of that embeddedness, perhaps surprisingly, is *character*. Character can be made available discursively in the psychoanalytic therapies.

A further distinction must be made between the similar seeming concepts: Unknowability and Uncertainty. Unknowability is an ontological state of World and Self located in time; it is objective. Uncertainty refers to a state of Dasein; it is *subjective*, a state of Being and Mind. Unknowability can be one of the reasons for Uncertainty but there are others; they have to do with how Dasein sees its World and itself, what it considers and looks for, but also *what it permits itself to see*.

Postmodernism concerns itself first and foremost with the interface between Self and World. That interface which, less obviously, is of equal importance to Existentialism is, by its nature interreferential; on a micro level, World and Self are constantly affecting each other, often in unknowable ways. The Existential piece that interests us here, is that Meaning and Absurdity are formed *at the interface* in the same interreferential way.

---

1 This includes some things that, while unknowable *now*, might become knowable in the future when new ways of finding out or measuring are developed. An understanding of Consciousness might well fall into this category.
2 A bodily example can serve to illustrate these points. As I sit here, I know nothing about what my heart is doing except, by inference, that it must be beating. If someone performs an echocardiogram by applying an ultrasound to my chest, we could know much more about what my heart is doing by looking at the image of it that appears on the ultrasound's video display. But to perform these measurements, I would have to lie in a particular position and perhaps hold or release my breath; these activities would alter what my heart is doing and the measurements we would make.

Dasein: the bridge between Self and World

Existentialists such as Sartre and Camus, in developing their ideas about Absurdity and Meaning, did not really "get it" that Heidegger (1975/1982) had already somewhat paved the way for them. There are many reasons for this. Perhaps the most basic of them is that they did much of their work before serviceable translations of Heidegger were even available. Another is the fact that they were French and, with the Nazi occupation of France and Heidegger's Nazi connections, they found him hard to stomach. Finally, Heidegger and Sartre were each supremely arrogant and, with their modes of thought and writing being *so* different, found little means or reason to make common cause (Bakewell, 2016).

Very briefly, Heidegger's concept of Dasein can be seen to lead to Existentialist ideas about Being. For our purposes here, the significant aspect of Dasein is that it links Human Beings and World. Existence (the usual as opposed to the philosophical translation of Dasein) involves a being *there*, some kind of characterization of the *manner and nature* of the Self's (my term now) location in World. There are the three ways of Being-in-World—Everydayness, Thrownness, and Fallen—with the first two speaking to Meaning and the third to Absurdity. Then there are the specifics of the geography the Self attaches itself to. Dasein renders a Human Being and World inseparable in the same way as the concept of Self that insists on a Bio-Psycho-Social Self does. An intact Dasein combines two ways of Being—Thrownness and Everydayness—a regression to a state of Fallenness represents a failure of Dasein [the Self]. We would have to consider Thrownness the state of Being that *requires* Consciousness because it involves the awareness of life's finitude and the inevitably of death (the banishment of both is entailed in Fallen states).

Keeping all of this in mind, let us turn to Culture and Society.

Culture and society

Culture has not much been a subject of Existentialist or Phenomenological inquiry. Consciously or Unconsciously, it has been assumed. The philosophers performing these inquiries in Europe during the first half of the 20th century did not question the implications of the fact that they pertained to Western Europe and further to what might loosely be called the intellectual classes of Western Europe. Mid-century clinical American writers *implicitly* added North America to their geographical considerations and "white" to the class of people they pertained to. They did not specifically consider what the search for Meaning was about for people outside of these classes; it is likely that Heidegger would simply have considered them to be immersed in Everydayness (*Alltäglichkeit*).

If it is argued that being human entails an orientation towards Meaning, then, varying from culture to culture and person to person, Meaning is to be found, not in any particular order, in work, play (as either participants or observers), relationships, and in the pursuit of *higher goods*, whatever these might entail. In Asia, the latter might involve honoring one's parents and ancestors, while in Europe and America it would involve the pursuit of social goods and, in Judaism, loving kindness (*chesed*) and healing the world (*tikun olam*). Religion has been both a source of Meaning and of Absurdity. Meaning, Value, and Happiness *all* have a cultural component. Although they demonstrate some degree of overlap, it is important to remember that they are discreet components of Being. Vast amounts of writing exist on all of these topics; there is not a great deal that can be said *in brief* about them that would not be trivial.

We are learning much more about what happens when a society changes in catastrophic ways for some of its members. The situation faced by Jews and other marginalized, depreciated groups in Nazi Germany during the Holocaust readily jumps out at us. Both the Fallen deaths in the gas chambers and life in the Absurdity of the Concentration Camps are relevant here. Frankl's (1959/2006) writing on the search for Meaning is grounded in his experiences as an inmate of the Camps and is searingly applicable.

> Only those prisoners could keep alive whom, after years of trekking from camp to camp had lost all scruples in their fight for existence; they were prepared to use every means, honest and otherwise, even brutal force, theft and betrayal of their friends in order to save themselves. We who have come back, by the aid of many lucky chances or miracles ... we know: *the best of us did not return.*
>
> (pp. 5–6, italics added).

And,

> Man *can* preserve a vestige of spiritual freedom, of independence of mind, even in such terrible conditions of psychic and physical stress [as existed in the concentration camps]. It is this spiritual freedom—which cannot be taken away—that makes life meaningful and purposeful.
>
> (pp. 65, 67).

And,

> The way in which a man accepts his fate and all the suffering it entails, the way in which he takes up his cross, gives him ample opportunity—even under the most difficult circumstances—to add a deeper meaning to his life.
>
> (p. 67)[3]

---

3 The last two are highly reminiscent of Camus' (1942/1991) Sisyphus.

In the late 20th and early 21st centuries we have, in addition to Third World genocides resulting from cultural degradation, seen significant patterns of migration and emigration. These cultural trends have brought emigres to our societies suffering from PTSD and the aftereffects of torture and malnutrition. In some instances, Western societies have offered these emigres psychological as well as physical care, but in others they have been largely ignored or rejected.

The American Dream

A unique organizing principle that integrates all of these areas for people in the United States, *Americans*, is the pursuit of the *American Dream*. It formulates a right to a meaningful and good life. It includes meaningful relationships but requires a satisfactory sense of Vocation and possibility. Appearing first in the Colonial[4] and early Post-Colonial period (McCullough, 2019), it focused on pioneer settlers pushing West in search of an opportunity that was uniquely American. Often involving great sacrifice, the meaning to be found in the Dream did not necessarily include immediate personal satisfaction and gratification but rather that pioneers were laying the groundwork for a meaningful, good life for their children and grandchildren. The *elements* of the Dream, not the Dream itself, gradually morphed over the 19th and 20th centuries from the Way West and a sense of personal freedom and possibility (if you weren't a slave) to more individually formulated components. The Dream became more of an umbrella encompassing these growingly diverse elements. Towards the end of the 20th century, perhaps dating from the lost Vietnam war, the Dream *began* to show its age and its possibilities became curtailed. By the early 21st century, society had begun, nationally and globally, to fail its members. Institutional possibility, regardless of socio-economic class, had shrunk; there was no more room at the inn.

Across class and profession, the 1950s were the heyday of white, male possibility, with brown and female possibility *beginning* a decade later. (This is, of course, an oversimplification, but a meaningful one.) Incomes were compatible with a fulfilling life; they would begin to become less so perhaps three decades later. These broad trends were fully reflected in American Psychoanalysis. Psychiatrists coming home from the war impressed by the effectiveness of brief, psychoanalytically oriented psychotherapy in restoring to function soldiers disabled by what was then called Combat Fatigue (and is now called PTSD) sought out psychoanalytic training. Serendipitously, these new (to American society as a whole) therapies had captured the public's imagination in an era still-lacking in effective psychotropic medication (the first antidepressants were

---

4 Indeed, elements of the Dream could be found in Pre-Colonial myths involving searches for the fountain of youth or the seven cities of gold, whose streets were said to be paved with the precious metal.

not to appear until the early 1960s). It became the golden age of psychoanalytic practice. (Senior analysts were often known to *only* see patients in five, occasionally four times weekly analysis and imagined things would always be that way.) Similar trends could be seen in the Academy. Public universities mushroomed in the postwar years[5] with doctoral programs expanding to train the faculty to staff them. Meanwhile, an expanding postwar economy insured stable employment and rising salaries that offered a secure and meaningful life.

As a result, the Social environment remained stable, and the issues that brought people to seek therapy or analysis were either intrapsychic or relational. There are, however, a number of important caveats here. The first is that relational problems as a source of mental illness and psychopathology were only poorly understood during this period and, at best, only dealt with implicitly in therapy. Although Existential Psychoanalysis *was* getting off the ground in the 1950s and Sullivan's Interpersonal Psychotherapy was established, both schools, as a percentage of available therapists, were minute. More important still, this social environment of stable promise that did not cause psychic pain and suffering (the reasons, after all, for seeking treatment in the first place) *really only applied to white men*. The insoluble problem for women seeking therapy during this period was that, by and large, neither they or their (mostly male) therapists could see that Western society offered a repressive environment or, if they could see it, could not imagine that there was a way they could struggle against it and prevail. (It is equally pointless to even imagine, at the time, that reasonable social possibility, let alone psychotherapy, could exist for black [sic] or homosexual [sic] people.)

These trends, both the positive and the exclusionary, were to change as the second half of the 20th century unfolded. Work tended to become less of a reliable source of meaning and became, instead, a battle for security. As sources of meaning began to fail, an element of social Absurdity began to enter American life. If we were to look to the role of macro-cultural trends in these changes, three events stand out: the triple assassinations of the Kennedy brothers and Martin Luther King; our engagement in and loss of the geopolitically as well as morally corrupt Vietnam war; and the Nixon impeachment. They signaled a growing disparity between the American Dream and life as it was. Thinking back clinically to those events occurring a generation ago, it is interesting that, while we were at times deeply affected by them, they remained for the great majority of us psychically external[6] and hence not a subject of Therapeutic Discourse.

With the advent of the 21st century, the American Dream was in trouble. We grow into Meaning as we grow into the Culture that defines it. Social change can impact Culture so as to make the usual sources of Meaning

---

5 The University of California under the leadership of Clark Kerr epitomized this trend.
6 PTSD occurring in men and women who served in Vietnam (Lifton, 1973) being an obvious exception to this observation.

unavailable. If we look at the three index occupations we have considered—traditional (20th century) white- and blue-collar industry,[7] the Academy, and Psychoanalysis—we see declining incomes relative to inflation, a decline in meaningful employment, employment security, and an increasing awareness of life's growing Absurdity.

Manufacturing moved overseas as American labor lost its competitiveness. Plant closures and increasing automation drove people (mostly men) out of work or forced them to work for much-reduced salaries. They (again by-and-large) did not see their failure to adapt as a psychological problem but rather as a failure of government to return them to the social conditions of a half-century earlier. Plagued by untreated depression and rising suicide rates, they tended to seek palliation in drugs and alcohol rather than psychotherapy. A further shift in these problems occurred from brown urban to white urban/suburban and rural populations. What became clear in all of this was that external societal changes were at least contributing to and at most causing intrapsychic changes, that is, psychopathology. The psychopathology was best discussed in Existentialist terms (Frankl, 1959/2006; May, 1958). This knowledge did not, however, find expression in the allocation of societal resources to address the problem which, in descending order, were devoted instead to interdiction of the supply of illicit drugs, treatment (particularly of drug overdoses), and ways of improving the current fit of sub-populations to the world in which they lived.[8]

Members of the Academy faced similar problems during the early 21st century, if their responses to them were less desperate. As the capacity of the college and university system expanded, the markets for its graduates declined. A bachelor's degree, which had formerly constituted a ticket to a white-collar job, no longer did so; students also often graduated from college with no sense of vocation and deeply in debt. Meanwhile, the faculty positions that the postwar expansion of graduate education was designed to fill had indeed been filled by the end of the century. While an increasing demand for graduate degrees in industry and business persisted, the same could not be said for liberal arts training. For roughly the first decade of the new century, graduates perceived a worsening job market but retained the conviction that positions would eventually come their way. The human adjustments and depressions that followed when it began to appear that such convictions were misplaced did lead some numbers of graduates to seek psychotherapy or reduced fee psychoanalysis. By the second decade, a reassessment had taken place in which students realized that they would never find college teaching positions in their chosen fields. That left adjunct positions, secondary school teaching

---

7 Information technology constituting an obvious and dramatic exception to this trend.
8 Without this last effort people, usually the young, who could change or leave did so, leaving behind a bitter population even less able to cope.

and applied jobs in industry.[9] Faculties were slow to admit to the problem but, when they did, began counselling applicants about the realities of their job prospects and offering their students seminars in seeking employment outside of the academy. A corollary to these trends was an increasing demand for graduate training in the professions without the realization that these jobs were changing as well, often for the worse.

Psychoanalysis as a profession manifests similar trends although they appeared perhaps three decades earlier and were met with higher levels of denial. It is in the nature of the practice of our profession that it has brought with it some degree of social isolation, particularly so for training analysts whose practices often include some guarantee of psychoanalytic work in the analysis of candidates[10] that insulates them economically. The tremendous costs of psychoanalytic training, payable in both time and money, also encouraged candidates to deny their predicament. The incursion of reality in the 21st century led denial to give way to disavowal in which reality was acknowledged but individuals continued to act as if this was not the case.

As Psychoanalysis began to be seen as undesirably anachronistic it became harder to attract new patients to it. As this trend expanded in the 21st century, more and more established Psychoanalysts began to refer to themselves in the way they interfaced with the community—web sites, business cards, social conversations—as *Psychotherapists*. Falling incomes led the profession to appeal less to highly paid white male Psychiatrists and more to a wider, gender neutral range of professionals who came to the field with briefer, less costly, professional training.

My own experiences can serve as an illustration of these dilemmas. First committed to psychoanalytic training while still a medical student, I sought that training at the then-new San Diego Psychoanalytic Institute in 1975. The community was in the midst of a phase of exponential growth in which the founding fathers (no mothers here) and original candidates had full practices. Such was not my experience in training (I took my first control case at a fee of $1.25 per session), but I assumed time and graduation would solve the problem. I graduated in 1981 and was generally well thought of. When a year had gone by with things no better for me or my classmates, I made the unusual decision that I would make a geographic move so I could have the professional life I found meaningful (the only thing unusual here was my willingness to move). I began doing research and found Minneapolis, a developing Psychoanalytic community on a par with San Diego circa 1970. Before I left, the then Dean in San Diego assured me, with his full practice,

---

9 Graduates of doctoral programs in physics, for example, found that their math skills were in high demand in the financial services industry, particularly in investment analysis.

10 This varied from institute to institute. A training analyst in a Midwestern institute told me sometime in the 1990s that his institute had 60 TAs with many(?), including himself, never having analyzed a candidate.

that this was only a temporary blip and my move was unnecessary. I made the move in early 1983 and the practice I imagined came with it.[11] As it turned out, my experience in San Diego was not a blip but the start of a national trend[12] that would find the average American psychoanalyst with, if lucky, a single analytic patient.

All of these groups shared a transition from denial to disavowal in which the personal failure of the Dream was acknowledged but possibility was retained. Doctoral programs continued to exist without faculty jobs, and Psychoanalytic Institutes largely staffed by faculty without psychoanalytic practices continued to train psychoanalysts. These situations came to more and more resemble that faced by Sisyphus (Camus, 1942/1991), who was able to successfully find personal Meaning in an Absurd World.

Although we don't label it as such, patients often come to us with a combination of internally created problems (infantile psychopathology) in conjunction with personal failures of the American Dream. In past years (and to some extent still), our tendency as psychoanalysts has been to prioritize material from the infantile past as being of central importance in the treatment of our patients. In an extreme form of this prioritization, these present-day issues arising in the *Umwelt* and *Mitwelt* have been labeled as resistances and interpreted as such. I have posited that such a therapeutic stance becomes a power transaction (Leffert, 2013, Chapter 1) that drives a patient into rebellion or passive submission and impairs Therapeutic Action. In recent years, fewer analysts and therapists have taken this position.

Ellen, a 28-year-old single woman, had had several years of twice-weekly psychoanalytic psychotherapy in another city that had focused, with good results, on her highly ambivalent relationship with her father. Both her social phobia and periodic attacks of eczema were much improved. After completing a Doctorate in Latin American literature and finding a post-doc at the University of California, she sought therapy with me for depression. It emerged that her mother, who quit her practice as a lawyer to raise a family and never returned to work, had suffered from a moderate untreated depression for much of Ellen's life. Ellen felt that her mother was often angry at her and kept her distance. Her own depression had followed on her repeated lack of success in even being interviewed for a tenure track position.

There were two ways I could formulate Ellen's situation. One would be to posit that her mother's not figuring in the prior therapy was due to resistance and that her therapist had been shortsighted in not interpreting it. Now it had reappeared in the depression and I was being offered a chance to deal

---

11 I had no expectations that things in Minneapolis would be any different from San Diego; only that this time I was getting in on the ground floor.
12 The reasons for the decreasing popularity of psychoanalysis are multiple, if not particularly obscure. Like so many other changes in World, they are often met by psychoanalysts with a kind of eco-denial.

with it. Alternatively, Ellen's relationship with her mother had not been sufficiently problematic to appear in the earlier Therapeutic Discourse and the absence of depression at that time could be seen as confirming of that. From this perspective, what was happening now was *new*. While it led to an examination of her relationship with her mother, its origins lay in the present, in Ellen's inability to actualize the career that she had worked so hard for: that she, like her mother, was locked out of the career she had aimed for. The *Meaning* of this disappointment, and the *Absurdity* that accompanied it, was that of an Existential failure, one that also mobilized from the infantile past, the fear that she would end up like her mother. The depressive identification with her confirmed this.

The maternal piece was the easier of the two to treat. As Ellen began to talk about her mother, her childhood anxieties about being like her, emptily depressed, emerged. What was new was her ability to talk about them in the context of a safe relationship (with me), lacking in the ambivalence that she felt for her father. An interpretation that it was her mother's depression and not her own that she suffered from proved quite successful in dealing with it. What remained was the more difficult problem facing Ellen in the present. The vocation she had trained for—studying and teaching the connections of South American magical realism to the work of the American authors of the 1930s and 40s—seemed unlikely to materialize. While no longer depressed, she was in the midst of grief over this loss. With work, Ellen *was* able to craft a meaningful substitute: a renewable lectureship and a careful plan to write in her area of interest. We will see how this unfolds in the future with a distant possibility of the tenure track job she wants in the background.

Anxieties—ecological and political

Before discussing ecological and political anxiety we must consider the clinical disagreements concerning whether or not they should even be a subject of Therapeutic Discourse. The extreme negative position is that they should not, that they act as a resistance to talking about the intrapsychic and the unconscious, and that feelings about them— for both patient and therapist—are too highly charged for such discourse. A corollary to this position is the so-called Goldwater Rule put in place by the American Psychiatric Association. It states, in effect, that it is unethical for Psychiatrists to offer opinions concerning the mental health and diagnoses of public figures whom they have neither examined personally nor received permission from to discuss.

My own position is that to ignore an Existential crisis in the *Umwelt* and act "therapeutically" as if doesn't exist is Absurd. I would also posit that we have, as therapists, a moral obligation to speak out about such issues and to actively engage our patients about them *when the usual issues of therapeutic tact and timing make it appropriate to do so*. The extreme comparison would be to analyses conducted in Germany in the 1930s as if nothing was going on outside, in the streets of Berlin or Vienna. (A group of German analysts, headed by Boehm, attempted to keep the Berlin Psychoanalytic Institute up and running during the Nazi years and do just that.) I have no idea how widespread my views are, but I have seen no Discourse on them in our literature. I believe that many therapists and analysts feel as I do. However, I recently had occasion to speak with a senior colleague—whose therapeutic stance I would otherwise describe as Relational and Contemporary—on the subject of political anxiety. He did not feel that any sort of active role was warranted on the subject, and when I asked what he did when his patients brought up these issues and their distress about them he replied that he "listened."

Broadly speaking, the very new term *Ecoanxiety* (or Eco-anxiety) can be defined as anxiety about how we see our world as headed for or already in the midst of a series of cataclysmic disasters. (*Eco-grief* is an accompanying emotion.) Public discourse on the subject began with the publication of *Silent Spring* (Carson, 1962/2002) in 1962. The current political situation of the Trump presidency in which he and his appointees actively *choose* to put the United States on a course that exacerbates environmental degradation—not to mention questioning or denying its existence or claiming that it is a hoax perpetrated by the "Swamp"— makes it impossible to separate the two; the political and the ecological. As long as we keep this in mind, a separation for heuristic purposes can be worthwhile.

We need to recognize that while majorities of Human Beings do not talk openly about climate change, they *do* talk about "politics" (with great acrimony), decay in their lives, their experience of and belief in life to have been much better in the past, and the experience of not being able to get ahead in their lives (however they choose to define *getting ahead*). A loss of personal Meaning is implicit throughout. An expression of these trends can be found in fiction, the cinema, and the particular forms of Mythopoesis (Slochower, 1970) demonstrated in both. There is now a large body of dystopian literature and science fiction written around end-of-the-world and end-of-humanity-as-we-know it themes, often set in a post-apocalyptic world or universe. These novels seldom reach the best sellers list. What do reach these lists are (usually) multi-volume series that are set in mythical worlds or alternative universes. They often contain mythical beasts, magical swords, and quests. They range from *The Lord of the Rings* to *A Game of Thrones*. What these genres have in common is that they tend to be *somewhat* more popular among men than women. What they also have in common is that nearly all of the time heroes and heroines or humanity as a whole triumph over threats and evils. In addition to the gratifications they offer that usually have to do with sex and aggression they also serve up antidotes to a lived life that somehow fails or falls short. They are attempts at *play*, as are the videogames they sometimes give rise to, ways of mitigating stress and seeking mastery. Dystopian fiction serves as a way of trying to manage very real fears about what the future holds for us and the World we live in. Interestingly, our patients don't talk much about these things and, again, we usually don't bring them up. The growing popularity and legality of recreational and prescription drugs and alcohol represent other, maladaptive ways of trying to cope with these problems.

Taken together, these all constitute folk remedies for precisely the Existential problems we are proposing to resolve: How do we find something, *anything*, meaningful as we live in an often-Absurd world? We are seeking Sisyphus' solution (Camus, 1942/1991) rather than Meursault's (Camus, 1942/1989).

The Ecoanxieties

Although there is a growing body of interdisciplinary literature on the subject of anxiety related to environmental deterioration, there is disagreement concerning just *what* the term refers to. Gifford and Gifford (2016) distinguish between the effects of local climate catastrophes on the mental health of those individuals living in their midst and those connected to them and Ecoanxiety. They define the latter as "characterized by severe and debilitating worry about risks that *may be insignificant* and is not associated with the more proactive behavior associated with habitual ecological worrying" (p. 292, italics added). Another way of saying this is that Human Beings suffering from Ecoanxiety are not those who have directly experienced environmental catastrophes. Pihkala (2018) distinguishes "direct psychological and existential impacts" from more subtle indirect impacts on "vast numbers of people" (p. 1). Albrecht (2005), an environmental philosopher, coined the term, *Solastalgia*, with its origins in the terms *solace* and *desolation*. It refers to "the pain experienced when there is recognition that the place where one resides and that one loves is under immediate assault (physical desolation)" (p. 45). The very sense of belonging to a place, a sense of *home*, is under attack. Irrespective of these classifications, the National Wildlife Federation (NWF, 2011) estimates that 200 million Americans will eventually experience psychological stress related to environmental change.

It is best to speak of Ecoanxieties in the plural because the term signifies *a group* of related emotions and the defenses (individual *and* group) that they give rise to. We are dealing with two interreferential processes: Human Beings' reactions to present day acute climate change and catastrophe and the future—almost unthinkable—changes in our planet and loss of life that massive global warming will bring about. (As I write this, the now annual crop of Category 5 hurricanes suggests that the Caribbean and certain southeastern coastal areas of the United States are becoming uninhabitable.) Climate pessimism is the widely held belief that Human Beings are not up to the task of addressing this problem and we will ultimately be overwhelmed by it. What this would mean is that societies *would*, in the end, reorganize themselves at a smaller, more local level. Although getting from point "A" to point "B," as it were, would be excruciating, the final result, arguably, might not be so bad.

In contrast to eco-pessimism, we have eco-commitment, a dedication to doing what we can to improve the environment and combat global warming. This can be done individually or as part of a dedicated group. It is a way of seeking and finding meaning in this Absurd world where the Absurdity often goes unaddressed.

If we are to stick to Existential distinctions (the point of the present volume) a different set of considerations comes into play. People who are direct victims of local environmental catastrophes must also contend with elements of PTSD. Arguably, the entire population must contend with a suite of worsening climactic events—including massive storms, rising sea levels, catastrophic droughts, heat waves and wildfires—as global warming continues to accelerate, combined with the environmental degradation due to industrial exploitation and the collapse of infrastructure. Some of these trends are amenable to reversal; others are not. Opportunities for such reversal are rapidly decaying. People respond in different ways: anxiety, depression, grief, psychological and intellectual denial among them. I have encountered most of these in my practice.

I live and practice in Santa Barbara, California where I see patients in person and via telephone and Skype (Leffert, 2003), the latter mostly from the Midwest. In Santa Barbara, we have over the years been threatened by a number of serious forest fires that were ultimately contained with some lost homes but no loss of life. Many of us (myself and my family on two occasions) were ordered to evacuate several times. Montecito, our suburb immediately to the southeast of us, was particularly threatened but ultimately protected. The flames, however, were terrifying: A patient fleeing on the coast highway at night told me she had imagined she was driving through hell. Towns to the south of us lost houses, and in Ventura, an adolescent psychiatric hospital, Vista Del Mar, burnt to the ground. Patients and staff were evacuated and, for a time took up residence at the county fairgrounds.

A result of the fires was to denude the low mountains above Montecito of ground cover and, the following winter, unusually heavy rains released a series of mudslides and avalanches of boulders, many the size of automobiles. The devastation was shocking. Twenty-one people and some dozens of houses were lost as a result. It seemed we all knew people who had lost houses or people who had been killed or knew people who knew people who had been killed. Flooding caused by the slides cut US 101 to the south for two weeks, severing our link with Los Angeles.

A number of my patients evacuated their homes multiple times. Others, in the face of repeated orders to evacuate that proved to be "false alarms," found that their anxieties extinguished and they refused to leave. Prior to the mudslides I had begun seeing a woman, we'll call her Louise, for an untreated depression. Among other issues, she had an infant with significant congenital problems that would require multiple surgeries to (hopefully) correct. She had a very close, warmly ambivalent relationship with a parent who, horribly, was carried away and killed by the slide. The mutilated body was found several days later, and the house had been wrecked by mud and boulders. Louise was thrown into what I would describe as a state of enraged grief that supplanted her depression. She was well aware that the complexity of her parental relationship made the death harder for her to deal with. She regretted things she had done or not done, said or left unsaid. Her rage was directed at the city and the county whom she felt, with some justification, had botched the handling of a reservoir overflow, the evacuation order, and contributed to if not caused the death. She joined a lawsuit against the local governments as a means of seeking retribution and validation of her loss rather than any financial gain. Louise had no thoughts of climate change as it might apply to these events; they felt local to her. This was true as well for myself and other patients and friends; there was, surprisingly, *locality* rather than Existentiality. By this, I mean that they felt like individual events rather than something about a larger, all-encompassing change in the nature of World and Self.

Surprisingly, I found that most of my patients and friends had relatively minimal emotional reactions to these events. The same was largely true of myself with one exception: the first time we were told to evacuate. I was considering staying behind with some thoughts of using a garden hose to keep the roof wet when I walked outside and, a half mile or so away, saw a column of flame a couple of hundred feet high. I felt a combination of elemental fear and the sense of impossibility of standing up to it. These feelings subsided for me and for others replaced by feelings of camaraderie (shared diners in the town some of us evacuated to overnight) and bearing up in the face of adversity, similarly to what it feels like to live through a power failure. (Where were you when...? Etc.) The fact that we had an intact house to return to helped a lot. I would view this as Eco-denial and Eco-disavowal both on an individual and a group (read social network) basis.

I also work with patients at a distance, patients who have not directly experienced environmental crises or disasters. They, and it is more likely for women to speak about this than for men, *do* experience global warming and industrial damage to the environment as an Existential crisis, that the world and life itself is being degraded. The danger experienced is global: It refers to the death of the human species or the end of civilized life as we know it (Pihkala, 2018). Although personal death is a familiar Existential problem, the death of *all of us*, first seen in the Cold War of the last century, is a very different sort of problem: It deprives us of the ability to pass anything on. (One of the Thrown ways we deal with our own deaths.) Even if one acts in ways to try to mitigate these trends, some feelings of helplessness inevitably remain.

If a patient does not broach the subject of environmental decline and climate change I will, at some point consistent with tact and timing and some relevance to current events, ask for thoughts about climate issues. If they have little or nothing to say about the issue, I will not pursue it. If patients *do* start talking about it, or about a current disaster—the devastation that Hurricane Maria wrought on Puerto Rico, for example—I say that I share their concerns and that I welcome talking about the subject. If a patient has experienced some environmental trauma in the past, that situation will be mobilized but, if not, I do not find a resurgence of infantile material; the fears remain World-based. Although I have never done so, I believe that to offer any kind of genetic interpretation of a patient's concerns—unless *they* have first led us there—would produce an iatrogenic regression.

In keeping with these clinical observations, Doherty and Clayton (2011) posit three classes of psychological reactions to climate change. The first they call the *direct*: extreme or traumatic responses to acute climactic events or catastrophes as they occur in an individual's life. The second is the *indirect*: threats to what they call emotional well-being and we know to be Subjective Well-Being (Diener, 1984) posed by concerns about perceived future risks. Finally, what they define as the *psychosocial*: the lived, chronic, social, and community effects of climate change, heat, droughts, floods, migrations, and the like.

The literature on the treatment of Eco-anxiety as a part of individual Psychotherapy and Psychoanalysis is limited and disappointing. A number of analysts and psychotherapists (Lertzman, 2016; Orange, 2016; Weintraub, 2013) *have* written on psychoanalysis and climate change. Unfortunately, their writing is not on the Therapeutic Situation as it is impacted by global warming, but rather the application of psychoanalytic concepts and defenses (mostly Kleinian concepts and defenses) to large groups and whole societies. (As we shall see, sociologists, anthropologists and social network theorists are much more knowledgeable on these subjects than we are.) Although we are justified in our concerns about maintaining the relevance of psychoanalysis to modern life, in this area we do best in supplementing the interdisciplinary studies being written on the subject and less in trying to supplant them with metapsychologically derived concepts. I have found very limited writing about climate change and psychotherapy outside of psychoanalysis. An article in the *Philadelphia Inquirer* (Nobel, 2007) describes a therapist, Melissa Pickett in Santa Fe, New Mexico who sees "40 to 80 eco-anxious patients a month" in supportive psychotherapy. Sally Gillespie (2016) writes about dealing with issues of eco-anxiety in "therapeutic discussion groups" in which she describes what are clearly Existential fears.

With rising evidence of threats to existence—the political threat of Nazism is as good an example as the ecological threat of global warming—Human Beings mobilize a variety of individual and group defenses to avoid thinking about them. Norgaard (2011), a sociologist, has studied the effects of climate change on "Bygdaby," a pseudonym for an actual rural community in western Norway.

Extreme warmer weather came to Bygdaby in the late 1980s (Norgaard, 2011); it reached a maximum in the fall and winter of 2000–2001, the warmest in 130 years, with severe flooding across the entire region. What winter there was came late, and the ice on the nearby lake (which had drawn people from far and wide for recreational purposes), when it did appear, was too thin to be safe. Skiing was limited to a single artificial run.[13] Bygdaby suffered economically from a decline in tourism. Both older and younger generations (some of whom had *never experienced the usual winter climate*) were found shaking their heads and speaking of "climate change." Communities around the world have similar stories to tell. Because of the difficulty distinguishing between weather

---

13 Climate had become *Absurd*.

and climate, it could not be said with certainty that these changes *were* climate change but the inhabitants were experiencing a difference. The "sociologist in Norgaard" was interested in her observation that, while everyone noticed the difference in the weather and knew what climate change was, they went about their everyday (*alltäglich*) life *as if it did not exist.*

Earlier explanations for these reactions have rested on information deficit models (Bulkeley, 2000): If people knew more they would act. In fact, the reverse seems to be the case: The more people know about climate change, the less emotional they are about it. A possible explanation for this (Norgaard, 2011) observation is that people can tolerate anxiety without catastrophe for only so long until they are exhausted by it and shift into disavowal.[14] People live in two separate realities, that of climate change and that of everyday life; while Norgaard labels this a state of *denial, disavowal* (knowing *and* not knowing) is probably closer to the truth.

This latter state of disavowal is an instance of Heidegger's Everydayness or *Alltäglichkeit* in which the individual is unreflectively present, dealing only with what they find to be *at hand* (*Vorhandenheit* or *Zuhandenheit*). This, again in the language of Phenomenology, is a simultaneous state of Everydayness and Thrownness with the latter offering the possibility of true engagement along with the risk of dealing with death or lapsing instead into a fallen state. Here, there is an instance of facing personal death but also the risk of societal or racial death and the end of people existing to receive the inheritance of what we have to pass on. This reflects back on us as individuals who in part deal with the thrownness of Death by the passing on of ourselves to our descendants and our accomplishments to society or community.[15] Consistent with these observations is that while the people of Bygdaby could speak of climate change, there was no local political discourse on the subject; it was perceived as an issue for *national* discourse. In the process, the need for local action was abrogated; it was the business of the national government and nothing need be done in Bygdaby.

Lest this should be considered a local phenomenon of western European civilization, we find similar patterns among historically marginalized peoples struggling with climactically induced changes to their way of life. It is seen in the Native villages of northwestern Alaska (as described by anthropologists Marino & Schweitzer, 2016) where the inhabitants have lived successfully for millennia in areas that have experienced major increases in coastal flooding. Detailed knowledge of climate and the harvesting of plant and animal species are encoded in generations of oral traditions. Iñupiat communities, for example, "witness a changing landscape that is altering subsistence practices,

---

14 This morning's newspapers (July 9, 2019) have front page pictures of drivers standing on their car roofs talking calmly on their cell phones in Washington DC where their cars were submerged as a result of flash flooding. The stories make no mention of climate, only weather.
15 The latter is a part of what satisfaction we derive from our work as psychotherapists.

threatening livelihoods and modern infrastructural development, and increasing the risk of life-threatening conditions" (p. 202). Severe coastal erosion has triggered debates among local residents and governmental agencies about the relocation of whole villages that have, up until now, received scant political attention. As media attention has come to the Native communities of Alaska's northwest coast, it has produced discrepancies between the measured but accurate narratives of the inhabitants and the catastrophic accounts of the journalists. Portraying the residents as helpless victims robs both the narratives *and* the inhabitants of their Meaning.

Meanwhile, in the United States, climate skepticism remains a major force on a national level (Fiske, 2016). Although it makes sense to talk about the intrapsychic processes (denial, disavowal, projection, splitting etc.) that operate in individuals and groups in communities experiencing climate catastrophes (like my own community, Santa Barbara, CA) or long-term environmental degradation, they gain only limited traction on a national level. Referring to *denial* (as in climate denial) does not make sense—disavowal and climate change *suppression* are explanatory terms demonstrating greater value. Suppression takes place "inside the Beltway" through the efforts of lobbying, corporate, and political interests and has been so successful that significant numbers of climate hoax believers exist and repeated Gallup polls show that, by a small majority, Americans don't believe that they will be threatened by climate change in their lifetimes. "Climate skepticism seems to be a uniquely American *belief system* with its own exceptional constellation of elements in resistance to pronouncements of scientists, the use of science to set environmental policy, fear of government intrusion, and support for entrenched interests of fossil fuel industries that support a dominant life style" (Fiske, 2016, p. 323, italics added): Europeans or South Pacific islanders, all living in areas that will be obliterated by rising sea levels are much more of one mind with their governments. In treating this as an intrapsychic process, the few psychoanalysts writing on the subject (Lertzman, 2016; Orange, 2016; Weintraub, 2013) do us a disservice: Suppression is much better understood through discourse on the mechanics of power (Foucault, 2000; Lukes, 2005) that we will consider below. This national trend lessens in some coastal states and decreases markedly on the local level of communities on the front lines of coastal erosion and flooding, or forest fires and droughts.

Political Anxiety

I am using the term Political Anxiety to signify the Existential threats that are experienced as a result of governmental and societal failures that lead us to feelings of anxiety, powerlessness, and, probably a more apt term, *despair*. It is a sense that our society is failing us and our government is unresponsive at best and a causal agent at worst. The fact that many of the issues that give rise to these feelings have to do with a degrading environment and governments' failures in dealing with it make it hard to separate the ecological from the political.

A majority of Americans experience Donald Trump at the center of these problems and his presidency as an intellectual and moral failure. Some, correctly I think, see him as a symptom (albeit a life-threatening one) of multiple socio-political problems rather than their cause. He, and roughly a third of the population who support him (his base), instill rage, contempt, and, ultimately, fear in people globally as well as nationally. (It must be realized that this third believes in these things and consider the rest of us to be the problem. Making sense of this involves the question of how you deal with irreducible Subjectivity.)

As clinicians, to address these problems with patients is to move into uncharted territory, *terra incognita*. Although others have been here before us (think Nazi Germany and the South American dictatorships), they have not sent back records of their experiences, their traumas, perhaps wanting instead to put it behind them.[16] Similar issues arose in 1950s America— the communist witch hunts instigated by the investigating committees of Congress and the Senate and the fears of nuclear war—but again there was no writing to suggest that these might have been subjects to be taken up in psychotherapy or analysis. We can only proceed with these issues as we find them in clinical practice.

As near as I can tell, I have one or possibly two patients who voted for Donald Trump. They say nothing about politics. The remainder of my patients are outspoken Independents or Democrats. About half of them are engrossed in their personal lives and have nothing much to say about politics or the news. The other half have a great deal to say about both. Sometime during the run up to the 2016 election, I indicated a willingness to talk about politics as an Existential state of our country; what I heard back ranged from rage and anxiety to the worsening of endogenous depressions. It was helpful in all of these cases to validate the emotions, share them where I could, and draw the distinction between what was internal and what was external where I couldn't.

As a result of these inquiries, it became clear that the central issue in all of this is power—who has it, who doesn't, and the uses that are made of it. I have written about power a number of times (e.g., Leffert, 2010, 2013) as it pertains to organized psychoanalysis and the Therapeutic Situation and will draw on some of those arguments here. The two major contributors to the field are perhaps Foucault (1980, 1979/1995) and Lukes (2005). These authors write about power (*not* violence or torture) as *the* instrument of social control without parallel but come at the subject from very different directions.

To offer an argument in highly condensed form, almost two centuries ago, Marx and Engels (1845/1998) posited that power and capital were one in the same, that they determined membership in social class, and that one's *membership*

---

16 There is an oral history held by the American Psychoanalytic Association documenting psychoanalysts' *flight* from Nazi Germany and Austria and Muriel Gardiner's (a physician and later a psychoanalyst in training in Vienna in the 1930s) memoir (1983) of her work with the Austrian underground.

in a class determined one's reality—for our purposes here, climate-reality.[17] Foucault (1980) was particularly interested in the relations between power and knowledge, which he deemed to be inseparable: hence power-knowledge and knowledge-power. In trying to understand the realities of climate change, the linkage of the two is of particular relevance to the individual trying not to be at the mercy of ruling classes and their aims and motives. This brings us to Lukes (2005) who identified dominated and dominating classes in all social systems with language being an essential tool of power.

Lukes (2005) addressed the question of why dominated classes accept the dominance of ruling elites. Such elite groups are defined by three properties (Dahl, 1958): They must be discreet groups; their preferences must run counter to other groups; *and they must prevail in realizing their preferences*. This can be achieved in a number of ways. At the most basic level, it is *overt action of any kind* that achieves an elite's ends. Subtler, is an elite's ability to *limit public discourse to only those subjects that the elite finds innocuous*. Setting agendas and the evocation of social or political values are tools with which to bring this about. But as Lukes uniquely points out, the subtlest of all is the *invention or modification of language* in ways that make it impossible to even talk about a particular conflict over the aims of an elite. (Orwell (1949/1961) got this with his three dicta: *War is Peace, Freedom is Slavery*, and *Ignorance is Strength*.)

As one reads this and thinks about the political situation we find in early 21st century America, warning lights should begin to flash (or bells go off, your choice). We find a number of at-times-competing power elites that, as an illustration of Lukes' (2005) use of language, we mistakenly call *interest groups*. There are at least four: corporate elites, populist elites, liberal elites, and the newly-christened "progressive" elites (the last are actually *radical* elites but, again, language has been used to limit and sanitize discourse). These elites sometimes compete, that is, act to dominate each other, and sometimes share interests in their pursuit of power. They all have particular, fairly obvious interests pertaining to climate change, some of which are short-term and others are self-destructive. In Existentialist terms, a society constructed in this way along a dimension of power is, for at least some and potentially all of its classes, an Absurd society.

We find several dominated classes in 21st century America and some large groups attempting to be independent and retain freedom. (We *really* don't like, that is, resist, applying such nomenclature to ourselves.) We currently live in a social situation in which the dominated classes believe they can

---

17 In India, for example, there is a great water shortage; members of the lower classes (woman actually) stand waiting in the middle of the night to collect water in plastic containers from trucks that arrive late. People from the social upper classes *hire* trucks to deliver truckloads of water *to* them. To bring this closer to home, during last years' drought in Montecito, California where water was rationed, residents trucked in water to water their lawns until they were massively fined for doing so (we don't live in India, after all).

identify the class(es) that is attempting to dominate them (whether this is true is admittedly uncertain). Red and Blue come readily to hand as definitions, as long as we remember things are subtler and more complex than that. The members of these groups *all* believe they are living in and trying to find their way in an Absurd world; however, exactly *what* they find Absurd differs markedly, albeit with some overlap. There is, for example, almost universal agreement that the functioning of national government (life within the beltway) is Absurd. However, how members of different groups view a Trump rally, with its chants of "lock her up" or "send her home," differ dramatically. Trump is, of course, either a savior/entertainer or a contemptible demagogue depending on who you are. While members of these groups find common meaning in such things as having a secure home or access to health care (for themselves certainly, but, sometimes, not necessarily for the "other"), in others, like climate or owning firearms, they differ sharply. Political anxiety is an issue of great complexity because it calls into question the Existential standard of *subjective* personal meaning as some kind of overarching standard. This ultimately leads to the necessary addition of other standards, morals, ethics, values, aesthetics and Subjective Well-Being if we are to truly address what is meaningful and truly works in World. It should be obvious that arriving at conclusions in these areas is no easy task.

Comprehensive descriptions of these groups and their relations are difficult at best. Levels of experienced Absurdity in our culture are perhaps higher than they have ever been. We can say that Thrownness is hard to come by these days, Fallenness is all too common and large numbers of Human Beings are left to settle for, at best, Everydayness.

The inner world—the Microbiome

Up until recently, Existential relationships with World could be left unspecified—there was only the world outside of the Self to be considered. All that has changed. It has been known, probably for a couple of centuries, that we carry in our gastrointestinal tract living bacteria—probably three pounds or so of them. (The Microbiome also includes the bacterial populations of the body's surface and orifices.) Among them are roughly 150–200 common species of bacteria in the gut (Dinan, et al., 2015) and 1,000 species that are less frequently found. Aside from the capacity of some of these bacterial strains to cause disease in the individual Self or to be spread to others by individuals acting as vectors, these bacteria used to be considered inert. Indeed, they have been experienced as unhygienic and some number of people periodically *cleanse* themselves as a way of getting rid of them. Others have come to see them as healthy, again in a fairly non-specific way, and people often consume strains of "healthy" bacteria, called *probiotics*, so as to colonize their GI tracts with them. (Current studies suggest that, by lessening the diversity of the Microbiome, indiscriminate ingestion of probiotics is not healthy.) What we have recently come to understand, however, goes far beyond this (Archie &

Tung, 2015; Clarke, et al., 2013; Cryan & O'Mahony, 2011; Dinan, et al., 2015; Foster, 2013; Gershon, 1999; Malan-Muller, et al., 2017; Roberts, et al., 2018; Sampson & Mazmanian, 2015; Sarkar, et al., 2016; Yang, Wei, Ju, & Chen, 2019): "Our bacteria" effect not only food cravings but also how we feel physically and emotionally and how our brains develop. From an Existentialist perspective, two things stand out about the influence of the Microbiome on the Self. The first is that its effects on the Self occur *outside of its consciousness*—always problematic for Existentialism and Phenomenology (see Chapters 1–3). The second is the Absurdity of these effects on a Being that prides itself on its self-reflectivity. To use the vernacular in order to stress this Absurdity, we are saying that a gut full of shit influences who we are as Human Beings. The Microbiome, as we shall see, acts on the Self in three ways: chemically and hormonally through the circulatory system, directly on the brain through the Vagus nerve, and apparently (it's too new to be sure) through bacteria that actually *live* in the brain (Roberts, et al., 2018).

What is being defined is a Microbiome-Gut-Brain axis (Cryan & O'Mahony, 2011). It is a *bidirectional* axis. The Gut-Brain part of the axis involves the collection of relay ganglia located in the Gut that, along with the Vagus nerve are now described as a Second Brain (Gershon, 1999)—an *enteric nervous system*. It includes neurons assembled into ganglia and wrapped in glial cells, much like the "first" Brain, and is the only other such arrangement in the body. The Vagus nerve has been demonstrated (Porges, 2009, 2011)[18] to have vast capacities for the bidirectional exchange of information between the Brain, the gut, the cardiovascular system, and the striated muscles of the face. Porges developed what he called a Polyvagal Theory of reciprocal influence between brain and body. He defined two axes—the Brain-Heart-Vagus-Circuit (BHVC) and the Brain-Heart-Face-Circuit (BHFC)—by which this *reciprocal exchange of information* takes place. How this information is affected by the particular bacterial population of an individual's Microbiome is not yet known or understood. "While advances in metagenomic technologies have revealed the composition of the human gut microbiota from early infancy through old age, far less is known about the physiological impact this microbiota has on host health including that of the brain" (Dinan, et al., 2015, p. 3).

In addition to the Vagal component (the sympathetic and parasympathetic elements of the enteric nervous system) (Dinan, et al., 2015) of the MGB axis, the communication between Microbiome and Brain, there are other elements—a spinal component of the nervous system, and the neuroimmune and the neuroendocrine systems. A moment's reflection should suffice to realize that these components of the axis all have the capacity to cause illness and suffering and that modifying the Microbiome probiotically and prebiotically ought to, potentially be able to ameliorate or cure a large number of diseases.

---

18 See Leffert (2013, 2016) for a discussion of the activities of the Vagus nerve.

There effects on the Self's Being and capacity for Meaning are, at this time, still more obscure.

As an indication that we are dealing with a valid premise, Yang and colleagues (Yang, et al., 2019) reviewed the literature since July of 2018 on the effects of regulating intestinal microbiota on anxiety symptoms. They found numbers of basic studies demonstrating that gut microbiota can regulate brain function through the microbiome-gut-brain axis mediated by the Vagus nerve (Porges, 2009). They found 21 studies done in the *past year* that attempted to treat anxiety symptoms by modifying the Microbiome. Their authors did so by either modifying its bacterial population by introducing strains of cultured bacteria (pro-biotic) or by diet modifications such as adjustments of fermentable saccharides (non-probiotic, *pre-biotic*). Ingested together, the two are referred to as psychobiotics (Sarkar, et al., 2016). fourteen of the twenty-one studies demonstrated a reduction in anxiety symptoms: 36% of the studies that used probiotics showed this effect while *86%* of those using non-probiotic, pre-biotic interventions showed improvement.

Most psychobiotic research (Sarkar, et al., 2016) is based on rodent models which assess anxiety, depression, and motivation. Desbonnet and colleagues (2010) used early maternal separation in male rat pups to induce stress and accompanying depression and anxiety. A control group was untreated whereas one studied group was given the SSRI citalopram and a second group received the probiotic *Bifidobacterium infantis*. The two studied groups showed a normalization of the symptoms, with the pro-biotic group demonstrating a down-regulation of the Hypothalamic-Pituitary-Adrenal (HPA) axis. Sarkar and colleagues have found widespread validation of these results. A frequently quoted study (Messaoudi, et al., 2011) of probiotic effects on rats and humans demonstrated improved mood in a sample of normal, asymptomatic humans. The mechanism of action of the probiotics is as yet poorly understood. It *is* known (Sarkar, et al, 2016), however, that bacteria–brain signaling along the Microbiome-Gut-Brain axis operates through increasing the electrophysiological stimulus-thresholds of enteric neurons. This occurs through their exposure to the fermentation products produced by *Bifidobacterium longus*. Gut bacteria can also directly produce neurotransmitters through the metabolism of otherwise indigestible fibers—those of the Jerusalem artichoke, for example. It is clear that we have the beginnings of a large and complex narrative concerning the actions of the inner world on the Self through the MGB axis.

Malan-Muller and colleagues (2017) took their review farther, looking at the Gut Microbiome and its role in anxiety- and trauma-related disorders. They looked at the MGB axis and its role in the programing of the Hypothalamic-Pituitary-Adrenal (HPA) axis early in life. They saw this early, emerging research—and it *is* early—as pointing to critical factors in the development of mental health and illness. Other studies (Clarke, et al., 2013; Dinan, et al., 2015) look at the effects of the Microbiome on normal development.

It has so far been shown that the Microbiome exerts a macro influence on the Self: It influences Being with a very broad brush. If it shapes the details, and it might, we do not yet understand how. Studies (Archie & Tung, 2015; Clarke, et al., 2013; Dinan, et al., 2015) are beginning to pursue this influence by looking at how the Microbiome influences social behavior—a major pathway for the effect of World on Self that involves both Meaning and Absurdity. The social brain carries with it obvious evolutionary advantages based on the benefits of mutualism in social and physical survival. At this point in time, studies have focused on Autistic Spectrum Disorders (ASDs) and ASD-like disorders in mice and, to a much lesser extent, in humans. Studies of Germ Free (GF) mice and the maternal environment in which mice develop in utero and are raised in thereafter point to a connection between gut microbiota and the development of autistic spectrum mice. Going back to an earlier observation, these are social observations based on only the broadest of brushstrokes.

In a groundbreaking study of stress at a similar level of emotional resolution, the authors (Tillisch, et al., 2013) looked at human stress using functional Magnetic Resonance Imaging (fMRI). Healthy women without gastrointestinal or psychiatric symptoms were given an FMPP (Fermented Milk Product with Probiotic) containing *Lactobacillus* and *Bifidobacterium*. fMRIs were administered to measure brain response to an emotional-faces-attention task and resting level brain activity before and after they received the cocktail. They found the FMPP consumption "was associated with reduced task-related response of [this] distributed functional network ... containing *affective, viscerosensory,* and *somatosensory cortices*. Alterations in intrinsic activity of resting brain indicated that ingestion of FMPP was associated with changes in midbrain connectivity, which could explain the observed differences in activity during the task" (p. 1394, italics added).

We have been looking at how the Microbiome impacts the Self who is in much less control of himself than he thinks he is. Let's now turn to the impact of the external world.

The mechanics—the Social Network and the Mirror Neuron System

If we look at the way that the outer World impacts Self, we find two sorts of effects: that of the *Umwelt*—the physical world—and that of the *Mitwelt*—the social world. If the former is a matter of perception and how the Self *subjectively* processes what it perceives and then experiences (it reached 108.7° F in Paris yesterday, an all-time record; we feel the heat *and* think about global warming), the latter is more complex (we transmit social information to each other over great distances and degrees of separation). Phenomenologically we are looking at how World acts to influence Meaning but, operationally, the issue involves the mechanisms, social and perceptual, through which self is embedded in the matrix of World. The Social Network and Mirror Neuron Systems act on the Self in complementary ways: the latter operates in groups and between individuals in visual contact with each other (or easily capable of being so), while the former acts amorphously, sometimes at great distances, and integrates the impact of the physical world as well. In Phenomenological terms, these mechanisms mediate the Self's Being-in-World, that is, Being *there*, or Dasein. In the discussions of Absurdity, we have lost track of Dasein that really underlies it. It is the *there* in Dasein that we formulate for ourselves —through the mechanics of the Social Networks we embed ourselves in and the Mirror Neuron System we use to connect ourselves to it—that determines the outcome of Meaning or Absurdity.

The Mirror Neuron System (MNS)

Since their discovery in the right inferior frontal cortex of macaque monkeys in the mid-1990s (Gallese, Fadiga, Fogassi, & Rizzolatti, 1996), mirror neurons have been shown to play a central role in the exchange of social information. They were subsequently (Iacoboni, 2007, 2008; Iacoboni, et al., 2005; Iacoboni, et al., 1999) identified in the prefrontal motor, visual, and somatosensory cortexes of Human Beings. The MNS is a shared processing system (Leffert, 2016) in which the same cells process images of Self and Other. Combined with the Brain-Heart-Face-Circuit, the MNS constitutes the *biological engine of intersubjectivity*. It is the engine of Being-in-World. The activity of the engine is completely unconscious, causing the same problems that many of the other mechanisms we have discussed do for classical Phenomenological and Existentialist thought. (The purpose of the present volume has been, in part, to develop new ways of dealing with this discrepancy.)

The MNS produces *embodied simulation*, defined (Ferrari & Gallese, 2007) as "an automatic, unconscious, and pre-reflexive functional mechanism, whose function is the modeling of objects, agents, and events" (p. 74). It leads to an epistemic grasping of World that is essential if we are to be able to tease out Meaning from Absurdity. It acts to grasp motor acts in others. Its grasp of a motor act also involves its *context* as part of a causal sequence of actions that produce a sought-after result (the MNS will distinguish between identical motor acts embedded in different functional sequences). The MNS acts independently of whether we actually repeat an action (a patient crosses their legs and we cross ours) or simply experience our perception of their action and think about performing it.

The MNS also acts to mirror emotions and facial expressions—disgust (Ferrari & Gallese, 2007), for example. "Witnessing an emotion in others or experiencing it in oneself both activate the same area of the brain, the insula" (Leffert, 2016, p. 43). This suggests that the first- and third-person experiences of emotion and expression involve a shared mental substrate. The perception of the facial expressions of others—people close to us and people of public importance we see in the media—has a great deal to do with how we assess Meaning in World and the things (or people) we find Absurd. The actions of the MNS that allow an individual to recognize themselves in a mirror are unique to Human Beings. The MNS also plays a significant role in development. It provides the infant with an innate capacity for bidirectional intersubjective exchange (Leffert, 2010) with their mother. This constitutes a break with more usual psychoanalytic thinking that draws on Freud, Mahler, and Bowlby. Bråten (2007) thus posits what he refers to as an *altercentric* capacity for mirroring in infants and adults that is sensitized—but not created—by nurture in the first months of life. The innateness of this capacity and of the MNS can be demonstrated in photographs of the infant's capacity to mirror their mother's facial expressions at as early as age *20 minutes*. Here we have a bridge between Existentialism (Being with or *Mitsein*) and psychoanalytic developmental psychology and psychopathology.

A failure in sensitization of the MNS would lead to attachment psychopathology: *Existentially*, this would be expressed in deficiencies in the ability to find Meaning in life and would lead to Absurdities. The addictions constitute prime examples of such Absurdity; they involve a capitulation in the battle to find Meaning. The machinery of the MNS can also be defective from birth. Such defects would also limit sensitization. While their seriousness is variable, the most obvious would entail Autistic Spectrum Disorders. Part of the defect here would lead to a failure to be able to comprehend that other Human Beings think and feel as we do; the ability to develop a Theory of Mind (ToM) (Baron-Cohen, Tager-Flusberg, & Cohen, 2000; Gallagher & Frith, 2003). To the extent that Meaning is derived from intimate relationships, a functioning MNS is essential for the development of Meaning and its absence can lead only to Absurd relationships. These aspects of Meaning and Absurdity—that involve the making and breaking of affectionate social bonds (Bowlby, 1979[1977]/1984)—have not been much considered by Existentialist authors, perhaps as a result of their own psychological deficits in this area.

John, an unmarried attorney in his late 30s, sought treatment because of feelings of chronic isolation. Even the idea of psychotherapy with another person seemed foreign to him; it only came to him after he had stumbled on a newspaper columnist who dispensed psychological advice. As John talked to me about the people (very few) in his life it was as if they were not people in their own right, with any thoughts, feelings, or motivations of their own. By no means at the autistic end of the spectrum, John's capacity for a ToM was nevertheless damaged. People were *social dispensers* for him to use—or rail against, or get depressed, or anxious about, when they failed to supply what he needed. The obvious diagnostic question was how could John's disorder be distinguished from a more usually diagnosed condition: Narcissistic Personality Disorder. The answer is that he lacked expressly narcissistic pathology; he was without evidence of grandiosity and, more importantly, he showed no susceptibility to narcissistic injury. On perhaps a half-dozen occasions over the first few sessions I consciously crossed my legs to see if John would mirror me; he did not.

John was not a patient I would ever consider using the couch with—I *wanted* him to have the input of my facial expressions, trusting that he would eventually learn to decipher them. Over the course of a very long therapy, I gradually introduced him to the idea of what people actually were and how often they reacted pretty much like he himself did. His beginning sense of this was much reinforced by his experience that they treated him in a different and rewarding way when he kept this in mind. I have had patients who simply never "got it": although they did benefit somewhat from therapy and the therapeutic relationship I offered. I have on occasion indirectly heard that one or two of these patients had regressed significantly post-termination.

The Social Networks that make us who we are

In seeking to understand our Social Networks and how they define us, we are led to the work of Christakis and Fowler (2009) that I introduced in Chapter 1. Social Networks are groups of individuals, we will call these individuals *nodes*, that are connected to each other by "lines" of relationship; each line between two nodes represents one degree of separation (friends). Two nodes connected to each other through another node (friends of friends) demonstrate two degrees of separation, and so on. Networks break down after about three degrees (friends of friends of friends) of separation. The number of first-degree connections a node has varies, with some nodes having many connections, being centrally located, so to speak, in a network, while others are more peripheral, having at times only a single social connection. Information, called *contagion*, is passed from node to node, measurably through three degrees of separation. For our purposes, what is most important about this process is that it occurs unconsciously; neither donor nor recipient is aware of its taking place. Indeed, we are largely unaware of being a part of such networks—it can, however, be pointed out to us. Thus, we can know we are members of some organization—a psychoanalytic institute is a very good example—but it takes more effort to recognize the social network implications of such belonging. Staying with institute networks for a moment, they are configured by power relations connections (Leffert, 2010, Chapter 7), and chosen psychoanalytic theories serve as powerful contagions within the network. The strength with which these nodes cohere might be called *receptivity*, and their resistance to coherence with outside nodes or networks can be called *immunity*. The Existential takeaway which we have to deal with here is that our Being-in-the-World, again in terms of Meaning versus Absurdity, is being shaped by large amounts of information we are receiving but aren't aware of. Curiously enough, the strength of contagions has less to do with the amount of geographic separation and much more to do with the degree of separation in the network.

Nodes can also be members of very large Social Networks called *Superorganisms* (Christakis & Fowler, 2009). Beyond describing the behavior of Superorganisms such as human waves of standing nodes making their way counterclockwise around an arena at a sporting event, they have not been much studied. The concept of superorganisms having minds of their own merits consideration.

Contagion can be *felt*. Fashion serves as a good example. For many years, knit shirts with the Polo™ of the horse and rider (and the alligator decades before *it*) just somehow felt right to have and wear, then, not so much. Moving on to more difficult contagions, individual countries often comprise a single superorganism; we could describe the package of contagions that cause them to cohere *nationalism*. Nationalism, of course, can operate for good or ill. The members of such a superorganism can be relatively receptive or immune to outside contagions. In the United States today (2019), we are in the midst of serious problems with contagion. We have split, socially and politically, into two superorganisms whose members experience at times great antagonism for each other and are immune to each other's contagion. The political divide has, to a significant degree, overcome the nationalistic connection. Local social networks are sometimes able to overcome the immunity. These networks involve many different kinds of contagion so individuals are not limited to defining each other one dimensionally in terms of a single vector, in this case the political one. Local governments are sometimes able to function in this way. So, although I am convinced that my experience (and my friends' experience) of the nightmare of the Trump presidency we are living with is accurate I, *at the same time*, realize that there is this other network of people that feel just as strongly that their views, opposites of mine, are the correct ones (while some few of them may actually be evil, the great majority are not; they are people similar to myself in many ways). The ontology is then taken up with dueling Absurdities, but the members of the two superorganisms do also have many Meanings in common. Reminding ourselves that nearly all of us are Human Beings can offer the beginnings of a path out of the mess our country currently finds itself in.

A number of things should stand out in this chapter. Meaning and Absurdity exist at the interface, psychological and physical, between Self and World. This is where the search for Meaning (Frankl, 1959/2006) takes place. As therapists, we have to address very different things: how a patient's psychopathology interferes with or precludes conducting such a search, but also how globally rife Absurdity is in our early-21st century World, the world we and our patients must contend with. This latter problem has taken the chapter and our work with patients down strange and confusing pathways that we are unaccustomed to pursue; indeed, many of us feel we have no business doing so. If, however, we consider the engagement of Absurdity and the quest for Meaning a part of Care (Leffert, 2016, Chapter 6), it is hard to see that we have any choice.

References

Albrecht, G. (2005). "Solastalgia" A new concept in health and identity. *PAN: Philosophy, Activism, Nature, 3,* 41–55.

Archie, E. A., & Tung, J. (2015). Social behavior and the microbiome. *Current Opinion in Behavioral Sciences, 6,* 28–34.

Bakewell, S. (2016). *At the existentialist café: Freedom, being and apricot cocktails.* New York: Other Press.

Baron-Cohen, S., Tager-Flusberg, H., & Cohen, D. J. (2000). *Understanding other minds: Perspectives from developmental cognitive science* (2nd edn). Oxford: Oxford University Press.
Bowlby, J. (1984). The making and breaking of affectional bonds. In J. Bowlby *The making and breaking of affectional bonds* (pp. 126–160). London: Tavistock. (Original work published in 1979).
Bråten, S. (2007). Altercentric infants and adults: On the origins and manifestations of participant perception of others' acts and utterances. In S. Bråten (Ed.), *On being moved: From mirror neurons to empathy* (Vol. 68, pp. 111–136). Amsterdam: John Benjamin's Publishing Company.
Bulkeley, H. (2000). Common knowledge? Public understanding of climate change in Newcastle, Australia. *Understanding of Science, 9*, 313–333.
Camus, A. (1989). *The stranger* (M. Ward, Trans.). New York: Vintage Books. (Original work published in 1942).
Camus, A. (1991). The myth of Sisyphus. In A. Camus, *The myth of Sisyphus and other essays* (J. O'Brien, Trans.) (pp. 3–138). New York: Vintage Books. (Original work published in 1942).
Carson, R. (2002). *Silent spring*. New York: Houghton Mifflin Company. (Original work published in 1962).
Christakis, N. A., & Fowler, J. H. (2009). *Connected: The surprising power of our social networks and how they shape our lives*. New York: Little, Brown and Company.
Clarke, G., Grenham, S., Scully, P., Fitzgerald, P., Moloney, R. D., Shanahan, F., et al. (2013). The microbiome-gut-brain axis during early life regulates the hippocampal serotogenic system in a sex-dependent manner. *Molecular Psychiatry, 18*, 666–673.
Cryan, J. F., & O'Mahony, S. M. (2011). The microbiome-gut-brain axis: From bowel to behavior. *Neurogastroenterology & Motility, 23*, 187–192.
Dahl, R. A. (1958). A critique of the ruling elite model. *American Political Science Review, 52*, 463–469.
Derrida, J. (1982). Différance. In J. Derrida, *Margins of philosophy* (A. Bass, Trans.) (pp. 1–27). Chicago: University of Chicago Press.
Desbonnet, L., Garrett, L., Clarke, C., Kiely, B., Cryan, J. F., & Dinan, T. G. (2010). Effects of the probiotic Bifidobacterium infantis in the maternal separation model of depression. *Neuroscience, 170*, 1179–1188.
Diener, E. (1984). Subjective well-being. *Psychological Bulletin, 95*, 542–575.
Dinan, T. G., Stilling, R. M., Stanton, C., & Cryan, J. F. (2015). Collective unconscious: How gut microbes shape human behavior. *Journal of Psychiatric Research, 63*, 1–9.
Doherty, T. J., & Clayton, S. (2011). The psychological impacts of global climate change. *American Psychologist, 66*, 265–276.
Elliott, A., & Spezzano, C. (1996). Psychoanalysis at its limits: Navigating the postmodern turn. *Psychoanalytic Quarterly, 65*, 52–83.
Ferrari, P. F., & Gallese, V. (2007). Mirror neurons and intersubjectivity. In S. Bråten (Ed.), *On being moved from mirror neurons to empathy* (pp. 73–88). Amsterdam: John Benjamins Publishing Company.
Fiske, S. J. (2016). "Climate skepticism" inside the Beltway and across the Bay. In S. A. Crate & M. Nuttall (Eds), *Anthropology and climate change: From actions to transformations* (2nd ed., pp. 319–335). London: Routledge.
Foster, J. A. (2013). Gut feelings: Bacteria and the brain. *Cerebrum, 9*, 1–9.
Foucault, M. (1980). *Power/Knowledge: Selected interviews & other writings 1972–1977* (C. Gordon, L. Marshall, J. Mepham & K. Soper, Trans.). New York: Pantheon Books.

Foucault, M. (1995). *Discipline and punish. The birth of the prison* (A. Sheridan, Trans.). New York: Vintage Books. (Original work published in 1979).
Foucault, M. (2000). *Power* (R. Hurley & Others, Trans.). New York: The New Press.
Frankl, V. E. (2006). *Man's search for meaning* (I. Lasch, Trans.). Boston: Beacon Press. (Original work published in 1959).
Gallagher, H. L., & Frith, C. D. (2003). Functional imaging of "theory of mind". *Trends in Cognitive Sciences, 7*, 77–83.
Gallese, V., Fadiga, L., Fogassi, L., & Rizzolatti, G. (1996). Action recognition in the premotor cortex. *Brain, 119*, 593–609.
Gardiner, M. (1983). *Code Name Mary: Memoirs of an American woman in the Austrian underground*. New Haven: Yale University Press.
Gershon, M. D. (1999). The enteric nervous system: a second brain. *Hospital Practice, 34*(7), 31–52.
Gerson, S. (2004). The relational unconscious: A core element of intersubjectivity, thirdness, and clinical process. *Psychoanalytic Quarterly, 73*, 63–98.
Gifford, E., & Gifford, R. (2016). The largely unacknowledged impact of climate change on mental health. *Bulletin of the Atomic Scientists, 72*, 292–297.
Gillespie, S. (2016). Climate change imaginings and depth psychology: Reconciling present and future worlds. In J. P. Marshall & L. H. Connor (Eds), *Environmental change and the world's futures: Ecologies, ontologies and mythologies* (pp. 181–195). London: Routledge.
Heidegger, M. (1982). *The Basic problems of phenomenology* (A. Hofstadter, Trans. Rev. ed.). Bloomington: Indiana University Press. (Original work published in 1975).
Heidegger, M. (2010). *Being and time* (J. Stambaugh & D. J. Schmidt, Trans.). Albany: State University of New York. (Original work published in 1927).
Husserl, E. (1983). *Ideas pertaining to a pure phenomenology and to a phenomenological philosophy*, Book 1 (Original work published in 1913).
Iacoboni, M. (2007). Face to face: The neural basis of social mirroring and empathy. *Psychiatric Annals, 37*(4), 236–241.
Iacoboni, M. (2008). *Mirroring people: The new science of how we connect with people*. New York: Farrar, Strauss and Giroux.
Iacoboni, M., Molnar-Szakacs, I., Gallese, V., Buccino, G., Mazziotta, J. C., & Rizzolatti, G. (2005). Grasping intentions of others with one's own mirror neuron system. *PloS Biology 3*, e79.
Iacoboni, M., Woods, R. P., Brass, M., Bekkering, H., Mazziotta, J. C., & Rizzolatti, G. (1999). Cortical mechanisms of human imitation. *Science, 286*(5449), 2526–2528.
Leffert, M. (2003). Analysis and psychotherapy by telephone: Twenty years of clinical experience. *Journal of the American Psychoanalytic Association, 51*, 101–130.
Leffert, M. (2007). Postmodernism and its impact on psychoanalysis. *Bulletin of the Menninger Clinic, 71*, 15–34.
Leffert, M. (2010). *Contemporary psychoanalytic foundations*. London: Routledge.
Leffert, M. (2013). *The therapeutic situation in the 21st century*. New York: Routledge.
Leffert, M. (2016). *Phenomenology, uncertainty, and care in the therapeutic encounter*. New York: Routledge.
Leffert, M. (2018). *Psychoanalysis and the birth of the self: A radical interdisciplinary approach*. London: Routledge.
Lertzman, R. (2016). *Environmental melancholia: psychoanalytic dimensions of engagement*. London: Routledge.

Lifton, R. J. (1973). *Home from the war*. New York: Simon & Schuster.
Lukes, S. (2005). *Power a radical view* (2nd edn). New York: Palgrave Macmillan.
Malabou, C., & Derrida, J. (2004). *Counterpath* (D. Wills, Trans.). Stanford: Stanford University Press. (Original work published in 1999).
Malan-Muller, S., Valles-Colomer, M., Raes, J., Lowry, C. A., Seedat, S., & Memmings, S. M. J. (2017). The gut microbiome and mental health: Implications for anxiety- and trauma-related disorders. *OMICS A Journal of Integrative Biology*, 1–18. doi:10.1089/omi.2017.0077
Marino, E., & Schweitzer, P. (2016). Speaking again of climate change: An analysis of climate change discourses in Northwestern Alaska. In S. A. Crate & M. Nuttall (Eds), *Anthropology and climate change: From actions to transformations* (2nd edn) (pp. 200–209). London: Routledge.
Marx, K., & Engels, F. (1998). *The German ideology*. Amherst: Prometheus Books. (Original work published in 1845).
May, R. (1958). Contributions of existential psychotherapy. In R. May, E. Angel, & H. F. Ellenberger (Eds), *Existence* (pp. 37–91). New York: Simon & Schuster.
Mayer, E. (2018). *The mind-gut connection: How the hidden conversation within our bodies impacts our moods, our choices, and our overall health*. New York: Harper Collins.
McCullough, D. (2019). *The pioneers: The heroic story of the settlers who brought the American ideal west*. New York: Simon & Schuster.
McGowan, J. (1991). *Postmodernism and its critics*. Ithaca: Cornell University Press.
Messaoudi, M., Lalonde, R., Voille, N., Javelot, H., Desor, D., Nedji, A., et al.(2011). Assessment of psychotropic-like properties of a probiotic formulation (Lactobacillus helveticus R0052 and Bifidobacterium longum R0175) in rats and human subjects. *British Journal of Nutrition*, *105*, 755–764.
Nisbett, R. E., & Wilson, T. (1977). Telling more than we can know: Verbal reports on mental processes. *Psychological Review*, *84*, 231–259.
Nobel, J. (2007). Eco-anxiety: Something else to worry about. *The Philadelphia Inquirer*, April9.
Norgaard, K. M. (2011). *Living in denial: Climate change, emotions, and everyday life*. Cambridge: MIT Press.
NWF (2011). The psychological effects of global warming on the United States: And why the U.S. mental health care system is not adequately prepared. *National Forum and Research Report*, February, 2012.
Orange, D. (2000). Zeddies' relational unconscious: Some further reflections. *Psychoanalytic Psychology*, *17*, 488–492.
Orange, D. (2016). *Climate crisis, psychoanalysis and radical ethics*. London: Routledge.
Orwell, G. (1961). 1984. New York: Signet Classics. (Original work published in 1949).
Pihkala, P. (2018). Eco-anxiety, tragedy, and hope: Psychological and spiritual dimensions of climate change. *Zygon Journal of Religion and Science*, *53*, 545–569.
Porges, S. W. (2009). Reciprocal influences between body and brain in the perception and expression of affect: A polyvagal perspective. In D. Fosha, D. J. Siegal, & M. F. Solomon (Eds), *The healing power of emotion: Affective neuroscience, development and clinical practice* (pp. 27–54). New York: W.W. Norton & Co.
Porges, S. W. (2011). *The polyvagal theory: Neurophysiological foundations of emotions attachmentcommunication self-regulation*. New York: W.W. Norton & Co.
Roberts, R. C., Farmer, C. B., & Walker, C. (2018). The human brain microbiome; there are bacteria in our brains! Paper presented at the Annual Meeting for the Society for Neuroscience, November 2018.

Safran, J. D. (2006). The relational unconscious: The enchanted interior, and the return of the repressed. *Contemporary Psychoanalysis, 42*, 393–412.

Sampson, T. R., & Mazmanian, S. K. (2015). Control of brain development, function, and behavior by the microbiome. *Cell Host & Microbe, 17*, 565–576.

Sarkar, A., Lehto, S. M., Harty, S., Dinan, T. G., Cryan, J. F., & Burnet, P. W. J. (2016). Psychobiotics and the manipulation of the bacteria-gut-brain signals. *Trends in Neurosciences, 39*, 763–781.

Sartre, J.-P. (2013). *Nausea* (L. Alexander, Trans.). New York: New Directions. (Original work published in 1938).

Slochower, H. (1970). *Mythopoesis: Mythic patterns in the literary classics*. Detroit: Wayne State University Press.

Tillisch, K., Labus, J., Kilpatrick, L., Jiang, Z., Stains, J., Ebrat, B., et al.(2013). Consumption of fermented milk product modulates brain activity. *Gastroenterology, 144*, 1394–1401.

Tversky, A., & Kahneman, D. (2000). Rational choice and the framing of decisions. In D. Kahneman & A. Tversky (Eds), Choices, values, and frames (pp. 209–223). Cambridge: Cambridge University Press. (Original work published in 1986).

Weintraub, S. (Ed.). (2013). *Engaging with climate change: Psychoanalytic and interdisciplinary perspectives*. London: Routledge.

Yang, B., Wei, J., Ju, P., & Chen, J. (2019). Effects of regulating intestinal microbiota on anxiety symptoms: A systematic review. *General Psychiatry, 32*, 1–9.

Zeddies, T. J. (2000). Within, outside and in between: The relational unconscious. *Psychoanalytic Psychology, 17*, 467–487.

6 Meaning, Subjective Well-Being, Thrownness, and Death

A summing up

Introduction

Over the course of this book we have tracked the presence of Absurdity in modern life through Psychoanalysis, Human Biology, Neuroscience, Philosophy, and Interdisciplinary Studies. There seems to be a significant divergence between the writings of the European Existential philosophers (for our purposes here, let's say Husserl, Heidegger, Sartre, and Camus) and their sort-of contemporaries, the *clinical* Existentialists (Boss, Frankl, May, and Yalom). The difference is the relative absence of writing about what should be called, Phenomenologically, relations between Human Beings[1] and what clinically, has been subsumed by Relational Psychoanalysis. This involves the analysis of here-and-now relationships between patients and therapists and the here-and-now relationships that patients and therapists have with others in their lives. These in turn have to a degree supplanted but not replaced the analysis of transferences located in the genetic past (Gill, 1982). Indeed, some of the richest *emotional* clinical writing, describing both patient and therapist is to be found in the work of Existential clinicians like Frankl (1972, 1959/2006) and Yalom (2009, 1989/2012).

The fundamental distinction between Existentially-based therapies and the various clinical schools of Psychoanalysis and the non-analytically based modes of therapy (e.g. Cognitive Behavioral Therapy (CBT), Dialectical Behavioral Therapy (DBT), and Eye Movement Desensitization and Reprocessing Therapy (EMDR)) is not that it necessarily seeks to disavow or replace them. It is rather that it requires us, with piercing honesty, to confront, and help our patients to confront, the Existential issues of living uniquely as Human Beings. These can be reduced to a few seemingly simple things: the presence of Absurdity, the search for Meaning, the finiteness and impermanence of life, and Death and our unavoidable anxieties about it. It would seem implicit in

---

1 Heidegger *did* become interested in clinical work later in life when he turned to Boss and participated in the Zollikon Seminars (1987/2001), but this work still did not delve into emotionality. Heidegger dealt with human relations, the *Mitwelt*, mostly in terms of Everydayness, the Being-with of the German *Volk* that was largely unreflective.

these observations that the absence of at least an Existential component to Psychoanalysis or Psychotherapy will leave significant therapeutic issues unaddressed and lead to a more limited therapeutic outcome than one might hope for.

Being, as we have seen, takes place at the interface between Self (the Bio-Psycho-Social Self) and World, a fact that Heidegger dealt with through his concept Dasein, Sartre through his dictum of "*Existence precedes Essence*" (1947/2007), and other Existential authors (e.g., Camus, 1942/1989, 1942/1991; Frankl, 1959/2006; Yalom, 1980) who describe the search for Meaning and the Deconstruction of Absurdity as taking place in World. "Deconstruction is a way of preserving particular aspects of meaning, often contrary ones that have been lost in [the] reliance on structure" (Leffert, 2010, p. 8). Structures of thought and observation that rely on taxonomy (inevitably involving the formation of Identity Categories) to seek out ways of Being can bury Meaning in Absurdity. Taxonomy freezes Meaning by encoding the absolute relationships between things (*choses*) and leaving no place for other relationships. Deconstruction is a tool that questions structure and offers a *post-structural* approach, a fundament of Postmodernism, to Being that releases Meaning from determinism.

None of the Existential Philosophers have focused at all on happiness and well-being. This has happened (or not happened) in spite of the fact that they are, after all, Existential states of Human Being; very desirable ones at that. The area of Interdisciplinary study that does take up these issues is Subjective Well-Being (SWB) (Diener, 1984) (see Chapter 4 for a discussion of SWB) and the area of psychology to which it applies is Positive Psychology (Leffert, 2017). The latter is often poorly understood and draws to itself at times undeserved criticisms and even contempt. It is possible that these philosophers have not thought much about happiness and SWB because they were not part of their lives or even their expectations. As I have written (Leffert, 2017) psychoanalysis and psychotherapy underwent a sea change in the late 20th century from striving to understand pain to seeking to heal or cure it. It is a still more recent phenomenon to aim not simply for the amelioration of the negative but for a transit into the world of the positive.

The problem we face is how well (or poorly) the various concepts—Meaning, SWB, Happiness, Thrownness—interface with each other. Meaning and Thrownness, for example, fit well together, as do SWB and Happiness. Although Meaning *can* fit into SWB and Happiness, it is not clear that it is necessary, and it is hard to see how Thrownness fits into either of them. When the Existentialists write about Meaning, however, they write about extreme situations entailing a particular individual's life on the edge—Sisyphus (Camus, 1942/1991), Meursault (Camus, 1942/1989) or Roquentin (Sartre, 1938/2013) —that involves Thrownness at least of a sort, but not Happiness. In considering these ways of Being Existentially, it is necessary to consider their relation to Death and the inevitability *it* brings with it: the death of the subject. We have, so far, not been particularly successful in our Existential understanding of Death; It is, after all, another of the hard problems (like Consciousness). A final attempt will be made here.

There is another aspect to what might be called "life at the border;" what takes place between Self and World. What has not been considered is that this space is now additionally populated by one or more electronic devices customized by the individual first for the Self and, as a distant second, for the World. Since the millennium, these devices have become parts of the Self, a Self, now part biological human and part machine, that has become a *Cyborg*. Although there is a developing body of literature on the subject, by and large it looks to the future in which the little machines we take for granted have morphed into things that fuse us all into a single Cyborg entity. We are interested in a more current, more modest view of what we are dealing with in our daily lives and how they might require us to reconsider the spaces of Meaning and Absurdity and the Connectedness (Christakis & Fowler, 2009) of the *Mitwelt*.

Subjective Well-Being

The piece that we have to add to Existentialist thought in this chapter is Subjective Well-Being (SWB)[2] as a major component of the wider field of Positive Psychology. It is a piece that is largely unknown to psychoanalysts if not to psychotherapists. *Briefly*, the field studies what makes people happy and how to measure it. It owes its origins to the seminal works of Ed Diener (2009a; 2009b; 2009c). A foundational conflict in the area—does happiness arise as a *subjective state* or in adherence to certain *external goods*—dates back to ancient Greece and the writings of Democritus and Plato, respectively. Contemporary Hedonics researchers, among whom Diener retains pride of place, focus on subjective state. As studied today, we assign equal weight to the *Subjective* and *Well-Being* parts of SWB. Kahneman (1999/2003) would like to offer objective criteria for happiness but is left with the realization that, in practice, self-assessments of SWB involve judgments made on-the-fly, so to speak, judgments *made under uncertainty* (Kahneman & Tversky, 1979/2000) employing heuristics and biases. The experience of SWB derives from a conscious assessment of happiness that involves both a cognitive, judgmental and an emotional, hedonic component. The assessment is both contextual and contingent (another problem for Kahneman). Clinically, it is a lack of Well-Being that often brings our patients to us. What we come to discover is that they make choices in the face of Uncertainty that they expect to make them happy only to find out that their Heuristics are false and have led them instead to repeated *un*happiness.

What we know about a person's SWB derives from what they tell us. They reference judgments made on the fly (Schwartz & Strack, 1999/2003) that are aspects of *life representation*. Immediate events (context) and mood (contingency) influence life representation. These authors also found that objective life circumstances only account for 5 percent of the variance in SWB; its subjective

---

2 See Leffert (2017), Chapter 6 for a more comprehensive discussion of Subjective Well-Being.

experience is a product of the Self-World (Heidegger's *Eigenwelt*). The attempted reconciliation of these findings with the ability of some life experiences—for Jews in Nazi Germany and African Americans in the pre-Civil Rights South for example—to totally overshadow the Self-World has perplexed SWB researchers from the start. Assessment involves a *target* the individual aims for and a *standard* to evaluate success. The Availability, Representativeness, and Simulation Heuristics are used in this process.

Rather than assessing on-the-fly judgments, we are more interested in an individual's long-term experience of Well-Being. These long-term experiences have been found (Diener, 1994) to be both stable and valid. "A case can be made for the dependency of Subjective Well-Being on the living out of culturally approved norms over the course of the life cycle involving the successful interdigitation between generations within a particular society" (Leffert, 2017, p. 142). Social factors correlating with SWB vary cross-culturally: In poorer societies (Diener & Diener, 1995), they vary with financial satisfaction, whereas, in more affluent societies, they correlate with fulfilling family and social relationships. Both cross-culturally and intra-culturally (Suh, Diener, & Updegraff, 2008) individuals assess their SWB differently, depending on whether they have a collectivist allocentric or an individualistic autocentric view of themselves.

The argument for the beneficial effects of Subjective Well-Being on the human condition should not be taken for its converse: that the goal is the eradication of negative affect. (Such affects are an essential and unavoidable part of human experience and learning.) SWB researchers (and Existentialist philosophers and clinicians) do not much take the neuroscience into account when studying it or other topics. Negative affects function as motivators, they drive constructive change, and they aid in the development of cognitive reappraisal systems. *However*, and it is a big however, the neuroscience tells us that chronic and persistent negative affect globally shapes experience and changes the brain—the functional neuroanatomy of the Self.

Anxiety as a class of experience, a fundamental response of the FEAR system (Panksepp & Biven, 2012), profoundly interferes with SWB. Wright and Panksepp (2012) locate such anxieties as secondary and tertiary responses of the GRIEF/PANIC system. They involve emotional and cognitive experiences deemed unrealistic *in the present* that include PTSD, Phobias, Panic Disorder, and Generalized Anxiety Disorder (GAD). SWB *cannot even exist* in the presence of these conditions.

Burgdorf and Panksepp (2006) offer discussions of the neurobiology of positive affects, finding several distinct forms related to "sub-neocortical limbic brain regions we share with other mammals" (p. 173). There is also evidence that the amygdala, much involved with anxiety, is *not* involved with positive affect; SWB thus arises in a separate system or group of systems. The neurobiology of Subjective Well-Being is a complex and neuroanatomically diverse matter, the study of which could aid us in understanding its stability and openness of SWB to change (Davidson, et al., 2003).

Meaning, Absurdity, Thrownness, Happiness, and Subjective Well-Being

If these ontological spaces more or less encompass the Existentialist universe, it is not clear that they can be integrated beyond a certain point. To illustrate just how difficult it can be to piece them together, let's look at life in one of the world's most miserable places to live—the slums of Calcutta (or Kolkata to free it from its Orientalist (Said, 1979) constraints). By looking at Happiness at the Margins, so to speak, it is possible to study it in the absence of uxorious gratifications. Unfortunately, little research on the happiness and well-being of people living in poverty has so far been conducted to study the effects of material deprivation on SWB. At its lowest levels, income has the largest effect on SWB (Veenhoven, 1991) through its ability to fulfill basic needs rather than add-ons such as automobiles or vacations (cellphones have since moved to a more ambiguous position). At the same time, psychologically or physically painful stimuli have been shown to, over time, display a lessening effect on SWB; this is thought to be a result of a *diminishing responsiveness* to such stimuli. At higher income levels, people tend to value relationships above material gratification. To study the relation of income and material possessions to life satisfaction (we are then left to consider how it relates to the issues of SWB we are studying) Bitwas-Diener and Diener (2001/2009) interviewed 83 residents of the Calcutta slums. They fell into three groups: those living in slum housing, sex workers (prostitutes) living in brothels, and homeless individuals living on the streets. By choosing disparate groups the authors (Bitwas-Diener & Diener, 2001/2009) hoped to find and study rich variations in the experience of poverty.

Dominique LaPierre (1983/1988) in *The City of Joy*, her fictionalized account of life in the Calcutta slums describes people trying, in the face of the direst of circumstances, to make of life what they can, using personal strengths and positive psychology. Bitwas-Diener and Diener (2006, 2001/2009) set out to explore and measure Subjective Well-Being in these populations. For our purposes, studying the Existential consequences of life's circumstances, it is important to note that they divided Life Satisfaction into three domains: Material Domains such as food, income, and housing; Social Domains such as romantic relationships, friends, and family; and Self-related Domains like Self, morality, physical appearance, and intelligence. They found that Life Satisfaction differed significantly in impoverished populations among the three domains, leaving us to draw conclusions about Meaning, Absurdity, Thrownness and Happiness.

Life satisfaction was measured by the Satisfaction With Life Scales (SWLS) that correlate well with Subjective Well-Being. Among all three groups of slum dwellers (Bitwas-Diener & Diener, 2001/2009) overall life satisfaction, while low (as compared to middle income Calcutta college students), was not *as* low as might be expected. Life satisfaction correlated strongly with objective measures of income (a correlation that was lost as incomes increased even modestly). These low global measures did not correlate with specific domain satisfactions, particularly the Self-related domains, which could be quite high. "Together, the multiple measures approach to SWB research produced a picture of Calcutta's poor as a group that, while living in sub-standard conditions are satisfied with many areas of their lives" (p. 274). Social and family relationships are particularly important to housed slum dwellers' sense of well-being where their relative absence in the pavement dwellers and sex workers was a major source of dissatisfaction. *None* report the overall suffering we might at first expect. "Rather, they believe they are good (moral) people, they are often religious (religion has been shown to correlate with SWB). They have satisfactory social lives and enjoy their food ... the complete picture focusses on the positive aspects of the respondent's lives" (p. 275).

Sabera is a 38-year-old slum dweller (Bitwas-Diener & Diener, 2001/2009) who lives in a single concrete room in a slum tenement with her husband and five other family members. She had five children—two daughters died when they were very young. She spends her days doing housework, cooking, and sewing for a living. Despite the deaths of her daughters she reports "my son gives me the most joy" and eagerly looks forward to his getting a job in a bakery. Married since the age of 15, she says that her husband, a tailor, is a major source of happiness in her life. She describes daily prayer as her most important regular task. When asked about life's challenges, she doesn't mention poverty or crowded living conditions or her young daughters' deaths but rather the work it will take to save for her two living daughters' dowries. Sabera sounds to us to be an enviably happy woman who does not share the more elaborate concerns of those earning large (comparatively) incomes.[3] Her life clearly has Meaning to her.

As the authors (Bitwas-Diener & Diener, 2001/2009) summarize,

> [I]t should be apparent that while the poor of Calcutta do not lead enviable live, *they do lead meaningful lives.* They capitalize on the non-material resources available to them and find satisfaction in many areas of their lives. Perhaps it is time we turned from an overused deficits model of understanding poverty to a more *positive strengths model.*
>
> (p. 276, italics added)

As it is a mistake to consider patients as a homogenous population, it is also a mistake to think of the slum dwellers in that way. Individuals respond in different ways based on the particulars of their Development, relationships, and Acts of Fate. As a result, one finds some dwellers of the slums living in subjective Absurdity while most do not. There is, of course, a global Absurdity at work here: Earth *could* be a planet of plenty capable of supporting a reasonable

---

[3] In Western society, it is found that happiness increases with income to an annual salary of $75,000 at which point it ceases to have a causal effect.

population in dignity and comfort. The fact that it does not is Absurd, an absurdity that we all have a role in and seem incapable of addressing.

What have we learned about our Existential questions from an examination of a Third World life of poverty? Bitwas-Diener and Diener (2006) were able to separate out cognitive aspects of SWB such as satisfaction and happiness from emotional aspects such as overall mood and particular feelings like joy and affection. The Existentialists have not been much interested in these distinctions. Although positive experience has much to do with Meaning and Happiness (Leffert, 2017), it has not been much thought about by the Existentialists let alone studied among populations; what I have been about here and throughout this volume is indeed a reworking of Existentialist concepts from a necessary interdisciplinary perspective.[4] It seems likely that Heidegger would have seen these things as Everyday (*Alltäglich*) concerns, not involving higher order Thrownness, a point that we will want to consider, but whose relevance to the question of Meaning is subject to doubt.

In these studies of Meaning, both from the perspectives of Existentialism and Subjective Well-Being, we are taking a macro rather than an individual view of the subject. While we work clinically with the absence, loss, or development of personal Meaning in the individual Human Being, it is important to keep an eye on the broader picture as well, something that (I hope) permeates my own work but can easily be lost in the immediate concerns of the Therapeutic Situation.

Meaning

There is a tendency among Existentialist and Phenomenological authors to make Meaning into some sort of higher-order goal to which is attached a certain *importance* or even *nobility*. It becomes, then, a form of metacognitive knowledge that is gleaned from reflections on the experiences of Human Beings. As Frankl (1959/2006) puts it,

> Man's search for meaning is the primary motivation in his[sic] life, not a "secondary rationalization" of instinctual drives. This meaning is unique and specific in that it must and can be fulfilled by him alone; only then does it achieve a significance which will satisfy his own *will* to meaning.
> (p. 99)

Heidegger (1975/1982, 1927/2010) implicitly takes the same position. He would place Meaning within the realm of Thrownness, that state of attuned Being-in-the-present in which the inevitability of Death is a foundation for life's meaning. It stands in opposition to the fear of Death that includes a fantasy that it is avoidable. Camus takes a similar stance. In *The Stranger*

---

4 Psychoanalysis is currently in the early stages of a similar reworking.

(Camus, 1942/1989), Meursault, who has lived a meaningless life (in his eyes as well as ours), finally finds meaning in the rage of the crowd at his upcoming public execution for the meaningless murder of an Arab he committed in a daze. Sisyphus (Camus, 1942/1991), who has led what Heidegger would call an empty, fallen life, is assigned a meaningless, repetitive task in Hades. As he performs it—pushing a huge boulder up a hill only to have it slip from his hands at the top and roll down requiring Sisyphus to walk down the hill and repeat it—he makes personal, subjective meaning out of the time for his thoughts as he walks down the hill.

We are so used in our *intellectual* pursuits of these kinds of arguments, reasoning forwards from hypotheses, that we do not stop to think that we are dealing with a top-down ontology. There is no *empirical* evidence cited here, no bottom-up reasoning. (To their credit, however, they are useful illustrations.) This is not the case for the writings of the Existential clinicians (e.g., Boss, 1963; Heidegger, 1987/2001; May, 1969; May, Angel, & Ellenberger, 1958; Yalom, 1980, 1989/2012). I would include here the more recent contributions of Stolorow and his colleagues (Stolorow, 2011; Stolorow & Atwood, 1992; Stolorow, Orange, & Atwood, 2002), who work with a more Phenomenological bent but are concerned with meaninglessness, pain, and death (Stolorow (2011) writes meaningfully and autobiographically about his own losses in ways that suggest he has been unable to come to terms with death). They start off clinically with patients who are suffering meaningless, unhappy lives that they cannot get ahead of. Neither the philosophers nor the clinicians treat happiness as an important part of these Existential considerations; indeed, suffering can *at times* be inferred from their work to be some higher order of experience.

Taking a more general top-down view of meaning, people in Western society find meaning in vocations and relationships. Specific kinds of human interactions involving, for example, rendering Care, are associated with Meaning. Meaning is Subjective; some people find meaning in sports and competitions, either as participants or as observers. Meaning also comes in new forms. Currently, many people seem to find Self-Meaning in exploring their DNA and their ancestry, seeking out roots and relations. The capacity to find Meaning for oneself is a psychological function, in the older language, one of the ego functions; it can be impaired through deficit or conflict and can be the subject of Psychotherapy. Over the course of this book, I have discussed many patients who presented with a sense of meaninglessness in their lives and worked with them in a search for Meaning. The origins of their sense of meaninglessness were multifactorial: development marred by trauma and deficit; conflict-based inhibitions of a more neurotic nature; and damage done by World or physical impairment of the Self. Like any other configuration of symptoms, one does not psychoanalytically address Meaning directly by identifying the problem and presenting a plan to solve it. (Whether or not this could be done in a Cognitive Behavioral Therapy approach remains questionable to me.) In each case, a sense of personal Meaning was regained through addressing specific underlying problems.

SWB researchers have studied the presence and prevalence of happiness and well-being in different general populations or sub-populations. Their basic measure of life satisfaction is the eponymous Satisfaction With Life Scale (SWLS) (Diener, Emmons, Larsen, & Griffin, 1985). It is a five-item scale that measures global life satisfaction, asking how satisfied people are with their lives and their goal accomplishment. It has been in use for decades, has been repeatedly validated, and correlates with other measures of well-being. The SWLS does not ask about Meaning. Although SWB researchers have not concerned themselves with philosophical issues or arguments concerning Meaning, they *have* studied how individuals find personal meaning in various geographically diverse populations at differing socio-economic levels.

Objective research into perceived Meaning of Life, understood to be an important part of Subjective Well-Being, has in the past been quite limited. Because Psychology and Psychotherapy have focused for so long on the quantification and elimination of the negative in life experience, SWB in general and Meaning in particular have come rather late to the table of Academic Psychology. Well-being researchers consider personal Meaning a sub-category of SWB. As Ryff observed in 1989, many of the available measures of positivity have been studied for reliability and validity and suffered from some narrowing of their perceived usefulness as a result. She appears unaware of an important thread of psychological research (Crumbaugh, 1977; Crumbaugh & Maholick, 1964; Reker & Cousins, 1979; Schulenberg, Baczwaski, & Buchanan, 2014) that has aimed to quantify the search for Meaning particularly as it relates to its Existential roots in the clinical and philosophical work of Viktor Frankl (1959/2006, 1969/2014). Since the millennium, SWB and Meaning have been extensively studied through the development of different psychometric scales

Frankl (1959/2006) developed the concept of Noögenic Neurosis to describe failures to the Human Condition, specifically a failing of the "will to meaning" (*Der Wille zum Sinn*), an Existential frustration, that separates Human Beings from other living things. He contrasted it with the Psychoneuroses. Frankl had found that 89 percent of people surveyed felt that life had to have some *purpose*, the will to meaning. To respond to the wholesale critiques of Frankl's work—that Existentialism accepts intuitive and subjective as well as empirical knowledge— Crumbaugh and colleagues (Crumbaugh, 1977; Crumbaugh & Maholick, 1964) set out to psychometrically study the will to meaning and determine if the concept of Noögenic Neurosis in fact reproducibly defined a discrete category of psychopathology. They, and investigators who came after them, were interested in validating Frankl's therapeutic approach—logotherapy— but their conclusions would also be valid for other Existentially-based psychotherapies. Crumbaugh and Maholick first developed the Purpose in Life Test (PIL), a 20-item test that asked participants to rate elements of purpose and life satisfaction using a seven-point scale: Interest, for example went from completely bored (1), to neutral (4), to exuberant, enthusiastic (7). They define "purpose in life" (arguably a re-statement of meaning-of-life (MoL)), as "the ontological significance of life from the point of view of the experiencing individual" (p. 201). Crumbaugh then developed a complementary scale—the Seeking of Noetic Goals Test (SONG)—also a 20-item test that asked about things like "ultimate life meaning" and "bothered by uncertainty in life." (Schulenberg et al., (2014) have subsequently validated the SONG as a measure of depression and psychological stress.) Crumbaugh found that PIL and SONG together successfully separated normal from abnormal populations and predicted therapeutic outcomes in patients treated with Frankl's approach.

Since then, Steger and colleagues (Steger, Frazier, Oishi, & Kaler, 2006) having developed a new measure, the Meaning of Life Questionnaire (MLQ) and Schnell (2009) has developed the Sources of Meaning and Meaning of Life Questionnaire (SoMe). They argue that better measurement tools will advance research able to assess therapeutic outcomes in the areas of both personal Meaning and SWB. Measurement of the MoL is difficult because it is, of necessity, a very individual thing, but *it is not impossible*. Steger and colleagues are critical of previous measures because of their high correlation with negative and positive affect and mood: "The investigation of potential correlates, antecedents and consequences of meaning of life are hampered if items are included in meaning measures that tap these related constructs" (p. 81).

The Meaning of Life Questionnaire (MLQ) is a ten-item survey (Steger, et al., 2006) that is divided into two subscales—Presence and Search—of five items each. There is a seven-point scale that ranges from "Absolutely True" (1) to "Absolutely False" (7) for each. "I understand my life's meaning," for example, is a Presence subscale item, and "I am looking for something that makes my life feel meaningful" is a Search subscale item. The authors present evidence from three studies that the MLQ is a reliable measure of the presence of and search for Meaning in life and that it represents an improvement over the PIL and SONG tests. Although previous scales indicated an improvement in personal Meaning as a result of psychotherapy, they could not distinguish it from confounding variables such as an amelioration of depression or anxiety. The MLQ is able to avoid covariance with these other factors. They found that "Meaning seems to be an indicator of a healthy and appreciated life and deserves greater attention in empirical investigations of human functioning" (p. 89). For our purposes, this conclusion is of particular importance since it is reached independently of Existentialist theorizing and provides confirmatory evidence for much of what has been discussed over the course of this volume.

A problem with the MLQ (Steger, et al., 2006) and the other scales of Meaning we have discussed is that they lack separate positive and negative scales with which to assess Meaning in Life. Since we are particularly interested in the failures in Meaning that can be grouped under the term *Absurdity*, we are left to judge them by inference alone. The Sources of Meaning and Meaning in Life Questionnaire (SoMe) (Schnell, 2009) comes much closer in the assessment of Absurdity. It offers separate scales that measure positive and negative dimensions of meaning: *Meaningfulness*, a sense of meaning and belonging, and *Crisis of Meaning*, life as frustratingly empty and devoid of Meaning. Schnell sets out, as do many Meaning in Life researchers, to investigate Frankl's (1959/2006) two premises: that the will to Meaning is what makes us human and what separates us from other creatures, and that its frustration can result in Existential symptoms that can look like psychological symptoms. Her aim, as well as that of Steger and colleagues, is to control for covariance with negative *and* positive factors such as depression, anxiety, boredom, neuroticism, satisfaction, positive affect, and Subjective Well-Being. the aim of the SoMe is to provide a simultaneous assessment in an individual of the positive and negative aspects of Meaning in Life. The scales yield separate triangles of data: Meaningfulness vs. no meaningfulness, Crisis of Meaning vs. no crisis of meaning, and some Meaningfulness and some Crisis of Meaning vs. Neither meaningfulness nor crisis of meaning. The questionnaire investigates four broad areas: self-transcendence—vertical involving something greater than the Self and horizontal involving relationships with others—self-actualization, order, and Well-Being and relatedness.

So, we have a philosophical and clinical approach to Meaning and Absurdity and a series of empirical studies of Meaning and, by extension, Absurdity that offer tools with which to study individuals or individual patients. The empirical studies offer that Unicorn of data: objective studies of the Subjective. This is a situation in which the whole *is* greater than the sum of its parts—taken together, the three approaches offer a much more powerful set of tools with which to study Meaning and Absurdity than any one of them would if taken singly. They offer as well a degree of cross validation that is hard to come by in the clinical behavioral sciences.

I want to move on to make another attempt at understanding the Meaning of Death (being dissatisfied, perhaps understandably, with the attempts I have made so far), perhaps the greatest enigma that confronts Human Beings.

Death and Death Anxiety

Death Anxiety is as old as Consciousness. Its roots lie deep in prehistory when it was only one of the many incomprehensible things that early humans and some of the hominins before them had to deal with. It, along with joy in living, are the ultimate regulators of homeostasis (Fotopoulou & Tsakiris, 2017) that distinguish us as Human Beings from other animals. They are, biblically speaking, a blessing and a curse. It is biologically hard-wired into us: Even animals that do not possess Autonoetic Consciousness seem to experience something like it. It is contained in the experience that prey have of predators. Death Anxiety exists at least as far back as the early Paleolithic (Leffert, 2018). This combined package led to the innovation of religion, the idea that there was some higher power who could take care of these (then) *unknowable* things. The appearance of funereal practices in the archaeological record is suggestive of both: the fear of death, an attempt to negotiate the passage from life to death, and the advent of Autonoetic Consciousness. Another marker is the presence of ornamentation—in dress, caves, or implements—which would require the presence of Consciousness. How far back are we talking about? Difficult to say. We do know of funeral practices and the presence of early "cemeteries" in a cave in what is now Spain, dating back 200,000 years. Recoverable evidence of ornamentation goes back around 50,000 years. So these proto-Existentialists were struggling with some of the same issues—Death, World, climate change—that we are.

The disastrous climate changes we are now living with (and their almost daily worsening) are unconsciously experienced as threats to personal Existence, the highly evolved representative of homeostasis. I live in California with its ever-longer seasons of raging Wildfires and now massive "controlled" power shutdowns that are supposed to limit the fires but don't: the failure on a governmental and corporate level to provide us with the homeostasis we have come to expect from them give me what, for lack of a better term, I would term an experience of Existential instability. If I add the sense of failure of our national government, I feel assaulted from all sides: My patients and friends tell me they experience the same things.

If we want to establish the phylogenetic bonafides of Death Anxiety we need look no further than the work of Jaak Panksepp (Panksepp, 1998, 2009; Panksepp & Biven, 2012). Panksepp found empirical evidence through cross-mammalian and cross-vertebral studies of seven biologically hard-wired core affects, one of which is FEAR. He defined for each, based on functional neuroanatomy, Primary, Secondary, and Tertiary affective states. Primary affect, in this case FEAR, is a midbrain function. It is a subject for debate whether these Primary affects include a component that we might best term EXISTENCE-FEAR. Certainly, such a component *does* exist in Secondary affects. It is the Tertiary component involving the cerebral cortex that poses uniquely (perhaps? probably? certainly?) for Human Beings the conscious knowledge and terror of Death that builds on primary and secondary FEAR.

Death is not a subject that usually comes up in contemporary Psychoanalysis and Psychotherapy unless patients have a terminal illness, or a chronic one that will become terminal, or have lost loved ones. As such, dealing with Death in treatment usually morphs into dealing with grief and mourning. This constitutes a major shortcoming present in much of contemporary therapeutic work. Enter Existentialism and Phenomenology. The position of these philosophers is not that dying is looked forward to and desired (although in the case of illness it *may* be), but rather that the finiteness of life, a finiteness we all must confront or deny, brings with it is an essential factor in life's having Meaning. The FEAR of Death is universal. It is the price of self-awareness, Consciousness, or auto-noetic consciousness, however we wish to term it. Yalom (2009) begins his personal account of the terror of dying with a quote from the 4,000-year-old Gilgamesh Epic, "Sorrow enters my heart. I am afraid of death." William James (1902/1982) looked to *transience*, both of the Self and its accomplishments, as giving rise to the need for religion. He famously referred to it as *the worm in the core* (of the apple) that ruined life and gave rise to religion. Phenomenology arose as the philosophical response to the problem; changing it instead to a bitter but essential part of the apple.

Death Anxiety is universal and has been extensively studied *outside* of Psychoanalysis but also *within* Existential Psychotherapy. Everyone, with the exception of some people at the very end of life, experiences some dread of Death: Success at living, well, *Existentially*, and the experience of Thrownness does not eradicate it or seek to do so. It is when Death becomes a pathological focus of Being or when the anxiety is rampant throughout one's existence, one's dreams, and one's hopes for the future that Death should become a subject of therapeutic inquiry.

Most therapists and analysts are unfamiliar with the literature on Death Anxiety and take the position with their patients that Death Anxiety is not anxiety about Death, but rather a displacement from some other fear. Vaillant (2002), in his work with subjects of the Harvard Adult Development Study, instead of taking the displacement route, offers a more advanced developmental view of dealing with Death based on Erikson's (1950/1963) last of the eight ages of man: *Integrity*. It involves the ability to keep one's Identity, one's *Self*, intact in the face of physical and mental decline. He offers a thoughtful and compassionate approach but does not consider Death Anxiety, its origins, course, or treatment. Neither he or Erikson consider the fact that Death Anxiety is present throughout the life cycle and is, if anything, *more* prevalent in young adulthood. As therapists, we tend to only find anxiety about Death in our patients when we start to listen for it (Vaillant does not appear to have heard about Death Anxiety from the subjects of his multi-decade study of Adult Development). Rather than serving as a displacement, facing our fear of Death can act in the opposite direction: Facing the reality of Death can lead us to making decisions to change our lives, making them meaningful in new ways. Yalom (2009), who has written extensively on the subject, makes this point with his patients. In his numerous clinical examples, he describes how many patients have sought him out for consultations or therapy precisely *because* they are much taken up with this Existential problem and know, from his writings, that he is attuned to its importance as a therapeutic concern.

Phenomenologically, Death and Death Anxiety can be engaged predominantly in any of the three modes of Being—Thrownness, Everydayness, or Fallenness—with the mix varying with age and circumstance. Yalom (2009) argues that the Consciousness of Death (or the finiteness of life experienced through a life-changing event) can serve as an agent of change that can shift a person's mode of Being from the Fallen or Everyday to the Thrown. If Consciousness, that is, Autonoetic Consciousness, of Life and Death can be an identifying feature of Thrownness, then *Un*consciousness, that is, the Repression of Life and Death as a traumatizing issue, is an identifying feature of Fallenness.[5] This shift

---

5 Everydayness represents a more complex situation. It is not driven by a fear of Death but rather manifests an unawareness of it, an in-the-momentness; an individual can be moved out of it, in the direction of Thrownness or Fallenness, through lifechanging events or, in the case of the former, through therapy.

into Thrownness is one that we can facilitate in our patients through therapy. Modern medicine has facilitated remaining in a Fallen state as it has enhanced the idea that death is avoidable or at least delayable for long periods of time and current experiments in cloning offer the possibility (or fantasy) that it can be dispensed with entirely.

Death Anxiety and a sense of personal Meaninglessness are closely related. (Ecoanxiety, as we discussed in the preceding chapter, has roots in both.) The sense that we have acted on World and the people around us for the benefit of both, a lasting benefit that may be passed on to future generations, mitigates against Death Anxiety and Meaninglessness. The hope that, as a therapist, I can offer my patients change for the better, change that they can in turn pass on to those around them, is, along with the relief of pain and suffering, one of the major things that gives *my* work Meaning. Yalom refers to this wish or expectation rather poetically as "rippling." This kind of legacy is not a personal one and certainly does not yield a personal immortality of lasting fame—such a wish is very much a Fallen one. Homer's story of Achilles (1998) taken from the *Iliad* illustrates this problem. As the story goes, Achilles was offered, as a youth, the choice of a long, happy life, or a short, heroic one as a great warrior. In the former, he would have good family and friends, die loved by all, be remembered for a generation or two and then forgotten. In the latter, he would be famous throughout the ages: This is the choice he makes, a Fallen choice. But, like much that comes from Homer's gods, there is irony here. Achilles does get his immortal fame, but for what? As is most widely known, it is for his weakness, not his skill as a warrior, for his *Achilles heel*. For those more familiar with the *Iliad*, he is also well known for his dishonorable desecration of the body of Hector, the prince of Troy and family man he had just bested in a duel.

Arguably, the treatments for Death Anxiety can be subsumed under the term *Consolation*. They differ only somewhat when a person has a terminal illness or when they do not. (Life itself can, albeit with some debate, be considered a bi-terminal—birth and death—situation.) Consolation derives from two sources: human relationships, including therapeutic relationships, and religion. There is an important distinction to be made here. Religion can be a source of consolation in that a belief in some higher caring entity is a source of solace. To the extent, however, that it is used to support a belief in everlasting life, that is immortality, it encourages Fallenness. Religions are, indeed, somewhat schizophrenic on the subject. Some do promise everlasting life in Heaven or Paradise (and the flipside—Hell), but others do not. Judaism speaks mostly of sleep and turning to dust, of going quietly into the eternal night. Many years ago, the Rabbi of the Congregation I then belonged to told me that he saw the role of religion, and, by extension his role, as helping people to cope with life's transitions. These included celebrations of marriages and developmental milestones but also the great transitions: Birth and Death. All religions prescribe carefully structured ways of mourning that comfort people in their grief, but an important function of all clergy is to visit the dying. The fact that, as therapists, we sometimes find ourselves moving into this role with patients has not been much written about (Yalom, 2009, is, again, an exception). But is becoming an ever-more-important part of the Therapeutic Situation.

In the case of Death Anxiety, present or appearing when Death does *not* seem to be on the horizon, it falls particularly on us as Psychotherapists and Psychoanalysts to help our patients deal with it. We must recognize a number of causes for such anxiety. Although we find conflict-based and attachment-based Death Anxiety, we must not lose sight of the forest for the trees. Interpreting the psychopathology does not address the Existential elements of Death and *we must address both*.

Charles

Many years ago, Charles, an investment banker in his 50s, consulted me as a Psychiatrist because he was suffering with restless leg syndrome. This proved fairly easy to treat but, in the process of my getting to know him, he told me a story. It seemed that his firm had decided to offer employees at his level a complete physical at the Mayo Clinic free of charge. Although Charles felt fine, he had chosen to avail himself of the opportunity. To make a long story short, they found that he had lung cancer. A lung was removed. A past smoker, the functioning of Charles's remaining lung was borderline. His oncologists elected (the need was uncertain) to treated him with radiation and chemotherapy and the remaining lung began to develop pulmonary fibrosis, a progressive condition that would gradually damage its function still further. It seemed a very real possibility that the radiation and chemotherapy had caused the fibrosis. Charles told me in his stoical way that he had been the victim of two acts of Fate. If he had declined the physical, he would not have known about the cancer and could have had several years of happy life, and if he had declined the post-surgical therapies, he would probably not have developed the progressive (and ultimately to-be-fatal) fibrosis.

There was little in Charles's past or childhood that bore on the subject. He led a restrained family life, loving his wife and children but not very emotional about it. In a few months of work, we were able to get past his stoicism and reach his anger at the situation he found himself in. Charles denied a fear of Death, "I know I will die of this eventually," he told me. "Since I don't know when, there's no point in my making myself unhappy by thinking about it." I had to agree. Charles was neither psychologically minded nor, more importantly, psychologically *interested*. I left him with the assurance that I was there for him and that I wanted to hear from him if things changed. I felt dissatisfied with what I was able to do for him but I felt it was my job to live with the dissatisfaction, not push him where he did not want to go.

He called me two years later. The fibrosis had worsened and he was in considerable respiratory distress. Charles's doctors were not particularly forthcoming on the subject: He had figured out that, as things were going, he was headed for an excruciating death by suffocation. He wanted to talk to me about dying, about what to do about the mechanics of Death. He felt that he didn't want to burden his family with any of this, and I offered my de facto acquiescence to his choice (if I had this to do over again today I would have pushed him to talk to his wife and offered to see them together to help them talk about it.) Charles remained unafraid of Death; it was the manner of this death that (rightly) terrified him. I told him that, if I were in his position, I would be terrified too. (By doing so I was making human contact with this stoical man and giving him permission for his feelings.) His doctor had prescribed opiate patches to relieve his respiratory distress. He then asked me what would be the result if he used four of them at once. I was well aware of the laws concerning assisted suicide but, throughout my career, I have had very strong ideas about my obligations to my patients to relieve pain and suffering. I told him that if he did that, he would slip peacefully into unconsciousness, stop breathing, and pass away. He would not know what was happening. He was silent for a long moment, then he thanked me. What was known and left unsaid was what he was asking (for information and permission) and how I was answering him. I thought it was even more powerful configured without speech. We chatted for a bit about how his family was doing, what *he* did—following professional sports remained an interest—and said goodbye for what I knew would be the last time (I did tell him that he should feel free to call me at any time if he needed to.) I practiced in a very small city. Two weeks later, I heard through the "grapevine" that he had died peacefully. I offer up Charles's story as an example of what can be accomplished in helping a patient to approach death, with only modest therapeutic tools.

Dennis

In contrast, Dennis, a reflective and self-observant clinical psychologist, living in another city, sought me out via Skype in his late 60s because of severe Death Anxiety that amounted to terror. In his early 30s he had suffered a mild heart attack and was left to wonder what life had in store for him. There was a history of heart disease in both of his parents' families, with two uncles having died suddenly of unexpected of heart attacks. An analysis in the 1970s and a re-analysis in the 1980s never addressed this issue, instead attempting to reconstruct more or less Oedipal issues related to his father's heart condition and his uncles' deaths. (Indeed, when he suffered a third MI in 1989, he simply did not return to the re-analysis—without being conscious of his anger and disappointment in both analysts.) The tendency for repeated MIs was addressed medically—the 1989 MI proving to be his last—but, 20 years later, he suffered an acute attack of Congestive Heart Failure. Although successfully managed with medication, Dennis's researches told him that *this* was what was going to kill him—he just didn't know when and his doctors were either unwilling or unable to tell him how long he had to live.[6] The episode ratcheted up his anxiety, and my writings on Existentialism (Leffert, 2016, 2018) and therapy and analysis via telephone (and now Skype and FaceTime) (Leffert, 2003) led him to contact me for a consultation. In such instances, I always suggest two or three in-person sessions to start with, and Dennis was happy to come and see me the following week.

I got all of this information in our first two meetings. I did not take a more standard narrative history because I knew *Dennis was not here for that* and would think unfavorably of me as being just like the other disappointing therapists he had seen in the past. In the way he talked about himself, his life and the people he knew, it emerged that Dennis belonged to a category of Human Beings that I have come to call the *Psychologically Solitary*. By this I mean people who usually have spouses, family, and friends and connections with World but experience themselves as *fundamentally isolated and alone*. He, his thoughts and feelings, did not feel known (*connaître*) to others even if at times he could see that they were.

I looked directly at him and asked him to take his time and tell me *exactly* what he was afraid of. "It's not being dead that so frightens me," he replied, "although I don't much care for the fact that I will *end*, lose all my experiences and my family, and seeing my children grow into their lives. It is the process of dying that is terrifying." "So, tell me exactly what is terrifying you about the dying," I directed. Two things frightened him. A loss of control: He was immobilized and *ending* and he couldn't move or do anything about it and the feeling of dying that he imagined as a black, downward, spiraling. This I could immediately help with and I asked him if he had ever received ether. It emerged that he had had a tonsillectomy at age five, which he had not thought of in his adult life. He had been physically held down while an ether cone was slapped on his face and he spiraled down into blackness. I told him that I had seen this before where people constructed dying experiences out of often unconscious memories of childhood anesthesia. "Killing two birds with one stone," I thought to address Dennis's solitariness along with the terror in the here and now of our relationship. "While I haven't experienced this particular terror," I told him, "I have had my own encounters with fears of death, and *I had the same experience with ether* as a child that you did." I held myself out to him as someone who could help him through both the terror and the isolation—to have taken any other kind of stance would, I felt, only serve to validate his feelings of separateness from humanity. He described this as "freeing"; the thoughts remained but the terror seemed to "evaporate."

---

6 This was one of the cases in which the fact that I was also a physician who was well-versed in Internal Medicine was essential to my understanding of my patient. I knew that it was impossible to answer Dennis's terrible question precisely and that it was too soon to answer it even in the most general of terms (Dennis's now eight-year healthy survival has been re-assuring to us both).

Coming to terms with his two Existential anxieties—fear of Death, as opposed to fear of dying, and the pain of being psychologically alone—then went on to make up the essence of Dennis's therapy.

Empirical studies of Death Anxiety

Having gone through some of the Existential ideas about Death and our subjective experience of them, we find, as we did with Meaning, that there is an empirical literature on the evaluation and measurement of Death Anxiety. Empirical researchers describe Death Anxiety as a fairly stable personality trait consisting of negative cognitive and emotional reactions to Death and dying. Templer (1970) began to study Death Anxiety in the mid-1960s and developed a Death Anxiety Scale (DAS) that is still in widespread use today. It consists of 15 statements (e.g., "I fear dying a painful death" and "The sight of a dead body is horrifying to me") that were initially posed in a true/false format but have more recently been administered by asking subjects for an evaluation of each item on the familiar five-point scale ranging from "strongly agree" to "strongly disagree." For our purposes, as interesting as the DAS might be, it is more interesting to take note of the fact that its development must indicate a significant rise in empirical and research interest in both Death and Death Anxiety. Prior to the mid-60s, these issues were disavowed and subject to taboos (much as cancer and mental illness were) both within and outside of the Healthcare communities.

It should be noted that, contrary to the expectations of the non-existential therapist, Death Anxiety researchers (e.g., Thorson & Powell, 1992) find such anxiety to be in no way unusual and very much a part of the normal emotional makeup of Human Beings. There are now many different approaches to measuring it. It remains very hard to validate these measures and most rely on their comprehensibility and face-validity. An exception is the Threat Index (Neimeyer, 1994/2015) that grows out of the now little-remembered foundational theories of George Kelly (1955/1963) to be found in his Psychology of Personal Constructs. Kelly's is a proto-dialectical constructivist theory (Hoffman, 1998) that anticipates contemporary relational work by a half-century and offers a replicable basis for measuring an individual's personal constructs about Death and Dying. What this means is that we all construct our own subjective realities of Death and, as therapists, we ought to try to engage our patients around the ways they construct their experiences of life in this area as we do in others.

Neimeyer (1994/2015) offers two critiques of the (then) existing Death Anxiety research: that it is "intellectually impoverished" in its definitions of Death Anxiety and that it fails to focus on Existential issues such as the experience of Death as an affirmation of Life. In contrast, the Threat Index (TI), devised by Krieger, Epting, and Leitner (1974), is fundamentally different, grounded in Kelly's (1955/1963) core psychological constructs that define identity and existence. It is used to identify an individual's personal constructs surrounding death. When these core constructs are challenged, we experience a Threat with Death being the "prototypical challenging event."

To assess Death Threat, The TI, administered in a structured interview format, has two phases: construct elicitation and element placement. In the elicitation phase, the subject is presented with three cards, each describing a situation. In the example Neimeyer (1994/2015) uses, one card (there are 19 different cards) says, "you discover you have leukemia and have only a few weeks to live." Another says, "A terminally ill patient dies after months of unrelievable pain." The third card is always the one that says simply "Death": It is employed to maintain the subject's focus. The subject is then asked to state an important way in which any two of the statements differ from the third. A subject responds that "two seem unpredictable while one seems predictable." This is then recorded as one of the ways the subject construes Death. The process is repeated with the 19 statements until 30 different constructs of Death are obtained. In the element placement phase, the subject is then asked to apply each construct to themselves or their Life, their ideal Self or their ideal Life, and their Death. (In the case of the example: Is your Life, your ideal Life, or your Death predictable or unpredictable?) As originally administered, the TI offers therapists a rich perspective on an individual's experience of Death and its place in their Life but it is difficult to score and compare multiple subjects. As a result, Krieger and colleagues (Krieger, Epting, & Hays, 1979) developed a shorter, self-administered form of the test that obviated the need for a trained interviewer.

Wong and colleagues (Wong, Reker, & Gesser, 1994/2015) observe that the focus on Death Anxiety research has been accompanied by a paucity of studies on other attitudes towards death. They posit that both Death Anxiety and Death Acceptance are related to the pursuit of personal meaning (Frankl, 1972, 1959/2006). To some extent, both are always present. Death Acceptance involves a cognitive acceptance of the finitude of life and, emotionally, some degree of equanimity or peace with that reality. These two components represent Confrontation and Integration. None of these are unitary concepts and are, by their very nature, as complex as the Selves that experience them. We seek personal meaning, and a source of our fear of death is our inability to find it. Consistent with this is Erikson's (1950/1963) last (eighth) stage of Development: the struggle between integrity and despair. Integrity involves a review of one's life—aspects one finds meaningful and shortcomings and regrets—that is a normative part of this final stage. In place of fear of Death, or coincident with it, Wong and colleagues identify three types of Death Acceptance: Neutral, Approach, and Escape Acceptance. (An alternate way of Being to Death Acceptance is, of course, Death Avoidance.) Both Death Anxiety and Death Acceptance are related to the search for personal Meaning. Neutral Acceptance involves accepting Existential reality; Approach Acceptance involves belief in some form of afterlife or reincarnation; and Escape Acceptance offers relief from present pain and suffering. For our purposes as therapists, what is to be learned here is that Death Anxiety, while at times pathological, is a normative part of Human Existence with phylogenetic roots going back to the primary core emotion FEAR.

We find in this empirical work many categories defining how we experience Death that we have not previously identified as therapists but can be used in clinical work. Therapists working with their patients in this way (e.g., Firestone & Catlett, 2009) do not see it as a replacement for other forms of exploratory Psychotherapy and Psychoanalysis but a necessary addition to it. The premise for this addition is that, uniquely in Human Beings, the awareness of Death, first appearing in childhood, and the Death Anxiety that follows leads to some normative denial of the inevitability of Death that is accomplished via the deployment of pathological defenses. Although many people are able to work through the denial of Death on their own, many are not.

Firestone and Catlett (2009) posit that the core pathological defense against Death Anxiety is what they call the *fantasy bond*. It involves an idealized connection to an idealized other (parents, family, spouse). Such a bond vanquishes Death. It is a bond that, unlike attachment, is a form of bondage because to violate it is to face the reality of Death. It also crowds out the real connections between people and the intimacy that goes along with them. They see the fantasy bond as hidden beneath other defenses—denial, transference, and enactment, for example—that must first be dealt with interpretively. These involve negative views of Self and World: a defensive retreat from Self and Life. The result of this process is gratification through fantasy rather than through lived Existence and the aim of therapy is to uncover the defenses that obscure it. As we have seen, the hallmark of gratification in a lived life is the acceptance of its transience, of the inevitably of Death.

Technologically enhanced Human Beings

Since the millennium, there have been fundamental changes in Dasein—the relation of *Self* to *There* (the *Mitwelt*). But if we are going to understand these additive changes in the connectedness of Human Beings, and the qualitative changes in the *Mitwelt* that technology has produced, we will have to go back much further—say, 20,000 years or so. I plan to offer only a brief account of these early changes: a different narrative of some Ancient, Early Modern (1500–1800), and Modern (1800–2000) events that will lead us to a novel view of the present, a Post-Phenomenological view.

Background

The roots of the connectedness that Christakis and Fowler (2009) wrote about go back to the pre-linguistic competence found in primate phylogeny and later involved groups of roughly 150 hominins: the social group size—Dunbar's number—that has been traced back at least to the Neolithic period. One hundred and fifty is also an upper limit mandated by the size of the Human neocortex (Dunbar, 1993, 2016). Speech and language, when they appeared, added to small group cohesiveness, and writing, when it appeared a few millennia ago, allowed for connectedness between groups of Selves at a distance. Literacy of a minority made this early transfer of information possible.[7]

Johannes Guttenberg introduced the movable type printing press into Europe ca. 1450. While the eponymous bible printed in 1452 was of long-term importance, the printing press, by the end of the 15th century, made information available through hundreds and then thousands of books (Pettegree, 2011) and allowed the *rapid* dissemination of information at a distance. (A broadside of Martin Luther's 95 theses written in Wittenberg in 1517 and generally credited as the start of the Protestant Reformation was printed and disseminated throughout much of Europe at a rate surpassing that of the news of the event.) What changed in that half-century was not peoples' brains, but the quantity of information people received and how they expected to receive it. Nothing much else happened for 500 years (newspapers offered only a more refined and systematized version of these 16th century broadsides). The appearance of printed books and broadsides allowed their authors to enter World more rapidly and to *connect* with others in a much larger *geographic* space than had previously been possible.

Partial literacy was sufficient for the dissemination of information. Whereas only a minority of people were literate at the beginning of the Early Modern Period (1500), a majority could read by its end (1800). The period also saw the advent of widespread personal correspondence allowing for the transmission of commercial information but, more importantly for our purposes, the maintenance of social relationships at geographic distance.

The 19th century saw the invention of the telegraph and wireless, which made possible the more or less instantaneous transmission of information; these allowed people to also think differently *about* information. The 20th century, with the advent of motion pictures, telephones, radio, and television, allowed for the direct and immediate transmission of *emotion* as well as cognitive information among individuals and groups. The rapid growth and financial success of these media prove how much Human Beings crave such connectedness. All of these devices *functioned more or less on demand* (radio and television content is *scheduled*—less so now—requiring individuals to plan for them) to quantitatively add to the Self's relationship with World. It was towards the end of the last century, with the advent of computers and cellphones, that things changed qualitatively.

Cyborgs

Webster's Dictionary (*Merriam-Webster's Dictionary*, 2004) defines a Cyborg as a bionic human. As we have understood the term, it refers to Human Beings

---

7 Most of the cuneiform tablets of the second and third millennia B.C.E. pertain to the shipping and accounting of commercial goods.

whose disabilities have been corrected or *whose capacities have been enhanced* by the implantation of mechanical or informational communicational devices (ICTs). (Such implanted devices already exist to offer limited corrections of some blindness (Stingl, et al., 2013), deafness, and motor issues.) We have not considered the effects of devices that remain external to the physical body —that is, cellphones (the potential for an implantable cellphone is probably only a decade or two away)—on the Self.

Intersubjective cellphone usage must impact two areas of the Brain: the Social Brain and the area of the Brain involved in Self-representation. The Social Brain concerned with intersubjective communication consists of the Right Pre-Frontal Cerebral Cortex and the Mirror Neuron System (Ferrari & Gallese, 2007; Gallese, 2005, 2009) connecting it to other parts of the Brain (see Chapter 1, this volume and Leffert, 2013, for further discussions or this material). Largely text-based communication can be partially converted to sensory images recovered from perceptual memories that remain largely unconscious. Self-Representation has been shown (Uddin, Iacoboni, Lange, & Keenan, 2007) to be the province of Cortical Midline structures of the Brain, which can exist in default or active states. The Self-representation includes the aspect of Self that enters Cyberspace and leaves a presence there. An important way to approach the study of the kind of Cyborgs who inhabit a Cyberspace of their own creation[8] is as ethnographers (Hakken, 1999) examining them from the perspective of social and cultural reporters who delineate the nature of the space and the social relations of those who inhabit it.

"Computer theorists use the term *cyberspace* to refer to the notional social arena we 'enter' when using computers [and cellphones] to communicate" (Hakken, 1999, p. 1). It constitutes a new social formation created by Advanced Informational Technology (AIT): It is a particular species of culture. The goal of the Cyberspace ethnographer is not to create new discourses (in a space already replete with discourse) but rather to try to sort out all that is going on there in a way that promotes meaning.

Cellphones fundamentally changed the Self and the way social groups functioned. Socially and Informationally, they offer a new pathway for mentalizing homeostasis (Fotopoulou & Tsakiris, 2017). Christakis and Barabási (Onnela, Arbesman, Gonzáles, Barabási, & Christakis, 2011) were on to this when they observed that while social networks had been largely constrained by geography, "larger social units, enabled by modern technology and political organization, offer dramatically different opportunities for social interactions and for group assembly over larger geographic ranges" (p. 1). Srivastava (2008) makes the observation that usage of the internet and the cell phone expanded at equal rates in the 1990s—only to see cell phone usage skyrocket globally in the new millennium. (In 2002, the number of cell phone lines in both the industrial and the

---

8 There are other kinds of Cyborgs, such as, for example, a blind Self with an implanted artificial retina (Stingl, et al., 2013).

developing world surpassed the number of land lines. By 2006, there was one cell phone line for every three inhabitants of the *planet*.) What the internet and cellphones both offered individuals and groups of individuals was the opportunity for the Self to enter a new third space (the first and second spaces being the self and the physical-social world of relating selves and others), Cyberspace.

There were geopolitical consequences to the explosion in cellphone usage: its epicenter shifted from North America and Europe to Asia. As we have come to live in an Informational Society (Donner, 2008), we had come to create a now-shrinking social world (not coincident with the geopolitical third world) of people and social units lacking cellphones. Cellphones were invented to be, well, these convenient little telephones you could carry around and call people with when you wanted. (While they are certainly that and people *do* call other people with them, they have rather become powerful little computers that are functionally parts of ourselves.) What cellphones have become, since the advent of the millennium, *was neither foreseen or predictable.*

Cellphones and their usage developed along two separate lines—the informational and the intersubjective—that unpack Heidegger's ontological locations of the Self's Being, the *Umwelt* ant the *Mitwelt* in the technological world of the 21st century. (I posit, following Idhe (2012), that this is a Postphenomenological undertaking—a difficult term that will be discussed below.) The Development of informational usage of cellphones was a two-step process. The first involved the ability to use search engines such as Google and commercial websites that came with the advent of cellphone internet access. This allowed an individual to *carry on their person* instant access to the informational world. The next step was the appearance of mobile apps on cellphones—an unanticipated event when the iPhone 1 appeared on the market a decade ago (last year, 178 *billion* apps were downloaded globally). The choice of apps allows an individual to create their own Subjective *space* (Bachelard, 1958/1994), an interface residing in the electronic *Umwelt* and *Mitwelt*.[9] The choice of apps determines how an individual reaches out to World. They constitute a Personal Construct.

The second line of Development involves Social Media, major components of which are Facetime, Twitter, and Podcasts. They entail reaching out to the electronic components of others posted on the internet and posting aspects of oneself for others to interact with. This creates a complex ontological space. We are projecting an aspect of Self into cyberspace that is available to others and can be interacted with by them and changed by them in our conscious presence or our absence. The aspect of the projected Self can also be a fantasied object or Self-representation. These interactions define Cyberspace as a Third Space that we enter as Cyborgs, relate to, and are changed by. We leave a presence there even when it is not attended to by our conscious

---

9 One customizes one's Cyberspace in the same way one selects a dwelling place, a house or apartment, and then stocks and furnishes it in keeping with one's interests, needs, and fantasies.

Minds. Game playing makes up a significant part of cellphone usage by roughly half of the people who have them. Games can involve solitary play against machine or fantasied opponents or can involve groups taking on fantasied tasks or quests in computer-generated worlds, with or without opponents; all of these can change the Social Self.

At least some mention of sex and the internet is called for here. Although addiction to online pornography—with the internet serving as far and away the major porn dispenser—and online sexual seduction and abuse are receiving (rightly so) considerable attention and study because of their universal destructiveness, the use of cellphones as a part of normative non-addictive sex between consenting adults has not been much studied.

This narrative of this Third Space is incomplete, taking up the device-like ("DT") (Wellner, 2016) and intersubjective aspects of cell phones and their usage in a limited way. It fails to consider the driving motivations behind their precipitous rise in usage and even their sometimes addictive quality: People *need* to be connected to other people and to World, and, given the opportunity, seek to increase these connections electronically. Although there are great commercial, scheduling and informational communication uses for cell phones, the *force* of their rise grows out of an overwhelming social need for connectedness (Christakis & Fowler, 2009). This need can constitute a healthy reaching out or a pathological addiction. The field of cellphone research is evolving so rapidly that even comparatively recent accounts (e.g., Katz, 2008) are becoming obsolete. It is difficult to keep up with how *cellphones are rewiring Social Networks*. Cellphone *dependency* as a predictor of depression and anxiety is already (Lapierre, M. A., Zhao, & Custer, 2019; Park, Yong-Chan, Shon, & Shim, 2013) a subject of considerable study. It is also clear that cellphone usage and the reasons for it differ among the generations; something that is beginning to be studied (Twenge, Martin, & Spitzberg, 2019). At a foundational level, cellphones are, for good or ill, taking up a much bigger piece of the Self and, again to summarize, people like or crave this.

Something should be beginning to be apparent about the introduction and exploding usage of cellphones in global society. If we look at this usage Phenomenologically (Heidegger, 1975/1982), we find that it falls into each of the three categories of Being— Everyday, Thrown, and Fallen. People can seek information and connectedness with others for purposes that fit into each of them. Coming back to the central themes of the present volume, we find that much (?), some (?) of cellphone usage is Absurd and involves dialing out (pun intended) of the real World in favor of a Fallen World without Meaning. Absurdity and Meaning can apply to the *Mitwelt* and the *Umwelt* of Cyberspace. This should become a subject of Therapeutic Discourse; mostly, it does not. Although we may hear from our patients about Fallen uses of cellphones—internet porn or mindlessly surfing the web—we have largely not yet added them to our lists of things to ask about.

A final note on Postphenomenology

Looking over this chapter, what strikes me is that there is a lot more work to be done on the issues that I have tried to tie together here. The chapter does not succeed in its purpose of tying up loose ends but, instead, systematically organizes the topics to be considered in a subsequent volume. The subject that the present volume has not engaged is the new field of Postphenomenology, the origins of which are generally attributed to Don Idhe (Idhe, 2012; Selinger, 2006). What seems to have driven Idhe's thinking about this field, which he also terms *Experimental Phenomenology*, is the appearance of technology—post-Husserl, post-Heidegger, post-Merleau-Ponty—and the reworking of Phenomenology that its appearance requires. I consider these arguments, interesting as they are, to be unnecessarily narrow. They ignore, for example, the advent of Neuroscience, a very similar kind of unfolding to Technology and they also insist on cleaving off Existentialism from Phenomenology—the reverse of the position I have taken for some years (Leffert, 2017, 2018; present volume). One cannot, for example, discuss Being-in-World, that is Dasein, without also discussing Network Studies, either from the perspectives of Latour (1999, 2005) or Christakis (Christakis & Fowler, 2009). The term that I am going to use instead, and develop in a subsequent volume, is *Interdisciplinary Phenomenology*. What I will propose is that Existentialism/Phenomenology is the most powerful epistemological discipline that we possess, but that, to fully realize its potential, it must be taken out into the wider world.

References

Bachelard, G. (1994). *The poetics of space* (M. Jolas, Trans.). Boston: Beacon Press. (Original work published in 1958).

Bitwas-Diener, R., & Diener, E. (2006). The subjective well-being of the homeless, and lessons for happiness. *Social Indicators Research, 76*, 185–205.

Bitwas-Diener, R., & Diener, E. (2009). *Making the best of a bad situation: Satisfaction in the slums of Calcutta Culture and well-being: The collected works of Ed Diener* (pp. 261–278). New York: Springer. (Original work published in 2001).

Boss, M. (1963). *Psychoanalysis and Daseinanalysis*. New York: Basic Books.

Burgdorf, J., & Panksepp, J. (2006). The neurobiology of positive emotions. *Neuroscience & Biobehavioral Reviews, 30*, 173–187.

Camus, A. (1989). *The stranger* (M. Ward, Trans.). New York: Vintage Books. (Original work published in 1942).

Camus, A. (1991). The myth of Sisyphus. In A. Camus, *The myth of Sisyphus and other essays* (J. O'Brien, Trans.) (pp. 3–138). New York: Vintage Books. (Original work published in 1942).

Christakis, N. A., & Fowler, J. H. (2009). *Connected: The surprising power of our social networks and how they shape our lives*. New York: Little, Brown and Company.

Crumbaugh, J. C. (1977). The seeking of noetic goals test (SONG): A complementary scale to the purpose in life test (PIL). *Journal of Clinical Psychology, 33*, 900–907.

Crumbaugh, J. C., & Maholick, L. T. (1964). An experimental study in existentialism: The psychometric approach to Frankl's concept of noogenic neurosis. *Journal of Clinical Psychology, 20*, 200–207.

Davidson, R. J., Kabat-Zinn, J., Schumacher, J., Rosenkranz, M., Muller, D., Santorelli, S. F., et al.(2003). Alterations in brain and immune function produced by mindfulness meditation. *Psychosomatic Medicine, 65*, 564–570.

Diener, E. (1984). Subjective well-being. *Psychological Bulletin, 95*, 542–575.

Diener, E. (1994). Assessing Subjective Well-Being: Progress and opportunities. *Social Indicators Research, 31*, 103–157.

Diener, E. (Ed.) (2009a). *Assessing well-being: The collected works of Ed Diener*. New York: Springer.

Diener, E. (Ed.) (2009b). *Culture and well-being: The collected works of Ed Diener*. New York: Springer.

Diener, E. (Ed.) (2009c). *The science of well being: The collected works of Ed Diener*. New York: Springer.

Diener, E., & Diener, M. (1995). Cross-cultural correlates of life satisfaction and self-esteem. *Journal of Personality and Social Psychology, 68*, 653–663.

Diener, E., Emmons, R. A., Larsen, R. J., & Griffin, S. (1985). The satisfaction with life scale. *Journal of Personality Assessment, 49*, 71–75.

Donner, J. (2008). Shrinking fourth world? Mobiles, development and inclusion. In J. E. Katz (Ed.), *Handbook of mobile communication studies* (pp. 29–42). Cambridge: MIT Press.

Dunbar, R. (1993). Coevolution of neocortex size, group size and language in humans. *Behavioral and Brain Sciences, 16*, 681–694.

Dunbar, R. (2016). *Human evolution: Our brains and behavior*. Oxford: Oxford University Press.

Erikson, E. (1963). *Childhood and society* (2nd edn). New York: W.W. Norton & Co. (Original work published in 1950).

Ferrari, P. F., & Gallese, V. (2007). Mirror neurons and intersubjectivity. In S. Bråten (Ed.), *On being moved from mirror neurons to empathy* (pp. 73–88). Amsterdam: John Benjamins Publishing Company.

Firestone, R. W., & Catlett, J. (2009). *Beyond death anxiety*. New York: Springer.

Fotopoulou, A., & Tsakiris, M. (2017). Mentalizing homeostasis: The social origins of interoceptive inference. *Neuropsychoanalysis, 19*, 3–28.

Frankl, V. E. (1972). The feeling of meaninglessness: A challenge to psychotherapy. *American Journal of Psychoanalysis, 32*, 85–89.

Frankl, V. E. (2006). *Man's search for meaning* (I. Lasch, Trans.). Boston: Beacon Press. (Original work published in 1959).

Frankl, V. E. (2014). *The will to meaning: Foundations and applications of logotherapy*. New York: Plume Books. (Original work published in 1969).

Gallese, V. (2005). Embodied simulation: From neurons to phenomenal experience. *Phenomenology and the Cognitive Sciences, 4*, 23–48.

Gallese, V. (2009). Mirror neurons, embodied simulation, and the neural basis of social identification. *Psychoanalytic Dialogues, 19*, 519–536.

Gill, M. M. (1982). *Analysis of transference* Volume I. *Theory and technique*. New York: International Universities Press.

Hakken, D. (1999). *Cyborgs@Cyberspace. An ethnographer looks to the future*. London: Routledge.

Heidegger, M. (1982). *The basic problems of phenomenology* (A. Hofstadter, Trans., Rev. ed.). Bloomington: Indiana University Press. (Original work published in 1975).
Heidegger, M. (2001). *Zollikon seminars: Protocols-conversations-letters* (F. Mayr & R. Askay, Trans.). Evanston: Northwestern University Press. (Original work published in 1987).
Heidegger, M. (2010). *Being and time* (J. Stambaugh & D. J. Schmidt, Trans.). Albany: State University of New York. (Original work published in 1927).
Hoffman, I. Z. (1998). *Ritual and spontaneity in the psychoanalytic process*. Hillsdale: The Analytic Press.
Homer (1998). *The Iliad* (R. Fagles, Trans.). New York: Penguin Books.
Idhe, D. (2012). *Experimental phenomenology* (2nd edn) *Multistabilities*. Albany: SUNY Press.
James, W. (1982). *The varieties of religious experience*. New York: Penguin Books. (Original work published in 1902).
Kahneman, D. (2003). Objective happiness. In D. Kahneman, E. Diener, & N. Schwartz (Eds), *Well-being: The foundations of hedonic psychology* (pp. 3–25). New York: Russell Sage Foundation. (Original work published in 1999).
Kahneman, D., & Tversky, A. (2000). Prospect theory: An analysis of decisions under risk. In D. Kahneman & A. Tversky (Eds), *Choices, values, and frames* (pp. 17–43). Cambridge: Cambridge University Press. (Original work published in 1979).
Katz, J. E. (Ed.). (2008). *Handbook of mobile communication studies*. Cambridge: MIT Press.
Kelly, G. A. (1963). *A theory of personality: The psychology of personal constructs*. New York: W.W. Norton & Co. (Original work published in 1955).
Krieger, S. R., Epting, F. R., & Hays, L. H. (1979). Validity and reliability of provided constructs in assessing death threat. *Omega*, 20, 87–95.
Krieger, S. R., Epting, F. R., & Leitner, L. M. (1974). Personal constructs, threat, and attitudes towards death. *Omega*, 5, 299–310.
LaPierre, D. (1988). *The city of joy*. New York: Grand Central Publishing. (Original work published in 1983).
Lapierre, M. A., Zhao, P., & Custer, B. E. (2019). Short-term longitudinal relationships between smartphone use/dependency and psychological well-being among late adolescents. *Journal of Adolescent Health*, 5, 607–612.
Latour, B. (1999). *Pandora's hope: Essays on the reality of science studies*. Cambridge: Harvard University Press.
Latour, B. (2005). *Reassembling the social: An introduction to Actor-Network-Theory*. Oxford: Oxford University Press.
Leffert, M. (2003). Analysis and psychotherapy by telephone: Twenty years of clinical experience. *Journal of the American Psychoanalytic Association*, 51, 101–130.
Leffert, M. (2010). *Contemporary psychoanalytic foundations*. London: Routledge.
Leffert, M. (2016). *Phenomenology, uncertainty, and care in the therapeutic encounter*. New York: Routledge.
Leffert, M. (2017). *Positive psychoanalysis: Aesthetics, desire, and subjective well-being*. New York: Routledge.
Leffert, M. (2018). *Psychoanalysis and the birth of the self: A radical interdisciplinary approach*. London: Routledge.
May, R. (1969). *Love and will*. New York: W.W. Norton & Co.
May, R., Angel, E., & Ellenberger, H. F. (Eds) (1958). *Existence: New directions in psychiatry and psychology*. New York: Simon & Schuster.
Merriam Webster's Dictionary (2004) (11th edn). Springfield: Merriam-Webster Inc.

Neimeyer, R. A. (2015). The threat index and related methods. In R. A. Neimeyer (Ed.), *Death anxiety handbook: Research, instrumentation, and application* (pp. 61–101). London: Routledge. (Original work published in 1994).

Onnela, J.-P., Arbesman, S., Gonzáles, M. C., Barabási, A.-L., & Christakis, N. A. (2011). Geographic constraints on social network groups. *Plos One*. doi:10.1371/journal.pone.0016939

Panksepp, J. (1998). *Affective neuroscience: The foundations of human and animal emotions*. Oxford: Oxford University Press.

Panksepp, J. (2009). Brain emotional systems and qualities of mental life: From animal models of affect to implications for psychotherapeutics. In D. Fosha, D. J. Siegal, & M. F. Solomon (Eds), *The healing power of emotion: Affective neuroscience, development, and clinical practice* (pp. 1–26). New York: W.W. Norton & Co.

Panksepp, J., & Biven, L. (2012). *The archaeology of mind: Neuroevolutionary origins of human emotions*. New York: W.W. Norton & Co.

Park, N., Yong-Chan, K., Shon, H. Y., & Shim, H. (2013). Factors influencing smartphone use and dependency in South Korea. *Computers in Human Behavior, 29*, 1763–1770.

Pettegree, A. (2011). *The book in the Renaissance*. New Haven: Yale University Press.

Reker, G. T., & Cousins, J. B. (1979). Factor structure, construct validity and reliability of the seeking of noetic goals (SONG) and purpose in life (PIL) tests. *Journal of Clinical Psychology, 35*, 85–91.

Ryff, C. D. (1989). Hapiness is everything or is it? Explorations on the meaning of psychological well-being. *Journal of Personality and Social Psychology, 57*, 169–181.

Said, E. W. (1979). *Orientalism*. New York: Vintage Books.

Sartre, J.-P. (2007). *Existentialism is a humanism* (C. Macomber, Trans.). New Haven: Yale University Press. (Original work published in 1947).

Sartre, J.-P. (2013). *Nausea* (L. Alexander, Trans.). New York: New Directions. (Original work published in 1938).

Schnell, T. (2009). The Sources of Meaning and Meaning of Life Questionaire (SoMe): Relations to demographics and well-being. *The Journal of Positive Psychology, 4*, 483–499.

Schulenberg, S. E., Baczwaski, B. J., & Buchanan, E. M. (2014). Measuring search for meaning: A factor-analytic evaluation of the seeking noetic goals test (SONG). *Journal of Happiness Studies, 15*, 693–715.

Schwartz, N., & Strack, F. (2003). Reports of Subjective Well-Being: Judgmental processes and their methodological implications. In D. Kahneman, E. Diener, & N. Schwartz (Eds), *Well-Being: The foundations of hedonic psychology* (pp. 61–84). New York: Russell Sage Foundation. (Original work published in 1999).

Selinger, E. (Ed.). (2006). *Postphenomenology: A critical companion to Idhe*. Albany: SUNY Press.

Srivastava, L. (2008). The mobile makes its mark. In J. E. Katz (Ed.), *Handbook of mobile communication studies* (pp. 15–27). Cambridge: MIT Press.

Steger, M. F., Frazier, P., Oishi, S., & Kaler, M. (2006). The meaning of life questionnaire: Assessing the presence of and search for meaning of life. *Journal of Counseling Psychology, 53*, 80–93.

Stingl, K., Bartz-Schmidt, K. U., Braun, B. D., Bruckmann, A., Gekeler, F., Greppmaier, U., et al.(2013). Artificial vision with wirelessly powered subretinal electronic implant alpha-IMS. *Proceedings of the Royal Society*, 1–8. https://doi.org/10.1098/rspb.2013.0077

Stolorow, R. D. (2011). *World, affectivity, trauma*. New York: Routledge.
Stolorow, R. D., & Atwood, G. E. (1992). *Contexts of being*. Hillsdale: The Analytic Press.
Stolorow, R. D., Orange, D., & Atwood, G. E. (2002). *Worlds of experience: Interweaving philosophical and clinical dimensions in psychoanalysis*. New York: Basic Books.
Suh, E. N., Diener, E., & Updegraff, J. A. (2008). From culture to priming conditions: Self-construal influences on life satisfaction judgements. *Journal of Cross-Psychology, 39*, 3–15.
Templer, D. I. (1970). The construction and validation of a death anxiety scale. *The Journal of General Psychology, 82*, 165–177.
Thorson, J. A., & Powell, F. C. (1992). A revised death anxiety scale. *Death Studies, 16*, 507–521.
Twenge, J. M., Martin, G. M., & Spitzberg, B. H. (2019). Trends in U.S. adolescents' media use, 1976–2016: The rise of digital media, the decline of TV, and the (near) demise of print. *Psychology of Popular Media Culture, 8*, 329–345.
Uddin, L. Q., Iacoboni, M., Lange, C., & Keenan, J. P. (2007). The self and social cognition: the role of cortical midline structures and mirror neurons. *Trends in Cognitive Sciences, 11*, 153–157.
Vaillant, G. E. (2002). *Aging Well*. New York: Little, Brown and Company.
Veenhoven, R. (1991). Is happiness relative? *Social Indicators Research, 24*, 1–34.
Wellner, G. P. (2016). *A post phenomenological inquiry of cell phones: Genealogies, meanings, and becoming*. Lanham, Maryland: Lexington Books.
Wong, P. T. P., Reker, G. T., & Gesser, G. (2015). Death Attitude Profile revised: A multidimensional measure of attitudes toward death. In R. A. Neimeyer (Ed.), *Death anxiety handbook: Research, instrumentation, and application* (pp. 121–148). London: Routledge. (Original work published in 1994).
Wright, J. S., & Panksepp, J. (2012). An evolutionary framework to understand foraging, wanting,and desire: The neuropsychology of the SEEKING system. *Neuropsychoanalysis, 14*, 5–39.
Yalom, I. D. (1980). *Existential psychotherapy*. New York: Basic Books.
Yalom, I. D. (2009). *Staring at the sun: Overcoming the terror of death*. New York: Jossey-Bass.
Yalom, I. D. (2012). *Love's executioner: And other tails of psychotherapy*. New York: Basic Books. (Original work published in 1989).

Index

References to footnotes consist of the page number followed by the letter 'n' followed by the number of the note.

1960s, and Existential Psychology 75–77

aboriginal healers 4
Abstract art, and Existentialism 74
Absurdism: and Camus xvi–xvii, xviii, 53, 58–59, 61, 64; and Kierkegaard 61–62; and Meaning/Desire 117; and Sartre 63; and Schopenhauer 40–41; and the Self 115; *see also* Absurdity; Camus, Albert; Psychotherapy and Psychoanalysis of the Absurd
Absurdity: Absurdity defined 108–109; Absurdity in Being xii–xiii; and addictions 166; and American Dream xix, 146–147; and cellphone usage 196; and Culture and History xix, 140, 142; Dasein as illness of xi, 109; and Development across life cycle 127–128; Developmental Absurdity 132; and Fallenness 144; and Meaning xvii, xviii, 109, 111–112, 182; and Meaning/Thrownness/Happiness/Subjective Well-Being 174, 177–179; as necessary psychotherapeutic component 173–174; neuroses as species of xii; pathological narcissism as species of xii; and politics 160–161, 168; and Sartre's *Nausea* 57; and Sartre's view of religious Existentialism 56; and Sources of Meaning and Meaning of Life Questionnaire (SoMe) 182–183; *see also* Absurdism; Camus, Albert; Psychotherapy and Psychoanalysis of the Absurd
Academic Psychology 181

Achilles story (*The Iliad*, Homer) 186
addictions: and Absurdity 166; and cellphone usage 196
Advanced Informational Technology (AIT) 194
aestheticism 45
affective neuroscience xviii, 32, 116, 119–120
Alaska, Native villages of northwestern Alaska 157–158
Albrecht, G. 153
Alcoholics Anonymous, Serenity prayer 63
Alltäglichkeit see Everydayness (*Alltäglichkeit*, Heidegger)
American detective fiction writers (1930s) 53, 59
American Dream xix, 146–151
American Existentialist Psychotherapy 33
American Psychiatric Association: asylums and foundation of 5; "Goldwater Rule" xix, 151
American Psychoanalysis 146–147, 149–150
American Psychoanalytic Association (APsaA): Kleinian analyst's Plenary Address 89n22; The Lawsuit, certification and control of institute curricula 14–15; number of members 2, 3; oral history re. psychoanalysts' flight from Nazi Germany and Austria 159n16
American Psychological Association 15
Andrews, F. M. 126
Angel, E. 81; *Existence* (May, Angel, Ellenberger, eds.) 8, 85

Angst 37, 97–98; *see also* anxiety
Annette case 95–96, 120
Anoetic Consciousness xv–xvi, 51, 116, 119, 130
anti-Semitism 35, 112, 114
Anxiety: and *Angst* 97–98; and Existential Psychotherapies 81, 96–99; Existential vs. Neurotic Anxiety 81; vs. Fear 94n27, 96–97; and fear of death 98; and folk psychopharmacology (1960s) 77; Freud's theories 9, 96–97, 98; Generalized Anxiety Disorder (GAD) 176; in Kierkegaard 37, 38; and Microbiome 163; and Subjective Well-Being (SWB) 176; *see also* Death Anxiety; Ecoanxieties; Political Anxiety
aporia 27
"An Appointment in Samarra" (Mesopotamian tale) 94
apps, and cellphones 195
archeology of knowledge (Foucault) xv, 35n3
Aristotle 124; *The Metaphysics* 10
Aron, Raymond xvi, 51
Arzy, S. 118
associations (patient's) 6, 8
asylums 5
attachment psychopathology 166
Attachment Theory xi, 9, 13–14, 166
Auchincloss, E. L. 133
Augustine 36
Autistic Spectrum Disorders (ASDs) 164, 166
Autonoetic Consciousness: and the brain 117, 118, 131; and Camus' *The Stranger* 112; and child development 132; and Death Anxiety 183, 184, 185; as defined by Tulving xv–xvi, 51; and Evo-Devo 59; and Memory 130; not in Everydayness 113–114; Tertiary autonoetic emotions 120; and Thrownness xvi, 51
Availability Heuristic 123, 176

Bachelard, G. 102n31
Bakewell, S., *At the Existentialist Café* 51, 54
Barabási, A.-L. 194
Barnett, L. 85
Barrett, W. 39, 53, 54, 57
Baudelaire, Charles, *Les Fleurs du Mal* 42
The Beatles 76

Beauvoir, Simone de: and birth of Existentialism xvi, 51; and Camus' Absurdism, rejection of 62; and Existential psychology 104; and Freedom as key issue 54; and Heidegger 74; and Kierkegaard 56; Sartre-Beauvoir "golden couple" and fame 53; Sartre-Beauvoir relationship and Existentialism as cultural movement 52
becoming (Being towards) 37, 80
Being: Crises of 27; givens of 92; Heidegger's concept of xv, xviii; illnesses of 47, 58; vs. no-Being 80; state of vs. neurosis/psychosis 71, 81
Being of Human Beings: clinical theories based on xvii; and Consciousness/Unconsciousness 140–141; and Culture and Society xix; Dasein as 51–52; and Meaning in the face of Absurdity 140; and Ontology, subset of 64; as philosophy's subject (Heidegger) 49; as purview of psychology xv; and Sartre's "existence precedes essence" 56
Being towards (becoming) 37, 80
Being-in-the-World: and Absurdity xi; and Daseinanalysis 88; and Existential Psychology 71, 104; Heidegger's three ways of Being-in-World 144; and Network Studies 197; and Phenomenology xii; and the sixties in America 77; and Social Network/Mirror Neuron Systems 165; and Social Networks 167; systems automating ways of Being-in-World 111; *see also* Dasein (Heidegger)
the believed, vs. the knowable xii
Bergmann, Martin S. 10, 26, 34, 75
Berkeley, George 40
Berlin Psychoanalytic Institute 152
Biases *see* Heuristics and Biases
Binswanger, L. 33, 37, 70, 74, 81, 88; Ellen West case 72, 74
Biological needs (of sex and survival) 89
Bion, Wilfred R. 1, 72n7; "selected fact" concept 18–19, 23
Bio-Psycho-Social Self xviii, 80, 115–116, 118, 128n10, 140, 144, 174
Bipolar Disorder 47
Birksted-Breen, D. 25
Bitwas-Diener, R., Kolkata (Calcutta) slums study 177–179
Blass, R. B. 17–18, 19–20, 21–22

Boehm, Felix Julius 152
Boss, M.: Daseinanalysis 87–88; Dr. Cobling case 72–74, 89, 90; and Existentialist Psychotherapy 33, 70; and Heidegger 49, 74, 88, 173n1; and Kierkegaard 36–37; relations between Human Beings, focus on 173; Zollikon Seminars (Heidegger and Boss) 173n1
Boston Change Process Study Group 9, 91n24
Bounded Rationality 121, 122, 123
Bowlby, J. 9, 166
brain: Brain-Heart-Face-Circuit 162, 165; Brain-Heart-Vagus-Circuit 162–163; Brain-Self 131, 142; and cellphone usage 194; Cortical Midline Structures 118, 129; development of 128–129; Left Brain and Right Brain 50, 117–118, 122, 129, 130–131; Microbiome-Gut-Brain axis 162–163; Mind-Brain systems 119; Mirror Neuron System xix, 129, 164–167, 194; Second Brain 162; Self-Representation 118, 194, 195; Social Brain 194
Bråten, S. 166
Brentano, Franz 47
British Middle Group 8, 11, 36, 46, 58, 72
British Psycho-Analytical Society 72n6
Britton, R. 19
Bronstein, A. A. 23, 24, 24n24
Burgdorf, J. 176
Butler, Harry 13–14

Calcutta (Kolkata) slums study 177–179
California wildfires (US) 154–155, 158, 184
Camus, Albert: Absurdism and discrepancy between Self and World xvi–xvii, 58; Absurdity and freedom 63–64; Absurdity and Heidegger's concepts of Being xviii; Absurdity and "leap of faith" 61–62; Absurdity and suicide 61, 111, 123n9; acceptance of Absurd condition/the subjective 62; *Caligula* (play) xvii, 52–53, 59, 63–64; doing philosophy writing novels 53, 76; Existence question 60–61; Existential failure, concept of xi; and Existential psychology 70, 72, 104; and Existentialists, different views from 109; in Existentialists list 34; and Heidegger 144; and Kierkegaard, foreshadowed by 39; and Kierkegaard's relationship with Christianity 37; life in Nazi-occupied France 112–113; and Meaning 62–63, 64, 104, 111–112, 174, 179–180; and Nietzsche, foreshadowed by 39; and nihilism xviii, 61, 62, 64, 111–112; *Notebooks* 53; and Picasso's *Guernica* 74; *The Plague* (novel) 53; and Psychotherapy/analysis of the Absurd 53, 109, 111–113; *The Rebel* (essay) 53; relations between Human Beings, no writing about 173; and Sartre, relationship with 52–53; "Three Absurds" xvi, xvii, 52–53, 59; *see also The Myth of Sisyphus* (Camus); *The Stranger* (Camus)
Care: CARE system (Panksepp) 96, 119; and Everydayness 49, 63, 113, 114; Existentialism as clinical theory of care 69; and Greek healers 4; and Meaning 180; professions focused on 11, 13; and Self-World interface 168; theories of 1; and Thrownness 50
Carson, Rachel, *Silent Spring* 77, 152
cases: Annette 95–96, 120; Charles 187–188; Constance 86, 96; Dennis 188–190; Diana 86–87; Dr. Cobling (Boss) 72–74, 89, 90; Ellen 150–151; Ellen West (Binswanger) 72, 74; John (in his 30s) 166–167; John (in his 70s) 133–134; Louise 154–155; Russell S. 100–104, 113, 114, 116, 121, 124, 125–127
Catholic Church: heresy and outlawing of healers 4; pastoral counseling 4–5
Catlett, J. 192
CBT (Cognitive Behavioral Therapy) 90, 174, 180
CCM (Comparative Clinical Methods) project 23–25, 26
cellphones: and addiction/dependency 196; and Connectedness 193, 196; and game playing 196; and homeostasis xx, 194; and Human Beings as Cyborgs xx; impact on Brain 194; impact on Self and social groups 194–195; informational usage 195; intersubjective usage 194, 195, 196; and sex 196
character 143
Charles case 187–188
child development: and Absurdity of development across life cycle 127–128;

child development courses 13; Existential Development 131–133; and Mirror Neuron System 165–166
Christakis, N. A. xx, 25, 43, 140, 167, 192, 194, 197
Civil Rights Movement (US, 1960s) 76
"civilized man" concept 42
Clayton, S. 156
climate crisis: and Death Anxiety 184; and disastrous effects of Self on World 140; and power elites 160; *see also* Ecoanxieties
climate skepticism 158; *see also* Eco-denial; Eco-disavowal
clinical moments, in conferences/study groups 17, 23
Cobling case (Boss) 72–74, 89, 90
Cognitive Behavioral Therapy (CBT) 90, 174, 180
Cohen-Solal, Annie 53
communism 43, 52
Comparative Clinical Methods (CCM) project 23–25, 26
complex systems xviii, 115–116
concentration camps, Frankl on 82–83, 145
connaissance, vs. *savoir* 79
Connectedness xx, 111n4, 116, 175, 192–193, 196; *see also* cellphones; Social Networks
Consciousness: Anoetic Consciousness xv–xvi, 51, 116, 119, 130; and Death Anxiety 183–184, 185; and emotions 119; and Evo-Devo 59; neuroscience of xv–xvi, 51; Noetic Consciousness xv–xvi, 51, 113, 116, 119, 130; and Phenomenology xv, 47; and Psychoanalysis 59; in Sartre 56–57; and Thrownness 144; and Unconsciousness 140–141; *see also* Autonoetic Consciousness
Consolation 186–187
Constance case 86, 96
constructions, theories as 22
constructivism, dialectical (Hoffman) 17, 19, 27, 78n15
contagion (Social Network Theory) 25, 43, 167–168
Contemporary Psychology xvii–xviii
Cooper, S. H. 17–18, 20–22
"counterpath" concept (Malabou/Derrida) 26, 49, 143
countertransference xiii; transference-countertransference 74

couples therapy 14
Crises of Being 27
Crumbaugh, J. C. 181–182
Culture and History: chapter overview xviii–xix, 140; American Dream xix, 146–151; Consciousness and Unconsciousness 140–141; culture and society xix, 144–146; Dasein as bridge between Self and World 144; Ecoanxieties xviii, xix, 141, 151–158; illustrative case (Ellen) 150–151; illustrative case (John, in his 30s) 166–167; illustrative case (Louise) 154–155; Microbiome xix, 141–142, 161–164; Mirror Neuron System 164–167; Political Anxiety xviii, xix, 141, 151–153, 158–161; Social Network System 164–165, 167–168; Unknowability 141, 142–143
culture and society xix, 144–146
Cyberspace 194, 195, 196
Cyborgs xx, 175, 193–194, 195; *see also* cellphones

Dasein (Heidegger): about Heidegger's concept xiv, xv, 36, 37, 49–50, 79–80; Absurdity as illness of xi, 109; Bio-Psycho-Social Self as 21st century formulation of xviii, 115; as bridge between Self and World 144, 174; as condensation of World, Being-in-the-World, Existence concepts xii; and Consciousness/Unconsciousness 141; and Despair 99; and digital connections between Self and World xx; and Existential Psychotherapies 78–80; and Existentialism, sociology of 35; and Network Studies 197; and neuroanatomy 117; and Phenomenology 51; and Social Network/Mirror Neuron Systems 165; and technology 192; and Uncertainty 143; *see also* Being-in-the-World
Daseinanalysis 49, 72–74, 84, 85, 87–89, 104, 109
Death: and Being-towards-not-Being 80; and Camus' *The Myth of Sisyphus* 61; and Everydayness xx, 93; and Existential Psychotherapies 80, 91–96; Existential understanding of 174; and Fallenness xx, 57, 80, 133; in fiction 93; in Frankl 83; Freud's "Death Instinct" concept 46, 80; in Heidegger

48, 49–50, 83, 93; and humor 94; and Meaning xix, 93; and Psychoanalysis 92; Psychological Schools focusing on 9; and religion 93; in Sartre 56–57, 83; Schopenhauer on 45; and Thrownness xx, 80, 93, 133, 155, 179, 185; and Viennese *fin de siècle* café society xv, 42, 43, 44, 45–46, 48; in Yalom xviii, 92–96, 98, 184, 185–186, 187

Death Acceptance xx, 191

Death Anxiety: classification and quantification of xx; and Consciousness 183–184, 185; and Consolation 186–187; Death Anxiety Scale (DAS) 190; and displacements 94–95, 185; empirical studies 190–192; and Everydayness xx, 185; and Fallenness xx, 50, 185–186; and fantasy bond 192; and FEAR system 184; and Gilgamesh Epic ("Sorrow enters my heart. I am afraid of death") 184; and Happiness xix; history of 183–184; and homeostasis, as regulator of xx, 183, 184; illustrative case (Charles) 187–188; illustrative case (Dennis) 188–190; illustrative case (John in his 70s) 133–134; and Meaning xix, 93, 191; and Meaninglessness 186; and Phenomenology xii; as psychotherapeutic component 173–174, 185; and religion 183, 184; and standard psychotherapy xii; and Subjective Well-Being (SWB) xix; Threat Index (TI) 190–191; and Thrownness xix, xx, 186

Death Avoidance 191

decadence, and Viennese *fin de siècle* café society 41–42

decision-making theories 121–124

deconstruction: and Meaning 174; Metapsychologies as subjects of xi

Democritus 124, 175

Dennis case 188–190

Depersonalization 60

Depression, vs. Despair 99

Derealization 60

Derrida, Jacques: cleavage between subject and object, critique of 72; "counterpath" concept 26, 49, 143; *différance* concept 3, 17, 21n21, 27, 49, 142–143

Desbonnet, L. 163

Descartes, René 48, 88

Desire: and Absurdism xvii, 58–59; and Mastery 132; and Psychotherapy/analysis of the Absurd 114, 116–117

Despair: vs. Depression 99; in Erikson 191; and Existential Psychotherapies 81, 99–100; in Heidegger xiv; in Kierkegaard 37–38, 44; Political Anxiety as 158; Sartre's *Nausea* concept as illness of 58

Deurzen, Emmy van 89, 91

Development: Absurdity of across life cycle 127–128; biology and psychology of xviii, 128–131; and Culture and History 140, 142; Developmental Absurdity 132; Erikson's theory xv, 50, 128; Evo-Devo 59, 123n8, 130, 132; Existential Development 131–133; Existential Psychology's failure to study 110; Freud's psychosexual developmental theory 18; and Psychotherapy/analysis of the Absurd 111, 116; and therapy taking place "in the present" 92

Dialectical Behavioral Therapy (DBT) 173

dialectical constructivism (Hoffman) 17, 19, 27, 78n15

Diana case 86–87

Diener, E.: Kolkata (Calcutta) slums study 177–179; Subjective Well-Being (SWB) 124, 125, 126, 175

différance concept (Derrida) 3, 17, 21n21, 27, 49, 142–143

Dinan, T. G. 162

Distributed Processing Systems 117

Doherty, T. J. 156

Dos Passos, John 57

Dr. Cobling case (Boss) 72–74, 89, 90

Drive, and Mastery 132

D-T scale 126

Dylan, Bob 76

Ecoanxieties xviii, xix, 141, 151–158, 186

Eco-commitment 153–154

Eco-denial 155, 157, 158

Eco-disavowal 155, 157, 158

Eco-grief 152

Eco-pessimism 153

Ego Psychology 8, 16, 18, 22, 71

Egypt, healing arts in pharaonic times 4

Eigenwelt see World of the inner Self (Heidegger's *Die Eigenwelt*)

Ellen case 150–151

Ellen West case (Binswanger) 72, 74
Ellenberger, Henri F. 81; *The Discovery of the Unconscious* 4, 41, 42, 43; *Existence* (May, Angel, Ellenberger, eds.) 8, 85
Elliott, A. 142
embodied simulation 165
emigres (20th-21st centuries) 146
emotional clinical writing 173
emotions: and Existential Psychotherapies 84; and Existentialism xvii; and motion pictures/telephones/radio/television 193; neuroevolutionary basis of 116, 119–120
empathic interest 102
Encounter groups/movement 14, 77
Engels, Friedrich 159–160
Epigenesis 128, 132
episteme 41
epistemology 64, 110, 142
Epting, F. R. 190, 191
Erikson, Erik: *Childhood and Society* 128; eight stages of Man xv, 50, 185, 191; fear of death and anxiety 98
European history (1848-WWII), and Existentialism 35
"European Spring" (1848) 35, 43
European thought, sea-change (ca. 1885) 41
Everydayness (*Alltäglichkeit*, Heidegger): about Heidegger's concept xii, xv, xviii, 49, 50, 173n1; and Care 49, 63, 113, 114; and cellphone usage 196; and culture 144; and Death xx, 93; and Death Anxiety xx, 185; and Eco-disavowal 157; and Happiness 179; and Meaning 63, 144, 179; and Nietzsche's *Thus Spoke Zarathustra* 39; and Noetic and Anoetic Consciousness xvi, 51; and Political Anxiety 161; and Psychotherapy/analysis of the Absurd 110, 112, 113–114, 118, 119, 120; and theory as construction 22; and therapists' work xiii
Evo-Devo 59, 123n8, 130, 132
Existence: and Camus' *The Myth of Sisyphus* 60–61; *existenz* (Kierkegaard) xiv, 36, 37; Meaning in Human Existence (or *Existenz*) 89; Phenomenological concept xii; Sartre's "existence precedes essence" xvi, 54, 55–56, 85, 111, 131, 132–133, 174; *see also* Being-in-the-World; Dasein (Heidegger)

Existential Development 131–133
Existential Psychology *see* Existentialism-based Psychotherapy and Psychoanalysis
Existential Psychotherapy Center of Southern California (Los Angeles, US) 84
Existentialism: beginning with Beauvoir/Sartre/Aron meeting (Montparnasse, Paris) xvi, 51; birth of and applications to Psychotherapy/analysis xiii–xviii, 32, 34; bridge between psychology and philosophy 35; establishing list of Existentialists 34–35; and European history (1848-WWII) 35; Existentialist family tree 32, 33; French Existentialism xvi, 33, 36, 52, 53, 55; and happiness/well-being, lack of interest in 174; and impressionist/abstract artists 74; and Phenomenology, relation to xii–xiii, xiv, 34; philosophic non-linear history of 32; Postmodern critique of Modernist Existentialism xix; and Psychoanalysis 9; as psychopathology of Human Being 70; and relationships between Human Beings, lack of interest in 173; search for Meaning as *the* Existentialist Problem 38; shortcomings of due to absent knowledges xix; sociology of 35; *see also* Existentialism-based Psychotherapy and Psychoanalysis; Existentialists (mid-20th century psychoanalytic theoreticians); Parisian café society (1930s-)
Existentialism-based Psychotherapy and Psychoanalysis: chapter overview xvii–xviii, 32; contemporary and classical literature on 84–85; Daseinanalysis 49, 72–74, 84, 85, 87–89, 104, 109; Existential philosophers vs. clinical Existentialists 173; Existential Psychology, appearance and overview 69–71; Existential Psychology, failure to address the Absurd 108–110; Existential Psychology, failure to study Development 110; Existential Psychology, origins 71–75; Existential Psychology, the sixties 75–77; Existential Psychology today 84–86; Existential Psychology, two problems (Camus/Interdisciplinary Studies) 104; Existential Psychotherapies, vs. other

therapies 10–11, 77–78, 85–86; illustrative case (Annette) 95–96, 120; illustrative case (Constance) 86, 96; illustrative case (Diana) 86–87; illustrative case (Russell S.) 100–104; Logotherapy 83, 84, 85, 88, 181; North Americans and the British 89–91; therapy and Anxiety 81, 96–99; therapy and Dasein 78–80; therapy and Death/Being-towards-not-Being 80; therapy and Death (Yalom's approach) 91–96; therapy and Despair 81, 99–100; therapy and Freedom, internal lack of 81; therapy and Freedom, Sartrean Human Freedom 55; therapy and legacy/vibrancy/dialogue 85; therapy and Meaninglessness 33, 81–84, 85, 108; therapy and Representativeness Heuristic 8; *see also* American Existentialist Psychotherapy

Existentialists (mid-20th century psychoanalytic theoreticians) 8, 9

Existentially Displaced Person 82

existenz: Kierkegaard's concept xiv, 36, 37; Meaning in Human Existence (or *Existenz*) 89

Expected Utility Theory 121, 123

Experimental Phenomenology (Postphenomenology) xi, xiv, xx, 192, 195, 197

Externalization 112

Eye Movement Desensitization and Reprocessing Therapy (EMDR) 173

Die Fackel (*The Torch*) 44n13

Fairbairn, Ronald 72

Fallenness (Heidegger): about Heidegger's concept xii, xv, xviii, 50; and Absurdity 144; and Autonoetic Consciousness xvi, 51; and Camus' *The Myth of Sisyphus* 61, 114, 180; and cellphone usage 196; and Daseinanalysis 88, 89; and Death xx, 57, 80, 133; and Death Anxiety xx, 50, 185–186; and Despair 99; and Heuristics and Biases 121; and life without choice 55; and Meaning, search for 26; and Nietzsche, as applied to 40; and Political Anxiety 161; and Psychotherapy/analysis of the Absurd 110, 113, 114, 118, 120; and religious consolation 186; and Stoltzfus' definition of the absurd 109n1; and theory as construction 22; and Unconsciousness 185

family therapy 14

fantasy bond, and Death Anxiety 192

Faulkner, William 53, 59

Fear: and *Angst* 97; vs. Anxiety 94n27, 96–97; FEAR system 119, 176, 184, 192

Ferrari, P. F. 165

Firestone, R. W. 192

Fiske, S. J. 158

Fliess, Wilhelm 6

Foley, J. 64

folk medicine/healing, and origins of Psychotherapy/Psychoanalysis 3–5

folk psychology 77, 93, 97, 124

folk psychopharmacology 77

Foucault, Michel: *The Birth of the Clinic: An Archeology of Medical Perception* 79; cleavage between subject and object, critique of 72; *The History of Madness* 5; knowledge, archeology of xv, 35n3; knowledge and power 14n16, 159, 160; *regard médical* 79, 101

Fowler, J. H. xx, 25, 43, 140, 167, 192

Framing, and Prospect Theory 123

France: May-68 76, 77; Nazi occupation of xvi, 53, 59n24, 60, 62, 64, 76, 112, 144; Paris Commune 35

Franco-Prussian War (1870) 35

Frankl, V. E.: concentration camps 82–83, 145; emotional clinical writing 173; and Existential psychotherapy 70, 81; Logotherapy 83, 181; *Man's Search for Meaning* 82, 84–85; and Meaning 104, 109, 112, 179, 181, 182, 183; Noögenic Neurosis 181; relations between Human Beings, focus on 173

Freedom: in Camus 63–64; and Existentialist Psychotherapies 55, 81; in Fromm 83–84, 103; in Kierkegaard (free will) 37; and Meaninglessness 83–84, 109; in Sartre (Human Freedom) xvi, 52, 54–55, 57; in Yalom xviii, 91

French Existentialism xvi, 33, 36, 52, 53, 55; *see also* Sartre, Jean-Paul

French Postmoderns 36, 78n15

Freud, Anna 20, 70n2, 72n6

Freud, Sigmund: "Actual Neurosis" concept 97; anxiety, theories of 9, 96–97, 98; *Arbeiten und Lieben* ("work and love" dictum) 75; *Autobiographical*

Study 38; child-mother relationship 166; *Civilization and Its Discontents* xiv, 38; cleavage of subject and object and objective truths of patients' lives 36n4; couch, rationale behind 6; Death, fear of and anxiety 98; Death Instinct/Drive 46, 80; early proto-psychoanalytic practice and healing arts 4; early years as neurologist/psycho-analyst 6; Ego, Id, Superego as clinically irrelevant construct 12; Ego, Id, Superego vs. World and Self 70; the Ego-Psychological 6, 8; and Existential psychology 70; hypnosis 6; *Inhibition, Symptom, and Anxiety* 39n9; Marcuse's synthesis of Marx and Freud 77; May's respect for 75; and Modern Psychology, birth of 12–13; on Nietzsche 38; Oedipus complex 26; psychosexual developmental theory 18; replacing "neurotic misery with everyday unhappiness" 109; schizophrenia 72n7; *Standard Edition* 74n12; *Studies in Hysteria* 16; the Topographic 6; transference 6–7, 18; Unconscious 39, 48n18, 120–121; and Viennese *fin de siècle* café society 43n12, 46; writings of as obfuscating contemporary *connaissance* 11–12; *see also* Psychoanalysis
Freudian School 9, 81, 89n22, 91–92, 99
Fromm, E. 81, 83–84; *Escape from Freedom* 103
Führer principle 49n19

Gallese, V. 165
game playing, and cellphones 196
Gardiner, Muriel 159n16
Gazzaniga, M. S. 50
General Systems Theory (GST) 115
Generalized Anxiety Disorder (GAD) 176
Genet, Jean 53
genocides 146
German psychoanalysts (1930s) 151–152, 159n16
Gesser, G. 191
Giacometti, Alberto 53
Gifford, E. and R. 153
Gilgamesh Epic, "Sorrow enters my heart. I am afraid of death" 184
Gill, M. M. 1
Gillespie, Sally 156

"Goldwater Rule" (American Psychiatric Association) ix 151
Greece, healing practices in ancient Greece 4
Greek philosophy, happiness and the good life 124, 175
Grief: Eco-grief 152; GRIEF system 176
Grimm's Fairytales 93
group therapy 14
Guntrip, H. 72
Gut-Brain 162–163
Guttenberg, Johannes 193

Hakken, D. 194
hallucinogens 77
Happiness: and culture 145; and Death Anxiety xix; and Everydayness 179; Existentialist philosophers' lack of interest in 174; and external goods vs. subjective state debate 175; and Greek philosophy 124, 175; and Meaning 125; and Meaning/Absurdity/Thrownness/Subjective Well-Being 174, 177–179; and Postmodernism 125; and Subjective Well-Being (SWB) 174
Harry Potter books 93
Harvard Adult Development Study 185
Hays, L. H. 191
healing arts, and origins of Psychotherapy/Psychoanalysis 3–5
Hegel, Georg Wilhelm Friedrich 40
Heidegger, Martin: *The Basic Problems of Phenomenology* 49; Being, concept of xv, xviii; *Being and Time* 48, 49, 49n19, 50; "being is the proper and sole theme of philosophy" xv; and Boss 49, 74, 88, 173n1; and Camus 144; Death 48, 49–50, 83, 93; Despair xiv; and Existential psychology 70, 72; and Existentialism, atheistic strand of 55; *Führer* principle 49n19; and Husserl, breaking with 34, 48, 50; and Husserl, taught by 48; and Intersubjectivists, influence on 69; and Nazism 48–49, 144; and Nietzsche's work, knowledge of 39n8; as one of the "Big Four" existentialists/phenomenologists 34, 35; philosophy as study of ontology xv, 49; relations between Human Beings, no writing about 173; and Sartre 51, 74, 144; Subjectivity xiv; temporality 50; translation issue 74, 144; "What is Metaphysics?" 51; Zollikon Seminars

(Heidegger and Boss) 173n1; *see also* Dasein (Heidegger); Daseinanalysis; Everydayness (*Alltäglichkeit*, Heidegger); Fallenness (Heidegger); Thrownness (Heidegger); World of other Human Beings (Heidegger's *Die Mitwelt*); World of the inner Self (Heidegger's *Die Eigenwelt*); World of things and animals (Heidegger's *Die Umwelt*)
Heisenberg, Werner: participant-observer concept 36n4; Uncertainty Principle 36, 143
Hemingway, Ernest 53, 59
Heuristics and Biases: Availability Heuristic 123, 176; and Psychotherapy/analysis of the Absurd xviii, 111n4, 116, 120–124; Representativeness Heuristic 8, 19, 123, 176; Simulation Heuristics 176; and Subjective Well-Being self-assessments 175
Hillel the Elder 69
historicity xv, 47, 50, 92, 100
History *see* Culture and History
Hoffman, I. Z., dialectical constructivism 17, 19, 27, 78n15
Holistic System (of Self) 115
Holocaust 145
Holtzman, P. S. 1
homeostasis: and cellphones xx, 194; Death Anxiety as regulator of xx, 183, 184
Homer, Achilles story (*The Iliad*) 186
hominins 183, 192–193
Human Beings *see* Being of Human Beings World of other Human Beings (Heidegger's *Die Mitwelt*)
Human Condition xi, xviii, 17, 71, 91, 133, 181
Human Freedom (Sartre) xvi, 52, 54–55, 57; *see also* Freedom
humor, and Death 94
Husserl, Edmund: "bracketing a term" concept 21n21, 27; everyday vs. objective science 48; and Existentialism/Phenomenology, father of 47, 48; and Existentialist Psychology 74; in Existentialists list 34; first principle (existing through being conscious) 54; and Heidegger, relationship with 34, 48, 50; Intentionality 47; intersubjectivity 48; Phenomena, clinical distortion and consciousness 47–48; relations between Human Beings, no writing about 173; "return to the things themselves" xii, xv, xvi, 34, 47, 50, 51, 73, 85, 142; transcendental intersubjectivity 48
hypnosis, Freud's practice of 6

idealism 41
Identity Categories 174
Idhe, Don 195, 197
immunity, and Social Networks 25, 167, 168
Impressionism: Impressionist art and Existentialism 74; Viennese Impressionism 43, 45–46
Informational Society 195
inhibition (*Hemmung*, Nietzsche) xiv–xv, 39
Institute for Contemporary Psychoanalysis (Los Angeles) 16
Institute for Psychoanalysis (Chicago) 16
Intentionality, in Phenomenology xv, 47
Interdisciplinary Phenomenology xviii, 197
Interdisciplinary Studies 11, 15, 21, 32, 104, 110–111, 120, 156, 173
Internal Working Models (IWM) 118, 122, 129
International Psychoanalytic Association (IPA) 3, 14, 23; number of members 2
internet 194–196; *see also* cellphones
Interpersonal School 8, 9, 72, 75, 90, 92, 147
interpretations: Existential interpretations 111, 127, 133–134; and first psycho-analysts 7
interreferentiality xviii, 17, 42, 94n27, 115, 128, 143, 153
Intersubjective School 9, 11, 16, 36n4, 69, 71n5, 75, 81, 99
intersubjectivity: biological engine of (Mirror Neuron System) 165–166; and cellphone communication 194, 195, 196; in Husserl 48; in Sartre's *No Exit* 56
Iñupiat communities 157–158
Irreducible Subjectivity xiv, 19, 39, 47, 56, 108, 110, 124, 159

Jacquette, D. 45
James, William 184
Janaway, C. 45
Janet, Pierre 6n10, 13
Janik, A. 41
Jaspers, Karl 55
John (in his 30s) case 166–167

John (in his 70s) case 133–134
Johnston, W. M. 35n1, 43, 45, 46
Journal of the American Psychoanalytic Association, papers on theoretical plurality 2, 17–22
Journal of the British Society of Phenomenology 84
Journal of the Society for Existential Analysis 84
Joyce, James 53
Judaken, J. 53
Jungians 84

Kahneman, D.: decision-making and risk ("Prospect Theory" paper) 121–124; decision-making and Uncertainty 8, 18, 19, 121; hedonic psychology 124, 125, 175
Kant, Immanuel 40, 49
Kaufmann, Walter 34
Kelly, George A. 190
Kennedy, John F. and Robert F., assassinations of 77, 147
Khan, Masud 72
Kierkegaard, Søren: and animal nature of Man, struggling with xiv, 38; anxiety (*Angst*) and freedom (free will) 37, 38; and Camus 37, 39; Christianity and Church, love-hate relationship with 36, 37; Christianity and search for meaning xiv, 38; in chronic crisis of Being 36–37; *The Concept of Anxiety* 38; *Concluding Unscientific Postscripts to Unscientific Fragments* 37; despair as illness of the Self 37–38, 44; early psychologist xiv, 38; and Existential psychology 70; and Existentialism, religious strand of 55, 57; Existentialists starting off from 32, 33; *existenz* xiv, 36, 37; *Fear and Trembling* and Absurdism 61–62; as one of the "Big Four" existentialists/phenomenologists 34, 35; and Phenomenology, definition of 47; pseudonyms 36, 37; Regine Olsen, relationship with 36; relational truth xiv, 36; and Sartre xvi, 39, 52; and Sartre's "Existence precedes essence" xvi, 55–56, 132–133; *The Sickness unto Death* 37–38; subjectivity and becoming 37; suffering 44, 88; translations of his works 74; and Viennese *fin de siècle* café society 43, 44
King, Martin Luther, Jr. 76, 77, 147

Klein, Melanie 9, 11–12
Kleinian School 9, 18, 20, 72n6, 72n7, 81, 89n22, 99, 156
knowledge: archeology of knowledge (Foucault) xv, 35n3; the believed vs. the knowable xii; *connaissance* vs. *savoir* 79; history of xv; Meaning as metacognitive knowledge 179; and power xiii, 14–15, 159, 160; social and scientific elements of 28
Kolkata (Calcutta) slums study 177–179
Kraus, Karl 44, 46n16
Krieger, S. R. 190, 191

Lacanians 84
LaFarge, L. 17–19, 20, 21–22
language, and power 160
LaPierre, Dominique, *The City of Joy* 177
Laplanche, J. 87, 133
Latour, Bruno xviii, 197; *We Have Never Been Modern* 28
Leffert, Mark, "Telephone Analysis" paper (2003) 10
Leitner, L. M. 190
"life at the border" (between Self and World) 175
life representation, and Subjective Well-Being (SWB) self-assessments 175–176
life satisfaction: Calcutta (Kolkata) slums study 177–179; and income levels 177–178; and personal Meaning 124; Purpose in Life Test (PIL) 181–182; Satisfaction With Life Scale (SWLS) 177, 181
literacy, and Connectedness 193
Loewald, H. W. 134–135
Logotherapy 83, 84, 85, 88, 181
"Lost Generation" intellectuals 51
Louise case 154–155
Luft, S., *The Routledge Companion to Phenomenology* (Luft and Overgaard, eds.) xv, 47
Lukes, S. 159, 160
Luther, Martin 37, 193

McGowan, J. 142
Madison, G. 85
Mahler, Margaret 166
Maholick, L. T. 181–182
Main, Mary 1
Major Depressive Disorder 47
Malabou, C. 26, 49, 143
Malan-Muller, S. 163

Man: animal nature of xiv, 38; eight stages of (Erikson) xv, 50, 185, 191; problem of xiv, 38
Marcel, Gabriel 55
Marcuse, Herbert, *One-Dimensional Man* 77
Marino, E. 157–158
Marx, Karl 77, 159–160
Marxism 43, 52; Neo-Marxism 64, 110
Mastery (in Development) 132
May, Rollo: *Existence* (May, Angel, Ellenberger, eds.) 8, 85; and Existential Psychotherapy xvii, 70, 71, 78, 80–81; and Freud/Freudian Psychoanalysis 75, 80; and Heidegger, Kierkegaard, Nietzsche 74; and psychoanalytic techniques, criticism of 98, 108; relations between Human Beings, focus on 173; and Sartre's *Nausea* character 58; and William Alanson White Institute 16
May-68 (France) 76, 77
Meaning: and Absurdism 58, 117; and Absurdity xvii, xviii, 109, 111–112, 182; and Absurdity/Thrownness/Happiness/Subjective Well-Being 174, 177–179; and American Dream xix; and Camus 62–63, 64, 104, 111–112, 174, 179–180; and Care 180; and cellphone usage 196; and children 132; and culture 144–145; and Culture and History xix, 140, 142; and Daseinanalysis 89; and Death xix, 93; and Death Acceptance 191; and Death Anxiety xix, 93, 191; and deconstruction (Postmodernism/Post-Structuralism) 174; and Everydayness 63, 144, 179; vs. Existential failure xi; as the Existentialist Problem 38; and Existentialist Psychotherapy/analysis 33, 85, 108, 116–117; and Fallenness 26; and Frankl 104, 109, 112, 179, 181, 182, 183; and Happiness 125; and Heuristics and Biases 121; in Human Existence (or *Existenz*) 89; and interpretation 133; and life satisfaction 124; Meaning of Life Questionnaire (MLQ) 182; measurements (objective and subjective) of personal meaning xix–xx; as metacognitive knowledge 179; and Mirror Neuron System 165, 166; and Phenomenology xii; and Political Anxiety 161; and politics 152; and Psychoanalysis of the Absurd 33, 90, 109–110, 111–113, 116–117, 118, 119–120, 134–135; as psychotherapeutic component 173–174; and Purpose in Life Test (PIL) 181–182; and Sartre 57, 58, 60, 62–63; and Satisfaction With Life Scale (SWLS) 177, 181; scales/questionnaires 181–183; and Seeking of Noetic Goals Test (SONG) 182; and the sixties 77; Sources of Meaning and Meaning of Life Questionnaire (SoMe) 182–183; and Subjective Well-Being (SWB) 181; and Subjectivity 180; and taxonomy 174; and Therapeutic Situation xvii, 179; and Thrownness 63, 144, 174, 179; top-down view of 180; *see also* Meaninglessness
Meaning of Life Questionnaire (MLQ) 182
Meaning Therapy 83
Meaninglessness: and Death Anxiety 186; and Existentialist Psychotherapies 33, 81–84, 85, 108; and Freedom 83–84, 109; multifactorial origins of 180; and Psychoanalysis of the Absurd 33, 116; Psychological Schools focusing on 9; Yalom on 91
Medical Model 88
Memory: and Culture and History 140; memory systems 130–131; Narrative Memory 129–130, 131; Procedural Memory 111n4, 129–130, 131; Semantic Memory 111n4; Syntactical Memory 129–130
mental illness: asylums, sanitaria and spas 5; birth of modern psychiatry 5–6; first psycho-analysts 6–7
Merleau-Ponty, Maurice 52, 104
Mesopotamian tale ("An Appointment in Samarra") 94
Messaoudi, M. 163
metacognitive knowledge, Meaning as 179
Metapsychologies (theory theories): vs. atheoretical psychoanalytic/therapeutic conversation 26–27; and clinical process, grown out of 26; vs. clinical theory 1–2, 11; as constructs xi–xii; and. Depression 99; and *différance* 27; multiple vs. single Metapsychology problem xiii; vs. Ontology 85; and psychoanalysts' education/training 15; and psychotherapists' education/

training 13; as social truth (not telling any truths about World) 27–28; and theoretical eclecticism 16–17; and theoretical plurality 17–18, 21–22; theory of theory theories 25–26; and validity issue 22
Meursault (character) see *The Stranger* (Camus)
Microbiome xix, 141–142, 161–164; Microbiome-Gut-Brain axis 162–163
Middle Group see British Middle Group
migration (20th-21st centuries) 146
Mind-Brain systems 119
Mirror Neuron System xix, 129, 164–167, 194
Mitwelt see World of other Human Beings (Heidegger's *Die Mitwelt*)
Modern Psychology 12–13
Modernist Existentialism, Postmodern critique of xix
Molnar-Szakacs, I. 118
multiple models 17, 19, 20–21; see also theoretical plurality
mysticism 42
The Myth of Sisyphus (Camus): and Absurdism xvii, 52, 59; and American Dream 150; and Death 61; and ecological/political anxieties 153; and Fallenness 61, 114, 180; and Frankl 109n3; and Heuristics and Biases 121, 123; and Meaning (not Happiness) 174; and Meaning vs. Absurdity 111–112; overview 60–63; and Russell S. case 103; and Thrownness 114, 180
Mythopoesis 152

narcissism, as species of Absurdity xii
Narcissistic Personality Disorder 166
Narrative Memory 129–130, 131
nationalism, as superorganism 168
Nausea (Sartre): Nausea concept 37, 58, 60; novel 52n20, 54, 57–58, 83, 103, 121, 143, 174
Nazism: crimes of and Existential Psychology 81–82; German analysts during Nazi years 151–152, 159n16; and Heidegger 48–49, 144; Holocaust 145; Nazi occupation of France xvi, 53, 59n24, 60, 62, 64, 76, 112, 144; Nietzsche's "superman business" and the Nazis 38n7; origins of and Viennese oppressed working class 43
Neimeyer, R. A. 190, 191

Neolithic period 192–193
Neo-Marxism 64, 110
Neo-Pragmatism 58, 64, 110
Neo-Romanticism 41–42
Network Studies 32, 197; see also Social Networks
neural hardware (of Self) xviii, 116, 117–118
neuroanatomy 115, 116, 117–118
neurobiology 110, 176
neuroevolutionary basis (of human emotions) 116, 119–120
neurophilosophy 115
neuroscience: affective neuroscience xviii, 32, 116, 119–120; of Consciousness xv–xvi, 51; interdisciplinary approach 10, 15; and metapsychologies 26; and Postphenomenology 197; and Psychoanalysis 9, 28; on psychotherapy courses 13; of the Self 116; and Subjective Well-Being (SWB) 176; thinking neuroscientifically 78n15; Workspace Theory 18; see also brain
neuroses: "Actual Neurosis" concept (Freud) 97; Noögenic Neurosis vs. Psychoneuroses (Frankl) 181; as species of Absurdity xii; vs. state of Being 71, 81
New Center for Psychoanalysis 12
New York Psychoanalytic Institute 12
New York University, Ego Psychology and Relational Psychoanalysis 16
Nietzsche, Friedrich: and animal nature of Man, struggling with xiv, 38; and Camus 39; early psychologist xiv, 38, 39; and Existential psychology 70; and Existentialism, atheistic strand of 55; Freud on 38; Heidegger's knowledge of 39n8; ill health and Dionysus 38; inhibition (*Hemmung*) xiv–xv, 39; nihilism xiv, 39; as one of the "Big Four" existentialists/phenomenologists 34, 35; Paganism and search for meaning xiv, 38; and Sartre 39; and Schopenhauer, influenced by 40; "superman business" and the Nazis 38n7; *Thus Spoke Zarathustra* 39–40, 43–44; translations of his works 74; and Viennese *fin de siècle* café society 40, 43–44
nihilism: and Camus xviii, 61, 62, 64, 111–112; and Nietzsche xiv; therapeutic nihilism 45, 46

214　*Index*

Nisbett, R. E. 121
Nixon, Richard, impeachment of 147
"noble savage" concept 42
nodes (Social Network Theory) 25, 167
Noetic Consciousness xv–xvi, 51, 113, 116, 119, 130
Noögenic Neurosis (Frankl) 181
Norgaard, K. M. 156–157

Oedipus complex 26
Olsen, Regine 36
one-person psychology 18
online pornography 196
Ontology: Being of Human Beings as subset of 64; vs. Metapsychology 85; and Phenomenology xv, 47, 85; philosophy as study of (Heidegger) xv, 49
Orwell, George 160
Overgaard, S., *The Routledge Companion to Phenomenology* (Luft and Overgaard, eds.) xv, 47

Panic Disorder 176
PANIC system 119, 176
Panksepp, Jaak xx, 96, 118, 119, 176, 184
Paris Commune 35
Parisian café society (1930s-): Beauvoir/Sartre/Aron meeting (Montparnasse, Paris) xvi, 51; and Existentialism 33, 35; French Existentialism and fiction 53; friendships and hatreds 53; Merleau-Ponty and Camus 52–53; Sartre and birth of French Existentialism 52; the "Sartre phenomenon" 53; Sartre-Beauvoir relationship and Existentialism as cultural movement 52; social circles including writers and artists 53; *see also* Beauvoir, Simone de; Camus, Albert; Sartre, Jean-Paul
participant-observer concept 36n4
pathological narcissism *see* narcissism
perception: studies of 40n10; and World of things and animals (Heidegger's *Die Umwelt*) 164
Phenomenology: beginning of in *fin de siècle* Vienna cafés xv; concepts xii; Consciousness xv, 47; defining (Luft and Overgaard) xv, 47; development of and applications to Psychotherapy xiii–xvii; and Existentialism, birth of xvi; and Existentialism, relation to xii–xiii, xiv, 34; and Existentialist Psychotherapy 32; family tree of Existentialism, Phenomenology 33; and fear of death 184; Intentionality xv, 47; and Ontology xv, 47, 85; Postmodern critique of xiii, xix; and Psychoanalysis 9; shortcomings of due to absent knowledges xix; sociology of 35; Temporality xv; and Therapeutic Discourse 18; Unconsciousness xv, 47; *see also* Interdisciplinary Phenomenology; Postphenomenology (Experimental Phenomenology)
philosophy: "being is the proper and sole theme of philosophy" (Heidegger) xv; doing philosophy writing novels (Camus) 53, 76; and Psychoanalysis 9, 28; study of Ontology as (Heidegger) xv, 49
Phobias 176
Picasso, Pablo 53; *Guernica* 74
Pickett, Melissa 156
Pihkala, P. 153
placebo effect, and primitive healing 4
Plato 36, 124, 175
Play: PLAY System 119; Play Therapy 132
Political Anxiety xviii, xix, 141, 151–153, 158–161
politics: and Absurdity 160–161, 168; and Meaning 152; and Social Networks 168; *see also* power
Pontalis, J. B. 87, 133
Porges, S. W. 162
pornography, online pornography 196
Positive Psychology 116, 174, 175, 177
Postmodernism: critique of Modernist Existentialism xix; critique of Phenomenology xiii, xix; deconstruction and Meaning 174; and epistemology 64; French Postmoderns 36, 78n15; and Happiness 125; knowledge and power 15; multiple psychoanalytic languages and Postmodern tools 17; and Psychoanalysis 9; and Psychotherapy/analysis of the Absurd 110; Subjectivity 17; Uncertainty 17; Unknowability xix, 17, 142–143
Postphenomenology (Experimental Phenomenology) xi, xiv, xx, 192, 195, 197

Post-Structuralism: cleavage between subject and object, critique of 72; deconstruction and Meaning 174; *différance* concept 3, 27–28; and epistemology 64; and French philosophy 36; non-linearity xiii, 3; and Psychotherapy/analysis of the Absurd 110; and theory as construction 22; Unknowability 142
Post-Traumatic Stress Disorder (PTSD) 7, 83n19, 95, 97, 146, 147n6, 154, 176
power: and institute networks 167; and knowledge xiii, 14–15, 159, 160; and language 160; and Political Anxiety 159–161; and Therapeutic Situation 159; 'witchcraft' as power relations term 4; *see also* politics
primal scream therapies 14
Primary Emotional Systems 119–120
primary process cognition 119n6
Primary Process Emotionality 119–120
primate phylogeny 192
printing press (ca. 1450), and Connectedness 193
probiotics 161, 163, 164
Procedural Memory 111n4, 129–130, 131
projection, and first psycho-analysts 7
Prospect Theory 121–124
psychiatry: birth of modern psychiatry 5–6; origins of 13
Psychoanalysis: American Psychoanalysis 146–147, 149–150; and Consciousness 59; and Death 92; different psychoanalytic theories 8–9; vs. Existential Psychology 75, 85–86, 92; vs. Existential therapies 173–174; and Existential toolbox, as sometimes-useful subset in xii; and Existentialism/Phenomenology 9, 69, 70; interpretations 7; and neuroscience 9, 28; Nietzsche and *fin de siècle* psychoanalysis xiv; and philosophy 9, 28; and Postmodernism 9; primary process cognition 119n6; prioritization of infantile past over *Umwelt/Mitwelt* issues 150; projection 7; Psychoanalytic Situation 22, 26–27; vs. Psychotherapy 2n2; resistance 6; taught on psychotherapy courses 13; taught on Social Work courses 14; as Theory of Man xvii, 71; transference 6–7, 18; Unconscious 12, 90; *see also* Freud, Sigmund; Psychoanalysis and Psychotherapy, brief history of; Psychotherapy and Psychoanalysis of the Absurd
Psychoanalysis and Psychotherapy, brief history of: chapter overview xiii; focus on macro-historical trends 2; healing arts and origins of psychotherapy/analysis 3–5; history and phenomenological inquiry 3; mental illness, asylums and birth of modern psychiatry 5–6; mental illness, neurological symptoms and first psycho-analysts 6–7; metapsychology and *différance* 27; metapsychology and validity issue 22; metapsychology as social truth (not telling any truths about World) 27–28; metapsychology vs. atheoretical psychoanalytic/therapeutic conversation 26–27; metapsychology vs. clinical theory 1–2; post-1950 explosion in psychoanalytic theory 7–9, 75; post-2000 lack of major innovations in psychoanalytic theory 10; Psychoanalysts as innovators (Extenders, Modifiers, and Heretics) 10, 26; Psychoanalysts' education and training 13n15, 14–15; Psychoanalysts marketing themselves as Psychotherapists 3n5, 149; Psychoanalysts/therapists, groups and numbers of 2–3; Psychoanalysts/therapists' education and clinical relevance of past theories 11–12; psychoanalysts/therapists' practice and Comparative Clinical Methods project 22–25, 26; Psychology of Being and Existentialism 10–11; Psychotherapists' education and training 12–14; science, the social and the psychoanalytic hybrid 28; theoretical eclecticism 16–17; theoretical plurality 2, 15, 16–22; theory of theory theories 25–26; transfer of information and Social Network Theory 25; *see also* Psychoanalysis; Psychotherapy and Psychoanalysis of the Absurd
Psychoanalytic Institutes 150
psychobiotics 163
Psychodynamic Psychotherapy 91, 92
Psychologically Solitary People 189
Psychology: as academic discipline 12; Being of Human Beings as purview of xv; Modern Psychology 12–13

psychopharmacology 13, 46, 47, 99, 110; folk psychopharmacology and the 1960s 77
psychoses, vs. state of Being 71, 81
Psychotherapy *see* Psychoanalysis and Psychotherapy, brief history of, Psychotherapy and Psychoanalysis of the Absurd
Psychotherapy and Psychoanalysis of the Absurd: chapter overview xviii; Bio-Psycho-Social Self 115–116, 118, 128n10; Camus' Absurdism 53, 109, 111–113; defining Absurdity 108–109; Desire 114, 116–117; Despair 99; Development 110, 111, 116; Development, Absurdity of across life cycle 127–128; Development, biology and psychology of 128–131; Development, Existential Development 131–133; Developmental Absurdity 132; emotions, affective neuroscience and neuroevolutionary basis of xviii, 116, 119–120; Existential and Metapsychological therapies' failure to address the Absurd 108–110; Existentialism, Phenomenology and Absurdity, family tree of 33; and Heidegger's Everydayness 110, 112, 113–114, 118, 119, 120; and Heidegger's Fallenness 110, 113, 114, 118, 120; and Heidegger's Thrownness 110, 112, 113, 114, 118, 120; and Heidegger's World of other Human Beings (*Die Mitwelt*) 110, 113, 135; and Heidegger's World of the inner Self (*Die Eigenwelt*) 110, 113, 115–117; and Heidegger's World of things and animals (*Die Umwelt*) 110, 113; Heuristics and Biases 111n4, 116, 120–124; illustrative case (Annette) 120; illustrative case (John) 133–134; illustrative case (Russell S.) 113, 114, 116, 121, 124, 125–127; Interdisciplinary approach 32, 110; interpretation, Existential 111, 127, 133–134; Meaning 33, 90, 109–110, 111–113, 116–117, 118, 119–120, 134–135; Meaninglessness 33, 116; neural hardware of Self xviii, 116, 117–118; and Post-Modernism/Structuralism 110; and Sartre's *Nausea* 58; Semantic and Procedural Memory 111n4; Social Connectedness 111n4;

Subjective Well-Being (SWB) 90, 116, 119, 124–127; temporality 110; and Unconscious 111
PTSD (Post-Traumatic Stress Disorder) 7, 83n19, 95, 97, 146, 147n6, 154, 176
Purpose in Life Test (PIL) 181–182

Queer Theory 26

rationality, Bounded Rationality 121, 122, 123
receptivity, and Social Networks 25, 167, 168
Reconstruction 81
Reflective Self 115, 116
Reik, T. 81
Reker, G. T. 191
Relational School 9, 16, 36n4, 71n5, 72, 75, 81, 90, 99, 173
relational truth (Kierkegaard) xiv, 36
Relational Unconsciousness 141
religion: and Consolation 186–187; and death 93; and Death Anxiety 183, 184; and Kierkegaard xiv, 36, 37, 38; and Nietzsche 43–44; religious vs. atheistic Existentialism 55–56; as source of Meaning and of Absurdity 145; and Subjective Well-Being (SWB) 178
Representativeness Heuristic 8, 19, 123, 176
repression: and Existential psychology 71n.3; and Freudian broken fragments (id, ego, superego) 70
resistance, and first psycho-analysts 6
Risse, G. L. 50
Roquentin (character) *see Nausea* (Sartre)
Rudden, M. 23, 24, 24n24
Rudolf, Crown Prince of Austria 46
Russell S. case 100–104, 113, 114, 116, 121, 124, 125–127
Ryff, C. D. 181

Samberg, E. 133
San Diego Psychoanalytic Institute 149–150
sanitaria 5
Santa Barbara wildfires (California, US) 154–155, 158, 184
Sarkar, A. 163
Sartre, Jean-Paul: *Being and Nothingness* xvi, 54–55, 57, 80, 85; and Camus, relationship with 52–53; and Camus' Absurdism, rejection of 62–63;

Consciousness and the other 56–57; Death 56–57, 83; "existence precedes essence" xvi, 54, 55–56, 85, 111, 131, 132–133, 174; Existentialism, birth of xvi, 51–52; Existentialism, religious vs. atheistic 55–56; *Existentialism is a Humanism* 54, 55–56; and Existentialist psychology 70, 72, 104; *The Flies* 52; and Heidegger 51, 74, 144; Human Freedom xvi, 52, 54–55, 57; "Is Existentialism a Humanism" (lecture) xvi, 53; and Kierkegaard xvi, 39, 52; and Kierkegaard's relationship with Christianity 37; "L'enfer, c'est les autres" 56–57; literature as mode of action 53; and May-68 events 76n14, 77; and Meaning 57, 58, 60, 62–63; Nausea (concept) 37, 58, 60; *Nausea* (novel) 52n20, 54, 57–58, 83, 103, 121, 143, 174; and Nietzsche 39; *No Exit* (play) 54, 56–57; as one of the "Big Four" existentialists/phenomenologists 34, 35; and Picasso's *Guernica* 74; relations between Human Beings, no writing about 173; Sartre-Beauvoir "golden couple" and fame 53; Sartre-Beauvoir relationship and Existentialism as cultural movement 52; subjectivity 62
Satisfaction With Life Scale (SWLS) 177, 181
savoir, vs. *connaissance* 79
Schacter, D. L. 83
Schnell, T. 182–183
Schnitzler, Arthur 42, 46
Schopenhauer, Arthur: on death and suicide 45; in Existentialists list xiv, 34; idealism and skepticism 41; and Nietzsche, influence on 40; "the Thing Itself" 41; and Viennese *fin de siècle* café society 40, 42, 43, 44–45; *The World as Will and Representation* 40–41, 44
Schore, Allan N. 117
Schorske, C. E. 43
Schulenberg, S. E. 182
Schweitzer, P. 157–158
science: and Husserl (everyday vs. objective science) 48; and the social 28; and Viennese Impressionism 43
Second Brain 162
Seeking of Noetic Goals Test (SONG) 182
"selected fact" (Bion's concept) 18–19, 23

Self: belief in (1960s) 75; Bio-Psycho-Social Self xviii, 80, 115–116, 118, 128n10, 140, 144, 174; Brain-Self 131, 142; and cellphone usage xx, 194–195; Despair as illness of the Self (Kierkegaard) 37–38; and Existential Development 131; Holistic System of 115; and interpretation 133; mother and development of 131; nature and origins of 28; and Neo-Romanticism 41; neural hardware of xviii, 116, 117–118; and psychological development 129; Psychological Schools focusing on 9; and Psychotherapy/analysis of the Absurd 110; Reflective Self 115, 116; and Social Media 195–196; Social Self 196; and Viennese *fin de siècle* café society xv; *see also* Self and World; World of the inner Self (Heidegger's *Die Eigenwelt*)
Self and World: Dasein as bridge between Self and World 144, 174; Dasein expansion via digital connections between Self and World xx; fragmentation of and abstract/impressionist artists 74; vs. Freudian broken fragments (id, ego, superego) 70; "life at the border" between Self and World 175; *see also* Culture and History
Self Psychology xvii, 2n4, 8–9, 10–11, 16
self-actualization 14
Self-experience xviii, 115, 118
Self-reflection xviii, 115, 118, 119, 120, 140
self-reporting scales 126
Self-Representation 118, 194, 195
self-understanding 14
Semantic Memory 111n4
Senden, Marius von 40n10
Sensitivity Training movement 14, 77
sex: anxiety from (Freud) 9; Biological needs of 89; and cellphones 196
Shakespeare, William, *The Taming of the Shrew* 64
Shane, M. and E. 134–135
Simulation Heuristics 176
Sisyphus *see The Myth of Sisyphus* (Camus)
the sixties, and Existential Psychology 75–77
skepticism 41; benign skepticism 102
Sledge, Eugene B. 83n19
social activist movement (US, 1960s) 76

social behavior, and Microbiome 164
Social Brain 194
Social Connectivity 110; *see also* Connectedness; Social Networks
Social Media 195–196
Social Networks: and cellphone usage 194–195, 196; and development of Phenomenology xv; Social Network System 164–165, 167–168; Social Network Theory xix, 25, 28, 43, 116
Social Self 196
Social Work (as academic discipline) 12, 13–14
society and culture xix, 144–146; *see also* Culture and History
Sources of Meaning and Meaning of Life Questionnaire (SoMe) 182–183
space, subjective experience of 102n31
spas 5
Sperry, R. W. 117
Spezzano, C. 142
Srivastava, L. 194
Star Wars (film) 93
Steger, M. F. 182, 183
Steiner, J. 19
Stolorow, R. D. 180
Stoltzfus, B. 58–59, 108–109
The Stranger (Camus): and Absurdism xvii, 52; and doing philosophy writing novels 53; and ecological/political anxieties 153; and Heuristics and Biases 121; and Meaning 179–180; and Meaning (not Happiness) 174; and Meaning vs. Absurdity 112; Meursault's execution vs. assassination of Caligula 64; overview 59–60; and Unknowability 143
stress, and Microbiome 164
Structuralism 36
Subjective Well-Being (SWB): Calcutta (Kolkata) slums study 177–179; and Death Anxiety xix; and Ecoanxieties 156; and Happiness 174; and income levels 177–178; Interdisciplinary study of well-being 174; life representation and self-assessments 175–176; long-term experience of Well-Being 175–176; and Meaning 181; and Meaning scales/questionnaires 181–183; and Meaning/Absurdity/Thrownness/Happiness 174, 177–179; negative effects and anxiety 176; and neurobiology of positive/negative effects 176; and Political Anxiety 161; and Positive Psychology 175; and Psychotherapy/analysis of the Absurd xviii, 90, 116, 119, 124–127; Satisfaction With Life Scale (SWLS) 177, 181; Studies of 32
Subjectivity: in Camus 62; in Heidegger xiv, 114; Irreducible Subjectivity xiv, 19, 39, 47, 56, 108, 110, 124, 159; in Kierkegaard 37; and Meaning 180; objective studies of 183; and Postmodernism 17; in Sartre 62; Subjectively known xii, 96; *see also* intersubjectivity
suggestion: advertent/inadvertent suggestions 5; explicit/implicit suggestions 5; and Freud's early practice 4; and healing/pastoral counseling 4–5; Psychoanalysts' depreciation of clinical use of 5; Psychotherapists' use of 7
suicide: and Absurdity (Camus) 61, 111, 123n9; Schopenhauer on 45; and Viennese *fin de siècle* café society 46, 61, 111
Sullivan, H. S. 147
Superorganisms 140, 167–168
suppression, and climate change 158
Syntactical Memory 129–130
Systems Theory, complex systems xviii, 115–116

talk therapy 7, 13
taxonomy, and Meaning 174
technology: and Connectedness (19th–21st century) 193; and Dasein/*Mitwelt* 192; *see also* cellphones; Cyborgs
Templer, D. I. 190
temporality: in Heidegger 50; and Phenomenology xv; and Psychotherapy/analysis of the Absurd 110
theoretical eclecticism 16–17
theoretical plurality 2, 15, 16–22
theory, as construction 22
Theory of Man, Psychoanalysis as xvii, 71
Theory of Mind 166
theory theories *see* Metapsychologies (theory theories)
Therapeutic Action: and American Dream issues 119; and Attachment Theory 13–14; clinical theories of xi; and Comparative Clinical Methods

(CCM) project 24; and creative uncertainty, open to 89; and Daseinanalysis 88; and Depression 99; and Freud's Ego, Id, and Superego construct 12; and Primary Process Emotions 119; and prioritization of infantile past over *Umwelt/Mitwelt* issues 150; Psychoanalysts' tools of 7; Psychoanalysts' tools of and Existential Psychotherapists 84, 86; and therapist's caring attitude 9

Therapeutic Discourse: and Academic Dream issues 147; and cellphone usage 196; controversial concept 6; vs. "Dialogue" term 85; and ecological/political anxiety xix, 151; phenomenological form of 18; and Primary/Secondary Process emotions 120; vs. theoretical discourse 17

therapeutic nihilism 45, 46

Therapeutic Situation: and Anxiety 98; and Death Anxiety 187; and *différance* 3n6; and Ecoanxieties 156; and Existential Psychotherapies 69, 70, 77–84; and Meaning xvii, 179; and multiple models 20–21; and power 159; and Subjective Well-Being (SWB) self-reporting scales 126; and suggestions, implicit/inadvertent 5; and therapeutic bias 89; and transference 7

therapeutic space 101

Third Space (i.e. Cyberspace) 195, 196

Threat Index (TI) 190–191

Thrownness (Heidegger): about Heidegger's concept xii, xv, xviii, 49–50; and Autonoetic Consciousness xvi, 51; and Camus' *The Stranger* 60; and Care 50; and cellphone usage 196; and Consciousness 144; and Daseinanalysis 88; and Death xx, 80, 93, 133, 155, 179, 185; and Death Anxiety xix, xx, 186; and Eco-disavowal 157; and Meaning 63, 144, 174, 179; and Meaning/Absurdity/Happiness/Subjective Well-Being 177–179; and Nietzsche, as applied to 40; and Nietzsche's *Thus Spoke Zarathrustra* 39; and Political Anxiety 161; and Psychotherapy/analysis of the Absurd 110, 112, 113, 114, 118, 120; and Schopenhauer's view on death and suicide 45; and theory as construction 22; and therapists' work xiii

Tillisch, K. 164

time *see* temporality

Timms, E. 46n16

Tolstoy, L., *War and Peace* 93

The Torch (*Die Fackel*) 44n13

Toulmin, S. 41

transcendental intersubjectivity, in Husserl 48

transference: and Existential Psychotherapies 87; and first psycho-analysts 6–7; and Freudian psychoanalysis 18; vs. here-and-now relationships between Human Beings 173; transference-countertransference 74

Traumas 97, 119, 134; *see also* Post-Traumatic Stress Disorder (PTSD)

Trump, Donald 81, 141, 152, 159, 161, 168

truth: personal truth and postmodern project 142; relational truth (Kierkegaard) xiv, 36

Tuckett, D. 23–24, 26

Tulving, E. xv–xvi, 51

Tversky, A. 8, 18, 19; "Prospect Theory" paper 121–124

Umwelt see World of things and animals (Heidegger's *Die Umwelt*)

Uncertainty: and CCM method 24; and clinical situation 17; and decision-making 8, 18, 121–123, 125; Heisenberg Uncertainty Principle 36, 143; and Interdisciplinary world 110; and Postmodernism 17; Studies of 32; and Subjective Well-Being (SWB) self-assessments 175; and Unknowability 141, 143

Unconscious(ness): and emotions 119; and Existentialist Psychology xvii, 71, 115; and Fallenness 185; Freud's concept of Unconscious 39, 48n18; Freud's Dynamic Unconscious vs. unconscious systems 120–121; and neuroanatomy 117–118; and Phenomenology xv, 47, 48n18, 115; and Psychoanalysis 12, 90; psychodynamic unconscious and Right Brain/Left Brain 129; and Psychotherapy/analysis of the Absurd 111; Relational Unconsciousness 141

United States Department of Labor, Bureau of Labor Statistics, number of health professionals 3
Unknowability: and Postmodernism xix, 17, 142–143; and Uncertainty 141, 143

Vagus nerve 162–163
Vaillant, G. E. 185
Valuation, and Prospect Theory 124
Van Gogh, Vincent 74
Vetsera, Mary, Baroness 46
Viennese *fin de siècle* café society: aestheticism 45; Death xv, 42, 43, 44, 45–46, 48; and Existentialism 33, 35; *Jung Wien* generation 43, 44, 45, 61; and Kierkegaard 43, 44; Neo-Romanticism 41–42; and Nietzsche 40, 43–44; Ottakring suburb uprising (1911) 42–43; and Schopenhauer 40, 42, 43, 44–45; science, love of 43; suicide 46, 61, 111; therapeutic nihilism 45, 46; Viennese Impressionism 43, 45–46
Vietnam war 81, 146, 147

William Alanson White (WAW) Institute (New York) 12, 16
Wilson, T. 121
Winnicott, D. W. 72, 127–128
witchcraft 4
Withey, S. B. 126
Wittgenstein, Ludwig 45
Wong, P. T. P. 191
Workspace Theory 18
World *see* Being-in-the-World; Culture and History; Self and World; World of other Human Beings (Heidegger's *Die Mitwelt*); World of the inner Self (Heidegger's *Die Eigenwelt*) World of things and animals (Heidegger's *Die Umwelt*)
World of other Human Beings (Heidegger's *Die Mitwelt*): about Heidegger's concept xv, 49, 173n1; and Anxiety 98; and Camus' Absurdism xvi, xviii, 58; and cellphone usage 195, 196; and Cyborgs 175; and Daseinanalysis 88–89; and Despair 100; and Existential Psychotherapies 90; and metapsychologies 26, 27; and Mirror Neuron System xix, 164; and Political anxieties 141; and Psychoanalysts' prioritization of infantile past 150; and Psychotherapy/analysis of the Absurd 110, 113, 135; and the sixties 77; and Social Networks xix, 164; and technology 192
World of the inner Self (Heidegger's *Die Eigenwelt*): about Heidegger's concept xv, 49; and Anxiety 98; and Camus' Absurdism xviii; and Despair 100; and Psychotherapy/analysis of the Absurd 110, 113, 115–117; and Self-experience/reflection xviii, 115; and the sixties 77; and Subjective Well-Being (SWB) 176
World of things and animals (Heidegger's *Die Umwelt*): about Heidegger's concept xv, 49; and Anxiety 98; and Camus' Absurdism xvi, xviii, 58; and cellphone usage 195, 196; and Daseinanalysis 88–89; and Despair 100; and Ecoanxieties 141; and ecological/political anxiety 151; and Existential Psychotherapies 90; and metapsychologies 26, 27; and Microbiome xix; and perception 164; and Psychoanalysts' prioritization of infantile past 150; and Psychotherapy/analysis of the Absurd 110, 113; and Sartre's *Being and Nothingness* 54; and the sixties 77
Wright, J. S. 176
Wundt, Wilhelm 12

Yalom, Irwin D.: Death xviii, 92–96, 98, 184, 185–186, 187; emotional clinical writing 173; and Existential Psychology 10, 69; *Existential Psychotherapy* 85, 91; freedom xviii, 91; isolation xviii, 91; meaninglessness xviii, 91–92; mortality xviii, 91; relations, focus on 173; "rippling" wish/expectation 186
Yang, B. 163

Zaretsky, R. 112
Zimmer, R. B. 17–18, 19, 21–22